Competitive Strategies for the 21st Century

Competitive Strategies for the 21st Century

THEORY, HISTORY, AND PRACTICE

Edited by Thomas G. Mahnken

Stanford Security Studies
An Imprint of Stanford University Press
Stanford, California

Stanford University Press
Stanford, California

Printed in the United States of America on acid-free, archival-quality paper

Library of Congress Cataloging-in-Publication Data

Competitive strategies for the 21st century : theory, history, and practice / edited by Thomas G. Mahnken.
    pages cm
    "This volume grew out of a conference on 'Developing Competitive Strategies for the 21st Century,' which was held at the U.S. Naval War College in Newport, Rhode Island in August 2010."
    Includes bibliographical references and index.
    ISBN 978-0-8047-8241-8 (cloth : alk. paper) —
    ISBN 978-0-8047-8242-5 (pbk. : alk. paper)
    1. United States—Foreign relations—China—Congresses. 2. China—Foreign relations— United States—Congresses. 3. United States—Foreign relations—21st century— Congresses. 4. National security—United States—Congresses. 5. Strategic rivalries (World politics)—Congresses. I. Mahnken, Thomas G., editor of compilation.
    E183.8.C5C67 2012
    327.7305109'05—dc23

                                                                      2011052146

Special discounts for bulk quantities of Stanford Security Studies are available to corporations, professional associations, and other organizations. For details and discount information, contact the special sales department of Stanford University Press.
Tel: (650) 736-1782, Fax: (650) 736-1784

Typeset by Thompson Type in 10/14 Minion

To Andrew W. Marshall, mentor and friend

CONTENTS

ACKNOWLEDGMENTS

THIS VOLUME GREW OUT OF a conference on "Developing Competitive Strategies for the 21st Century," which was held at the U.S. Naval War College in Newport, Rhode Island, in August 2010. I would like to thank the conference participants, including the authors who appear in this volume as well as Paul Bracken, Patrick Cronin, Peter Dutton, Lyle Goldstein, Timothy Hoyt, Phillip Karber, John Maurer, Sally Paine, David Rosenberg, Robert Ross, Joshua Rovner, and Andrew Wilson for their contributions. I would also like to acknowledge the stellar support of the Naval War College Special Events Department, including Karen Sellers, Shirley Fernandes, and Al Lawton, as well as Cathy Hubert of the College's Strategy and Policy Department.

I would also like to thank the leadership of the Naval War College, Rear Admiral James P. Wisecup and Ambassador Mary Ann Peters, for their support of the project.

At Stanford University Press, I would like to thank Geoffrey Burn and Jessica Walsh for helping bring this project to print.

Finally, I would like to thank my wife, Deborah, and children, Thomas and Rachel, for enduring (more than they should) my absences and preoccupation with work.

ABBREVIATIONS

A2/AD	antiaccess/area denial
ABM	Antiballistic Missile
ASBM	Antiship Ballistic Missile
ASAT	antisatellite
ASCM	Antiship Cruise Missile
ASW	Antisubmarine Warfare
AT3	Advanced Tactical Targeting Technology
BAMS	Broad Area Maritime Surveillance
C3	command, control, and communications
C4ISR	command, control, communications, computer, intelligence, surveillance, and reconnaissance
CCP	Chinese Communist Party
CNP	Comprehensive National Power
CONUS	Continental United States
CS	Competitive Strategies
CVBG	Aircraft Carrier Battle Group
DADS	Deployable, Autonomous, Distributed Sensor Array
DARPA	Defense Advanced Research Projects Agency
DEAD	Destruction of Enemy Air Defenses

DoD	U.S. Department of Defense
DWADS	Deep Water Active Detection System
ECCM	Electronic Counter Countermeasures
EEZ	Exclusive Economic Zone
ELINT	electronic intelligence
EMCON	emission control
FDS	Fixed Distributed System
FOFA	Follow-on Forces Attack
GMLRS	GPS-guided multiple launch rocket system
GPS	global positioning system
HALE	High Altitude Long Endurance
HF	High Frequency
IADS	integrated air defense system
IED	improvised explosive devices
INF	Intermediate-Range Nuclear Forces
IRGC	Islamic Revolutionary Guard Corps
ISR	intelligence, surveillance and reconnaissance
JDAM	Joint Direct Attack Munition
JIEDDO	Joint IED Defeat Organization
JORN	Jindalee Over-the-horizon Radar Network
LACM	land-attack cruise missile
LADAR	laser-radar
LCS	Littoral Combat Ship
LEO	Low Earth Orbit
LOCAAS	Low Cost Autonomous Attack System
LRASM	long-range antiship missile
MCM	Mine Countermeasures
MRBM	medium-range ballistic missile
MSDF	Maritime Self Defense Force
MTR	Military-Technical Revolution

NASIC	U.S. National Air and Space Intelligence Center
NATO	North Atlantic Treaty Organization
NOC	Navy Operations Concept
OIF	Operation Iraqi Freedom
ONA	Office of Net Assessment
OTH/B	over-the-horizon/backscatter radar
PLA	People's Liberation Army
PLAN	People's Liberation Army Navy
QDR	Quadrennial Defense Review
RAP VLA	RAP vertical line array
RF	radio-frequency
RMA	Revolution in Military Affairs
ROK	Republic of Korea
ROTHR	Relocatable Over-the-Horizon Radar
RSAS	RAND Strategy Assessment System
SAC	Second Artillery Corps
SALT	Strategic Arms Limitation Treaty
SAM	Surface-to-Air Missile
SCDC	Strategic Concepts Development Center
SDI	Strategic Defense Initiative
SIGINT	signals intelligence
SLMM	Submarine Launched Mobile Mine
SOSUS	Sound Surveillance System
SRBM	short-range ballistic missiles
SS	Diesel attack submarine
SSBN	Nuclear-powered ballistic missile submarine
SSGN	Nuclear-powered cruise missile submarine
SSN	Nuclear-powered attack submarine
SURTASS	Surveillance Towed Sensor Array System
TBM	tactical ballistic missile

T/FDOA   time and frequency-difference-of-arrival

TLAM   Tomahawk Land Attack Missile

TLE   target location error

TRADOC   U.S. Army Training and Doctrine Command

UAS   unmanned aerial system

UAV   unmanned aerial vehicle

UUV   Unmanned Underwater Vehicle

WP   Warsaw Pact

CONTRIBUTORS

Ross Babbage is founder of the Kokoda Foundation, a not-for-profit research corporation that works closely with Australian government agencies on Australia's future security challenges. For the first five years of the foundation's existence, he served as its Chairman and Chief Executive Officer. He served as a special advisor to the Minister for Defense during the preparation of the 2009 Australian Defense White Paper. He also served on the Council of the International Institute for Strategic Studies. In addition, Professor Babbage is Managing Director of Strategy International (ACT) Pty Ltd, a defense consulting and education service delivery organization. He has served as a senior government official, a senior executive in the corporate world and also as a senior academic. Amongst his publications are: *A Coast Too Long: Defending Australia Beyond the 1990s* (Allen & Unwin, 1990) and *Rethinking Australia's Defence* (University of Queensland Press, 1980).

Gordon S. Barrass is a visiting professor dealing with strategic issues at the London School of Economics. During the last years of the Cold War he was Chief of the Assessments Staff in the Cabinet Office in London. He is author of *The Great Cold War: A Journey through the Hall of Mirrors* (Stanford University Press, 2009).

John A. Battilega is a Senior Technical Director of Science Applications International Corporation. He has been a senior consultant to the Office of the Secretary of Defense and the Intelligence Community for thirty years. He directed strategic research on the Soviet Union, Russia, and Eurasia from 1977–1999. Dr. Battilega was directly involved in the U.S. Competitive Strategies program throughout the decade of the 1980s. He has taught on the graduate faculty of the Graduate School of International Studies, University of Denver, and the U.S. Defense Intelligence College. He is a former Army officer and Vietnam veteran.

Dan Blumenthal is a resident fellow at The American Enterprise Institute for Public Policy Research as well as a current commissioner and former vice chairman of the U.S.–China Economic and Security Review Commission. Previously, he was senior director for China, Taiwan, and Mongolia in the Secretary of Defense's Office of International Security Affairs and practiced law in New York prior to his government service. At AEI, in addition to his work on the national security implications of U.S.-Sino relations, he coordinates the Tocqueville on China project, which examines the underlying civic culture of post-Mao China. Mr. Blumenthal also contributes to AEI's *Asian Outlook* series and is a research associate with the National Asia Research Program.

Michael S. Chase is Director of the Mahan Scholars Group at the U.S. Naval War College and previously served on the faculty of the College's Strategy and Policy Department. Prior to joining the Naval War College, he served as a research analyst with Defense Group Inc. and the RAND Corporation. He is the author of the book *Taiwan's Security Policy: External Threats and Domestic Politics* (Lynne Rienner, 2008). His recent publications include studies on Chinese nuclear force modernization and strategy, defense reform and domestic politics in Taiwan, Taiwan's defense spending debate, and contemporary U.S.-Taiwan security cooperation.

Owen R. Coté Jr. is Associate Director of the MIT Security Studies Program. He is also coeditor of the journal *International Security.* He received his PhD in Political Science from MIT, where he specialized in U.S. defense policy and international security affairs. He has written on U.S. nuclear weapons policy, avoiding nuclear terrorism, the sources of innovation in military doctrine, the future of naval warfare, and is also the author of *The Third Battle* (Naval War College Press, 2003), a history of how the U.S. Navy performed antisubmarine warfare during the Cold War.

Jacqueline Newmyer Deal is President and CEO of the Long Term Strategy Group, a Cambridge, Massachusetts–based defense consultancy. For the last five years, she has worked with the Director of the Office of the Secretary of Defense/Net Assessment on projects related to East Asia. She has held post-doctoral fellowships at the Belfer Center for Science & International Affairs at Harvard's Kennedy School of Government and the John M. Olin Institute for Strategic Studies in the Government Department of Harvard's Faculty of Arts & Sciences. She has been published in the *New York Times, Policy Review,* the *Weekly Standard,* and *War in History,* and she has been cited in a range of media outlets including *Newsweek.*

Andrew S. Erickson is an Associate Professor in the Strategic Research Department at the U.S. Naval War College and a founding member of the department's China Maritime Studies Institute (CMSI). He is an Associate in Research at Harvard University's John King Fairbank Center for Chinese Studies (2008–). Professor Erickson is coeditor of, and a contributor to, the Naval Institute Press book series, "Studies in Chinese Maritime Development," comprising *Chinese Aerospace Power* (2011); *China, the U.S., and 21st Century Sea Power* (2010); *China Goes to Sea* (2009); *China's Energy Strategy* (2008); and *China's Future Nuclear Submarine Force* (2007). He runs two research websites, www.andrewerickson.com and www.chinasignpost.com.

James R. FitzSimonds is a Research Professor with the Center for Naval Warfare Studies at the U.S. Naval War College, where he is director of the Halsey Alfa research and analysis group. His work centers on analysis of military issues in the Asia-Pacific region, including war-fighting balances and modernization trends. Professor FitzSimonds served for twenty-seven years in the U.S. Navy as both a surface line officer and intelligence officer, retiring in 2001 with the rank of captain. His operational assignments included USS *Blakely* (FF-1072), USS *Enterprise* (CVN-65), and the USS *America* (CV-66) Battle Group, where he served as Assistant Chief of Staff for Intelligence in the Persian Gulf during Operation Desert Storm. His ashore assignments included tours with the Chief of Naval Operations Current Intelligence Division, the Navy Operational Intelligence Center Detachment (Newport), the CNO Strategic Studies Group, the Net Assessment directorate of the Office of the Secretary of Defense, and the faculty of the Naval War College. He earned his BS from the U.S. Naval Academy in 1974 and MS from the Massachusetts Institute of Technology in 1980.

Paul S. Giarra is the President of Global Strategies & Transformation, a national defense and strategic planning consultancy. He was a Naval officer for twenty-four years and served as a naval aviator, a strategic planner, and as manager of the U.S.-Japan alliance in the Office of the Secretary of Defense. A graduate of Harvard College's last Navy ROTC class, the U.S. Naval War College, and Japan's National Institute for Defense Studies in Tokyo, he is a frequent international commentator on American and regional strategic issues in Asia and in NATO, including the strategic meeting engagement with China.

Daniel I. Gouré is a Vice President with the Lexington Institute, a nonprofit public policy research organization headquartered in Arlington, Virginia. Prior to joining the Lexington Institute, he was the Deputy Director, International Security Program, at the Center for Strategic and International Studies. He has held senior positions in both the private sector and the U.S. government. He spent two years in the U.S. government as the director of the Office of Strategic Competitiveness in the Office of the Secretary of Defense. He has taught or lectured at the Johns Hopkins University, Georgetown University, the Foreign Service Institute, the National War College, the Naval War College, the Air War College, and the Inter-American Defense College.

James R. Holmes is an associate professor of strategy at the U.S. Naval War College. Before joining the Naval War College faculty, he served on the faculty of the University of Georgia School of Public and International Affairs and as a research associate at the Institute for Foreign Policy Analysis, Cambridge, MA. His books include *Theodore Roosevelt and World Order: Police Power in International Relations; Chinese Naval Strategy in the 21st Century: The Turn to Mahan* (Routledge, 2007, coauthor); *Indian Naval Strategy in the 21st Century* (Routledge, 2009, coauthor); *Red Star over the Pacific: China's Rise and the Challenge to U.S. Maritime Strategy* (U.S. Naval Institute, 2011, coauthor); and *Nuclear Strategy in the Second Nuclear Age* (forthcoming, coeditor).

Bradford A. Lee holds the Philip A. Crowl Chair in Comparative Strategy at the U.S. Naval War College. A graduate of Yale College, he earned his PhD from Cambridge University and was a member of the Society of Fellows at Harvard

University, where he taught for eight years before coming to the Naval War College in 1987. At Harvard, Professor Lee was awarded the Levenson Memorial Teaching Prize as the best teacher among the assistant and associate professors. He has written extensively on strategy, diplomacy, politics, and economics in the affairs of modern states. He is now at work on a book entitled *On Winning Wars*, an analysis of how military operations translate into political results.

Thomas G. Mahnken is Jerome E. Levy Chair of Economic Geography and National Security at the U.S. Naval War College and a Visiting Scholar at the Philip Merrill Center for Strategic Studies at The Johns Hopkins University's Paul H. Nitze School of Advanced International Studies (SAIS). Professor Mahnken served as the Deputy Assistant Secretary of Defense for Policy Planning from 2006 to 2009. He is the author of *Technology and the American Way of War since 1945* (Columbia University Press, 2008) and *Uncovering Ways of War: U.S. Intelligence and Foreign Military Innovation, 1918–1941* (Cornell University Press, 2002). He is editor of *The Journal of Strategic Studies*.

Evan B. Montgomery is a Senior Fellow at the Center for Strategic and Budgetary Assessments. He has published on a wide range of topics, including nuclear proliferation, nuclear strategy, alliances, scenario-based planning, and U.S. Army modernization. He is the author of several reports in CSBA's Strategy for the Long Haul series, and his work has also appeared in *Foreign Affairs, International Security,* and *Security Studies*. He graduated from Villanova University with a BA in political science and sociology and received his MA and PhD in foreign affairs from the University of Virginia.

Stephen Peter Rosen is the Beton Michael Kaneb Professor of National Security and Military Affairs at Harvard University. He was the civilian assistant to the director, Net Assessment, in the Office of the Secretary of Defense; the Director of Political-Military Affairs on the staff of the National Security Council; and a professor of Strategy and Policy at the Naval War College. He participated in the President's Commission on Integrated Long Term Strategy and in the Gulf War Air Power Survey sponsored by the Secretary of the Air Force. He is the author of *Winning the Next War: Innovation and the Modern Military* (Cornell University Press, 1991), winner of the 1992 Furniss Prize; and *Societies and Military Power: India and Its Armies* (Cornell University Press, 1996).

James P. Thomas is Vice President and Director of Studies at the Center for Strategic and Budgetary Assessments, where he leads CSBA's research program focusing on the future of warfare. Earlier in his career, he served for thirteen years in a variety of policy, planning, and resource analysis posts in the Department of Defense, culminating in his dual appointment as Deputy Assistant Secretary of Defense for Resources and Plans and Acting Deputy Assistant Secretary of Defense for Strategy. He spearheaded the 2005–2006 Quadrennial Defense Review (QDR) and was the principal author of the QDR Report to Congress.

Barry D. Watts is a senior fellow at the Center for Strategic & Budgetary Assessments (CSBA). Prior to joining CSBA, he headed the Office of Program Analysis and Evaluation in the Defense Department (2001–2002). From retirement from the U.S. Air Force in 1986 until 2001, Mr. Watts was with the Northrop Grumman Analysis Center, which he directed during 1997–2001. During his Air Force career (1965–1986), Mr. Watts flew a combat tour in Southeast Asia in F-4s, taught logic and philosophy at the Air Force Academy, served twice in the Office of Net Assessment, and served in the Air Staff's Project Checkmate.

Toshi Yoshihara is John A. van Beuren Chair of Asia-Pacific Studies at the U.S. Naval War College. Previously, he was a visiting professor in the Strategy Department at the Air War College. He is coauthor of *Red Star over the Pacific: China's Rise and the Challenge to U.S. Maritime Strategy* (Naval Institute Press, 2010); *Indian Naval Strategy in the Twenty-First Century* (Routledge, 2009); and *Chinese Naval Strategy in the Twenty-First Century: The Turn to Mahan* (Routledge, 2008). He is also coeditor of *Asia Looks Seaward: Power and Maritime Strategy* (Praeger, 2008).

THE CONCEPT OF COMPETITIVE STRATEGIES Part I

1 THINKING ABOUT COMPETITIVE STRATEGIES

Thomas G. Mahnken

THE UNITED STATES today faces the most complex and challenging security environment in recent memory even as it must deal with growing constraints on its ability to respond to threats. Three challenges in particular are likely to influence U.S. national security in coming years. The first is the ongoing war with Al Qaeda and its affiliates: a protracted conflict that spans the globe with irregular adversaries using unconventional means. The second is the threat that nuclear-armed hostile regimes, such as North Korea and prospectively Iran, pose to U.S. allies and the stability of key regions. The third, and most consequential, challenge is the rise of China. Chinese military modernization promises to reshape the balance of power in Asia in ways inimical the United States and its interests. China may be able not only to deny the United States access to areas of vital national interest but also to undermine the alliances that have served as the foundation of regional stability for over half a century.

Although each of these challenges is very different, meeting each successfully will require the United States to formulate and implement a comprehensive long-term strategy. With the possible exception of the threat posed by the regime in P'yongyang, these challenges will likely remain defining features of the security environment for decades. Further, each demands a comprehensive response. Military power has a role to play, to be sure, but so too do other instruments of statecraft. The United States possesses a broad array of political, diplomatic, and economic tools that it has yet to fully bring to bear in dealing with these challenges. Nor should the United States meet these challenges alone. America's allies can and should play an important role as well.

Although it is axiomatic that states formulate and implement strategy with finite resources, the United States will face increasing constraints in coming years. For reasons of domestic politics as much as economics, resources for, and attention to, national security will likely be limited in coming years. These constraints make it increasingly clear that the United States can no longer seek to reduce risk merely by throwing money at the problem. Similarly, it cannot afford to simply do more of the same. Rather, U.S. leaders need to develop a well-thought-out strategy for competing over the long term. Specifically, the United States needs to clarify and prioritize its goals, conduct a net assessment of enduring U.S. strengths and weaknesses, and formulate and implement a strategy to leverage American competitive advantages against the range of competitors. Indeed, only by adopting such a strategy can the United States hope to achieve its objectives.

This volume emphasizes the need for a long-term strategic approach to the Sino-American competition. The chapters that follow acknowledge that formulating and implementing such a strategy is difficult for a variety of reasons, but they also demonstrate that such an approach is feasible because it has been done before, most recently during the period of U.S.-Soviet competition during the Cold War.[1]

At least since World War II, the United States has pursued a consistent set of objectives in Asia. These include defending U.S. territory, including the continental United States, Hawaii, Alaska, Guam, and the Northern Marianas; protecting U.S. allies such as Australia, Japan, and South Korea and quasi-allies such as Taiwan; assuring access to the global commons; and preserving a favorable balance of power across Eurasia. Over the last century, the United States has repeatedly used force when its territory or allies were attacked and when a would-be hegemon has threatened the balance of power in Eurasia.

The rise of China could again jeopardize these interests. Since the end of the Cold War, China has sought to expand its influence in the Western Pacific and constrict that of the United States. The expansion of Chinese military power, which has been underway for some time now, is already tipping the military balance against the United States and undermining the perceptions of U.S. commitment to the region and security guarantees to our allies. A preponderance of Chinese power in the Western Pacific would also jeopardize the free flow of goods, technology, and resources on which the United States and its allies depend.[2]

The competition between the United States and China is but the most recent case of a contest between a dominant power and an emerging one. Past examples include the competition between the United States and Great Britain that spanned the late 19th and early 20th centuries, that between Great Britain and Germany during the same period, and that between the United States and the Soviet Union during the second half of the 20th century.

Competition is not the same as conflict. Indeed, as used throughout this book, competition lies midway on a spectrum whose ends are defined by conflict and cooperation. In fact, elements of both cooperation and conflict can coexist in a competitive relationship. It is worth recalling, for example, that in the early 20th century Great Britain and Germany were both military rivals and highly interdependent economically. Prior to the outbreak of World War I, Britain was Germany's second-largest trading partner and its leading export market.[3]

To say that the United States is involved in a long-term geostrategic competition with China is not to prejudge its outcome. History contains examples of rising powers coming to blows with dominant powers, as Germany did twice with Great Britain during the 20th century. It also contains instances when competitions between emerging and established powers ended amicably, as when Great Britain accommodated the rise of the United States in the late 19th and early 20th centuries.

The U.S.-Soviet competition represents an intermediate case. Although the superpowers managed to avoid direct conflict for four decades, the Cold War was far from bloodless. It spawned conflicts that cost the United States alone more than 100,000 dead. And, indeed, on a number of occasions it led to direct combat between the United States and the Soviet Union, as when American and Soviet pilots clashed in the skies over Korea during the Korean War.

Today's circumstances differ considerably from those of the Cold War, and we should thus be wary of drawing too many analogies to it. During the Cold War, the Soviet Union was the overwhelming focus of U.S. national security policy. Today, the United States faces a range of challenges. As a result, the United States is unlikely to enjoy the sort of strategic focus it had in the decades after World War II. Similarly, during the Cold War, the United States pursued a strategy of containment across all dimensions of the U.S.-Soviet relationship—political, economic, ideological, and military. Today, the Sino-American relationship is more complex, incorporating elements of cooperation, competition, and conflict that vary in proportion across different elements of national power: The Sino-American military relationship tends toward the competitive, whereas the two powers' economic relationship has tended toward the cooperative.

Over time the United States developed a deep understanding of the Soviet Union and of the Soviet military. Today, however, there are substantial gaps in our understanding of competitors. Certainly there has been as yet no attempt to understand Chinese strategic culture, decision-making, strategy, operational art, and science and technology on the scale of the effort to understand the Soviet Union during the Cold War.[4] Most fundamentally, during the Cold War there was widespread agreement that the United States and Soviet Union were engaged in a competition, even as there was disagreement as to the character, course, and potential outcome of that competition. Today, the very notion that the United States and China are competing is contested.

Some American strategists are reluctant to cast the Sino-American relationship in competitive terms, fearing that to do so would breed conflict where none previously existed. Chinese strategists are less reticent when it comes to talking about competition with the United States. As Rear Admiral Yang Yi, the former director of the PLA National Defense University's Institute for Strategic Studies, said in an interview on the eve of Secretary of Defense Robert Gates's January 2011 visit to Beijing, "We hope the competition will be healthy competition."[5]

The Sino-American competition has been underway for some time but has largely been one sided. It appears, for example, that China began developing weapons to defeat U.S. forces in the mid-1990s as part of its reevaluation of the security environment after the collapse of the Soviet Union and the U.S. victory in the 1991 Gulf War.[6] Subsequent years have seen a major buildup of Chinese military power in the Western Pacific. The United States, however, has been slow to recognize and respond to the shifting military balance. Since 2001 Washington has focused its attention on fighting two land wars in Southwest and Central Asia. As a result, the military balance in the Western Pacific has begun to shift dramatically in favor of China and against the United States and its allies. This brings into question the ability of the United States not only to guarantee the status quo across the Taiwan Strait but also to assure U.S. allies in the region as well as to protect U.S. territory in the Western Pacific from attack.

America's allies in the region, alarmed by Chinese military modernization, have begun to take action. Japan's 2010 National Defense Program Guidelines call for a shift in Japan's defense priorities and deployments.[7] Australia's 2009 Defense White Paper envisions the expansion and modernization of its submarine force.[8]

The long-term competition with China could yield conflict, but it need not. Prognoses regarding the future arc of the Sino-American relationship vary and are in any event in the realm of speculation rather than accomplished fact.[9] Indeed, perhaps the most reliable way of averting conflict is to strengthen deterrence; a long-term strategy should aid that effort.

The time is thus right for the United States to adopt a long-term strategy for dealing with China, one that includes but is not limited to military means and one that fully includes U.S. allies and friends in the region.

THE CONCEPT OF COMPETITIVE STRATEGIES

States have formulated and implemented long-term strategies in pursuit of their aims for millennia. It was, however, only in the 1970s, during a period of similarly constrained resources, that a competitive strategies approach took hold within the U.S. government.[10] This section describes the competitive strategies approach and its key features.

Carl von Clausewitz famously defined war as "an act of force to compel our enemy to do our will."[11] The competitive strategies approach focuses on the peacetime use of latent military power—that is, the development, acquisition, deployment, and exercising of forces—to shape a competitor's choices in ways that favor our objectives. Specifically, the competitive strategies approach focuses on peacetime interaction among and between defense establishments.

Five features distinguish the competitive strategies approach from other methods of planning. First, it presupposes a concrete, sophisticated opponent. Strategy is concerned with how one applies one's resources to achieve one's aims. In the military sphere, it is concerned with how to employ military means to influence a particular competitor. Moreover, that competitor needs to be a strategic actor in that it must possess aims and formulate a strategy to achieve them.

Second, the competitive strategies approach assumes interaction between competitors. That is, it assumes that one competitor make strategic choices at least in part due to the actions of the other. Interaction need not be tightly coupled, however. Frequently a competitor's choices are only partially influenced by the other side's actions. The history of past competitions shows that states interact through the prism of their own strategic culture and preferences, domestic institutions, and bureaucratic politics.[12] The experience of the Cold War, for example, shows that action-reaction arms race models fall far short in explaining the actual course of the U.S.-Soviet competition.[13]

Third, the competitive strategies approach acknowledges that the choices competitors have open to them are constrained. States face a series of obvious limitations, including the availability of economic resources, personnel, and technology. But they also face other barriers, including those stemming from strategic culture. The competitive strategies approach seeks to identify and exploit those constraints.

Fourth, the competitive strategies approach acknowledges that interaction may play out over the course of years or decades. It is interested not only in influencing the use of forces but also in research and development, acquisition, and deployment over time. Competitive strategies may in fact employ time as a key variable. The competitive strategies approach also focuses on shifting perceptions of the utility of various types of forces. It may thus take years or decades to determine the full effect of a strategy.

Finally, the competitive strategies approach assumes sufficient understanding of the competitor to be able to formulate and implement a long-term competitive strategy, a task that requires not only an understanding of what a competitor is doing but also why he or she is doing it. Effective competitive strategies are predicated on an understanding of a competitor's decision-making process and doctrine.

ABOUT THIS VOLUME

The chapters that follow examine the theory and practice of competitive strategies. The first section explores the theory of peacetime strategic competition. In Chapter 2, Stephen P. Rosen reviews the logic of the competitive strategies approach as developed in the United States with an eye as to how it can be applied to current or future competitions. Bradford A. Lee's contribution in Chapter 3 discusses the two megaconcepts of strategy—rationality and interaction—and uses them to develop four types of strategy for peacetime competition and war: denial strategies, cost-imposing strategies, other ways of attacking the enemy's strategy, and attacks on the enemy's political system. The chapter evaluates some historical cases relevant to each of them, both in long-term peacetime competition and in war. Strategy is a difficult business, however, and in Chapter 4 Barry D. Watts explores reasons that it is difficult to formulate and implement strategy.

The essays that comprise the second part of the book focus on the practice of competitive strategies during the Cold War. Gordon S. Barrass's Chapter 5 examines the evolution of U.S. strategic thought and practice from the Nixon through the Reagan administrations. He argues that, although under Nixon and Ford the U.S. government began exploring competitive approaches to dealing with the Soviet Union and that under Carter the United States stepped up the pressure on Moscow, it was only under Reagan that such approaches were institutionalized. Daniel Gouré's Chapter 6 picks up the narrative by examining the development of net assessment as a discipline within the U.S. Defense Department and the origins and implementation of the Competitive Strategies Initiative. Finally, in Chapter 7 John Battilega explores the U.S. Competitive Strategies Initiative and Soviet reactions to it. He argues that initial Competitive Strategies Initiatives directly targeted what Soviet military thought viewed as key aspects of their approach. He notes, however, that some Soviet initiatives designed to deal with U.S. competitive strategies were already in motion when the United States launched the Competitive Strategies Initiative. Given the end of the Cold War and the collapse of the Soviet Union, estimating the effectiveness of Competitive Strategies against the Soviet Union is problematic.

The volume's Part III explores the U.S.-China military balance. In Chapter 8, James Holmes explores the nature of the U.S.-China competition from an American perspective through a discussion of enduring U.S. strengths and Chinese vulnerabilities. Then in Chapter 9 Jacqueline Newmyer Deal provides the Chinese view of the competition, examining the elements of China's strategy for competition and describing the Chinese leadership's assessment of China's progress. The chapters that follow explore the competition in greater detail. In Chapter 10, Dan Blumenthal examines the competition between U.S. power projection efforts and China's growing anti-access capabilities, while in Chapter 11 Owen Coté explores the undersea balance. And in Chapter 12, Michael S. Chase and Andrew S. Erickson describe China's nuclear and missile forces. They explain that China's growing missile force is emerging as one of the central elements of its anti-access approach and cornerstones of its strategic deterrence posture. They argue that China is currently moving toward a strategy based on a combination of "effective nuclear deterrence" and conventional deterrence based on the Second Artillery's growing conventional strike capabilities.

America's allies in Asia are an important element of the military balance and could play a central role in a long-term strategy for competing with

China. Toshi Yoshihara's Chapter 13 explores the maritime competition between China and Japan. He argues that Japan could severely complicate Chinese maritime ambitions in Asia if it engaged in competitive strategies that exploited Beijing's enduring vulnerabilities at sea. In Chapter 14, Ross Babbage explores China's military modernization from an Australian perspective and provides recommendations for how Australia and the United States can more effectively compete over the long term.

Finally, Part IV of the book explores strategies for the Sino-American competition. Jim Thomas and Evan Montgomery, in Chapter 15, and Paul Giarra, in Chapter 16, lay out approaches for the United States and its allies to pursue their interests more effectively in the face of Chinese military modernization. Finally, James R. FitzSimonds's Chapter 17 injects a note of caution regarding the prospects of competitive strategies. He notes that the United States has options for competing that it has not pursued because those options threaten deeply held cultural proclivities within the U.S. military officer corps—specifically issues relating to personal accountability and the dominant warrior ethos. Just as the United States needs to identify and exploit Chinese proclivities, its leaders must be aware of its own tendencies that inhibit effective competition.

NOTES

1. See also the essays in Williamson Murray, Macgregor Knox, and Alvin Bernstein, *The Making of Strategy: Rulers, States, and War* (Cambridge, UK: Cambridge University Press, 1994).

2. Aaron L. Friedberg, *A Contest for Supremacy: China, America, and the Struggle for Mastery in Asia* (New York: W. W. Norton, 2011), 6–7.

3. Paul M. Kennedy, *The Rise of the Anglo-German Antagonism, 1860–1914* (London: Allen and Unwin, 1982), 291–305.

4. See, for example, David C. Engerman, *Know Your Enemy: The Rise and Fall of America's Soviet Experts* (Oxford, UK: Oxford University Press, 2009).

5. "Political Trust Needed to Further Military Ties," *Global Times* (China), January 7, 2011.

6. David M. Finkelstein, "China's National Military Strategy: An Overview of the 'Military Strategic Guidelines,'" *Asia Policy* 4 (July 2007), 67–72.

7. "National Defense Program Guidelines for FY 2011 and Beyond"; retrieved on December 17, 2010, from www.kantei.go.jp/foreign/kakugikettei/2010/ndpg_e.pdf.

8. *Defending Australia in the Asia Pacific Century: Force 2030* (Canberra: Department of Defense, 2009). Retrieved from www.defence.gov.au/whitepaper/docs/defence _white_paper_2009.pdf.

9. For two sides of the debate, see Aaron Friedberg, "Menace," *The National Interest* (September/October 2009): 19–25; and Robert S. Ross, "Myth," *The National Interest* (September/October 2009): 19, 25–34.

10. David J. Andre, *New Competitive Strategies Tools and Methodologies,* volume 1, *Review of the Department of Defense Competitive Strategies Initiative, 1986–1990* (McLean, VA: Science Applications International Corporation, 1990).

11. Carl von Clausewitz, *On War,* edited and translated by Michael Howard and Peter Paret (Princeton, NJ: Princeton University Press, 1989), 75.

12. See, for example, the essays in Emily O. Goldman and Leslie C. Eliason, eds., *Adaptive Enemies, Reluctant Friends: The Impact of Diffusion on Military Practice* (Stanford, CA: Stanford University Press, 2003).

13. A. W. Marshall, "Long-Term Competition with the Soviets: A Framework for Strategic Analysis," R-862-PR (Santa Monica, CA: RAND Corporation, 1972).

2 COMPETITIVE STRATEGIES
Theoretical Foundations, Limits, and Extensions

Stephen Peter Rosen

THIS CHAPTER REVIEWS the logic of the competitive strategies approach as it was developed and applied by the U.S. Department of Defense from 1973 to 2010. By explicating the assumptions underlying the competitive strategies approach, this chapter makes it possible to specify how this approach differs from other approaches to strategy, as well as the conditions under which it may be applicable. The object is to begin to specify how the competitive strategies approach can be used in the future.

THE LOGIC OF COMPETITIVE STRATEGIES

Competitive strategies try to get competitors to play our game, a game that we are likely to win. This is done by getting them to make the kind of mistakes that they are inclined to make, by getting them to do that which is in their nature, despite the fact that they should not do so, given their resources. This can take place in war or in peacetime and is the result of conscious top-down choices or spontaneous bottom-up behavior. As we shall see, this approach to the development of strategy is fundamentally different from the rationalist approach, which assumes that actors will adopt the optimal strategy for themselves on the basis of the resources at their disposal and at the disposal of their enemies. It is an approach based on a view of human nature more akin to that which informed Greek tragedy, which depicted protagonists going to their doom because of what was inherent in their nature, or, more strongly, because of what was best in their nature, and what had made them great or admirable.

The competitive strategies approach proceeds from the assumption that actors are imperfectly rational. Beginning in the 1950s, economists realized that acquiring information is costly, and so actors will not acquire all the information that is available. They are not autistic, but neither do they constantly and completely pay attention to the external environment. They also make simplifying assumptions about the data they pay attention to. Hence, actors are episodically affected by external stimuli. They focus on very particular events and ignore other data, and they choose their reactions from a limited repertoire of preferred strategies. The competitive strategies approach of the 1970s thus rested on earlier work on bounded rationality by Herbert Simon and anticipated Michael Spence's Nobel Prize–winning work on the economics of information. The competitive strategies approach foreshadowed Scott Gartner's work on dominant indicators as well as constructivist work that focuses on the use of identity-appropriate "scripts" that actors follow in response to external stimuli.[1]

The competitive strategies approach goes beyond the insight that actors use limited information, however, and allows for the possibility that actors may be blind to the fact that they are damaging themselves by adopting a course of action. First and foremost, it incorporates a formal understanding of the blind spots and restricted freedom of action of large bureaucratic organizations. Bureaucratic organizations, by definition, have standard, routine ways of collecting information about the external environment and standardized routines for behaving in response to the information they collect. They are not organizationally aware of what is occurring if their routines are not set up to collect that information. They cannot respond in ways for which they are not trained and organized. They collect information internally on the basis of standardized procedures and reward individuals within the organization on the basis of their performance of tasks the organization values. The presumption is that successful organizations have collected information about their external environment and their internal behavior in ways that have allowed them to stay in business or even expand. But the organization may not change when the environment changes, and thus the routines for external and internal information collection and action may no longer be appropriate. All the incentives that motivate members of the organization reward the activities that already exist, not the activities that should exist. As I wrote in my book on military innovation, *Winning the Next War,* large organizations do not simply find it difficult to change, they are *designed* not to change. Innovation can occur but is not guaranteed.[2]

Arthur Marder's history of British naval operations in World War I provides one of the clearest and most dramatic cases of organizational informational dysfunction. The German U-boat campaign in 1917 was sinking more British merchant shipping than could be replaced by new construction. Great Britain was in imminent danger of being starved into submission. The Royal Navy was aware of the utility of convoys and routinely convoyed troop ships. It nonetheless refused to convoy merchant ships crossing the Atlantic to British ports, on the grounds that the number of merchant ships entering and leaving British ports was far too large to be convoyed, given the number of appropriate combat vessels in the Royal Navy. It knew how many merchant ships entered and left British ports every month because British port officials counted them. Of course, the Royal Navy was wrong. There were enough ships to convoy the ships at risk of being sunk by the German submarine force. The ships that had to be convoyed were the ships crossing the Atlantic bound for British ports, *not* all the ships entering and leaving British ports, most of which were engaged in coastal trade. The port authorities were not set up to collect data on the volume of trans-Atlantic shipping.[3]

The reader who objects that information problems may have been important a century ago but could not possibly be so today may wish to recall how difficult it was to shift how the U.S. Army collected information in Iraq so that it could generate statistics relevant to Iraqi population protection as opposed to numbers of enemy soldiers killed. As an exercise, the skeptical reader may wish to ask whether the United States spends more on the defense of Asia and the Pacific, as a percent of total defense expenditures, today than in 1990. One would find that the Department of Defense cannot answer that question because it does not maintain accounts with those budget categories. Hence, the somewhat counterintuitive assumption that an adversary may be led into self-destructive courses of action is entirely reasonable to analysts familiar with the routinely suboptimal behavior of large organizations.

Second, the competitive strategies approach was aware of the increasingly compelling evidence about the nature of individual decision making generated by the cognitive sciences and the ways in which human evolutionary biology shapes our ability to learn and make decisions. The biological aspects of human nature are important for the competitive strategies approach in at least two ways, both of which are explored in my book, *War and Human Nature.*[4]

Human beings do not learn from everything they experience. We can sit through lectures full of important information and remember essentially nothing. We live through experiences, and come to conclusions about what we should learn from them, that are completely the opposite of what others learn from exactly the same experience. What we learn is usually that what we thought before the experience has been validated by it. Human beings form persistent memories based on their experiences when they are exposed to stimuli that are emotionally arousing. Those memories persist and shape our interpretation of subsequent events.

As Ernest May has shown, French, British, and German political leaders behaved in 1939 and 1940 in ways that were shaped by their first successes in professional life.[5] Unfortunately for France, its military and civilian leaders had learned from their experiences that quick decisions early in crises were likely to be wrong and that slow and deliberate decision making was more successful. This was not an incorrect lesson to have learned, but it was exactly the wrong lesson on which to act when German tanks were executing the world's first blitzkrieg in May 1940, a moment in time when celerity, not deliberation, was necessary. The historian Marc Bloch recounted how he repeatedly observed French officers belatedly making decisions based on data on the location of German forces that was incorrect, given the rapidity of the German movement.[6]

The competitive strategies approach understands that organizations may be locked into routines that lead to error because they led to success in the past and that individuals may be locked into "lessons learned" that served them well in the past but that can be inappropriate at a given moment in time.

The competitive strategies approach also understands the character of fear. Although it employs the gray and neutral terms of "stimuli" and "response," in practice, the formulation of competitive strategies often began by asking, "What is the enemy's worst nightmare?" Taking actions that frighten the adversary is risky, but this strategy takes advantage of the fact that people who are stressed are not as capable of complex cognition that takes into account multiple factors. People who are afraid want to do something quickly and process fewer pieces of information. People who are afraid for long periods of time become stressed and depressed, which can reduce the amount of effort they put into decision making.

All of this analysis of organizational and human decision making can be combined in an approach to the development of strategy that understands the capacity of the adversary for error and delays in appropriately adapting behavior to the adversary's actions. It understands the opportunity that exists when the defender is relatively less afflicted with error or delay in certain areas of strategic interaction. It therefore places great emphasis on identifying areas of organizational or cognitive *asymmetry*. The competitive strategies approach does not assume that we are smart and the adversary is stupid. It acknowledges that both our adversary and we have blind spots but also that they are not the *same* blind spots. We see some things that the adversary is less able to see. In principle, we can take advantage of these cognitive asymmetries, as well as the asymmetries in material endowments referred to in the original specification of the nature of competitive strategies.

COMPETITIVE STRATEGIES: A CRITIQUE

How might one critique the competitive strategies approach, or, more usefully, identify when it might be appropriate? The most commonly encountered objection to the competitive strategies approach is that it is dangerous. Such strategies may be appropriate for an ongoing war. In peacetime, however, instead of shifting adversary behavior into more defensive or otherwise desirable courses of action, a competitive strategies approach could increase the likelihood of conflict or generally undesirable behavior, or so the objection goes. By engaging in behavior that puts pressure on adversaries to react, or that frightens them, defenders could make adversaries feel threatened. Actors may see threats even when there are none and could exaggerate threats when they do exist. Hence, the competitive strategies approach could increase levels of tension and animosity and perhaps even create those feelings where they did not previously exist.

This objection is significant in that it assumes that the adversary is both very sensitive to our actions and also will tend to overreact offensively to its perceptions of the defender. If these assumptions do not hold, then the adversary will react to a competitive strategy by taking note of the actions of the defender and doing more defensively, which is what is desired. If the assumptions do hold, however, the defender is likely to be dealing with an adversary who will react negatively to what the defender is doing *already* because, by assumption, the adversary sees most actions as threats and reacts offensively. The logical conclusion of this objection is either to acknowledge that we are already in a competitive interaction with the adversary, and so we should engage in it more thoughtfully, or that we need to take highly visible, convincing actions to reassure or appease the adversary. The appeasement strategy will be considered later in the section on socialization and is a serious option. However, the more common inference from the observation that competitive strategies are dangerous is that we should not deviate from what we are doing now. That inference is justified if what we are doing now is completely unprovocative, such that any deviation from it in the direction of higher levels of activity will activate an otherwise quiet adversary. But if the adversary is prone to see us as an enemy, sensitive to what we do, and likely to react offensively, a "freeze" reaction seems to be at best a temporarily effective response.

A second objection is that the dominant asymmetry is in attention and persistence, and it favors our competitors. We will initiate the competitive strategy; the adversary will react in the desired way, but we will change our minds, run out of money, or lose heart; and the adversary will not. Having started the competition, we will not sustain it, but the adversary will. This objection is true to the extent that competitive strategies focus only on adversary sensitivities. Competitive strategies, however, are as much about what the defender is inclined to do as they are about the characteristics of the adversary. As stipulated, competitive strategies must rest on enduring predispositions that make the defender likely to sustain a course of action, out of organizational or individual self-interest.

A third objection is that competitive strategies are irrelevant. Competitive strategies rest on the strong predisposition of adversaries to take certain actions. Given those actions, are they not likely to do what they are going to do, whatever the defender does? Competitive strategies may look like successes after the fact, but the claims for competitive strategies are like those of the rooster who takes credit for making the sun rise. The high level of effort put into Soviet air defenses may have been the result of the American B-1 bomber and cruise missile programs, but it really would have happened anyway given the bureaucratic interests and political power of the Soviet air defense command.

All strategies must deal with the counterfactual of what would have happened in their absence. This objection, however, is valuable in that it focuses our attention on the importance of intelligence that gives us feedback on the operation of the strategy as it is executed and not just after the competition is over. For example, if we could have tracked the year-to-year variations in Soviet air defense expenditures and compared them to variations in American offensive air-breathing nuclear weapons delivery programs, we could have had a better sense of whether there was some correlation in time, if not a cause-and-effect relationship.

Finally, it may be objected that the competitive strategies approach depends on predicting the behavior of the adversary. No one can do that, it could be asserted, and so the approach is preposterous. This objection, again, is not without merit if it is rephrased to say that without an adversary who displays predictable behavior, the competitive strategies approach will be difficult to execute. How strategy might be developed under conditions of uncertainty about the adversary is explored in the following section.

AN EXAMPLE

The discussion of competitive strategies approaches may benefit from a concrete example. A recently published history of Russian actions against Napoleon in the period 1807–1814 nicely illustrates the general description of the logic and preconditions of the competitive strategies approach. As Dominic Lieven describes, the most senior Russian leadership was presented with clear and credible intelligence that Napoleon was preparing to invade Russia.[7] They recognized that Napoleon as an individual was predisposed to deal with diplomatic difficulties by seeking a decisive battle with the army of an adversary, destroying it, and then seeking his surrender on favorable terms. This was the result of Napoleon's personal experiences, in which he had risen politically by winning battles, and it was a result of the internal characteristics of Napoleon's regime. Napoleon's internal legitimacy rested on his ability to deliver battlefield victories against external enemies. France depended on his being present at the imperial center for much of the year. Hence, to survive politically, Napoleon had to fight and win battles against external enemies quickly and decisively and then return to Paris. Napoleon's propensity to react to stimuli by waging and personally directing decisive battles was overdetermined.

The Russian leadership was also conscious of an information asymmetry. It knew more about the internal characteristics of Russia than Napoleon did. Russia had serious internal tensions that limited the ability of the regime to mobilize resources for offensive war, but it did have large amounts of geographic space and warhorses. Hence, a strategy of avoiding battle, drawing Napoleon in, mobilizing the resources of an invaded Russia, and harassing his rear and flanks with superior cavalry would deny Napoleon the ability to play the game that favored him and would make him fight the war that favored Russia.

Note, however, that this strategy required conscious choice. It was opposed by most Russian generals, resulted in the loss of Prussian allies who would fight only if Russia launched an offensive against Napoleon, and might have failed if Napoleon had adopted the more limited goal of creating an enlarged Poland that became the forward eastern base of anti-Russian military power. It also came close to failing when the Russian army, following the orders of the tsar, persistently declined to launch attacks on the French forces, leading to public discontent that reached into and included the tsar's family. The "natural" advantages of space, horses, Russian nationalism, and winter weather, in other words, did not by themselves produce victory.

Both the general statement of the logic of competitive strategies and the particular case of Russia against Napoleon highlight the assumptions underlying the competitive strategies approach:

- In the context of Russian-French relations in 1810, it was certain that Napoleon was inexorably hostile. There was no danger of turning a friend into an enemy.
- Napoleon's predisposition to solve problems by fighting battles was overdetermined. His behavior, within defined limits, was predictable.
- The tsar could, with difficulty, choose and execute one of several distinct strategies.

Suppose that any of those conditions did not hold. What might have been the alternative modes of strategy development? This question leads us to three very different approaches to strategy, which are embodied in the analysis of appeasement, or more properly socialization; Clausewitz; and the Chinese way of war, as elaborated by Francois Jullien, that rests on the importance of the tendency of things, not people.

ALTERNATIVE STRATEGIC PARADIGMS

Socialization

Suppose an adversary has some objectives that conflict with those of the defender but also others that are shared with the defender. Suppose the adversary is suspicious of the defender but is not convinced that one of them must sacrifice core interests and capabilities if they are to avoid war. What strategic approach might be most appropriate? The main objection to the competitive strategies approach is that a country that might live in harmony with the defender could be transformed into an enemy willing to wage war. If that is the case, how might an adversary be made into a country willing to satisfy the interests of the defender? Giving up a competitive strategies approach is not sufficient, as was previously argued.

The general intuition that adversaries can be made into friends goes back at least to the writings of John Maynard Keynes after the end of World War I.[8] By satisfying Germany's "legitimate" demands, Great Britain could have made Germany into a satisfied country, willing to uphold the international order that safeguarded the interests of Great Britain. To be sure, the interests of other countries might have been put at risk, but Britain would have benefited. This line of reasoning always foundered on the problem of how to ensure that an adversary would not simply pocket concessions and use its improved position to push for more concessions. Shared economic interests in peace and prosperity were clearly not enough and had not prevented World War I. Shared experiences in war against a common enemy clearly did not prevent the Soviet Union and the United States from becoming enemies after World War II.

The state of the argument as elaborated by Iain Johnston runs something like this.[9] Exposure to adversaries in an organizational environment in which there is day-to-day contact and the pursuit of common goals shifts the identity of actors. They see each other as more similar than different and adopt a perspective in which they seek gains for both parties. This is alleged to have happened in the front lines of opposing European powers on the Western Front in the first two years of World War I.[10] It is alleged to have occurred in multinational corporations[11] but did not occur in early-20th-century European trade, which is said to explain why there was protectionism in 1914 but not in the 1990s. This is alleged to happen in multinational arms control and diplomatic organizations. Close, sustained, substantive social interaction is the mechanism that produces a shift in the identities of actors, which can, over time, become sufficiently widespread as to create "zones of peace" in which warfare is unthinkable.

The merits of the arguments about the malleability of human social identity are impossible to evaluate fully in this chapter. However, because this strategic approach is often advanced in opposition to the competitive strategies approach, it is useful to note that the process of socialization does not seem to be incompatible with a competitive strategies approach because the fraternization of ordinary citizens has taken place at the same time that elites and organizations have adopted adversarial approaches. The issue has been whether adversary elites can control their populations to prevent fraternization. Limiting those elite efforts to block fraternization and socialization itself might be the objective of a competitive strategy.

Clausewitz and Strategy under Uncertainty

How should strategy be developed if it is assumed that an adversary's behavior is not sufficiently predictable to activate reliably adversary courses of action favorable to the defender? To some extent, this is the stance adopted by Clausewitz in *On War*.[12] Despite some measure of academic controversy, it appears reasonably clear that Clausewitz argues that there are severe constraints on what can be known about what the enemy is actually doing and even more severe constraints on what can be known about what that enemy will do. Clausewitz does instruct us to identify the enemy's center of gravity on the basis of knowledge of general characteristics, and he does remind us that the enemy is not passive and will react in ways intended to thwart our actions. However, this discussion includes little about anticipating what the enemy will do and nothing about what we can do to induce desired courses of action.

Instead, Clausewitz presents a series of observations that amount to a conclusion that, in war, resolution and persistence matter more than identifying the best course of action. War is a gamble, he tells us, with much left to chance. The virtues of a general include the ability rapidly to size up a battlefield but, more profoundly, a steadiness of character, slow to arouse but implacable in action. Above the level of the battle, it is the passions, not the reason, of the people that must be activated and channeled, directed by the political understanding of the monarch, who uses the art of his or her generals but controls them. Without being too much of a historicist, it is not hard to see in Clausewitz's writings the lessons of the Russian government and army with which he served in the war against Napoleon, filtered through the lens of the 19th-century German reaction against the Enlightenment, a reaction that deemphasized the role of reason and emphasized the role of the will and of the moral force in politics.

Strategy, in this view, becomes a matter of choosing a course of action that sustains the will of the army, government, and people in its resolve to continue a war. More finely calibrated decisions cannot, in the real world, be supported by what we can know. The last one standing will win, a point of view for which there is not a little historical support. Eric Larrabee, for example, has argued that the major strategic task for FDR in 1942 was to channel American popular passion away from Japan and toward Germany and to keep the American people engaged in the European theater in the long period before the invasion of France could responsibly be undertaken.[13] The point of the invasion of North Africa in 1942 was to place the American people in a war in which American soldiers were killing Germans and being killed by them. This done, the war would continue until American economic and demographic superiority ground down the Germans.

Shih and Human Agency: The Tendency of Things, Not Actors

In this view, it is hard to understand the enemy, and even harder to mobilize and guide one's own people. If, in contrast to the experience of the modern European city or nation-state, a polity is a large, multiethnic, multireligious, dispersed empire, surrounded by multiple loosely organized actors, one possible response would be to observe the general course of action that is being spontaneously adopted by the complex society over which the emperor presides and to align one's actions with the way things are already going.

To make a long and subtle argument short and simple, this is what Francois Jullien argues is the dominant tendency in Chinese thought.[14] The character of dominant trends, *shih,* is what is important, not the ability of humans to control the course of events. It is not the point of view of Sun Tzu, who was writing during the preimperial Warring States period, for kings who ruled much smaller and more compact domains. The old and persistent role of the *I Ching* in Chinese thinking is reflective of this worldview that does not have human agency at it center. The strategist must understand the logic of the forces that control or at least shape human activity, not the enemy. The strategist must do things that undirected forces will tend to make happen anyway, not try to channel his or her own country in ways that the strategist chooses. To give a contemporary example, if the diffusion of technology and interstate political rivalries drives states to seek nuclear weapons, go with this tendency, help states get nuclear weapons, and try to derive some benefit from doing so. If radical Islamic forces in Hezbollah and Hamas and Iran seek to harass and divert the United States, work with them, and push things along in the direction they are already moving.

WHEN CAN THE COMPETITIVE STRATEGIES APPROACH BE APPLIED?

Understanding the Nature of the Actors

The attempt to set out the underlying assumptions of the competitive strategies approach can help us understand when that approach is likely to be applied successfully. It is useful to recall that the competitive strategies approach had its origins in efforts to build strategies for a narrowly defined target, the Soviet military. The first assumption, concerning the predictability of the target, appeared at the time and in retrospect to have been satisfied. The Soviet military had formal mechanisms for indoctrinating officers into a uniform set of values and worldviews, a highly routinized military, analytical procedures, weapons development and procurement bureaucracies, well-structured incentives for components of the military to advocate increased resource allocations for themselves, relatively good insulation from competing social and political pressures to divert resources, and so on. The structured character of Soviet military behavior facilitated American analysis. That analysis was further assisted by a number of intelligence successes that gave the United States insight into how the Soviet military perceived American actions and an understanding of what the reactions were. Military systems dedicated to strategic air defenses were relatively visible to American overhead reconnaissance, and Soviet reactions to American submarine penetration of Soviet waters are said to have been monitored by intercepts of communications sent through undersea cables.

The American understanding of its tendencies and enduring resources were also straightforward when pointed out. By the 1960s, the U.S. Navy had an institutional history of over seventy years of consistent efforts to engage in long-range power projection, and the U.S. Air Force had an organizational record of at least forty years of persistent efforts to develop long-range bombardment. The services had well-established political constituencies in the civilian world. Systematic incentives to continue with programs in these areas were well entrenched. Moreover, military balances favored the offense over the defense in the case of long-range aircraft relative to air defenses and in the case of submarines versus antisubmarine warfare forces.

To the extent that the American business school literature of the 1970s inspired the competitive strategies approach, analysts were dealing with large corporate bureaucracies that were also well established with what came to be called "core competencies." The business school literature took these attributes of large industrial corporate bureaucracies and took the next step, of asking, "What business are we in?" That is, given the core competencies of the organization, how could resources be funneled toward them in a way that took most advantage of the organizations comparative advantages?

The competitive strategies approach was thus born out of the study of the behavior of large bureaucratic organizations that were, by design and history, relatively predictable in their behavior and responses. Study of organizational behavior could and did reveal the information necessary for the development of a competitive strategy.

It appears that the competitive strategies approach can be supplemented or extended to cover actors that are not Western and that do not have the attributes of long-standing bureaucratic organizations. To take one of the more prominent examples, the People's Republic of China is clearly non-Western in its cultural origins. The Chinese Communist Party (CCP) and the People's Liberation Army (PLA) have, however, become highly structured organizations. Chinese people join the Party and usually stay in it for decades, facilitating their socialization into a uniform set of values and views of the world. The Central Party School of the Central Committee of the CCP has formalized instruction for new Party members and programs for the recurring training and socialization of older Party members. Perhaps more importantly, the system of one-party rule provides systematic benefits to Party members and creates systematic tensions between the Party and the larger Chinese society. There is thus a set of embedded values and incentives that, in principle, should generate recurring patterns of behavior that can be studied externally to identify predispositions to action that can be activated by external stimuli to induce interactions favorable to the United States. The Iranian Army of the Guardians of the Islamic Revolution, usually referred to as the Islamic Revolutionary Guard Corps (IRGC), now has over thirty years of organizational history that can be studied. Many of the members of the leadership of the IRGC appear to have been part of that organization for many years, which would tend to increase our confidence that they had been socialized into a common set of IRGC values and worldviews. Some data are available about the content of the material used to socialize the leadership of the IRGC, and limited data are available about the incentives that are systematically presented to the members of it.

In the case of the CCP and the IRGC, the issue arises of whether culture plays a significant role in affecting the decision-making processes of the members of these two organizations. Culture can be defined as commonly shared values and shared understandings of why things happen in human society. My colleague Jacqueline Newmyer Deal and I have written extensively on how culture relevant to decisions about war, broadly defined, varies across different societies in ways that generate behavior that could not have been anticipated without reference to cultural factors. These cultural factors can be understood by reading the texts that shape the intellectual foundations of relevant individuals and by analyzing the social structures that culture creates and that in turn support and perpetuate it. They are neither unintelligible nor amorphous and can be used to improve our ability to understand and anticipate the reactions of adversaries in keeping with the competitive strategies approach. The unwillingness to incorporate cultural factors into the development of American military strategy, on the assumption that all actors behave in the same way, is possibly the biggest current obstacle to developing actor-appropriate competitive strategies.

There are nonetheless significant problems in developing competitive strategies for actors that are not long-standing, structured organizations. Radical

Islamic terrorist groups do not have stable bureaucratic structures and have relatively short histories. Members drift into and out of them and may not be reliably socialized. They tend to have highly personalized and idiosyncratic leadership that can change unpredictably. In addition, they are non-Western in their social origins, raising the question of whether they have values and preferred sources of information that make their behavior less intelligible to Western analysts. Highly personalized regimes such as that of North Korea may have decision-making processes that reflect not shared culture or patterns of organizational behavior but the whim of one person. The competitive strategies approach may need to have its basis in organizational behavior and theory supplemented by a number of additional bodies of knowledge.

With regard to highly personalized, small nonstate actors, the thinking and behavior of individuals becomes more decisive. A number of methodologies have been developed and used to improve our understanding of individual-level patterns of response. We have already referred to Ernest R. May's argument that the early formative professional experiences of British, French, and German actors explained significant aspects of their decision making in the Hitler-related crises of the 1930s. Rose McDermott provides data on how the medical histories and profiles of individual leaders shaped their behavior in international crises.[15] The work of Uri Bar-Joseph and my own work on the impact of stress on individual level behavior help us understand how the responses of leaders in high-stress situations may vary from that which has been visible in steady state interactions.[16] In the field of psychology, the Plomin Personality Inventory ("The Big Five") has displayed repeated value in characterizing the elements of personality that are stable across time and settings in ways that affect decision making in a personalized regime.

With regard to states that are governed by single leaders but that rule and react to larger host societies, there still remains no better analysis than that of Xenophon in his dialogue *Tyrannicus*.[17]

Understanding Ourselves

Although it is hard to understand others, it is harder to understand ourselves. The field of psychology has convincingly documented the unreliability of individual self-assessments with regard to personal attributes and competence. Organizational self-assessments have rarely displayed a realistic understanding of the strengths and weaknesses of the organization. The roles and missions of the American military are arguably more contested today than they have been since 1940. A major effort in the area of American self-assessment, at the level of the nation but also broken down by relevant organization and functional subcomponents of organizations, would be of great value but would have to be done by a very small group of individuals reporting in private to the chief of the organization.

The Nature of "the Game"

The competitive strategies approach finally depends on identifying interactions in which "the game" favors the defender. One possible problem today is that the United States has, for a variety of reasons, entered into games in which it can be forced to expend much larger amounts of material resources than the adversary. Terrorism and counterterrorism create clearly one such interaction in which the United States holds a "losing hand" in terms of levels of resources expended. In the case of the interaction of the United States and China, to take another example, it is not clear that there are material endowments that create useable competitive advantages for the United States over periods of time measured in decades. Identifying "games" that favor the defender in the current and future environment is a major theoretical and practical challenge.

NOTES

1. Scott S, Gartner, *Strategic Assessment in War* (New Haven, CT: Yale University Press, 1997).

2. Stephen Peter Rosen, *Winning the Next War* (Ithaca, NY: Cornell University Press, 1991), 2.

3. Arthur J. Marder, *From Dreadnought to Scapa Flow: The Royal Navy in the Fisher Era 1904–1919,* volume 4 (Oxford, UK: Oxford University Press, 1978), 64, 102, 118–119, 139–142, 150–152.

4. Stephen Peter Rosen, *War and Human Nature* (Princeton, NJ: Princeton University Press, 2005), 27–70.

5. Ernest R. May, *Strange Victory: Hitler's Conquest of France* (New York: Hill and Wang, 2000), 117, 129.

6. Marc Bloch, *Strange Defeat: A Statement of Evidence Written in 1940* (New York: W. W. Norton, 1968), 38, 45, 107–108.

7. Dominic Lieven, *Russia against Napoleon* (New York: Viking, 2010), 80

8. John Maynard Keynes, *The Economic Consequences of the Peace* (New York: Penguin, 1988).

9. Alastair Iain Johnston, *Social States: China in International Institutions 1980–2000* (Princeton, NJ: Princeton University Press, 2008).

10. Tony Ashworth, *Trench Warfare 1914–1918: The Live and Let Live System*[o] (New York: Holmes and Meier, 1980).

11. Helen Milner, *Resisting Protectionism: Global Industries and Politics of International Trade* (Princeton, NJ: Princeton University Press, 1988).

12. Carl von Clausewitz, *On War*, trans. and ed. Michael Howard and Peter Paret (Princeton, NJ: Princeton University Press, 1976) book one, chapter 3, 102; book one, chapter 6, 117.

13. Eric Larrabee, *Commander in Chief: Franklin Delano Roosevelt, His Lieutenants and Their War* (New York: Harper, 1987), 138–141.

14. Francois Jullien, *The Propensity of Things: Towards a History of Efficacy in China* (New York: Zone Books, 1995).

15. Rose McDermott, *Presidential Leadership, Illness, and Decision Making* (New York: Cambridge University Press, 2008).

16. Uri Bar-Joseph and Rose McDermott, "Personal Functioning Under Stress," *Journal of Conflict Resolution* 52:1 (February 2008), 144–170.

17. Xenophon *Tyrannicus*, in Leo Strauss, *On Tyranny*, ed. Victor Gourevitch and Michael S. Roth (New York: Free Press, 1991).

3 STRATEGIC INTERACTION
Theory and History for Practitioners

Bradford A. Lee

AS WE MOVE DEEPER into the 21st century, practitioners need advanced strategic concepts. The road forward should begin with the most basic texts of classical strategic theory: Carl von Clausewitz's *On War* and Sun Tzu's *The Art of War*. From that fundamental basis, we can take as guideposts two megaconcepts of strategy, rationality and interaction, each of which has two faces. These four faces present key "theory of victory" problems with which all strategic practitioners have to grapple if they are to be effective. Even as strategists try to resolve their own side's problems, they should be looking hard for ways to exacerbate their adversary's difficulties. Four strategic concepts—denial, cost imposition, attacking the enemy's strategy, and attacking the enemy's political system—ought to be in the minds of American practitioners as they operate on the four faces of the adversary both in wartime and during peacetime competitions.

THE TWO MEGACONCEPTS OF STRATEGY

Clausewitz illuminated the importance for practitioners of the theoretical concepts of rationality and interaction more brilliantly than has any other theorist. Rationality is about the relationship between means and ends. Interaction arises from the fact that, as Clausewitz put it, "In war, the will is directed at an animate object that *reacts*."[1]

The first face of rationality is what social scientists call "instrumental" rationality. The key strategic question here is straightforward: Can the instruments available, the operational means (military and nonmilitary), be used and integrated in ways that will deliver the political objective? The second face of rationality is the "cost-benefit" calculus so revered by many social scientists. One of Clausewitz's most important passages frames this face of rationality: "Since war is not an act of senseless passion, but is controlled by its political object, the value of the object must determine the sacrifices to be made for it in *magnitude* and also in *duration*."[2]

The issue of cost drives us to come to grips with interaction, the second megaconcept of strategy, because the costs that one side incurs depend in significant measure on how the other side acts and reacts. Clausewitz warns that assessing how hard and well the enemy will fight is difficult.[3] And, as one moves from assessment to action, Clausewitz foresees further difficulty. In selecting courses of action, one tries to identify the action that will have the greatest desired effects, "the broadest and most favorable repercussions," on the enemy's ability and will to resist.[4] The problem is that "the very nature of interaction is bound to make it unpredictable. The effect that any measure will have on the enemy is the most singular factor among all the particulars of action."[5]

Difficulties may intensify as interaction with the enemy proceeds. Clausewitz is quite aware that the dynamics of interaction can cut against rationality. An effort to outdo the enemy in the military realm may trigger an escalatory spiral in which means "cease to be commensurate with ends" and rising costs cause "domestic problems" that lead to a ratcheting down of military action on one side.[6] But, in such a case, the other side has an incentive to carry on with a cost-imposing strategy, especially if it puts a higher value on the object, as for example North Vietnam did in its war with the United States over South Vietnam.

Clausewitz thus provides us with a daunting introduction to the problems of interaction that has a depressing resonance for American strategists. An acute sense of realism suffuses his text. But advanced strategic concepts need creativity as well as realism. Realism arises from anticipating the fog and friction that pervade the environment of war and the functioning of people and organizations under stress. Creativity brings to bear imagination and innovation on analysis and action.

To think creatively about mastering interaction, we would be well advised to reach back for inspiration to *The Art of War* attributed to Sun Tzu and based on pithy Chinese ideographs put on bamboo strips long before China was first unified. What emerges in bold relief on these bamboo strips is "hyperrationality." Sun Tzu holds out the ideal of winning without fighting or at least gaining the best possible political outcome with the most economical expenditure of military force.[7] He especially fears protraction of violent interaction because it imposes strain on the relationship between a government and its people by diminishing prosperity and generating fiscal "exactions" and also because it impairs the government's international position by giving third parties greater opportunity to take advantage of the conflict, as China, Russia, and Iran have been able to do with the "Long War" between the United States and Al Qaeda and Associated Movements (AQAM).[8]

Sun Tzu's hyperrational optimism depends crucially on his operational confidence with regard to interaction. Whereas Clausewitz sees interaction as very difficult to manage, Sun Tzu presents himself as its master. He points to three major ways of gaining competitive advantage over the adversary. The first is by achieving what we now call "information superiority." Sun Tzu plays up the value of human intelligence and deception, but the United States typically seeks an advantage in the information domain through technological means. His second way of mastering interaction is now known as "maneuver warfare." We can describe the glimmerings in his text of competitive advantage achieved in this way as positional advantage, timing and tempo advantage, and informational and psychological advantage.[9] American operational practice since 1991 comports well with these ideas.

The third way of mastering interaction that we can discover in Sun Tzu is much more alien to American operators and strategists. Translated by Samuel Griffith as "the strategist's keys to victory,"[10] I dub this approach "interaction games" and deem them to be the main operational manifestation of Sun Tzu's most important concept for practitioners, attacking the enemy's strategy, which I shall analyze later in this essay. The basic idea—important to other chapters in this volume—is to conceive of a course of action that will induce the enemy to blunder into a self-defeating reaction. A simple example would be to "offer the enemy a bait to lure him."[11] American operators typically want to find, fix, and fight enemy forces as directly as possible; Sun Tzu wants to proceed more indirectly by inducing the enemy to move into a trap or some other disadvantageous position. Here he mostly had in mind the achievement of an advantage in war fighting, but his logic applies to peacetime competition, too.

Clausewitz would take a dim view of Sun Tzu's hyperrationality supported by these creative ways of mastering interaction. He had a notoriously low opinion of the reliability of most intelligence; he believed deception and surprise to be overrated; and he distrusted clever or complex schemes of maneuver. For the Prussian, ingenuity was no match for the resolute application of force.[12] The Sun Tzuian counterargument would be that a Clausewitzian sense of realism crowds out a proper appreciation of the importance of creativity in a strategic leader or an operational commander. Although Clausewitz seemed to regard the options worth serious consideration in a given situation to be relatively few and rather obvious, Sun Tzu believed leaders with creative minds, entrepreneurial spirits, and different types of forces or instruments at their disposal could come up with many potentially effective combinations of means and ways to master interaction with adversaries at a reasonable cost.

Blending creativity with realism, practitioners have to ponder two key questions: Can they come up with a course of action that will lead to (or toward) a stipulated political objective at a level of cost and risk commensurate with the value of the object? How will adversaries, and other audiences as well, react militarily and politically to such a course of action? Practitioners on both sides of a conflict are bound to have major difficulties in handling the key issues of rationality and interaction captured in these questions. But to be strategically effective, they must not get so caught up in their own problems that they lose sight of those of the other side. Rather, they need to think creatively about how to exploit the adversary's difficulties in handling the two faces of each of the two megaconcepts.

The rest of this chapter will explore four faces of the adversary on which American practitioners can operate, looking into denial strategies, cost-imposing strategies, other ways of attacking the enemy's strategy, and attacks on the enemy's political system. These represent an overlapping series of strategic concepts. We shall identify and evaluate some historical examples of each of them. These examples demonstrate that the logic of the concepts applies to both mastering interaction in war and gaining advantage in peacetime competitions. We shall also draw from these examples some implications for possible future scenarios.

In evaluating strategies, we need to have in mind how they play out in enemy political systems (the second face of the interaction megaconcept). Clausewitz identifies three political endgames on the losing side. His preferred endgame is to render the enemy physically unable to carry on the conflict, but he recognizes that achieving this ideal result may require the winning side to pay a high cost. Accordingly, he points out two alternative endgames by which the adversary might give in to our political will: "Inability to carry on the struggle can, in practice, be replaced by two other grounds for making peace: the first is the improbability of victory; the second is its unacceptable cost."[13] In the 21st century, in conflicts against states possessing nuclear weapons, it seems inconceivable that the United States would be willing to run the risk of military operations that could largely destroy the enemy's physical ability to continue fighting, and, in wars against amorphous nonstate adversaries, it seems unlikely that the United States would be able totally to destroy their ability to carry on. If that is so, Clausewitz's two alternative endgames provide paths to victory worth exploring, though it may turn out that, to arrive at the best possible political outcome in a conflict, we have to plunge deeper into the dynamics of enemy political systems.

STRATEGIES OF DENIAL

In approaching the adversary's first face of rationality, the means-ends relationship, practitioners are prompted to adopt strategies that make it hard for the adversary to translate its operational means into the political ends that it desires. Here we are primarily looking for ways to make our adversaries conclude that victory for their side is improbable. The social science shorthand for such strategies is "denial."

Since the middle of the 20th century, the United States has made significant use of strategies of denial in war, especially by integrating air power with ground forces. For example, in 1950, even before the amphibious operation at Inchon, U.S. air power (much of it launched from aircraft carriers) in support of South Korean and American ground troops (hanging on desperately in the Pusan perimeter) kept the North Korean invasion force from winning a quick decisive victory. In 1972, American air operations allowed the South Vietnamese army to deny North Vietnam victory when the communists launched their Easter offensive.[14] In 1991, operational integration of air power and ground forces prevented Saddam Hussein from consolidating his conquest of Kuwait.

Denial operations serve to blunt the strategic effectiveness of surprise attacks. Developing and demonstrating the capability to execute such operations may serve to deter future attacks. If victory seems improbable to adversaries, it would be rational for those who contemplate an attack to hold back from launching it. Such is the prospect held out by advocates of major improvements in American "AirSea" capabilities against the threat posed by new Chinese military capabilities in the Western Pacific.[15] Here we see strategies of denial at odds with each other. China increasingly seeks to deny to the United States the military access necessary to protect allies and friends in the region. The United States increasingly must develop means and ways to keep its bases and forward-deployed forces from suffering a "knockout blow" from

Chinese missile strikes integrated with other air, submarine, surface, space, and cyber operations.

The most important historical case of a denial strategy in a peacetime competition has its intellectual point of departure in George Kennan's famous X article in *Foreign Affairs* in 1947, which introduced the notion of "containment" into the American strategic lexicon.[16] Containment was essentially a denial strategy for a long-term competition short of war with the Soviet Union. Kennan's creative thought rested on an insightful assessment of the Stalinist political system, especially of vulnerabilities that might eventuate in the "mellowing" of the USSR's foreign policy or even the breakup of the Soviet system as a whole. Kennan did not propose direct U.S. pressure on that system so much as he suggested denying the Soviets further foreign expansion. He was not specific about the forms containment should take and about how its effects would play on the vulnerabilities of the Soviet political system that he identified. Perhaps understandably in an open publication, he did not consider how the Soviets might try to outmaneuver efforts to contain them, for example by supporting wars waged by proxies or associated movements, which if successful would expand their influence and even if unsuccessful would impose significant costs on the United States. Though the theory of victory for the United States in Kennan's article was thus not complete or altogether coherent, one can make a case that containment as implemented in practice, and as supported by nuclear deterrence, did balk any straightforward Soviet theory of victory for the Cold War. But to capture the full contribution of American strategy to the outcome of the long-term competition with the Soviet Union, we shall later have to take into account other strategic approaches.

Even when strategies of denial succeed in blunting or deterring an attack, they have limited effectiveness in bringing about an optimal political outcome. For Clausewitz, the point of war is "to compel our enemy to do our will," but denial strategies often fail to do so in a durable manner.[17] For Basil Liddell Hart, the larger purpose of war is to create "a better state of peace," but denial strategies rarely produce such a favorable political outcome.[18] It is noteworthy that policymakers' desire for a favorable and durable peace tilted the debate in Washington in the summer of 1950 toward a decision to seek a unified Korea through an offensive north of the 38th parallel (which brought a greater war rather than a better peace).[19] Though denial operations against North Vietnam's Easter offensive of 1972 made possible the subsequent peace settlement, President Richard Nixon realized that the Vietnamese communist leadership put such a high value on gaining control over South Vietnam that the peace would not last unless the United States remained willing for years to come to use its air power in support of South Vietnamese ground forces against a renewed North Vietnamese offensive. Even the substantial drubbing inflicted on Iraqi military forces in 1991 did not resolve the basic long-term strategic problem posed by Saddam Hussein. In the Cold War, denial through mutually assured destruction helped to produce nuclear arms control agreements in the 1970s but did not move the long-term competition between the United States and the Soviet Union toward a "better state of peace" or even improve the overall American strategic position.

COST-IMPOSING STRATEGIES

When the value of the object is high for adversaries, and when at first they are denied victory, their political will is likely to stimulate new ways, or perhaps new efforts with old ways, to gain it. A logical response to this interaction dynamic by American strategists is to add a cost-imposing strategy to a denial strategy. If convincing the enemy of the improbability of victory is difficult, maybe the cost of continuing or renewing the conflict for such a willful enemy can be driven to a prohibitive level. A double-barreled approach might improve the odds of a favorable and durable political outcome.

Perhaps the best example of such an American strategy executed with explicit intent in a hot war is the campaign in the South Pacific theater against Japan in 1942.[20] It had a denial element: to prevent the Japanese from gaining bases from which they could interdict sea lines of communication between the United States and Australia. The most fervent proponent of the campaign, Admiral Ernest King, also saw the American wresting of Guadalcanal from Japanese control as the first step in a major counteroffensive that would give the strategic initiative thenceforth to the United States. More salient for our purposes, President Franklin Roosevelt articulated (in public and within the high command) a broader cost-imposing strategic intent. Assessing that Japanese productive capacity and logistical capabilities had already reached their limits in 1942, he saw the opportunity to tax the Japanese economy and reduce Japanese power even as the American war economy was still early in its mobilization.[21] The successful exploitation of that opportunity in 1942 was not "decisive" in the sense of guaranteeing the ultimate achievement of unlimited American political objectives, but it was "pivotal" in turning the tide and accelerating the currents that would lead to victory over Japan.

It is instructive to contrast success in the Pacific with the disappointing in-effectiveness of the strategic concepts that underpinned American ground and air operations in the Vietnam War from 1965 to 1968. Both sets of operations, supposed to ensure the survival of an independent, noncommunist South Vietnam, had denial and cost-imposing elements. General Westmoreland's search-and-destroy ground operations were to impose a heavy cost in casu-alties on the communist forces. The denial aspect depended on the assump-tion that the North Vietnamese leaders would come to recognize a "crossover point" where their personnel losses surpassed their capacity to replace them and that they would then make a projection that it would be impossible for them to win the war.[22] Air operations against North Vietnam would support a denial strategy by making it difficult for the communists in the north to supply their comrades fighting in the south. Beyond that, a gradual escalation in the intensity and northward reach of strategic bombing would impose a mounting cost on the North Vietnamese economy. The assumption here was that this economic cost would eventually become unacceptable to the com-munist leaders in Hanoi. With the prospect of victory waning and the costs of continued warfare rising, those leaders would make a rational decision to make peace on terms favorable to the United States and South Vietnam.

This double-barreled theory of victory was both creative and unrealistic. It did not rest on a solid assessment of the enemy and a shrewd anticipation of interaction dynamics. The flexibility of the Vietnamese communists' neo-Maoist operational doctrine and the proximity of cross-border sanctuaries made it possible for the enemy to maintain considerable control over the rate at which it suffered casualties. The massive material support to Hanoi from the Soviets and Chinese amply compensated for the amount of economic and logistical damage that American bombing imposed on North Vietnam. Per-haps above all in strategic significance, the value of the object for the enemy was so high that the level of acceptable cost for the communist leadership was greater than most American strategists were inclined to credit.

Cost-imposing strategies can play a significant role in a long-term peace-time competition. An excellent example provides intellectual inspiration for this volume. In 1972, when the draining of American resources in Vietnam was putting the United States at a competitive disadvantage in the larger Cold War, Andrew Marshall broached a creative case for a consciously conceived cost-imposing strategy against the Soviet Union.[23] By the 1980s all the Ameri-can military services, and other government agencies as well, were working up new courses of action and wielding new instruments that had some actual or potential cost-imposing effect on the Soviets.

Cost-imposing strategies are most effective against imperial powers, such as Japan in World War II and the Soviet Union in the Cold War, who have expansive political ambitions that outrun their economic or financial base and who, unlike North Vietnam in the Vietnam War, have no allies able to share the material burden. Sooner or later such "overstretched" powers are bound to come face to face with the limits of their productive capacity and logistical capability, with a fiscal crunch and perhaps even a government cash-flow crisis, with a spiral of price inflation and currency depreciation, or with a major balance-of-payments problem and acute shortages of foreign-exchange reserves.[24] After the Marshall study of 1972, the expansionist tendencies of Soviet foreign policy loomed larger, Soviet support for allies and associated movements became a greater material burden, the realignment of China added a big item to the Soviet enemies' list, and the growth rate of the Soviet economy decelerated apace. In the 1980s the Soviet state faced a fiscal crunch and a foreign-exchange crisis.

Limited opening of Soviet-era archives has not yet made possible any well-founded estimates of the increments of additional cost incurred by the Soviets in reacting to American actions and programs in the 1980s. The most eye-opening archival findings, by Yegor Gaidar, suggest that the external pressure with greatest effect at the margin in the "mellowing" of Soviet foreign policy under Mikhail Gorbachev came not from the American cost-imposing side of the "scissors" but from the income-cutting impact of the Saudi oil-production decision in 1985 that so dramatically drove down energy prices in 1986. With the resulting collapse of its most critical source of revenue and foreign-exchange reserves, the Soviet state spiraled ever deeper into fiscal and balance-of-payments crises, which in turn had the effect, according to Gaidar, of foreclosing options other than major foreign-policy concessions on Gorbachev's part in the late 1980s.[25]

As a complement to a cost-imposing strategy, depriving a political system of inputs or income vital to its economic viability can indeed have powerful effects. When the United States in 1941 imposed an oil embargo and exchange controls on Japan, the effect was for the worse: The Japanese responded with a surprise attack on Pearl Harbor and a remarkably successful offensive against Western imperial possessions in Southeast Asia and the Southwest Pacific.[26] Two major reasons that the effect was for the better in the Soviet case were that by 1986 Gorbachev was already predisposed to reappraise the value of the object and reassess Soviet strategy in the Cold War and that the Soviet military was under civilian control in a way that the Japanese military was not in 1941.

As a provisional generalization, one might say that strategies imposing mounting costs on the enemy may be pivotal in major hot wars and protracted cold wars, turning an unfavorable strategic situation into a more favorable one, or may accelerate an already advantageous process of attrition of enemy capabilities and will. But unless there is a reappraisal of the value of the object in the enemy political system linked to an internal power shift that brings new decision makers to the fore, cost-imposing strategies are likely to fall short of getting the enemy to do our political will in a durable manner. If that is so, it behooves us to bring into play strategies keyed on the two faces of the interaction megaconcept.

ATTACKING THE ENEMY'S STRATEGY

Strategists should recall that attacking the enemy's strategy is at the top of Sun Tzu's menu of options for how to win.[27] Two forms of interaction games are worth consideration, a reactive form and a proactive form. Both point toward manipulating interaction in ways that involve adversaries in a dynamic of defeating themselves. The proactive approach to inducing strategically self-defeating behavior on the enemy side is one that non-Western enemies of the United States use more readily than leaders who emerge from American strategic culture and educational institutions. The reactive approach, by contrast, is more easily found in the American strategic tradition.

The military operations at Yorktown in 1781 that proved decisive in securing the independence of the United States are a good example of such reactive counterpunching. In the summer of 1781 the British army commander Cornwallis based his force of more than 7,000 troops on the Virginia coast—the only place where a joint and combined operation of French naval forces and American and French ground forces had a good chance of closing a fatal trap on him. If his forces had remained at Wilmington, on the North Carolina coast, it is unlikely that Washington's army coming from the New York area could have reached that far south without melting away in the summer heat and humidity. If Cornwallis's forces had gone farther north than Virginia, the French naval commander de Grasse would have been unwilling to project his fleet that far from its base in the Caribbean. In looking for insight into how to attack an enemy political system, we shall later consider the reaction of the British political system to the capitulation of Cornwallis's army at Yorktown.

One does not have to go back so far in history to find conspicuous examples of enemies using proactive interaction games against the United States. Al Qaeda leaders seem to have assumed that the United States would react to the September 11, 2001, terrorist attacks by invading Afghanistan on much the same massive scale as the Soviet Union had done from late 1979. Subsequently, as Al Qaeda's associated movements opened new theaters elsewhere, the further assumption was that the United States would scurry to respond hither and yon. Such attempts to provoke or bait the adversary are characteristic of terrorist interaction games in many cases. The assumed strategic effect in this case was that the United States would ultimately bleed itself to bankruptcy, as Usama Bin Laden prognosticated in 2004.[28] We thus see here a compound concept of attacking the enemy's strategy, or its presumed strategic proclivities, and of imposing costs on the enemy.

As one would expect from the strategic culture in which Sun Tzu has long held pride of place, we can find examples of proactive interaction games in the Chinese military tradition, and not least in the repertoire of Mao Zedong. Having read Sun Tzu, and striving to stand out as a communist leader in the first phase of an insurgency from rural base areas against the Kuomintang government in the 1930s, Mao wanted "boldly to lure the enemy troops in deep" and then "annihilate them."[29] Intervening in the Korean War against the United States in 1950, Mao and his theater commander Peng Dehuai replayed the same game in a regional war, springing a trap on MacArthur's forces as they rushed headlong toward the Yalu River. In Peng's later Sun Tzuian telling: "We employed the tactics of purposely showing ourselves to be weak, increasing the arrogance of the enemy, letting him run amuck, and luring him deep into our areas."[30] The immediate operational result was the worst setback in American military history.

In the Taiwan Strait crisis of 1958, Mao sought to transport interaction games into the maritime domain. That September, he spoke to his colleagues of ensnaring "America's neck . . . in China's iron noose."[31] He had ordered repeated bombardment of Jinmen (Quemoy) and Mazu (Matsu), and the Eisenhower administration had responded, with evident reluctance, by linking the security of those two offshore islands to the defense of Taiwan, for which the United States had assumed a treaty obligation. Soviet leader Nikita Khrushchev had in turn warned Eisenhower that he would regard an American attack on the People's Republic of China (PRC) as an attack on the USSR. In these circumstances, Mao assumed that he had more leverage over the United States than vice versa.

All these examples of interaction games feature a weaker strategic actor trying to get a stronger adversary to engage in strategically self-defeating behavior. But Sun Tzu did not regard his "keys to victory" solely as a weapon of the weak, and neither should we. In many conflicts, the outcome is largely determined by which side, whether initially stronger or weaker in operational terms, ultimately defeats itself in strategic terms. If so, it makes sense for the United States as well as for its weaker adversaries to think about how to induce the other side to defeat itself.

Mastering interaction in such a sophisticated way is, to be sure, easier said than done. For interaction games to have good odds of producing the desired strategic effect, it is not necessarily enough to lure the enemy into a trap. Once in that trap, the enemy needs to be impaled on the horns of a dilemma. There must be no good option left open to it. The shock for the victim of a sudden attack or maneuver into a trap should, ideally, be followed by despair or panic over the difficulty of getting out of it and righting the reversal of fortunes. As usual with Sun Tzuian schemes of maneuver, psychological effects loom large in the theory of victory.

If the victim can wiggle off the horns and avoid getting stuck in the trap, it can not only deny its adversary a strategic victory but with adaptability can also turn the fortunes of war against its adversary in a subsequent round of interaction. The United States has been able to circumvent or bounce off the putative horns of a dilemma in the traps set for it that I have used as examples of proactive interaction games. But the United States has then had shortcomings of creativity in fully righting the reversal of fortunes.

After the 9/11 terrorist strikes, from Al Qaeda's unimaginative perspective, the United States only had two bad options in Afghanistan, a Soviet-style invasion or cruise-missile strikes of the sort that had redounded to Bin Laden's advantage with Muslim audiences in 1998. The United States was able in the fall of 2001 to improvise a more creative response to overthrow the Taliban regime. It did not, however, take out either the Al Qaeda or the Taliban leadership. A decade later, the outcome in the "AfPak" theater remained undetermined.

In the Taiwan Strait crisis of 1958, the United States was willing to stick naval forces into Mao's so-called iron noose. Taking that risk paid off. As American ships helped to supply Chiang Kai-shek's forces on offshore islands within range of PRC artillery fire, Mao did not attack them. Even as he backed off his earlier bluster to his Chinese colleagues, his bluster to his Soviet allies about a potential nuclear war over the Taiwan issue caused them to back away from him. American risk taking in 1958 had a disruptive effect on the Sino-Soviet alliance. Without firing a shot, the United States had potentially improved its position in the long-term competition with the Soviet Union. But more than a decade passed before a U.S. leader made a sustained, creative, diplomatic attempt to exploit the ever-growing rift between the Soviets and the Chinese.

In the Korean War, the stunning Chinese attack of late 1950 caused a panic-stricken MacArthur to react as if the United States were on the horns of a dilemma in Korea. In his view, it had to withdraw from the Korean peninsula and open a new theater, the Chinese homeland, not with American ground troops, but rather with air strikes, a naval blockade, and support for a cross-strait amphibious operation by Chiang Kai-shek's forces. While the Joint Chiefs of Staff gave more credence to MacArthur's case than their public utterances revealed, civilian policymakers rebuffed it. A new commander in Korea, General Matthew Ridgway, gave operational support to the policymakers' desire to hang on in Korea by developing increasingly effective ways of counterpunching against a series of Chinese offensives in the winter and spring of 1951. But then a risk-averse Ridgway missed a promising opportunity in June 1951 to terminate the war on favorable terms.[32] As a result, the war dragged on for two more years.

So far this discussion of attacking the enemy's strategy has drawn on examples from wartime cases (or, in the 1958 case, a crisis seemingly on the brink of war). But Sun Tzu holds out the ideal of achieving a major strategic edge without fighting. Beyond the use of deterrence in a cold war, can we usefully apply the concept of attacking the adversary's strategy to a peacetime competition?

Andrew Marshall in 1972, and Thomas Schelling before him in 1967, pointed out the potential importance of diverting or steering a peacetime adversary's strategy away from the courses of action, allocations of resources, and areas of competition that were most dangerous to one's own side and toward efforts that were less advantageous or even counterproductive to the other side. Marshall at that time focused on competition between Soviet and American nuclear force postures, but the concept of "competitive strategies" had potential application on a grander scale in the Cold War.[33] Schelling was impressed by fellow economist Burton Klein's observations about how strategic bombing operations from the west against Germany in World War II caused Hitler's government to divert about one-third of its war production to air defense of the homeland and away from the most dangerous threat to the Nazi regime, the Soviet ground advance from the east.[34] Of course, in the short term, a creative strategy of "diverting" or "steering" an adversary's strategy in a peacetime competition can produce only relatively small effects compared to what brute force can generate in a high-intensity war fought for unlimited political objectives. But there can be a cumulative and reinforcing series of diversionary effects over the long term in a cold war if enough well-chosen areas of competition are brought into play by one side and if strong vested interests or inflamed emotions develop on the other side in favor of allocations of resources that are strategically disadvantageous to it in the overall conflict.

ATTACKING THE ADVERSARY'S POLITICAL SYSTEM

Both hot wars and cold wars are ultimately competitions between political systems. Even as there is dynamic interaction in the operational arena between the military forces and nonmilitary instruments of the competing political systems, there is dynamic interaction within the different political systems on the different sides of the conflict. Leaders of political systems must maintain support from both their military counterparts and their population base (or, at least, "core support groups" within it) if they are to carry on the competition.[35] To compel the enemy to do your will means causing its political system either to disintegrate or to decide to give in to your peace terms.

A creative strategist ought to focus most intently on courses of actions that attack the enemy political system, that generate effects likely to cut away at the support that the political leaders on the other side need from within their system or the crucial inputs that they need from outside their system. A theory of victory for one's own side requires a theory of defeat for the enemy side, a set of assumptions about the political endgames that might play out in a particular political system as it comes under heavy strategic pressure. At first sight, making such an assessment seems to be extraordinarily challenging. But considering historical examples can help us see that some grasp of key characteristics of a political system is not beyond the reach of strategists if they are willing to make an intellectual effort or if they are able to draw on intelligence analysis focused on political systems, not just military systems.

Take, for example, the defeat mechanism at work within the British political system at the end of the American Revolutionary War. When news of Cornwallis's capitulation at Yorktown reached London in late 1781, it had a big psychological shock effect on Lord North, who as chancellor of the Exchequer was the king's notional prime minister. North had long doubted that the value of holding on in America was worth the cost of doing so, and the loss at Yorktown magnified those doubts. But, then as before, King George III rebuffed North's desire to give up and accept American independence. This time, however, there was an internal power shift in the British political system. Over the next several months after Yorktown, as members of Parliament reflected on what had happened, North lost his ability to muster majority support in the House of Commons. The parliamentary opposition took over and negotiated peace with the United States.[36] This political endgame reflected the rules that had come to govern the interaction among the monarch, ministers, and members of Parliament since the British revolution of 1688. American leaders did not know what George III or North really thought at any given time, but they were familiar with the rules of the British political game. They were also quite aware of divisions within the British political elite over the war.

Two centuries later, the United States was able to attack a very different political system in a cold war competition because it had developed and then updated the ability to anticipate Soviet political dynamics that might culminate in a favorable endgame. Kennan's X article of 1947 had foreseen the "mellowing" of Soviet foreign policy and even the "breakup" of the Soviet system. Among the circumstances that he judged likely to generate such political outcomes were problems of leadership succession in the Kremlin, tensions between the Soviet government and the Soviet people over the provision of consumer goods, and loss of ideological conviction.[37] All three of those circumstances were quite evident to key officials in the Reagan administration. To be sure, in the early 1980s no one, not even Richard Pipes, could reasonably anticipate the breakup of the Soviet Union by the early 1990s.[38] But "mellowing" was a realistic prospect. Ronald Reagan, like Margaret Thatcher, was quick to sense that Gorbachev was a new, more conciliatory kind of Soviet leader. Pipes and other staffers on the National Security Council focused on Soviet difficulties in earning foreign exchange, and CIA Director William Casey keenly appreciated how lower oil prices would make those difficulties much worse. It was increasingly apparent that the Soviet system could not meet consumer demand for food without massive imports to make up for shortfalls in the food supply from its chronically troubled agricultural sector. The basic intellectual ingredients for a strategy of attacking the Soviet political system were at hand at the top of the American political system.

For the United States to be effective in attacking adversaries' political systems in the future, it will have to attain the level of thought that went into understanding the Soviet system. Even though the United States has vast legions of academics and analysts, that level of thought is not much in evidence now. We still do not understand much about the nonstate political system that AQAM has been able to piece together in western Pakistan since 2001.

The bizarre North Korean political system remains opaque to us. The RAND Corporation has made a promising start with a series of studies on the Iranian political system, but there is only a shallow pool of experts on Iran in universities, think tanks, and government agencies who are equally at home with Iranian culture and strategic logic.[39] There is a profusion of experts on China, but we still know little about how Chinese political leaders and military leaders think and interact with each other about strategy.[40]

CONCLUSION

We are now in an era when the United States can no longer expect to overcome its strategic problems with sheer material superiority or overwhelming military force. If there are major interstate wars in the American future, they are likely to be fought against adversaries with nuclear weapons, and rationality suggests that the risk of escalation will constrain the use of overwhelming force by the United States. Furthermore, the logic of interaction suggests that adversaries will seek, and to some extent find, ways to sidestep American strategies predicated on material superiority. Yet another troubling prospect lurks in the material dimension of strategy: The economic and financial bases for material superiority are eroding in the United States. Unless a new wave of technological innovation and total-factor-productivity growth leads to an American economic resurgence, or unless there is an unexpected convergence by both political parties toward a sensible set of reforms of taxation policy and entitlement programs, a severe fiscal crunch looms dead ahead for the United States.

The Pentagon is very likely to be squeezed in such a crunch. The upshot is that enhanced strategic brains will have to compensate for diminished strategic brawn. Creativity will be at a premium. This chapter's excursion through an elaborate architecture of advanced strategic concepts points toward the sort of educational journey that American practitioners of strategy should be embarking on soon.

NOTES

The usual disclaimer in a publication by a U.S. Naval War College faculty member applies with special force to this essay: The author's views, especially about future contingencies, do not represent or reflect the views of the Naval War College, the U.S. Navy, or the U.S. government.

1. Carl von Clausewitz, *On War,* trans. and ed. Michael Howard and Peter Paret (Princeton, NJ: Princeton University Press, 1989), 149.

2. Ibid., 92.

3. Ibid., 77, 585–586.

4. Ibid., 485.

5. Ibid., 139.

6. Ibid., 585.

7. Sun Tzu, *The Art of War,* ed. Samuel B. Griffith (Oxford, UK: Oxford University Press, 1971), 77–79.

8. Ibid., 73–74.

9. In a metaphor that captures all the advantages of maneuver warfare, Sun Tzu highlights the prowess of a hawk (a forerunner of the unmanned aerial vehicle?), which can strike its target at the right time, from an unexpected place, and at a tempo with which the prey cannot cope. See Ibid., 92.

10. Ibid., 70.

11. Ibid., 66.

12. Clausewitz, *On War,* 75–76.

13. Ibid., 91.

14. Robert Pape, *Bombing to Win: Air Power and Coercion in War* (Ithaca, NY, and London: Cornell University Press, 1996), 195–210. Pape is the principal theoretical advocate of strategies of denial.

15. Jan van Tol, with Mark Gunzinger, Andrew Krepinevich, and Jim Thomas, *AirSea Battle: A Point-of-Departure Operational Concept* (Washington, DC: Center for Strategic and Budgetary Assessments, 2010).

16. X [George Kennan], "The Sources of Soviet Conduct," *Foreign Affairs,* 25 (July 1947): 566–582.

17. The quotation comes from the first page (75) of Clausewitz's *On War.* Later in his first chapter (80), he warns that the result of a war often is not final.

18. B. H. Liddell Hart, *Strategy,* 2nd rev. ed. (New York: Signet, 1974), 338.

19. In July 1950 there was apprehension in both the U.S. State Department and the Pentagon that unless the North Korean regime was eliminated, it would try another attack in the future. See U.S. Department of State, *Foreign Relations of the United States 1950,* vol. VII: *Korea* (Washington, DC: Government Printing Office, 1976), 452, 459, 503.

20. Bradford A. Lee, "A Pivotal Campaign in a Peripheral Theater: Guadalcanal and World War II in the Pacific," in *Naval Power and Expeditionary Wars: Peripheral Campaigns and New Theaters of Naval Warfare,* Bruce Elleman and S. C. M. Paine, eds. (London: Routledge, 2011).

21. "Address of the President Delivered by Radio from the White House," February 23, 1942, available at www.mhric.org/fdr/chat20.html; and Roosevelt to MacArthur, May 6, 1942, RG 4, Box 15, MacArthur Papers, MacArthur Memorial, Norfolk, VA.

22. Andrew F. Krepinevich, *The Army and Vietnam* (Baltimore: Johns Hopkins University Press, 1986), 141–179 *passim.*

23. A. W. Marshall, *Long-Term Competition with the Soviets: A Framework for Strategic Analysis* (Santa Monica, CA: RAND Corporation, 1972). The purpose of this study was to influence practice. For an earlier analysis pitched at an audience of theorists, see T. C. Schelling, "The Strategy of Inflicting Costs," in *Issues in Defense Economics*, Roland N. McKean, ed. (Cambridge, MA: National Bureau of Economic Research, 1967), 105–128.

24. The classic historical study of imperial "overstretch" is Paul Kennedy, *The Rise and Fall of the Great Powers* (New York: Random House, 1987).

25. Yegor Gaidar, *Collapse of an Empire: Lessons for Modern Russia,* trans. Antonina W. Bouis (Washington, DC: Brookings Institution Press, 2007). Since 1981 William Casey, and other American policymakers, had been trying to persuade the Saudis to drive down the price of oil, but the Saudi decision to do so in 1985 was probably motivated by their own economic interests. Compare Daniel Yergin, *The Prize* (New York: Free Press, 1993), 745–751; and Peter Schweizer, *Victory* (New York: Atlantic Monthly Press, 1994), 31–32, 99, 140–143, 154, 179, 203–205, 217–220, 232–233, 237, and 256.

26. Edward S. Miller, *Bankrupting the Enemy: The U.S. Financial Siege of Japan before Pearl Harbor* (Annapolis, MD: Naval Institute Press, 2007).

27. Sun Tzu, *Art of War,* 77.

28. Bin Laden video posted on Al Jazeera's website, November 1, 2004.

29. Mao Zedong, *Problems of Strategy in China's Revolutionary War* (Peking: Foreign Language Press, 1968; original version, Dec. 1936), chapter 5; and Mao's "Order to Lure the Enemy Deep into the Red Area, Wait until They Are Exhausted, and Annihilate Them," Nov. 1, 1930, in Stuart R. Schram, ed., *Mao's Road to Power: Revolutionary Writings, 1912–1949,* vol. III (New York: M. E. Sharpe, 1995), 656–657.

30. Peng's memoirs, as quoted in Eliot A. Cohen and John Gooch, *Military Misfortunes: The Anatomy of Failure in War* (New York: Free Press, 1996), 178.

31. Quoted in Chen Jian, *Mao's China and the Cold War* (Chapel Hill: University of North Carolina Press, 2001), 187.

32. Colin Jackson, "Lost Chance or Lost Horizon? Strategic Opportunity and Escalation Risk in the Korean War, April–July 1951," *Journal of Strategic Studies* 33 (April 2010): 255–289.

33. Marshall, *Long-Term Competition,* 33–38.

34. Schelling, "Inflicting Costs", 122, and Burton H. Klein, *Germany's Economic Preparations for War* (Cambridge, MA: Harvard University Press, 1959), 232–233.

35. I borrow the term *core support groups* from Jonathan Kirshner, "The Microfoundations of Economic Sanctions," *Security Studies* 6 (Spring 1997): 42.

36. Ian R. Christie, *The End of North's Ministry 1780–1782* (London: Macmillan & Co., 1958), 257–369.

37. X [Kennan], "The Sources of Soviet Conduct," 576–580.

38. Richard Pipes, "The Soviet Union in Crisis," text of speech given in Bonn, Cologne, and Paris, Oct. 1982, Pipes Files, Box 3, Ronald Reagan Presidential Library, Simi Valley, CA.

39. For the RAND studies, see Keith Crane et al., *Iran's Political, Demographic, and Economic Vulnerabilities* (2008); Jerrold Green et al., *Understanding Iran* (2009); Frederic Wehrey et al., *The Rise of the Pasdaran: Assessing the Domestic Roles of Iran's Revolutionary Guards Corps* (2009); and David E. Thaler et al., *Mullahs, Guards, and Bonyads: An Exploration of Iranian Leadership Dynamics* (2010).

40. Andrew Scobell, "Is There a Civil-Military Gap in China's Peaceful Rise?" *Parameters* 39 (Summer 2009): 4–20.

4 BARRIERS TO ACTING STRATEGICALLY
Why Strategy Is So Difficult

Barry D. Watts

WHY DOES THE DEVELOPMENT and, above all, execution of effective strategy almost always turn out to be so difficult? Why, to paraphrase Carl von Clausewitz's enduring insight regarding friction in war, does everything in strategy appear to be very simple in theory and yet turn out to be so difficult in practice?[1] Why is it, as John Collins concluded from experience teaching at the National War College, that strategy is a game that most anyone can play but one that only the most gifted participants "can play well"?[2] The aim of this chapter is to offer some answers to these elementary questions.

Because the answers hinge on the fundamental nature of strategic choice, the first step will be to clarify the concept of strategy. Although strategy may appear to be a simple concept, it is not. Most of us think we understand completely what the natural numbers (1, 2, 3, . . .) are. But in 1992 Thoraf Skolem proved that we cannot capture unambiguously what they are even in a formal mathematical language.[3] If anything, strategy is even more difficult to nail down, especially in the far more slippery semantics of a natural language such as English. I will therefore offer a sampling of definitions drawn from both military affairs and business before presenting six reasons why strategy is so difficult.

NOTIONS OF STRATEGY

This chapter, and this volume as a whole, focuses mainly on strategy in competitive rather than noncompetitive situations. In competitive situations, strategy looks outward, focusing directly on beating the opponent or adversary. In noncompetitive situations, by contrast, strategy looks inward, usually involving an irreversible commitment of resources to achieve some desired future, such as a corporation adapting itself to a changed business environment. In both cases, the strategic choices irreversibly close the door to the alternatives at a point in time. Although the distinction may be more a matter of degree than an either-or choice, it does suggest that the term *competitive strategies* is not redundant. As Andrew Marshall has emphasized, competitive strategies are both inward and outward directed: They build on one's enduring strengths while seeking to exploit the adversary's enduring weaknesses and vulnerabilities.[4]

One can legitimately apply the concept of strategy to a vast range of situations. It is this almost unlimited range of situations in which strategies can be applied that makes the underlying concept so elusive and complex that all of its important aspects cannot be captured in any single definition. A more realistic approach is to offer a range of alternative formulations that highlight different aspects or dimensions of strategy. Here are six drawn from military and business experience:

1. Strategy is the use of armed forces in the engagement to achieve the objectives of the war; strategy "decides the time when, the place where, and the forces with which the engagement is to be fought" (Carl von Clausewitz, 1831).[5]

2. Modern strategy is "the use that is made of force and the threat of force for the ends of policy" (Colin Gray, 1999).[6]

3. Strategy is "a heuristic solution to a problem"; in competitive situations, strategy is "usually an insight that creates or exploits a decisive asymmetry" (Richard Rumelt, 2007).[7]

4. Strategy is "managing the slow-moving variables in a strategic situation in order to change or reshape the situation in one's favor by influencing the options or possibilities that emerge over time" (Sidney Winter, 2008).[8]

5. Strategy in competitive situations is "fundamentally about identifying or creating asymmetric advantages that can be exploited to help achieve one's ultimate objectives despite resource and other constraints, most importantly the opposing efforts of adversaries or competitors and the inherent unpredictability of strategic outcomes" (Andrew Krepinevich and Barry Watts, 2009.)[9]

6. The concept of strategy "is usually is embedded in a notion of strategic choice, or choice. The idea is that you choose among alternatives, hoping to realize various consequences. And the quality of the strategy depends on how you define the alternatives and how accurately you can estimate their consequences" (James March, 2009).[10]

The first two formulations (by Clausewitz and Gray) have clearly been drawn from warfare—the use of armed force by states to achieve their ends. Gray's definition moves slightly beyond Clausewitz's in explicitly adding the threat of force to its actual use. He argues that an expansive understanding of Clausewitz "tells us that strategy is the use of tacit and explicit threats, as well as of actual battles and campaigns, to advance political purposes."[11] On this reading, military strategy includes nuclear deterrence as well as conventional conflict between states.

A shortcoming of both these definitions, however, is that they give little guidance as to how one might actually develop or execute a strategy to achieve specific ends. The other four definitions were selected with this in mind. Except for the fifth (Krepinevich and Watts), which was inspired by Rumelt's emphasis on seeking decisive asymmetries (or "edges of opportunity"[12]), the other notions are drawn from strategy experience in the business world. What Rumelt's, Winter's, and March's characterizations suggest is that our understanding of national security and military strategy can benefit from looking at business strategy.[13] For example, what does Rumelt mean when he insists that strategies are heuristic solutions to problems? Convinced that the future is not predictable, he maintains that strategies are always contingent guesses about how events will work out in the long run—an insight that provides one of the strongest reasons why strategy is so difficult.

Of the six definitions, the one that seems furthest from Clausewitz and Gray's relatively traditional formulations is Winter's notion of strategy as managing the slow-moving variables in a strategic situation to create exploitable edges of opportunity. Unusual as it may be, this definition provides a point of departure for doing strategy. Strategy begins, he counsels, by determining what the slow-moving variables in a given situation are that one can alter in one's favor. He offers reputations and personnel systems as examples of slow-moving variables that good strategy can change, though usually not very quickly. Thus, for Winter, executing a strategy tends to be a long-term endeavor, especially when it involves execution by large organizations such as a corporation or a military service.

The sixth definition (March's) emphasizes the importance of defining alternatives and assessing their likely consequences. He adds, though, that when one closely scrutinizes the strategic choices most organizations have made, it is rare to find a clear linkage between strategic decisions and anticipated or actual consequences. Winter makes the related point that, when one looks into the details of most case studies of strategic choice, the role of contingency looms large. These observations imply that strategy is not the sole determinant of strategic outcomes. Even in hindsight, it is often difficult to tease out the precise contribution strategy made to the eventual result.

If strategy is as multifaceted and elusive a concept as this brief discussion suggests, then it should not be surprising to discover that achieving strategic competency in real situations—especially in competitive ones against thinking adversaries—tends to be difficult. Military history is littered with instances of major strategic errors. Consider, for instance, Adolf Hitler's decision in June 1941 to invade the Soviet Union. As Andrew Roberts has stressed, "Out of every five Germans killed in combat—rather than in aerial bombing or through other means—four died on the Eastern Front."[14] The invasion of Russia, he argues, was Hitler's "cardinal error of the war," and the preponderance of German combat losses on the Eastern Front is the conflict's "central statistic."[15] Hitler, of course, compounded that strategic blunder with others, starting with his determination to convert the German Army into an instrument of racial extermination.[16] As the war on the Eastern Front unfolded, this brutal policy undercut partisan support for the Germans by Russians disaffected with Joseph Stalin's totalitarian regime, enabling Stalin to turn the war into a patriotic struggle to save the Russian homeland.[17]

REASON 1: STRATEGIES ARE ALWAYS HEURISTICS OR GUESSES ABOUT HOW EVENTS WILL EVENTUALLY PLAY OUT

One fundamental reason why strategy in competitive situations is difficult is the nature of the endeavor. Whether the strategist is trying to gain advantage in a peacetime competition such as the Cold War or is fighting to achieve victory in combat, the adversary seeks very different outcomes. The ultimate outcome depends on contingent interactions between the two sides and, therefore, is not predictable. The enemy, as military professionals often say, always gets a vote, and what the opposition chooses to do is often unexpected, surprising, and, most important, beyond our meager powers of prediction. The adversary "is a reacting, thinking being; he is not sitting still waiting for your onslaught but actively creating his own strategy . . . to foil yours."[18] For this reason alone, the eventual result of one's chosen strategy is not predictable in advance.

In wartime, of course, strategy faces the inherent unpredictability of battlefield events that can affect strategic outcomes. Consider the contingency of engagements and battles. As General Rupert Smith has observed:

Battle is an event of circumstance, no matter how much planning, exercising and drill precede it. The chances of victory are undoubtedly increased with proper preparation, but ultimately opponents fight the battle of the day: on another day, in the same location, with exactly the same forces, they would fight another battle in different circumstances.[19]

This view of contingency affecting outcomes has also emerged from attempts to model large-scale theater warfare accurately enough to get a sense of likely war outcomes. One of the more advanced theater models developed for this purpose during the 1980s was the RAND Strategy Assessment System (RSAS), which included a module for war between the North Atlantic Treaty Organization (NATO) and the Warsaw Pact (WP). The original motivation behind the RSAS was to improve analysis of the U.S.-Soviet strategic nuclear balance by developing an automated war-gaming tool that combined "the best features of political-military war gaming and analytic modeling" through the application of state-of-the-art artificial intelligence techniques.[20] Early in the project, though, RAND researchers realized that the RSAS had to be able to handle major conventional conflicts because U.S.-Soviet nuclear exchanges seemed most likely to occur as an escalatory step during a conventional theater war.[21] A major thrust of the RSAS development thus became modeling a nonnuclear NATO-WP conventional war in Europe.

RAND completed the first version of the new model (RSAS 2.0) in late 1986.[22] In 1988 Paul Davis, who had led the project, used the RSAS to make the point that because combat outcomes "are sensitive to *scores* of factors" and subject to "massive uncertainty," it is meaningless to talk about "best-estimate" or most likely war outcomes based strictly on computer models.[23] This is because even sophisticated models like the RSAS "tend to omit many of the most important factors in actual warfare including: maneuver phenomena; strategies employing surprise and deception; realistically imperfect decisions and behavior; and important aspects of readiness, mobilization, and sustainability."[24] To drive home the point, Davis assembled a list of over twenty political-military, strategic-tactical, force size, and technical variables, any one of which could, if changed, "flip a victory of the [Warsaw] Pact to a stalwart defense for NATO" and vice versa.[25] Interestingly, Davis reached this conclusion about the sensitivity of RSAS combat outcomes several years before three of his RAND colleagues demonstrated that even a very simple combat model could exhibit nonmonotonic behavior, meaning that if one side lost the fight under a given set of starting conditions, adding capabilities to that side could, counterintuitively, result in an even less favorable outcome.[26]

Such sensitive dependence of outcomes in mathematical models has been the subject of extensive study ever since Edward Lorenz discovered, in 1963, that the long-term results of running his simple atmospheric convection model were sensitively dependent on the number of decimal places used when entering the initial state data for the model.[27] The 1991 RAND paper on non-monotonicity in a simple combat model was, however, able to show that the observed "chaotic" behavior was structural rather than computational (that is, not due to rounding errors or time-step size).[28] Since the 1960s, this sort of "chaotic" behavior has been observed in a wide range of physical phenomena from solid-state physics and hydrodynamics to electronic circuits, mechanical and electromechanical systems, musical tones, population dynamics, planetary motion, business cycles, and, of course, weather models.[29] While existence of "strange attractors" in systems whose long-term states are highly sensitive to tiny variations in initial conditions shows that they are not "patternless," such behavior in a wide range of mathematical and physical phenomena strongly suggests that combat outcomes are unlikely to be predictable.

Further, competitions between individuals, large organizations, governments, or polities all involve human belief systems. It is difficult, therefore, to see how strategies in general could be other than heuristics or guesses about how events will play out under conditions of great uncertainty. Strategic choices, however rational they may seem, occur behind a veil of uncertainty as to how the unknowable future will unfold. As Michael Howard concluded in 1991:

> In formulating laws that will be either predictive or normative[,] social scientists have been no more successful than historians; for the number of variables is so incalculable, the data inevitably so incomplete. The theories they formulate are at best explanatory or heuristic. They can never be predictive.[30]

The economist Douglass North argues that there are two principal reasons why this is so. First, we "cannot know today what we will learn tomorrow which will shape our tomorrow's actions"; and, second, the world is nonergodic, meaning that the statistical time averages of future outcomes *can be*— and, more often than most people appreciate, *are*—persistently different from the averages calculated from past observations.[31] The future, to paraphrase the options trader Nassim Taleb, is "opaque. You see what comes out, not the script that produces events, the generator of history."[32] Or, stated in the more technical terms of computer science and mathematical logic, "There is no algorithmic process to determine the future—whether it's the future of a computer program, a thought process of the human mind, or the universe as a whole."[33] In the end, strategies are guesses about how the unpredictable future will unfold after the strategist has chosen and implemented a given course of action to address a major problem. Strategic choice itself is one element of the unseen "script" that produces the eventual, but unpredictable, outcome.[34]

REASON 2: STRATEGIC CHOICES ADDRESS "WICKED" PROBLEMS

Horst Rittel and Melvin Webber introduced the term *wicked problem* in 1973 to describe social planning dilemmas such as deciding where to locate a new freeway, how to modify school curricula, what tax rate adjustments to make, or how to deal with crime.[35] They argued that these problems, unlike "tame" ones such as building a safe highway bridge, are not given to engineering solutions. Tame problems can be stated in a relatively well-defined and stable way, have a definite stopping point, are amenable to solutions that can be evaluated as being right or wrong, belong to a class of similar problems that can be solved in a similar manner, and are open to trial-and-error solutions.[36] Wicked problems, on the other hand, lack a definite problem statement (because your ideas about solving it affect your understanding of what the problem is) and do not have stopping rules. Proposed solutions are better or worse rather than right or wrong, one wicked problem cannot usually be solved like another because each is novel and unique, and trial-and-error approaches do not work because any attempted solution changes the problem.[37] Finally, they lack an enumerable set of potential solutions or articulated set of permissible operations than can be mechanically applied to generate a definitive solution. In a nutshell, wicked problems "are messy, devious, and *reactive*."[38]

How does the dichotomy between tame and wicked problems relate to military affairs? T. C. Greenwood and T. X. Hammes have observed that there is increasing awareness within the Defense Department that wars involve a complex mixture of tame and wicked problems.[39] Especially in large-scale, high-intensity, predominately kinetic combat between combined-arms air, land, or naval forces, tame problems tend to be more common at the tactical level, whereas wicked problems are increasingly predominant at the operational and strategic levels. But even this rule of thumb has exceptions. In counterinsurgency operations, many of the tactical choices may be wicked as well.[40]

Wicked problems recall Clausewitz's observation that the outcome in war is never final.[41] A defeated enemy can always try to regain the upper hand in some later round of the struggle. A recent illustration is Operation Iraqi Free-dom (OIF), which David Kilcullen has identified as an exemplar of a wicked problem.[42] By invading Iraq in 2003, "the United States and its allies opened a second front before finishing the first [in Afghanistan], and without sufficient resources to prosecute both campaigns effectively."[43] In large part, the decision to invade Iraq appears to have been taken to eliminate the weapons of mass destruction Iraq was believed to possess. But it was also motivated in part by what proved to be the somewhat unrealistic view that overthrowing Saddam Hussein's Baathist dictatorship would allow the United States to establish a modern democracy in Iraq, thereby fundamentally transforming the strategic balance in the Middle East in favor of the United States and its allies.[44] The ini-tial strategic error of opening up a second front in the "War on Terror" before the finishing the first was then compounded by "confusing entry with vic-tory."[45] This misunderstanding of the strategic problem opened the door to the emergence of an insurgency led by foreign terrorists who could not be recon-ciled with the Shi'a-dominated national government the coalition put in place after Saddam Hussein's overthrow. These terrorists, in turn, were supported and enabled by various Iraqi insurgents—Kilcullen's "accidental guerillas"—most of whom could eventually be reconciled with the national government. However, from 2003 to 2006 the coalition pursued a top-down, national-level approach to reconciliation that proved unable to quell the growing violence and stabilize the country following the military "victory" of April 2003. Then, in February 2006, Al Qaeda, in Iraq's bombing of the al'Askariyya shrine at Samarra, one of the two holiest sites in Shi'a Islam, plunged the country into outright civil war between Shi'as and Sunnis, thereby both worsening and transforming the coalition's strategic problem.[46]

The dramatic turnaround in 2007 of the security situation in Iraq began even before the "surge" of U.S. troops under General David Petraeus. Signifi-cantly, this reversal of coalition fortunes came about in ways so unexpected as to underscore the wicked nature of the problem. As Kilcullen wrote in 2009,

> The pattern we are seeing runs counter to what we expected in the Surge and therefore lies well outside the "benchmarks" established by Congress with little awareness of field conditions. As noted, the original concept of the Joint Cam-paign Plan [for 2007–2008 developed under Petraeus and Ambassador Ryan Crocker] was that we (the coalition and the Iraqi government) would create security, which would in turn create space for a "grand bargain" at the national level. Instead, in 2007 we saw the exact opposite: a series of local political deals

displaced extremists, resulting in a major improvement in security at the local level, and the national government then began to jump on board with the program. Instead of Coalition-led, top-down reconciliation, this process is Iraqi-led, bottom-up, and based on civil society rather than national politics. Oddly enough, it seems to have worked better than anyone expected. . . . [W]e are indeed seeing improved security, and political progress—but at the local, not national, level. This is not what we initially expected; but the improvement in Iraqis' daily lives and the willingness to talk rather than fight is a real improvement nonetheless.[47]

The surge's near-term success was by no means the end of the "wicked" strategy problem that the United States and its allies have encountered in Iraq. To generalize from Kilcullen's analysis, strategic problems present shifting and evolving challenges to the strategist rather than static or fixed ones, and there is "no standard set of metrics, benchmarks, or operational techniques" that apply to all strategic problems or remain valid for any single strategic problem throughout its life cycle.[48] Small wonder, then, that strategy is so difficult.

REASON 3: RESOURCES ARE ALWAYS LIMITED AND CONSTRAIN STRATEGIC CHOICE

During his long career as a business strategist, Richard Rumelt has sought to answer in his own mind why he has encountered so much bad corporate strategy. In his experience, the foremost reason is the failure to recognize that the resources needed to execute strategies are inevitably finite and scarce.[49] This recognition is, of course, a traditional point of departure for economics. To recall one of the most trenchant statements of this fact, Charles Hitch and Roland McKean wrote in 1960 that:

> Resources are always limited in comparison with our wants, always constraining our action. (If they did not, we could do everything, and there would be no problem of choosing preferred courses of action.)[50]

The American intervention in Iraq provides stark evidence of a strategic choice being made without much foresight about the resources it eventually entailed. Consider the prewar estimates by senior Pentagon officials. In February 2003, less than a month before major combat operations began on March 19, Paul Wolfowitz told the House of Representatives' Committee on the Budget that press reports of OIF's likely costs being in the vicinity of $60 to $95 billion were not credible and suggested that Iraq's oil revenues of $15 to $20 billion a year could cover reconstruction following regime change.[51] True, before offering this estimate Wolfowitz cautioned committee members that all projections of a war's costs are "extremely uncertain"; he even cited the aphorism that prediction is dangerous, especially about the future.[52] Nevertheless, even the supposedly exaggerated prewar press reports of campaign costs in the neighborhood of $60 to $95 billion underestimated actual expenditures through fiscal year (FY) 2010 by factors of eight to as much as twelve, the cumulative bill for Iraq alone since 2001 having grown to around $750 billion.[53] Moreover, not all the bills arising from the U.S. adventure in Iraq have come due. Over and above the human costs in dead, wounded, displaced, or impoverished on all sides, the direct costs for Iraq alone will probably be at least $1 trillion.

Not only have the resources the United States has expended to prosecute the global War on Terror far exceeded going-in estimates, but Al Qaeda's announced strategic approach has been to prevail by imposing costs so disproportionately large on the United States and its Western allies that they will eventually give up. This exhaustion strategy parallels at least one of the approaches that the United States employed in the 1980s to defeat the Soviet Union. As Usama bin Laden stated in 2004:

> It is easy to provoke and bait this [U.S.] administration. All we have to do is to send two *mujahidin* to the furthest point East to raise a cloth on which is written al-Qaeda, in order to make the [U.S.] generals race there to cause America to suffer human, economic and political losses without achieving anything of note . . . so we are continuing this policy of bleeding America to the point of bankruptcy.[54]

In hindsight, it seems evident that, although American strategists overlooked the fact that resources are always constrained following the attacks on the World Trade Center and the Pentagon on September 11, 2001 (9/11), Al Qaeda's leaders did not. In Kilcullen's view: "Our too-willing and heavy-handed interventions in the so-called War on Terrorism to date have largely played into the hands of this AQ [Al Qaeda] exhaustion strategy, while creating tens of thousands of accidental guerillas and tying us down in a costly (and potentially unsustainable) series of interventions."[55] Given the intense emotions that the 9/11 attacks generated in the American body politic, George W. Bush's decisions to strike back with little regard for long-term costs in 2001 and, especially, in 2003 are understandable. But the limits of U.S. resources remained iron constraints on U.S. strategy after 9/11, nonetheless.

REASON 4: HUMAN RATIONALITY IS BOUNDED
AND PRONE TO SYSTEMATIC ERRORS

The rational-actor model of how humans make economic decisions—often referred to as *Homo Economicus* or economic man—has a history dating back to the late 19th century. In its canonical formulation, the model presumes that individuals make economic choices aimed at maximizing material payoffs based on the available information and their perceived self-interests (or marginal utility functions). The global rationality of neoclassical economic theory "assumes that the decision maker has a comprehensive, consistent utility function, knows all the alternatives that are available for choice, can compute the expected value of utility associated with each alternative, and chooses the alternative that maximizes expected utility."[56] Besides becoming a widespread assumption in 20th-century microeconomic models, by the 1960s U.S. intelligence estimates of future Soviet forces—especially forecasts of Soviet strategic-nuclear forces looking five to seven years ahead—also tended to presume a rational-actor model of Soviet decision making. On this view, Soviet force-structure choices were seen as being the result of a unitary, all-knowing decision maker, or a small group of decision makers, whose choices consistently offered "the highest probability of achieving the most preferred outcome."[57]

During the late 1950s, however, RAND's Andrew Marshall and Joseph Loftus grew increasingly skeptical of this view of Soviet decision making. The more they dug into the history of the USSR's nuclear forces during 1946–1961, the more evidence they found of puzzlingly suboptimal Soviet force-structure choices. They eventually concluded, "It was more plausible that the Soviet posture evolved as the result of decisions taken within a large bureaucratic structure than as the output of a small set of individuals working in a highly consistent manner."[58] In the mid-1960s, Marshall and others at RAND began arguing that progress in understanding decision making in large organizations such as American business firms by Richard Cyert, James March, Herbert Simon, and a small group of people at the Harvard Business School could provide the basis for better forecasts of decision making within large military organizations, including those of the USSR.

Herbert Simon was one of the first to offer an alterative to rational-actor models of human decision making. In a 1953 RAND paper he pointed out that the limited computational and predictive capabilities of human decision makers significantly constrain their ability to make utility-maximizing choices.[59] Later he argued that the limits humans face in obtaining information and performing computations make it probable that, in learning and choice situations, their decisions fall far short of the ideal of utility "maximizing" postulated by economic theory; organisms adapt well enough to "satisfice," but they do not, in general, "optimize."[60] In short, decision makers consider only a limited number of alternatives, have incomplete and inaccurate knowledge about the consequences of decisions, and choose actions that are expected to be satisfactory in light of the constraints.[61]

Meticulous behavioral experiments by various researchers, but especially by Daniel Kahneman and Amos Tversky, have confirmed Simon's rejection of *Homo Economicus*. The first joint research program Kahneman and Amos Tversky undertook was a study of various types of judgments about uncertain events, including numerical predictions and assessments of the probabilities of outcomes.[62] Their point of departure was the observation that most complex judgments humans make are intuitive in the everyday sense of coming to mind quickly and effortlessly, like precepts.[63] Intuitive judgments and responses occupy a position between the automatic operations of perception and the deliberate operations of reasoning, and these authors' first joint article in 1971 documented the systematic errors in statistical judgments to which even statistical experts are prone: "We were impressed by the persistence of discrepancies between statistical intuition and statistical knowledge, which we observed both in ourselves and in our colleagues."[64] For example, most people tend to attach great significance to early trends in their data, and a consistent trait of investors is overconfidence—thinking that they know more about a stock's value than they actually do.[65] Such research confirms the view that human rationality is not only bounded but prone to systematic errors unless subjected to statistical reasoning and analysis. These findings provide yet another reason why strategic competence is elusive.

REASON 5: THE TENDENCY TO CONFUSE GOALS WITH EXECUTABLE STRATEGIES

Beyond the structural reasons why strategy is difficult, there is also a long list of common strategic mistakes. Two that have often been repeated are conflating goals with strategies to achieve those goals and devoting insufficient effort and attention to execution. The first pitfall is readily illustrated with examples from the corporate world. More than one business firm has been tempted to formulate its "strategy" as doubling its market share in some period of time or becoming the dominant firm in a given business area or product line. But corporate "strategies" of this sort are not really strategies, only desired goals. By contrast, Gordon Moore and Andy Grove's decision in mid-1985 to shift Intel's core business from memory chips to microprocessors illustrates an executable strategy rather than a desired goal.[66]

In the case of U.S. national security strategy, it appears that congressional requirements have had the unintended consequence of encouraging the confusion between ends and means. The current mandate for the president to deliver annually to Congress a comprehensive "national security strategy report" derives from the National Security Act of 1947, as amended by the Goldwater-Nichols Act of 1986.[67] In recent decades, this requirement has been more often than not ignored. President George W. Bush, for example, submitted a national security strategy only twice, in 2002 and 2006. The deeper problem, however, is that these documents have increasingly consisted of the administration's foreign policy goals rather than concrete, executable strategies.

Consider the Bush administration's September 2002 national security strategy. Starting with the premise that the United States possessed "unprecedented—and unequaled—strength and influence in the world," the document announced that the United States would defeat the "catastrophic technologies in the hands of an embittered few" while seizing the opportunity to make "the world not just safer but better" through "a distinctly American internationalism" reflecting the union of U.S. values and national interests.[68] To achieve the overriding ends of defeating global terrorists and the threat of weapons of mass destruction, the document offered eight supporting goals as its "strategy": (1) championing aspirations for human dignity; (2) strengthening alliances to defeat global terrorism; (3) working with others to defuse regional conflicts; (4) preventing U.S. enemies from threatening the United States, its allies, and friends with weapons of mass destruction; (5) igniting a new era of global economic growth through free markets and free trade; (6) expanding the circle of development by opening societies and building democracy; (7) developing agendas for cooperative action with other main centers of global power; and (8) transforming America's national security institutions to meet the challenges of the 21st century.[69]

Do these subgoals constitute a coherent strategy? Take the last: transforming America's national security institutions to meet the challenges of the 21st century. The document states that the U.S. military would develop such things as advanced remote sensing and long-range precision strike capabilities, broaden its portfolio to deal with a wide range of scenarios, experiment with new approaches to warfare, and generally "maintain the forces to support our obligations."[70] In addition, intelligence warning and analysis would be strengthened, and U.S. diplomatic institutions would learn to "interact equally adroitly with non-governmental organizations and international institutions."[71] These were laudable goals, but they no more constituted an executable strategy that might achieve them against intelligent adversaries than a business firm's declaration that its "strategy" is to double its market share in the next three years.

If anything, this pattern of presenting foreign policy wish lists as strategies is even more pronounced in President Barack Obama's May 2010 national security strategy. The document's "strategy" emphasizes renewing American leadership by building "upon the sources of our strength at home, while shaping an international order that can meet the challenges of our time" and pursuing the world we seek "through an international system in which all nations have rights and responsibilities."[72] Toward these ends, the document establishes subgoals such as: strengthening homeland security; improving resilience through public-private partnerships; defeating Al Qaeda; pursuing the goal of a world without nuclear weapons; advancing peace and security in the greater Middle East; securing cyberspace; achieving balanced and sustainable economic growth at home and abroad; reducing the rapidly growing U.S. deficit; strengthening the power of our example by prohibiting torture and balancing security and transparency; promoting human dignity though a global health strategy and food security; and combating climate change.[73] While these many goals are certainly desirable, the document itself is extremely thin on how such ends as securing cyberspace, reducing the deficit, or advancing peace and security between Israel and the Palestinians might actually be achieved. Merely proclaiming these goals is not equivalent to a realistic strategy. It would be more accurate to title the 2002 and 2010 U.S. national security strategies as "national security objectives," a criticism that also applies to the 2006 version.

There are, of course, reasons for not detailing one's overall security strategy in public documents. Classic formulations of U.S. national security strategy during the Cold War, such as the President Dwight Eisenhower's October 1953 NSC (National Security Council) 162/2, "Basic National Security Policy," were classified even though the New Look's reliance on a massive atomic retaliatory capability to ensure a "strong, healthy and expanding U.S. economy" for the long term was openly discussed at the time.[74] Thus, one would not expect the details of American national security strategy to appear in unclassified documents written to fulfill legislative requirements. Instead, one would expect to find them in classified NSC documents.

The case of the Obama administration's 2010 national security strategy is especially interesting in that the unclassified document may be all there is. In June 2010, Andrew Krepinevich explicitly raised with an NSC staffer whether there existed a classified version of the administration's national security strategy. The reply he received was that the Obama White House "had not and would not" produce a classified version of its May 2010 national security strategy.[75] In this instance, then, one might reasonably conclude that declaring visionary goals has been taken to be strategy.

REASON 6: INSUFFICIENT EFFORT DEVOTED TO IMPLEMENTATION

A final common strategic pitfall is for leaders and decision makers to fail to devote sufficient effort to ensure that their strategy is actually implemented by the various individuals and organizations having execution responsibilities. The main reasons that execution requires so much attention in large institutions are limits on the organization's capabilities and the inevitable buildup over time of inertia and resistance to change. There is always the possibility that the strategy chosen by top leaders is simply not within the core competencies or resources of the institution. If the needed competencies cannot be developed, or if sufficient resources cannot be found, then the strategy is dead on arrival. A degree of self-knowledge is thus needed if an institution's strategy is to be executable.

As for inertia and resistance to change, top decision makers can also choose strategies that are incompatible with the core values, norms, or pre-existing commitments and practices of the organization. Today a new presidential administration has approximately 1,000 Senate-approved cabinet political appointments it can make, including over fifty in the Department of Defense (DoD).[76] Given the sheer numbers of political appointees in modern presidential administrations, ensuring that those further down the chain of command execute any given policy or strategy is no simple matter. Particularly on acquisition choices, the resistance individual military services can mount to decisions made by the secretary of defense or other top DoD political appointees can be truly astonishing. To paraphrase Clausewitz, military institutions, like their corporate counterparts, are capable of mounting resistance to unwelcomed strategic decisions that is inconceivable unless one has experienced it.[77] For this reason alone, execution is always central to strategy.

The last two reasons why strategy is so difficult in practice by no means exhaust the mistakes to which strategists are prone. Richard Rumelt has complied a list of no less than seven common "sins" that he has seen time and again in his years as a business strategist:

1. Failure to recognize or state that resources are scarce;
2. Failure to recognize or state the problem;
3. Problem not defined competitively;
4. False presumption of competence or causality;
5. Insufficient focus;
6. Mistaking strategic goals for strategy; and
7. Bad strategic goals.[78]

Regarding his fifth strategic "sin"—insufficient focus—Rumelt discusses the institutional problems of trying to satisfy too many different stakeholders and audiences and being unwilling to say "no" to those who disagree with the new strategy or prefer to continue doing what they have been doing. Such behavior underscores the importance of devoting attention and effort to implementation.

CONCLUSIONS

There are many reasons for thinking that developing and implementing strategy is astonishingly difficult in actual practice, however straightforward or simple strategy may appear in theory. Some of the reasons emerge from the very nature of strategic choices aimed at bringing about desired outcomes at some later time in an unpredictable future. Other reasons fall more into the category of recurring pitfalls and mistakes to which humans and their institutions are prone simply because people are biological organisms who "satisfice" most of the time and because their institutions are far from perfect. Consequently, strategy formulation and execution are likely to be a messy, fitful endeavor demanding vision, insight, and judgment that are rare even among talented individuals as well as enormous perseverance and effort in execution.

NOTES

1. As Clausewitz wrote, "Everything in war is very simple; but the simplest thing is difficult. The difficulties accumulate and end by producing a kind of friction that is inconceivable unless one has experienced war"; Carl von Clausewitz, *On War,* trans. and ed. Michael Howard and Peter Paret (Princeton, NJ: Princeton University Press, 1989), 119. The same can be said of strategy at every level.

2. John M. Collins, *Grand Strategy: Principles and Practices* (Annapolis, MD: Naval Institute Press, 1973), 235.

3. What Skolem proved was that "there is no consistent, categorical formal system having the natural numbers as its intended interpretation"; Howard DeLong, *A Profile*

of Mathematical Logic (Menlo Park, CA, and London: Addison-Wesley Publishing, 1970), 195. A categorical formal system is one all of whose models are isomorphic, that is, they can be put in one-to-one correspondence with one another.

4. A. W. Marshall, "Competitive Strategies—History and Background," unpublished paper, March 4, 1988, 1–2. Marshal has been the Pentagon's director of net assessment since 1973.

5. Clausewitz, *On War*, 128, 177, 194.

6. Colin S. Gray, *Modern Strategy* (Oxford, UK: Oxford University Press, 1999), 17 (emphasis deleted).

7. Richard P. Rumelt, "Some Thoughts on Business Strategy," PowerPoint presentation for a Center for Strategic & Budgetary Assessments (CSBA) seminar, September 25, 2007, slide 3.

8. Interview with Sidney G. Winter, December 17, 2008, conducted by Mie Augier and Barry Watts for an Office of Net Assessment (ONA) project on strategy.

9. Andrew F. Krepinevich and Barry D. Watts, *Regaining Strategic Competence* (Washington, DC: Center for Strategic & Budgetary Assessments, 2009), 19.

10. Interview with James G. March, January 23, 2009, conducted by Mie Augier and Barry Watts for an ONA project on strategy.

11. Gray, *Modern Strategy*, 17.

12. The search for "new edges of opportunity" (or "decisive asymmetries") has been especially intense in the personal computer industry. For examples of edges of opportunity in this industry, see Robert X. Cringley, *Accidental Empires: How the Boys of Silicon Valley Make Their Millions, Battle Foreign Competition, and Still Can't Get a Date* (New York: HarperBusiness, 1996), 138, 153, 18, 220, 236.

13. By the early 1960s, Andrew W. Marshall and his RAND colleague Joseph Loftus had concluded that business strategy and organizational theory could inform defense strategy.

14. Andrew Roberts, *The Storm of War: A New History of the Second World War* (London: Allen Lane, 2009), 603.

15. Roberts, *The Storm of War*, 588, 603.

16. Jürgen E. Förster, "The Dynamics of *Volksgemeinschaft*: The Effectiveness of the German Military Establishment in the Second World War," in *Military Effectiveness*, Vol. III, *The Second World War*, edited by Allan R. Millett and Williamson Murray (Winchester, MA: Allen & Unwin, 1988), 196.

17. John E. Jessup, "The Soviet Armed Forces in the Great Patriotic War, 1941–45," in Millett and Murray, *Military Effectiveness*, Vol. III, *The Second World War*, 259.

18. General Rupert Smith, *The Utility of Force: The Art of War in the Modern World* (New York: Alfred A. Knopf, 2007), 404.

19. Smith, *The Utility of Force*, 66.

20. Andrew W. Marshall, "Improving Analytic Methods for Strategic Forces," Memorandum for the Secretary of Defense, April 17, 1979, 1–2; Paul K. Davis and

Cindy Williams, "Improving the Military Content of Strategy Analysis Using Automated War Games: A Technical Approach and an Agenda for Research," RAND N-1894-DNA, June 1982, v.

21. Bruce W. Bennett and Paul K. Davis, "The Role of Automated War Gaming in Strategic Analysis," RAND P-7053, December 1984, 2.

22. Paul K. Davis, James A. Winnefeld, Steven C. Bankes, and James P. Kahan, "Analytic War Gaming with the RAND Strategy Assessment System (RSAS)," RAND Research Brief RB-7801, September 1987, 1.

23. Paul K. Davis, "The Role of Uncertainty in Assessing the NATO-Pact Central-Region Balance," RAND N-2839, December 1988, v.

24. Ibid., vii.

25. Ibid., 9.

26. J. A. Dewar, J. J. Gillogly, and M. L. Juncosa, "Non-Monotonicity, Chaos, and Combat Models," RAND R-3995-RC, 1991, v–vi, 4–6.

27. Ian Stewart, *Does God Play Dice? The Mathematics of Chaos* (Oxford, UK: Basil Blackwell, 1989), 133–139.

28. Dewar, Gillogly, and Juncosa, "Non-Monotonicity, Chaos, and Combat Models," 6–12, 42.

29. Edward Lorenz, *The Essence of Chaos* (Seattle: University of Washington Press, 1993), 151; Hao Bai-Lin (ed.), Chaos (Singapore: World Scientific Publishing Company, 1984), 67–71.

30. Michael Howard, *The Lessons of History* (New Haven, CT, and London: Yale University Press, 1991), 9.

31. Douglass North, *Understanding the Process of Economic Change* (Princeton, NJ, and Oxford, UK: Princeton University Press, 2005), 19, 69.

32. Nassim Nicholas Taleb, *The Black Swan: The Impact of the Highly Improbable* (New York: Random House, 2007), 8.

33. Charles Petzold, "Turing Machines That Run Forever," May 18, 2008, retrieved in November 2010 from www.charlespetzold.com/blog/2008/05/Turing-Machines-That-Run-Forever.html. For the basis of Petzold's statement, see *The Annotated Turing: A Guided Tour through Alan Turning's Historic Paper on Computability and the Turing Machine* (Indianapolis, IN: Wiley Publishing, 2008), 52, 277, 279, 330.

34. The classic Arab proverb I have often cited regarding the unpredictability of the future is one Rumelt first heard from Pierre Wack: *He who predicts the future lies, even if he tells the truth.* A more literal formulation is: *Even if predictions of the future turn out to be right, the reason is probably blind luck rather than an ability to peer into the future.*

35. Horst W. J. Rittel and Melvin M. Webber, "Dilemmas in a General Theory of Planning," *Policy Sciences* 4 (1973): 160.

36. Tom Ritchey, "Wicked Problems: Structuring Social Messes with Morphological Analysis," last modified November 2007, 1 (of the pdf version), retrieved on July 30, 2010, from www.swemorph.com/wp.html.

37. For additional insight into the uniqueness of wicked problems in counterinsurgency operations, see Anna Simons, "Got Vision? Unity of Vision in Policy and Strategy: What It Is, and Why We Need It," Strategic Studies Institute, Army War College, July 2010, v–vi, retrieved on August 25, 2010, from www.strategicstudiesinstitute .army.mil/pubs/people.cfm?authorID=779&email=false.

38. Ritchey, "Wicked Problems: Structuring Social Messes with Morphological Analysis," 1.

39. T. C. Greenwood and T. X. Hammes, "War Planning for Wicked Problems," *Armed Forces Journal* (December 2009); retrieved on August 25, 2010, from www.afji .com/2009/12/4252237.

40. Clear instances of tactical-level decisions having strategic consequences can be found in Kilcullen's account of the intervention to restore order by an Australian-led multinational force in East Timor in 1999; see David Kilcullen, *The Accidental Guerilla: Fighting Small Wars in the Midst of a Big One* (New York and Oxford, UK: Oxford University Press, 2009), 89–210.

41. Clausewitz, *On War*, 80.

42. Kilcullen, *The Accidental Guerilla*, 153.

43. Ibid., 43.

44. Ibid., 182.

45. Ibid., 44.

46. Ibid., 120–122.

47. Ibid., 182.

48. Ibid., 183.

49. Rumelt, "Some Thoughts on Business Strategy," slide 11.

50. Charles J. Hitch and Roland N. McKean, *The Economics of Defense in the Nuclear Age* (Cambridge, MA: Harvard University Press, 1960), 23.

51. Paul D. Wolfowitz in "Department of Defense Budget Priorities for Fiscal Year 2004," Hearing before the Committee on the Budget, House of Representatives, 108th Congress, 1st Session, Serial No. 108-6, February 27, 2003, 17–18; retrieved on July 30, 2010, from http://ftp.resource.org/gpo.gov/hearings/108h/85421.pdf.

52. "Department of Defense Budget Priorities for Fiscal Year 2004," No. 108-6, 8.

53. Amy Belasco, "The Cost of Iraq, Afghanistan, and Other Global War on Terror Operations since 9/11," RL33110, Congressional Research Service, September 28, 2009, CRS-9.

54. Kilcullen, *The Accidental Guerilla*, 29.

55. Ibid., 264.

56. Herbert A. Simon, *An Empirically Based Microeconomics* (Cambridge, UK: Cambridge University Press, 1997), 17.

57. A. W. Marshall, "Improvement in Intelligence Estimates through Study of Organizational Behavior," RAND D-16850-PR, March 15, 1968, 2.

58. Ibid., 1.

59. Herbert A. Simon, "A Behavioral Model of Rational Choice," RAND P-365, January 20, 1953, 15–16.

60. Herbert A. Simon, "Rational Choice and the Structure of the Environment," *Psychological Review*, 63:2 (1956), 129.

61. Simon, *An Empirically Based Microeconomics*, 17.

62. For an easily understood account of Kahneman and Tversky's research, see Justin Fox, *The Myth of the Rational Market: A History of Risk, Reward, and Delusion on Wall Street* (New York, HarperCollins, 2009), 175–178, 183–184.

63. Daniel Kahneman, "Maps of Bounded Rationality: A Perspective on Intuitive Judgment and Choice." In *Nobel Prizes 2002: Nobel Prizes, Presentations, Biographies, & Lectures,* edited by Tore Frängsmyr (Stockholm: Almquiest & Wiksell International, 2003), 481.

64. Kahneman, "Maps of Bounded Rationality: A Perspective on Intuitive Judgment and Choice," 450.

65. Fox, *The Myth of the Rational Market,* 177, 299.

66. Andrew S. Grove, *Only the Paranoid Survive: How to Exploit the Crisis Points That Challenge Every Company* (New York: Currency & Doubleday, 1996 and 1999), 89.

67. Catherine Dale, "National Security Strategy: Legislative Mandates, Execution to Date, and Considerations for Congress," Congressional Research Service RL34505, May 28, 2008, 3.

68. The White House, "The National Security Strategy of the United States of America," Washington, DC: September 2002, 1.

69. The White House, "The National Security Strategy of the United States of America," September 2002, 1–2.

70. Ibid., 29–30.

71. Ibid., 30–31.

72. The White House, "National Security Strategy," Washington, DC: May 2010, 1.

73. Ibid., 18, 19, 21, 24, 27, 31, 34, 36, 39, 46, 47.

74. The White House, "Basic National Security Policy," NSC-162/2, 19, 22; Herman S. Wolk, "The 'New Look'," *AIR FORCE Magazine* (August 2003), 82–83.

75. Colin Clark, "Strategy, What Strategy?" *DoD Buzz: Online Defense and Acquisition Journal,* June 29, 2010; retrieved on August 12, 2010, from www.dodbuzz.com/2010/06/29/strategy-what-strategy/.

76. Robert Longley, "Obama Builds His Cabinet," March 1, 2009; retrieved on February 10,, 2012, from http://usgovinfo.about.com/od/thepresidentandcabinet/a/

obamacabinet.htm; Henry B. Hogue, Maureen Bearden, and Terrence L. Lisbeth, "Presidential Appointee Postions Requiring Senate Confirmation and Committees Handling Nominations," Congresional Research Service, updated March 18, 2008, CRS-7 to CRS-9.

    77. Clausewitz, *On War,* 119.

    78. Rumelt, "Some Thoughts on Business Strategy," Slide 11.

THE PRACTICE OF COMPETITIVE STRATEGIES Part II

5 U.S. COMPETITIVE STRATEGY DURING THE COLD WAR

Gordon S. Barrass

DURING THE LATTER YEARS of the Cold War, the increasing pressure that United States brought to bear on the Soviet Union on a wide range of fronts helped bring the U.S.-Soviet competition to a peaceful end.

To understand the strategic lessons of that era, we need to consider whether the actions taken against the Soviet Union were simply a variant of an old-fashioned arms race or a more sophisticated competitive strategy. And, even if they were parts of a competitive strategy, it is important for us to know whether they were based on clear concepts and carefully articulated plans of action or were something more amorphous and ad hoc.

We should keep in mind that competitive strategy comes in two basic forms. As John Battilega succinctly puts it, there were "competitive strategies in the large," that is, the entire process of Defense Department investment based on competing with important aspects of the Soviet military posture over several decades, and there were "competitive strategies in the small," that is, the specific weapons programs that were part of the DoD's Competitive Strategies Initiative that was formalized in 1987.[1]

IN THE BEGINNING

America's strategy of "massive retaliation" gained new credibility with the testing in 1954 of a hydrogen bomb that produced a yield a thousand times greater than the atomic bomb dropped on Hiroshima. Although "massive retaliation" was a credible deterrent to threats against America's vital interests, it was not going to prevent the Soviet Union from competing with the United States in different ways around the globe and eroding its power.

At the RAND Corporation, which did much thinking for the Pentagon about the Soviet Union, a group of bright analysts were already pondering how the United States could respond. At the end of that year their thinking was encapsulated in a paper entitled "The Next Ten Years" that Andrew Marshall wrote together with Bernard Brodie and Charles Hitch.[2] They did not offer concrete suggestions as to what should be done, but they provided a way to think about extended peacetime competition. It would be several years before this concept generated any significant interest in Washington.

The 1962 Cuban Missile Crisis marked a turning point in American thinking about deterrence and competition. Many leading figures argued that compromises would have to be made to reduce the risk of returning to the brink of nuclear war. This approach fit with the widespread American faith that Soviet leaders could be coaxed into accepting a relationship with the United States that would not threaten American interests. The scientists and economists who were coming to dominate American thinking about the Soviet Union went so far as to assume that the Soviets would share their faith in the changing American calculus of nuclear deterrence.

As the Soviets seemed set to move into the ascendant position in the late 1960s, American strategists and policymakers were increasingly talking about "stability" and détente. The highly questionable assumptions on which détente was based reopened the debate on how the United States should respond to the rapid improvement in Soviet military capabilities.

President Richard Nixon advocated détente because, as a result of the Vietnam War, he saw no chance of the American people supporting tougher policies against the Soviet Union; Secretary of State Henry Kissinger, however, did so because of his Spenglerian pessimism about the decline of the West. They both felt that, as Soviet power was increasing rapidly, the United States should try to reach an accommodation with Moscow as soon as possible.

On the opposite side of the debate were a number of kindred spirits who might best be called "revivalists" because of their faith in the ability of the United States to revive its fortunes. Several shared the conviction that the Cold War would end only if America competed so strongly that the Soviet Union would give up. One of the most prominent and articulate revivalists was James Schlesinger, the director of strategy at RAND, who had just joined the Nixon administration. Over the next six years he held four defense-related posts—assistant director of the Bureau of the Budget, chairman of the Atomic Energy Commission, director of Central Intelligence, and then secretary of defense between 1973 and 1975.

THINKING ABOUT EXTENDED COMPETITION

Despite their advocacy of détente, Nixon and Kissinger were both interested in strengthening America's position. On taking over as secretary of defense in May 1973, Schlesinger said that he intended to "assure the military balance so necessary to deterrence and a more enduring peace" and "become increasingly competitive with potential adversaries."[3]

Few were surprised when, five months later, Schlesinger appointed Marshall as director of the Office of Net Assessment (ONA) within the office of the secretary of defense. ONA was tasked with undertaking something no one else in the government was authorized to do—provide regular comparative assessments of U.S.-Soviet military balance, in its various forms.

The timing was good. Despite the general malaise that pervaded America in the 1970s, some people in the political and military establishments were determined that America should regain its military preeminence. They could be divided into two broad groups, between which there were overlapping friendships and shared interests in what strategy could offer. The first group, who consisted of policymakers and scientists, was convinced that the dynamic interplay between America's scientific and entrepreneurial cultures, which had greatly facilitated the development of information technology, would ensure that the United States could sustain its lead over the Soviet Union. The second group, who were mainly from the services, believed that they needed to rethink fundamentally how they could fight and win against the Soviet Union without using nuclear weapons.

Marshall concentrated ONA's efforts on the extended peacetime competition and deterrence. He firmly believed that his responsibility was to diagnose problems, point to opportunities, and leave it to the secretary and others to write their own prescriptions.

A number of strands ran through Marshall's thinking during his early years at the Pentagon. First and foremost, he believed that the United States could no longer afford its early Cold War strategy of leading across the board; it needed to identify Soviet weaknesses and then shape the overall strategic arms competition toward those areas in which the United States enjoyed a sustainable competitive advantage. Over the next decade, this concept became a key building block in an increasingly sophisticated approach to "competitive strategies."

This way of looking at the long-term rivalry between the two superpowers highlighted three important and related questions. First, how did changes in the force posture or doctrine work as a "move" in the extended competition?

Second, how efficient was each competitor in using its resources to make these "moves"? Third, where did the United States stand relative to the Soviet Union in the overall competition?

These questions could be answered properly, Marshall argued, only if one understood that not just history and culture made the Soviets different from the Americans; their ideology, values, and preoccupations, also differed, as well as the ways in which the structure of their regime affected the way they viewed the outside world and responded to developments. Each side, Marshall believed, had its own rationality.

UNDER NIXON AND FORD: EXPLORING

ONA got off to a good start, in part because Marshall reported directly to Schlesinger and, in part, because they were good friends.

Work soon began on net assessments of three key balances: strategic nuclear, maritime (mainly surface naval warfare), and NATO versus the Warsaw Pact; a year later, ONA started studying the military investment balance. These net assessments, which were completed in 1977–1978, illuminated the basic contours of the competition in the military sphere and provided the intellectual seeds of many future programs.

While the research got underway, Schlesinger and Marshall continued sharing ideas on competitive strategy. One issue they discussed at length was arms control. "The debate in Washington centered on three big questions," Marshall recalled:

> Given America's lead in technology, was it to America's advantage to compete with the Soviet Union in developing anti-ballistic missile (ABM) systems? How should the United States respond to the increasing accuracy of Soviet missiles, which before long could enable them to destroy America's Minuteman missile force? Should it seek to ban missiles with multiple warheads or should it exploit its lead in this field?[4]

Nixon was so keen to increase stability that he refused to draw the Soviets into a long and costly competition over ABM, even though it would have required only modest American investments. Nixon did, however, give the go-ahead for MIRVs, which at U.S. insistence were excluded from the Interim Strategic Arms Limitation Treaty (SALT) that he and Leonid Brezhnev signed in Moscow in 1972.

Within months of the Moscow Summit, the United States obtained worrying intelligence revealing that, due a loophole in SALT, the Soviets were going to built far more heavy missiles than the United States had expected; each would be able to carry two to three times more MIRVs than the U.S. Minuteman. Once more, the calculus of deterrence would change; this time Moscow would be the winner.

Concern over the strategic balance gave an impetus to the development of a competitive strategy. Although Schlesinger explicitly disavowed any intention to acquire a destabilizing first-strike capability, he insisted that the United States should have "an offensive capability of such size and composition that all will perceive it as in overall balance with the strategic forces of any potential opponent."[5] Perception was a concept that would increasingly feature in the articulation of a competitive strategy.

Schlesinger also judged that the Soviet MIRV program was part of Moscow's long-term aim to deter the United States from using its strategic missiles for the defense of Western Europe. He responded with a declaratory policy that soon became known as the Schlesinger Doctrine. It was based on extensive research that he and Marshall had done at RAND on what the Soviets had said about nuclear war. In a speech in January 1974 Schlesinger warned the Soviet leadership that, if they attacked Europe, the United States would not only respond by using tactical weapons but would also use a few strategic missiles to strike remote targets on Soviet territory.

"The 'beauty' of this strategy," as Schlesinger likes to put it, "was that it played to Soviet gut reactions. Soviet leaders had said time and time again that they did not believe that nuclear war could be restrained once it had started. 'Limited Nuclear Options' would, therefore, make them very cautious and so reinforce deterrence."[6]

GETTING INSIDE THEIR MINDS

Exploiting "gut reactions" would become a potent tool of competitive strategy. To do that, however, one had to "get inside the mind" of one's adversary. American bright ideas about what would disconcert the Soviets, Marshall pointed out, might or might not be successful. Valuable insights into what would work, he believed, could be gained by closely observing how the other side had responded to what one was already doing, but the real gains came from asking why they had done it—and done it in that particular way. That was the key that would make it possible to exploit stock Soviet responses, sensitivities, fears, and—best of all—nightmares.

Concerns over the strategic nuclear balance also led Schlesinger and Marshall to pay more attention to the overall military balance, both conventional and nuclear—in terms not just of capabilities but also of the psychological and political effect that the changes in the various components could have on perceptions.

One area that needed urgent attention was Europe. As the Vietnam War wound down in the early 1970s, the U.S. military realized that Soviet forces had made enormous headway over the past decade. They had acquired a huge amount of impressive equipment and the 1973 Arab-Israeli War had demonstrated its effectiveness. The scale of the challenge was magnified by the fact that U.S. and NATO forces were, as General Alexander Haig, the supreme allied commander, Europe of the day, said, unfit for the purpose. Morale was low, and few commanders had thought of how they could stop a Soviet conventional assault without resorting to the use of theater nuclear weapons.

The time was ripe for a renaissance in thinking about strategy. The starting point came with a new approach to doctrine, particularly on how U.S. forces should fight the Soviets in Central Europe. It was called "active defense," and the author was General William DePuy, the head of the Army's Training and Doctrine Command (TRADOC). Instead of confronting Soviet forces in Europe with well-prepared static defense, the Army would henceforth counterattack with ground troops well beyond the front line. This was the biggest change in Army doctrine since World War II. In parallel, General David Jones, the commander of the U.S. Air Force in Europe, was trying to get the Air Force and the Army to work closely together so that they could win the first battle.

At the practical level, changes were already underway. Jones initiated an intensive intelligence effort to understand how his opponent would fight, which made it possible to develop special training programs that enabled American pilots to exploit Soviet weaknesses. The Air Force's "Red Flag" school would soon be producing pilots who had had realistic training in how to win against their Soviet adversaries, and plans were afoot for the Army to open a similar institution where troops could learn to fight against a division that was equipped and fought like the Soviets.

Thanks to exceptionally sensitive intelligence, the Navy knew more about its opponent than did the other services. In the late 1970s they were able to play sophisticated war games in which they could view the battle space through Soviet eyes; soon thereafter they formed a "Red Force" that would react like Soviet naval commanders.[7]

EXPLOITING COMPETITIVE ADVANTAGES

To blur the image of Soviets being ahead in the rivalry between the Warsaw Pact and NATO, U.S. forces needed to acquire new and compelling capabilities. Technological innovation offered some important new possibilities.

In 1973, the Defense Advanced Research Projects Agency and the Defense Nuclear Agency launched a research project that eighteen months later came to an immensely important conclusion: For certain tasks, improved guidance systems would soon make it possible to use conventional substitutes for nuclear weapons.[8] This discovery marked the beginning of what the Soviets called the "revolution in military affairs"—which stemmed from a mixture of changes in technology, organization, and doctrine. Marshall liked this term as it encouraged people in the United States to look at the organizational and operational concepts, not just at the new technology.

As early as December 1975, Yuri Andropov, the head of the KGB, was warning the Politburo that these new weapons could dramatically increase the ability of the Western alliance to mount a successful defense against a conventional attack. While the new technology itself played on Soviet fears, the concepts that would govern its use would worry them even more.

As public debate sharpened in the summer of 1976 over the future of the strategic balance, Marshall presented a memo to Secretary of Defense Rumsfeld that argued that, as the U.S. lead in the strategic nuclear field was being whittled away, the United States needed to erode Soviet confidence by reestablishing its preeminence in other aspects of the military balance. Marshall listed many ways in which this could be done. They included developing very-long-range SLBMs, mobile land-based systems, air-launched cruise missiles, improved guidance systems, ASW systems, real-time satellites, means of fooling Soviet information systems, and the targeting of both the bunkers used by the Soviet leadership and those that were command and control centers.

Rumsfeld shared Marshall's analysis and before leaving office authorized development of cruise missiles. He also approved development of the B-1 bomber. Marshall had done a paper for Robert Ellsworth, Rumsfeld's deputy, on the case for having the B-1. In that paper Marshall pointed out that Stalin had been deeply worried by the extraordinary devastation that U.S. strategic bombing had inflicted on Germany and Japan. Immediately after the war, Stalin had poured scarce resources into air defenses. Then American reconnaissance flights over Soviet territory, from the late 1940s through to the downing of the U-2 in 1960, ensured that air defense would become an enduring Soviet obsession.

Although the contract for 100 B-1s was not signed until 1982, the concept of a low-flying supersonic bomber played to Soviet fears, and the Soviet air defense forces leaped to the bait. The Soviets spent billions on developing the MiG-25, new surface-to-air missiles, and radar to counter this threat. The strategists in the Pentagon were pleased to see Soviet money spent this way rather than on more offensive weapons.

UNDER CARTER: BECOMING MORE COMPETITIVE

Although initially President Jimmy Carter was widely regarded as being weak on defense, three members of his administration had a reputation for being hawks—Harold Brown, his secretary of defense; Zbigniew Brzezinski, his national security adviser; and James Schlesinger, the former secretary of defense who served as Carter's secretary of energy. Brown, a distinguished scientist, had served as secretary of the Air Force from 1965 to 1969. During his four years as secretary of defense he again championed America's technological prowess and paid close attention to strategy.

A few months after taking office, Brown read the memorandum in which Marshall had set out for Rumsfeld a broad analytical framework for developing a competitive strategy. It was remarkable both for its long-term perspective and for its application of business-strategy concepts to the competition—for example, setting positive goals for the competition, exploiting Soviet weaknesses, and responding to Soviet strengths. Brown's comments on the memo demonstrated a shrewd appreciation of competitive strategy.

By this time, the rapid expansion of the Soviet surface and submarine fleets was creating a force capable of challenging Western naval power. In his first formal paper to Brown, in 1977, Marshall suggested that the United States should seek to reestablish clear maritime superiority. Brown's decision to do so was warmly welcomed by Admiral Thomas Hayward, the commander of the U.S. Pacific Fleet (1976–1978), who was pressing for the development of a global naval strategy.

Research by the Navy and ONA had revealed that a major vulnerability of the Soviet navy was that its missile-firing ships had to be told where their targets were. This information led the U.S. Navy to develop ways of neutralizing or destroying the sensors of command ships. In parallel, to reduce the vulnerability of its own ships, the U.S. Navy began deploying its surface firepower on a wider range of platforms and equipping its surface ships with antimissile defenses. As chief of naval operations (1978–1982), Hayward played a major part in bringing about this transformation.

Whereas the surface aspects of the maritime strategy contained little that was really "competitive," almost everything to do with ASW was extremely so, thanks to the close cooperation among a small number of people in the Navy and ONA. Marshall's carefully researched analysis and insights into ASW caught Brown's imagination and gave him the confidence to embark on a series of major programs.

Interesting new thinking about ASW was already underway. A decade earlier, some pioneering academic research had challenged American assumptions about what the Soviet navy would do in time of war. Later, intelligence showed that Soviet attack submarines would not be sent out into the Atlantic and Pacific to interdict troop convoys but would be held back to defend the "bastions" of the Barents Sea and the Sea of Okhotsk, in which the new Soviet SSBNs could be deployed now that they had long-range missiles. This would ensure that the Soviet Union would have a retaliatory nuclear capability.

Dramatic intelligence breakthroughs in the late 1970s helped the U.S. Navy to get further inside the mind of the Soviet naval high command.[9] As one U.S. Navy strategist put it, the aim was "to continuously reinforce in the Soviet mind the perception that it could not win a war with the United States . . . The key point is that the desired prospect must be *as perceived and measured in Soviet terms.*"[10]

Perception also continued to be a sensitive aspect of the strategic balance. Intelligence indicated that the Soviets would soon break free from "rough parity" and gain the ability, theoretically at least, to destroy all of America's land-based ICBMs in a first strike. While few believed that the Soviet leadership would seek to directly exploit this "window of vulnerability," there was broader agreement that the United States had to win the "battle of perceived capabilities." Marshall felt that net assessment was something whose time had come because the issue of where the United States stood vis-à-vis the Soviets had become a major political issue.

While the Carter administration debated its response to the buildup of Soviet strategic forces, Brown tasked Marshall and Walter Slocombe, Brown's deputy assistant secretary for international affairs, with recommending changes in U.S. targeting that would enhance deterrence. They concluded that Soviet leadership bunkers had to be a key target set.

In 1979, disillusioned by Soviet conduct on several fronts, Carter dramatically shifted U.S. policy and embarked on a far more competitive strategy. He asked Congress to approve the deployment of 200 "heavy" MX missiles, each with ten warheads, that would be well protected in an underground rail network that provided access to 4,600 firing points—far more than the Soviets could attack in a first strike. This would be the most expensive weapons program in history. Then, in December 1979, NATO announced its "twin track" decision. Unless Moscow agreed to sharply cut back its SS-20 force, NATO said the United States would begin deploying 108 Pershing II intermediate-range ballistic missiles and 464 ground-launched cruise missiles to Europe in late 1983.

Soviet concerns were soon compounded by Presidential Directive-59, "U.S. Nuclear Weapons Targeting Policy," which Carter approved in July 1980. Leaks to the press and other public statements left Moscow in no doubt that the Americans knew where the bunkers were and that it had the weapons to destroy them. In other words, if the Soviet leadership initiated nuclear war, they would be signing their own death warrants. In parallel, Brown announced that henceforth America would match the Soviet Union at any level of nuclear warfare. To its considerable surprise, Moscow now saw that the United States was adopting a Soviet approach to deterrence, based on conveying the message that it was ready to fight an extended nuclear war.

The Carter administration also geared up to push ahead with a more competitive strategy. One example of this was a strategy memo prepared by William Odom, the military assistant in Carter's National Security Council. In it, Odom recommended that if Carter were reelected he should compete selectively and make the Soviet Union face the full military, economic, political, and ideological power of the United States.[11]

The presidential election in November 1980 was, however, won by Ronald Reagan, the first American president to believe that the United States could compel the Soviet Union to end the Cold War. Reagan pursued that objective with a mixture of guile and steely determination.

REAGAN: PUTTING ON THE PRESSURE

Reagan's policy was based on the conviction that Soviet totalitarianism was an evil that the West could neither appease nor accommodate if freedom were to be preserved; his strategy was based on the equally firm conviction that the Soviet Union was in such serious economic trouble that an arms race would hasten its collapse.

Although the president did not begin signing strategy directives until 1982, the concept of a wide-ranging competition with the Soviet Union guided U.S. actions from the beginning of his administration.[12] Although Reagan was at times a "pile 'em high" arms-race man, he also had a rare understanding of Soviet weaknesses and a visceral instinct for exploiting them.

While Secretary of Defense Weinberger carried out Reagan's instructions to rapidly boost expenditure and procurement, the competitive aspects of the Pentagon's strategy were left to Fred Iklé, his undersecretary for policy. Iklé saw eye-to-eye with Marshall on the wisdom of exploiting Soviet weaknesses and fears; he articulated that concept in the first defense guidance written by the new administration. A few months after taking office, Iklé briefed labor leaders on Reagan's new approach: "We'll increase our military expenditures, steer it into channels that will make it increasingly difficult for the Soviets to compete with us, and at the same time we are going to work on denying them access to technology."[13]

Moscow was stunned that the military buildup was intended to be the largest in American peacetime history. The strategic forces were to receive 100 MX missiles; six new Trident submarines with ninety-six of the new, highly accurate D-5 missiles; 3,000 air-launched cruise missiles; and over 100 B-1 bombers to carry them. The United States also reiterated the commitment that Carter had given to NATO: If Moscow did not severely cut back its SS-20 missile force, then American Pershing II and cruise missiles would be deployed in Europe at the end of 1983.

In parallel, the United States made it clear that there would be a huge improvement in conventional forces—both for NATO and for the wider projection of power. This upsurge in funding made it possible for NATO to develop a competitive strategy that played a significant part in persuading the Soviet Union to end the Cold War.

As menacing as the planned U.S. buildup was, the first truly worrying change in American conduct came with a wide-ranging series of psychological operations designed to undermine Soviet confidence in their defenses. Almost immediately after Reagan's inauguration, sizeable numbers of U.S. military aircraft began flying straight toward the Soviet or East German frontiers, turning away only at the last minute. Then, in August and September 1981 a battle group of over eighty NATO warships passed through the Greenland-Iceland-UK Gap in radio silence and came close to Soviet territory before it was detected.[14]

These naval activities reflected the new U.S. maritime strategy, which was aimed at undermining the two key premises of the Soviet war plans—protecting its ballistic missile submarines and keeping U.S. naval carrier battle groups well beyond the points from which their aircraft could launch nuclear strikes against the Soviet Union. In keeping with this strategy, U.S. submarine force commanders even reportedly staged practice "sinkings" of Soviet SSBNs beneath the ice cap to demonstrate an ability to threaten these prized assets at will.[15]

Before the year was out, the General Staff made another disconcerting discovery. The lesser of their concerns was to find out that the Americans been tapping one of their naval communications cables; the greater was that that cable ran across the Sea of Okhotsk, the Far Eastern "bastion" in which Moscow thought that it had successfully protected many of its SSBNs from U.S. submarines.

The White House also set out to weaken the grip of the increasingly decrepit Soviet leadership over Eastern Europe, where the weakest point was Poland. In June 1982, just six months after martial law had been introduced in Poland to suppress Solidarity, Reagan and the Pope agreed to undertake a clandestine campaign to hasten the dissolution of the communist empire. From the Vatican's well-filled coffers and those of the Reagan administration, tens of millions of dollars were secretly channeled through to Solidarity.[16]

Reagan was equally determined to reverse Soviet gains in the Third World. By far the biggest effort went into arming the mujahedin fighting the Soviets in Afghanistan, which contributed significantly to the Soviet decision to withdraw from there in 1988. In addition, Reagan ordered the CIA to organize and support the Nicaraguan "Contras," a counterrevolutionary force that by the late 1980s was about 15,000 strong. At the same time, the Americans were backing anticommunist groups in Angola and Cambodia.

The administration's determination to deny Moscow access to advanced Western technology was reinforced by the *Farewell* Dossier that France's President François Mitterrand gave Reagan in July 1981. *Farewell* was the code name of a KGB colonel who had revealed to the French the extraordinary success Soviet intelligence was having in acquiring advanced Western technology, both legally and illegally.[17] While NATO governments began expelling most of the Soviet intelligence officers engaged in the illicit acquisition of technology, Gus Weiss, Reagan's intelligence adviser, took a different approach to exacerbating Soviet problems. Working with the CIA, he set out to ensure that some items did get through. These items included software that had "bugs" hidden deep in its programs. On one occasion, in June 1982, a "malfunction" generated such a huge pipeline explosion that it could be seen from space via American satellites. It is not yet clear at what point the Soviets caught on to what was going on.

Another well-established area of competition was space, where the Americans had a clear lead over the Soviets in all categories of satellites. The Americans were, however, growing concerned that the Soviets could "blind" or destroy American satellites during a crisis. Although the Americans were working on this issue, the Strategic Defense Initiative (SDI) that Reagan launched in 1983 posed a challenge to Moscow that went far beyond a "move" in a competitive strategy.

Although Soviet scientists cast doubt on the feasibility of the project, the Soviet leadership feared that the Americans had such a lead in technology that they would be able to open up a new arms race in space—and one in which the Soviet Union could not compete. Soviet leaders believed that if they did not constrain research and testing, the Americans would be able to develop new types of weapons for use on earth. This concern was made real in June 1984 when a U.S. ground-based missile intercepted the reentry vehicle of a Minuteman missile—an event that the United States publicized to great effect but never managed to repeat. SDI was one of several indications of Reagan's flair for disconcerting the Soviet leadership.

The Pentagon was becoming increasingly confident that they could deter the Soviet Union. A top secret and highly restricted review of the strategic balance done in 1983 "demonstrated convincingly," Marshall said, "that the United States was already in a rather good position and that was set to improve."[18]

COMPETITIVE STRATEGY IN ACTION

While the buildup and reequipment of Soviet forces in Central Europe gained momentum in the late 1970s, ONA intensified its efforts to establish how the Soviets would fight and identify the vulnerabilities in Soviet operational doctrine and practices. This led to the Pentagon deciding in 1978 to invest in "Assault Breaker" munitions and the associated targeting systems that could be used to thwart a massive Soviet armored offensive.

The research done by ONA and others had got underway just in time. In the late 1970s, the CIA began to receive reliable intelligence showing that Moscow was investing heavily in a new offensive strategy that, in the event of war, would enable Soviet conventional forces to defeat NATO before it had time to resort to the use of nuclear weapons. This is what was widely known as the Ogarkov Strategy, named after the marshal of that name who headed the Soviet General Staff. While a massive, high-speed armored offensive smashed through NATO's front line, 2,000 aircraft would attack all of NATO's nuclear weapons facilities and seek to pin down NATO aircraft for forty-eight hours.[19] The Soviet General Staff understood well that such capabilities would give them a military preeminence that would have a great psychological and political impact in Western Europe because it would undermine confidence in America's ability to defend its allies. When briefed on this intelligence at the end of 1981, General Bernard Rogers, SACEUR (Supreme Allied Commander, Europe), is reported to have said, "For the first time in my career, I really feel that I am getting inside the mind of my adversary."[20]

The fruits of the research done by DIA and ONA helped the Army and the Air Force develop the concept of the "Air-Land Battle." For the first time, U.S. forces contemplated a coordinated Army and Air Force counteroffensive to repel a Soviet armored onslaught. This concept soon evolved in what was called Follow-on Forces Attack (or FOFA for short), which NATO adopted as it strategy in 1985. The development of these concepts provided an intellectual framework in which the latest American technology could be adapted to the realities of the European battlefield.

With the deployment of Pershing II and Gryphon ground-launched cruise missiles in Europe at the end of 1983, the United States made another "move" that strengthened its overall position. Soviets leaders were wrong in fearing that Pershing II would be able to reach Moscow and thus destroy the city before they could order a retaliatory strike. They were on firmer ground when they feared that they might not be able to detect the far slower cruise missiles that certainly could reach Moscow and destroy their bunkers.

The deployment of the Pershing IIs and Gryphons had another far-reaching effect. With the introduction of the SS-20s (which could cover the whole of Western Europe but not reach the United States), the Soviet Union suddenly gained the capability of deterring Western Europe from using its tactical weapons in a conflict, because the United States had no theater nuclear forces that could inflict similar damage on the Soviet Union. With the arrival of Pershing IIs and Gryphons, the Soviets had lost that key advantage, which was such an important element in Ogarkov's new strategy.

As Marshal Sergei Akhromeyev, who replaced Ogarkov as chief of the General Staff, later put it, "The Soviet Union could not continue the confrontation with the United States and NATO after 1985. The economic resources for such a policy had been practically exhausted."[21]

PRESSING HARDER

Although Washington was not, it seems, in possession of such an authoritative and succinct Soviet assessment, President Reagan firmly believed that the Soviet Union was in economic trouble. Its weakness was the subject when Reagan met with four Soviet experts at the White House in April 1986. "We told him," Marshall recalled, "that the Soviet economy was far smaller than the CIA was claiming, the defense burden was extremely heavy, the cost of empire was a serious strain and the country was more critically dependent on its dollar earnings from oil and gas exports than we had earlier thought."[22]

These judgments certainly reinforced Reagan's determination to intensify the pressure. One of the main ways that this was done was by persuading Saudis to push down the price of oil. Not only did that give a much-needed boost to the flagging American economy, but it also slashed Soviet foreign exchange earnings.

In Europe, NATO looked stronger by the day as new weapons were linked to new strategic concepts and highly realistic training. "For the first time in our conventional rivalry," Marshall observed, "the Americans were really moving towards gaining the upper hand—not in defense, but in attack."[23] By using precision-guided munitions, for example, NATO aircraft would be able to destroy up to a hundred more targets than with previous conventional munitions. One of the greatest innovations was the "reconnaissance-strike complex," which was based on the ability of surveillance aircraft to identify targets far behind the front line—and eventually as far as 250 km away. High-powered computers could then locate aircraft already in the air that were near the target and had the right munitions—and then flash them the coordinates for the attack.

In 1987 NATO began demonstrating its new capabilities in a series of dramatic field exercises, one of which involved 120,000 men. Within months secret Soviet military journals ran articles warning that new technology was threatening tanks with obsolescence. The Soviet Minister of Defense Marshal Dmitri Yazov compounded the depression of his colleagues when he lamented that the West had developed electronic warfare capabilities that the Soviet Union simply could not match. This was another area in which the Americans had been exploiting their sustainable competitive advantage.

The Soviet General Staff had seen the writing on the wall. In the spring of 1988, the Warsaw Pact staged its first large-scale exercise that was purely defensive. In his first speech to the United Nations, in December 1988, Mikhail Gorbachev made the dramatic announcement that, over the next two years, Soviet forces would be cut by 500,000 men and six of its armored divisions in Eastern Europe would be disbanded. The Cold War, it seemed, was moving to a close.

LOOKING AHEAD

While Reagan stepped up the pressure on Gorbachev after their summit meeting in Geneva, Caspar Weinberger announced, in February 1986, that competitive strategy would be "a major theme" of the Department of Defense. This line fit nicely with Reagan's existing strategy, and he had probably agreed to it. As part of this process, a Commission on Integrated Long-Term Strategy was established to guide force development, weapons procurement, and arms control negotiations. Marshall led the group that produced a report on the security environment over the next twenty years. One of its key conclusions was that the Soviets were correct in their assessment that the advent of new technologies would revolutionize war and not merely make current forces marginally better at what they do.

In parallel, Weinberger had set up a task force to report on how to improve U.S. capabilities for mid- to high-intensity global conventional conflict with the Soviet Union and the Warsaw Pact. The task force's recommendations, made in 1987, were for unmanned air vehicles, long-range systems, low observables (for example, Stealth bombers), sensors, miniaturization, decoys, guided munitions, and the like—that, taken together, implied substantial changes to the Services' current acquisition programs. These recommendations touched on two highly sensitive issues—who had the responsibility for implementing competitive strategy and who would control the Pentagon's major acquisition programs. The Services claimed that they had already adopted competitive strategy. Over the next two years the services and the Joint Chiefs of Staff (JCS) killed off Weinberger's efforts to institutionalize competitive strategy.

Weinberger's failure to institutionalize competitive strategy, however, had little effect on the outcome of the Cold War. By then, the constituent elements of the strategy had gained considerable momentum, and Gorbachev was keen to seek an accommodation with the United States.

CONCLUSIONS

During the latter part of the Cold War, the United States did pursue an increasingly competitive strategy against the Soviet Union—one that played a major part not only in checkmating the Soviet threat but also in bringing the Cold War to a peaceful end. In essence, this strategy was based on exploiting America's "sustainable competitive advantage" and Soviet fears. Initially, competitive strategy dealt with the military aspects of the rivalry, before gaining greater traction in the context of Reagan's broader political approach to dealing with the Soviet Union.

Given the similarities of outlook, information and insights were easily shared and constructively debated, often outside official channels. Such an atmosphere encouraged sound instincts about what was the right thing to do. Some people who launched programs to siphon off Soviet military expenditure into wasteful projects thought it self-evident that there were significant and interesting payoffs to particular actions; they felt no need for long staff papers.

While the intensity of the Soviet threat facilitated acceptance of the strategy, success stemmed from the flair with which interest in it was generated. One of the key elements was the progress that Marshall and his wide range of collaborators made in "getting inside the mind" of their adversary.

There were clearly gains to be had from sustaining long-term advantages; identifying and exploiting Soviet "gut reactions" and fears would bring even great benefits. This was a prodigious undertaking that called for people who relished the intellectual challenge, were willing to battle against deeply entrenched conventional wisdom, and were well versed in the Russian language and Soviet culture and military affairs.

A sound understanding the Soviet threat depended on good intelligence. The heavy investments that the United States made in the technical collection of intelligence paid handsome dividends. Had the CIA and other Western intelligence services been more successful in recruiting Soviet and East European agents, they should have been better able to help the strategists gain a better understanding of Soviet rationality.

Historians will continue to be frustrated by the difficulties in establishing exactly what happened within the overall concept of the competitive strategy. The absence of a clear paper trail does, however, highlight a key element of the strategy—it was not an exercise in hard bureaucratic power but an exemplary use of soft power.

The United States should not, however, take too much comfort from that. The other point to be borne in mind is that the failure to institutionalize competitive strategy in the Pentagon did adversely affect the ability of the United States to respond to events in the post–Cold War era. The services claimed that their programs embodied competitive strategy. That was true, but the future they were looking at was a continuing old-style Cold War, not one in which there had been a "revolution in military affairs." The Russian armed forces have still not caught up with that revolution, but if the U.S. forces had embraced the "competitive strategy in the small" that was proposed in 1987, they would have been better able to respond effectively to the threats that have arisen in the past two decades.

Today, the United States lives in a more complex world than that of the Cold War era. The big double question now is whether and how the United States can create a new culture—not just within the Pentagon, but more widely within the administration—that would make it possible once again for the United States to focus its collective energies on competitive strategy.

NOTES

This paper draws on extensive discussions that I have had in recent years with Andrew Marshall and several other people closely involved with strategy during the latter part of the Cold War (see my book on *The Great Cold War—A Journey through the Hall of Mirrors* [Palo Alto, CA: Stanford University Press, 2009]), as well as additional valuable assistance that I have received from Barry Watts and Andrew May.

1. Correspondence with the author, October 11, 2010.

2. Bernard Brodie, Charles Hitch, and Andrew Marshall, "The Next Ten Years." Santa Monica, CA: RAND internal document, December 30, 1954.

3. Department of Defense, online SecDef Histories; retrieved on February 3, 2012, from www.defense.gov/specials/secdef_histories/bios/schlesinger.htm.

4. Barrass, *The Great Cold War,* 163.

5. Department of Defense, SecDef Histories; retrieved on February 3, 2012, from www.defense.gov/specials/secdef_histories/bios/schlesinger.htm.

6. Barrass, *The Great Cold War,* 181.

7. Christopher A. Ford and David A. Rosenberg, "The Naval Intelligence Underpinnings of Reagan's Maritime Strategy," *The Journal of Strategic Studies* 28 (April 2005), 392.

8. Dominic A. Paolucci, *Summary Report of the Long Range Research and Development Planning Program* (Falls Church, VA: Lulejian and Associates, Feb. 7, 1975), DNA-75-03055, SECRET (Declassified December 31, 1983). This report was sponsored by the Defense Nuclear Agency and the Defense Advanced Research Projects Agency.

9. Ford and Rosenberg, "The Naval Intelligence Underpinnings," 393.

10. Ibid., 395.

11. Barrass, *The Great Cold War,* 255.

12. NSDD 32 on "US National Security Strategy" was signed on May 20, 1982, and NSDD 75 on "Relations with the Soviet Union" on January 17, 1983.

13. Barrass, *The Great Cold War,* 264.

14. Ben B. Fischer, *A Cold War Conundrum: The 1983 Soviet War Scare* (Washington, DC: Center for the Study of Intelligence, September 1997), 4–10.

15. Ford and Rosenberg, "The Naval Intelligence Underpinnings," 394–395.

16. Barrass, *The Great Cold War*, 281–282.

17. Gus W. Weiss, "The Farewell Dossier—Duping the Soviets," *Studies in Intelligence*, 39 (1996), 121–126.

18. Barrass, *The Great Cold War*, 287.

19. There were two main sources for this intelligence. One was Ryszard Kuklinski, a colonel on the Polish General Staff who knew a lot about Soviet war plans and was a long-standing CIA agent. He defected to the United States in December 1980. See Benjamin Weiser, *A Secret Life: A Biography of Ryszard Kuklinski* (New York: Profile Books, 2004). The other was General Vladimir Polyakov of the GRU.

20. Barrass, *The Great Cold War*, 267.

21. S. Akhromeyev and G. Kornienko, *Glazami Marshala I Diplomata* [*Through the Eyes of Marshal and a Diplomat*] (Moscow: Mezhdunarodnye otnosheneii'a', 1992), pp. 315–316.

22. Barrass, *The Great Cold War*, 324.

23. Barrass, *The Great Cold War*, 339.

6 OVERVIEW OF THE COMPETITIVE STRATEGIES INITIATIVE

Daniel I. Gouré

IT HAS BEEN ALMOST forty years since the concept of a comprehensive U.S. strategy for long-term competitions was first broached.[1] In his *Long-Term Competition with the Soviets: A Framework for Strategic Analysis,* Andrew W. Marshall provided what one knowledgeable observer characterized as "a seminal contribution to US strategic thinking in the post–World War II era."[2] Marshall's study was published at a time when there was growing concern among policymakers that the struggle between Soviet Union and its allies and the Western democracies was evolving, at best, into a stalemate or, at worst, into a competition that the West was slowly losing. Emerging slowly from the wreckage of decolonization and the Vietnam War, there were many on both sides who saw the West, in general, and the United States, in particular, as entering a period of decline. Analyses of Soviet writings indicated that Moscow too viewed the period beginning in the 1970s as one in which the "correlation of forces" had begun to shift significantly in its favor. Moscow sought to devise a strategy that would allow it to capitalize on perceived sociopolitical and economic strengths so as to undermine containment and eventually encircle the West.[3]

Marshall appreciated what so few in the West did: that the struggle with the Soviet Union would be long and complicated and require the use of every tool at our disposal. But to engage in long-term competition with the adversary it would be necessary to develop both an accurate understanding of the other side and a set of basic postulates to guide specific applications of national power.

When he became the first director of the Office of Net Assessment (ONA), Marshall set out to systematize the study of the Soviet Union and develop a full-fledged methodology for conducting a long-term competition. What he could not know at the time was that the competition would be successfully concluded in his lifetime. Neither Marshall, the U.S. intelligence community, nor virtually any observer of the Soviet scene understood at the time—even up to the day the Soviet Union collapsed—the essential fragility of the communist regime. There were some studies, again generally sponsored by ONA, that indicated that the Soviet Union suffered from what might be called "imperial overstretch."[4] There were violent debates within the expert community regarding the Soviet defense budget and the burden that it placed on that country.[5] What was unknowable at the time was the progressive loss of credibility suffered by the Soviet government and the Communist Party of the Soviet Union with its own constituents. With the advantages of hindsight and access to some of the contemporaneous records of a number of Soviet decision makers and analysts, it is now clear that Moscow in the 1970s never saw itself in as strong a position as it was perceived to hold by the West. Moreover, whatever sense of potential the Kremlin leadership believed it possessed at the start of that decade had all but vanished by the early 1980s. Post–Cold War analyses clearly demonstrate that, while not the singular reason for the collapse of the Soviet Union, the competitive strategies approach, particularly as applied by the Reagan administration, did much to set the stage for subsequent events and for the eventual collapse of the Soviet Union and the Warsaw Pact.[6]

However much it contributed directly to the end of the Cold War, the competitive strategies approach proved extremely useful for assessing the nature of competitive environments and for developing cost-effective strategies for pursuing advantage in such situations. This approach remains relevant, particularly in developing strategies for today's complex competitive environments.

FROM NET ASSESSMENT TO COMPETITIVE STRATEGIES

Competitive strategies would not have been possible without the earlier effort to develop and demonstrate the methodology for net assessment. The demand for net assessment was driven by disagreements regarding the accuracy of extant assessments of military balance between East and West. There is a long Cold War history of Western analysts imputing to the Soviet Union capabilities it did not have while also failing to anticipate their acquisition of game-changing capabilities. Even access to critical high-level Soviet military writings did not resolve issues around motivations and intentions.

Secretary of Defense James Schlesinger's decision to create an Office of Net Assessment within OSD was driven by his experience at the CIA and specifically his unhappiness with the quality if the analyses performed there. In particular, it was clear that numbers alone did not tell the whole story of the U.S.-Soviet balance. Although the intelligence community became relatively adept at counting weapons, particularly with the advent of space-based imagery, it was not particularly adept at developing the deeper understanding necessary to explain how the Soviet Union was likely to employ them. Even less developed was the understanding of the role of history, national culture, domestic politics, and other influences on Soviet military behavior. Schlesinger wanted more:

> What Schlesinger sought was analyses of a type that other agencies were not engaged in or were doing in ways that could be improved upon, such as comparative cost of U.S. and Soviet military programs; the naval balance between the United States and the USSR; political and psychological aspects of military forces—how, for example, does deterrence actually work, viewed from a Soviet perspective?[7]

At the time, the RAND Corporation specialized in such "outside-the-box" thinking. By the early 1970s it already had established a long and impressive record in assessing various elements of the East-West competition from the nuclear doctrine and targeting, force planning metrics, Soviet leadership behavior, defense economics, and counterinsurgency operations. Its combination of regional and functional specialists provided the intellectual capital and data bases to support the conduct of net assessments.[8]

Andrew Marshall, the "godfather" of both net assessment and competitive strategies, had been working at improving the process of assessing and modeling the military balance between the United States and the Soviet Union. It became apparent to him that the so-called balance of power approach was inadequate not only as the basis for accurately characterizing a strategic relationship but also as a guide to action. Put simply, history showed that the biggest battalion did not always win. When the competition was political as well as military, static measures of capabilities were even less informative for policymakers.[9]

RAND analysts were able to draw on innovative thinking from a number of disciplines in the development of the concept of net assessment. The new field of business management provided one avenue of approach. Another source of inspiration was Soviet political-military thinking, which had developed an array of theories and modes of analysis around the idea of a "correlation of forces," generally military in nature or a broader sociopolitical variant, the "correlation of world forces." The correlation of military forces involved more than just numbers; it included qualitative factors that contributed to military capabilities and the conduct of operations. The correlation of world forces sought to weigh the full range of social, political, economic, and moral factors that contributed to a state's strength. Rooted in a Marxist-Leninist perspective, correlation of forces assessments were based on the idea of a historic competition between rival political systems.[10]

There are a number of serviceable definitions of net assessment. In its simplest form it involves the appraisal of military balances. More sophisticated definitions focus on the interaction between military and political factors or even on the "interactions of national security establishments in peace and war."[11] The analysis must be long-term, reflecting identifiable trends, and it must be at least two-sided, reflecting the interaction of the subject with its environment. A rather comprehensive definition of net assessment is provided by Thomas Skypek:

> Net assessment is a multidisciplinary approach to national security analysis that is comparative, diagnostic, and forward-looking. More precisely, net assessment is a framework for evaluating the long-term strategic political-military competitions in which states engage. As the word competition implies, net assessors view the interactions of states as inherently competitive rather than inherently cooperative. The aim of net assessment is to diagnose strategic asymmetries between competitors and to identify environmental opportunities in order to support senior policymakers in the making of strategy.[12]

Without necessarily disagreeing with any of the definitions already given, Paul Bracken's definition emphasizes the operational aspect of net assessment: "The best way to define net assessment is to understand that it is a practice. It isn't an art (like military judgment), nor is it a science (like chemistry). Rather, it's a way of tackling problems from certain distinctive perspectives that involve skills that can be improved."[13]

The net assessment process was guided by a relatively simple set of principles. The first was that net assessments had to be interactive; that is, they had to consider the behavior of a responsive antagonist. The second principle was that strategic behavior was the product of the operation of large and complex bureaucracies. The third was the need to take a long-term perspective and to take into account the potential unfolding of relevant trends. The fourth was the identification of asymmetries between the two sides, commonly termed strengths and weaknesses. The final principle was the need for means of testing hypotheses. This could be through scenario development, war gaming, or computer simulations, just to name a few.[14]

In one of his first published descriptions of a net assessment, Marshall included virtually all the essential principles:

> Our notion of a net assessment is that it is a careful comparison of U.S. weapon systems, forces, and policies in relation to those of other countries. It is comprehensive, including description of the forces, operational doctrines and practices, training regime, logistics, known or conjectured effectiveness in various environments, design practices and their effect on equipment costs and performance, and procurement practices and their influence on cost and lead times.[15]

THE COMPETITIVE STRATEGIES METHODOLOGY

It should not come as a surprise that the application of the higher forms of net assessment would lead to the search for a dynamic strategy to apply its insights.[16] This was competitive strategies (CS). The idea of competitive strategies reflected evolutionary developments across a range of fields from industrial psychology to group dynamics to computer-based modeling and simulation. For example, Michael Porter of the Harvard Business School pioneered the concept of business planning based on the central premise of continual competition among firms in the marketplace.[17] His work and that of other business sources were used by the Office of Net Assessment in the development of its theory of competitive strategies.

WHAT IS "COMPETITIVE STRATEGIES"?

As implemented in the Department of Defense, CS was both a process and a product. As a process, it was a method of systematic strategic thinking that allowed for developing and evaluating U.S. defense strategy in terms of a long-term competition. As a product, it was a plan of action (or a set of such plans) or simply a guide for helping the nation gain and maintain a long-term advantage in a particular competition:

> The goal of CS was, through systematic, long-range, strategic-competition planning, to make the US approach to the competition with the Soviets more efficient and effective to enhance deterrence and the security of the US and

its friends and allies. At bottom, DOD sought to contain the threat until, one hoped, things improved politically.

CS called for identifying and aligning enduring US strengths against enduring Soviet weaknesses (the particulars here depended upon which part of the competition was of immediate interest and on the goals established for the competition). This necessitated employing a three-step, chess-match-like methodology (three was considered the minimum) in a move/response/counter response sequence in order to create a new or improved military capability in high-leverage areas, thereby gaining and maintaining the initiative, shaping the competition, and achieving particular competition goals. All of this was to be done in the context of a planning horizon that extended 15–20 or more years into the future. The notion of "enduring" strengths and weaknesses involved dealing with things that, by their very nature, were hard to change, at least in the near term to midterm—thus the need to look out 15–20 years or more.[18]

A fundamental assumption of the CS methodology is that both sides operated in a resource-constrained environment. This led to an extended effort to understand the availability of resources to the adversary but also how that adversary allocated them. In the application of CS to Defense Department plans and programs, the idea of cost imposition (and to a lesser degree cost avoidance for the United States) played a role. One of the attractive features of the CS methodology was that it did not require that the proposed action take a particular form, say, for example, an increase in force structure or procurement of additional weapon systems. It could be argued that with its predisposition toward the "chess match" approach to competition that a CS-based strategy would favor changes in behaviors over increases in capabilities.

A criticism laid against the CS methodology was that it was neither new nor exceptional. It was asserted that, reductio ad absurdum, all good military or even corporate strategies were by definition competitive. Proponents of CS readily acknowledged that CS had been practiced in the past in various forms. It was not that CS was new per se; what was different was its codification in a set of basic principles and its institutionalization. From Sun Tzu to the present era, sheer genius has enabled some leaders to create and implement a successful CS campaign, albeit rarely over a protracted period. The United States could not count simply on the application of strategic genius or sheer luck in its competition with the Soviet Union. Therefore, the institutionalization of the CS methodology and the effort to force the system to take account of CS in the development of specific plans and programs was a way to enhance the formulation of strategy without reliance on the presence of genius. The approach required systematic thinking about the future and a clear audit trail from assumptions through analyses to recommendations.

The methodology required development of unvarnished assessments of both the strengths and weaknesses of the United States as well as those of the adversary. It made it an analytic crime to mirror image. In addition, the emphasis on enduring strengths and weaknesses required a different, broader, and more sophisticated approach to both data and intelligence than was typical of standard balance assessments and traditional forms of strategic planning. Enforcing a certain discipline or rigor on the defense planning and analysis processes could be considered a major contribution of the CS methodology.

As a process, CS was simple in principle yet difficult in application. It required a certain discipline of mind, breadth of understanding, and capacity to think like the adversary. One of the most obvious challenges to the application of the CS methodology was the requirement to think in the long term. Although all strategists claim to take a long-term perspective, this is rarely the case. Moreover, the Defense Department's dominant planning systems, the Planning, Programming, and Budgeting System and the Joint Strategic Planning System, are focused almost exclusively on the near term.[19]

Although it may seem odd, another challenging feature of the CS methodology was its assumption that the competition was long term. Although not explicitly ruling out the possibility that the U.S.-Soviet relationship could evolve into a less hostile interaction, CS neither hoped for such an outcome nor identified it as the aim of U.S. strategy. There was also nothing in the CS approach that rejected the reality of elements of cooperation between the two sides within a long-term competitive framework. There were critics of CS, including some in the U.S. government, who viewed the very idea of enhancing the ability of the United States to excel in a long-term competition with the Soviet Union as contributing to the problem.

Considering the instincts of the Pentagon's bureaucracy, it is amazing that CS was practiced at all, much less that it achieved as much as it did. CS is inherently two sided. It required the interaction of both Blue planners and Red analysts. Indeed, it placed the two on an equal footing, which tended to distress the Blue planners to no end. The "chess match" interaction could easily result in preferred, even cherished, U.S. strategies being challenged and potentially undermined.

CS, like any innovation in strategy, faced the twin challenges of acceptance and implementation. The history of applied CS in the DoD suggests that it was most successful when the problem being addressed was both critical and clearly recognized at very high levels and the scope of the effort was bounded. The examples cited by Secretary Weinberger in his annual reports to Congress, the penetration of Soviet air defenses by U.S. strategic bombers and U.S. efforts to counter the Soviet submarine threat, fit this description.[20]

COMPETITIVE STRATEGIES AT THE TOP

The heyday of competitive strategies, at least in terms of its official recognition and the attempt to apply it throughout the Department of Defense, came during the tenure of Caspar Weinberger as secretary of defense. Adoption of a competitive strategies approach to countering the Soviet threat reflected the view at the highest levels of the U.S. government that the United States was in an existential struggle against the Soviet Union and its allies for the future of the world. Nowhere in the Reagan administration's political doctrine was there the concept of total cooperation with the USSR. For Reagan, the issue was the terms of the competition. He understood that to replace containment with some military-based version of rollback would be to risk nuclear war. Therefore, he looked for other ways to compete.

Events at the time played to Reagan's firmly held convictions in the superiority of democratic capitalism over all other forms of government. Based on analyses he read before taking office as well as briefings he received from the intelligence community, the president concluded, in his own words, that:

> The Soviet economy was being held together by baling wire. In Poland and other Eastern-bloc countries, the economies were also a mess, and there were rumblings of nationalist fervor within the captive Soviet empire. If they didn't make some changes, it seemed clear to me that in time that Communism would collapse of its own weight, and I wondered how we as a nation could use these cracks in the Soviet system to accelerate the process of collapse.[21]

Two other events helped shape Reagan's approach to the East-West competition and establish a firm base on which to build a competitive strategies approach to strategic planning. The first was the rise of Solidarity in Poland, which offered the prospect of discrediting communism in Europe and weakening the Warsaw Pact. The second was the Soviet invasion of Afghanistan, which was the catalyst for the promulgation of the so-called Reagan Doctrine, which directed the provision of overt and covert assistance to anticommunist resistance movements around the world.

Reagan's overall strategy was to impose restraint on an expansionist Soviet Union by building up the U.S. military while forcing Moscow to spend ever-increasing amounts of resources not only to maintain military parity with the United States but also to support its friends and surrogates abroad.[22] In essence, the Reagan competitive strategy was based on increasing the horizontal competition between the United States and the Soviet Union, forcing the latter to spread its resources more widely. Some observers argue that the Strategic Defense Initiative was a form of competitive strategy, forcing the Soviet Union to invest in high-end electronics where they were comparatively weak. A simplified version of the same thesis would argue that, by seeking to devalue the ballistic missile, Reagan struck at the heart of Moscow's sole competitive advantage vis-à-vis the West.

It was Secretary of Defense Weinberger who most directly sought to translate Reagan's philosophy and political views into an action plan. In so doing, he sought to make CS a major tool in his department's efforts to craft a long-term strategy for defeating the Soviet Union. CS took a prominent place in the DoD's 1987 Annual Report to Congress, with Weinberger declaring "I have decided to make competitive strategies a major theme of the Department of Defense during the remainder of this Administration." In a series of memoranda to senior defense officials, Weinberger directed the department to implement the Competitive Strategies Initiative.[23]

It seems quite clear that Weinberger was drawn to the net assessment/competitive strategies approaches. His comment on how the United States should approach understanding the Soviet Union was classic net assessment: "By examining their military organization, their leadership . . . and even the broader trends in their society such as . . . demographics, we will not only know our enemy better, we will be able to attend to his weaknesses more effectively."[24] The connection to CS was made evident in an article Weinberger wrote for *Foreign Affairs*: "Implementation of our overarching strategy of secure deterrence requires an array of strategies that capitalize on our advantages and exploit our adversaries' weaknesses."[25]

Secretary Weinberger understood that the long-term competition with the Soviet Union was economic as well as military. The application of CS was intended to ensure a U.S. technological advantage over the Soviet Union while forcing that country to pay an increasing price for continuing the competition. In addition, Weinberger's Defense Department was challenged by the

Reagan administration's efforts to reduce what in current terms were exceedingly modest budget deficits. Hence, the CS approach, with the suggestion that cost avoidance could be factored into the development of specific proposals, offered some intriguing possibilities for the secretary.

Secretary Weinberger directed the establishment of the Strategic Concepts Development Center (SCDC) to develop operational-level ideas that could be applied in the near term with impact on the long-term military competition with the Soviet Union. The SCDC's greatest impact was in focusing the Defense Department's attention on the dominant competitive problem facing the United States: the threat the mass of Soviet and Warsaw Pact conventional forces on the Central Front in Europe. The efforts of the SCDC led to the development of concepts such as Assault Breaker, second-echelon attack, and Air-Land Battle, as well as to the Mutual and Balanced Force Reduction and Intermediate-Range Nuclear Forces arms control negotiations.[26]

Weinberger's successor as secretary of defense, Frank Carlucci, if anything went farther in his efforts to institutionalize CS within the Defense Department. He created a competitive strategies task force, a competitive strategies council, and a competitive strategies senior intelligence council. Carlucci continued to press the point made by Weinberger that a CS approach to defense planning could serve as an important adjunct to a broad range of DoD activities, including cost containment.

One natural operational outgrowth of the application of the CS methodology was the development of strategies of dissuasion. Formally adopted as a key element of U.S. defense planning only in the Rumsfeld Pentagon, dissuasion had roots in the CS approach. Based on a net assessment of a potential adversary's long-term enduring strengths and weaknesses, it was natural for CS planners to consider ways that the adversary could be induced not to pursue those courses of actions that either would minimize his growing stronger or make it more likely he would remain or grow weaker.[27]

During its heyday in the 1980s, CS clearly had a significant impact of U.S. defense planning. One of the best examples is the creation of the Maritime Strategy. By the 1980s, the United States and its allies faced a Soviet Navy of growing numbers and sophistication. There was growing concern that, if allowed to deploy into the trans-Atlantic and trans-Pacific sea lanes vital to U.S. efforts to reinforce forward deployed forces, the Soviet Navy could successfully isolate the United States from the main theaters of conflict.[28] The Maritime Strategy built on the established post–World War II practices of forward, offensive operations by carrier, amphibious, and attack submarine forces but emphasized their role in seizing the initiative from the Soviets in an initial stage of a conflict and posing a threat to Soviet littoral waters and critical land assets. The Maritime Strategy, which sought to shift the focus of U.S. naval power from a battle in the sea-lanes to the creation of a potential threat to the Soviet Union on its maritime flanks, came to full fruition during the 1980s. The Maritime Strategy was designed specifically to exploit the vulnerability of Soviet strategic missile submarines, which were increasingly deployed only in close-in waters and by so doing engendered a change in Soviet naval strategy and force deployments.[29]

The results were profound. The Soviet Navy responded by pursuing what was termed a bastion defense strategy, expending enormous resources to protect the close-in deployment zones for its strategic submarines and adding air- and sea-based assets for the purpose of defending Soviet territory against the threat of attack by carrier-based aircraft and naval cruise missiles. Defense analysts argued that the maritime strategy contributed to deterrence by posing the threat of attacks on Soviet strategic nuclear submarines early in a conventional conflict, thereby raising the specter of rapid and unpredictable escalation.

Although U.S. defense policy never made the explicit connection between CS and the Strategic Defense Initiative (SDI), many analysts have suggested that the Reagan-era initiative was based on "CS-like" thinking.[30] There were efforts undertaken to understand the effects of the U.S. pursuit of the SDI on Soviet behavior. A very sophisticated Red Team effort developed around the SDI (which continued up to the fall of the Soviet Union) to anticipate and, as needed, counter potential Soviet efforts to undermine U.S. defenses. This Red Team effort was almost always paired with parallel Blue Team activities in the familiar CS "chess move" format.[31] In addition, the question about the cost-imposing character of the SDI on the Soviet Union was also raised and analyzed.[32]

The Office of Net Assessment also pursued what might be viewed as a "hybrid" effort, somewhere between net assessment and competitive strategies, to understand the implications of emerging technologies for the future of warfare and the competitive position of the United States. The genesis for this effort was the thinking of various Soviet theoreticians on the subject of changes in technology and their implications for the future of conflict. Variously called the Military-Technical Revolution (MTR) or the Revolution in Military Affairs (RMA), the objective of this effort was not simply to identify potential revolutionary technologies but, more important, to understand how military organizations implemented the transition from one set of capabilities to others that were entirely different.[33] The RMA analyses identified a broad range of factors that contributed to revolutionary change in military capabilities, including new military doctrine, altered concepts of operations, and different military organizations. The work sponsored by the Office of Net Assessment sparked an intellectual frenzy in the defense community with literally hundreds of articles and books being written on some aspect of RMAs.[34]

The effort to explore the idea of an imminent RMA clearly influenced the thinking of the George W. Bush administration. The Bush administration came into office speaking the language of RMAs, suggesting that it might be time to skip a generation in weapons deployments to fully exploit the potential of emerging technologies. The new secretary of defense, Donald Rumsfeld, made the idea of transformation central to his vision of the future of the U.S. military. Many of the concepts for change he proposed appear to have had their roots in early assessments of the RMA.[35] In addition, defense planning during the Rumsfeld era focused a great deal of attention on implementing CS-based concepts of cost-imposing strategies, dissuading or shaping adversary behavior, and gaining or enhancing enduring U.S. military advantages. One of the challenges for planning in this era was the difficulty of identifying plausible adversaries as well as the lack of capacity in the intelligence and analytic communities to provide the same level of knowledge about prospective adversaries as had been available for the Soviet Union.

LESSONS FOR THE 21ST CENTURY

The impact of net assessment or competitive strategies on U.S. defense decision making has been profound. Net assessment has become a standard approach to intelligence analysis. Modern defense analysis clearly accepts both the need to assess the state of the competition from both sides and that it is important to consider the "intangibles" of belief systems, values, morale, and national character. It is now a well-established principle that good intelligence requires a deep knowledge of the adversary. The net assessment or competitive strategies process legitimized efforts to understand mind-set of adversary that, after initial efforts produced primarily out of RAND, had been downplayed. Works by Colin Gray and the late Laurent Murawiec on strategic culture and the mind of our adversaries were groundbreaking.

There have been only a limited number of attempts to apply the CS methodology to contemporary problems. The first step, as one analyst suggested, may be the intensive application of net assessment to an improved understanding of current competitions.[36] One of the most interesting of these is the edited anthology produced by the Nonproliferation Policy Education Center in 2000, *Prevailing in a Well-Armed World: Devising Competitive Strategies against Weapons Proliferation.* This volume is noteworthy, in part, because of the varied approaches taken by the contributors to the application of CS to counter proliferation.[37]

It is clear that the net assessment and competitive strategies methodologies are applicable to our current conflicts. Many of the improvements proposed by Major General Flynn to intelligence collection and assessment echo the need to apply lessons learned by net assessment and competitive strategies.[38] The characteristics of the global struggle against violent extremism would appear a textbook example of the type of competition that would be well served by the application of CS methods. Yet examples of application of the net assessment methodologies to the wars in Iraq and Afghanistan are relatively few in number.[39] Given the expectation that we will be involved in Iraq and Afghanistan for years to come, it would seem sensible for the Defense Department to develop a CS-based strategy for the region.

The CS methodology has demonstrated applications well beyond the walls of the Pentagon. In the aftermath of the fall of Baghdad, U.S. forces in Iraq found themselves confronted by a new, sophisticated, and agile adversary. Meeting the challenge posed by improvised explosive devices (IEDs), the Defense Department created a unique organization the Joint IED Defeat Organization (JIEDDO). JIEDDO's insight was to recognize that it was not fighting a weapons system or a tactic but a system capable of responding and evolving. To meet this challenge, JIEDDO created a competitive strategies group that "seeks to develop and provide JIEDDO with a continuous competitive advantage in the C-IED fight by anticipating second and third order effects of adversary adaptation in the use of IEDs in order to defeat IEDs as weapons of strategic influence."[40] At same time, the CS process also encouraged the examination of other forces that could prove transformative in military affairs. The research conducted on the RMA, coming at end of Cold War, was an impetus to efforts to understand the impact of IT on military operations and conflict. Other technology areas that have been under the net assessment "spotlight" include biotechnology, nanotechnology, and robotics.

Competitive strategies are extremely well suited to assessing the implications of globalization, in general, and the rise of China, in particular, for U.S. security. The Office of Net Assessment is conducting a range of analyses on the evolution of China, including the intersection of China's economic and technological progress and its future military power. This area is one that would clearly benefit from the kind of intensive and focused effort conducted in the 1970s and 1980s with respect to the Soviet Union.

The current mantra in national security for "whole-of-government" solutions to complex security problems would appear to invite the application of a CS methodology. What is the evidence that the application of the nonmilitary elements of U.S. power can achieve better results than a approach predominantly based on the use of military force? Even if true, which elements of power should be applied in a given situation and to what end? One wonders what a truly dispassionate application of the CS methodology to the problem of failing states would say about enduring U.S. advantages and weaknesses.

NOTES

1. Andrew W. Marshall, *Long-Term Competition with the Soviets: A Framework for Strategic Analysis* (U) (Santa Monica, CA: RAND Report R-862-PR, April 1972).

2. David J. Andre, *New Competitive Strategies: Tools and Methodologies, Volume I: Review of the Department of Defense's Competitive Strategies Initiative 1986–1990* (McLean, VA: Science Applications International Corporation, November 30, 1990), 2.

3. For example, see Foy Kohler, *Soviet Strategy for the 1970s: From Cold War to Peaceful Coexistence* (Coral Gables, FL: Center for Advanced International Studies, University of Miami, 1973).

4. See for example, Charles Wolf Jr., Keith Crane, K. C. Yeh, Susan Anderson, and Edmund D. Brunner, *The Costs and Benefits of the Soviet Empire, 1981–1983* (Santa Monica, CA: RAND Report R-3419-NA, August 1986).

5. Noel Firth and James Noren, *Soviet Defense Spending: A History of CIA Estimates, 1950–1990* (College Station: Texas A&M University, 1998), especially chapter 6.

6. John Hines, Ellis M. Mishulovich, and John F. Shulle, *Soviet Intentions 1965–1985, Volume I: An Analytical Comparison of U.S.–Soviet Assessments during the Cold War* (Washington, DCL BDM Federal, September 22, 1995); available at the National Security Archives, www.gwu.edu/~nsarchiv/nukevault/ebb285/index.htm.

7. Douglas Kinnard, *The Secretary of Defense* (Lexington: University of Kentucky Press, 1980), 171.

8. One history of the RAND Corporation is Alex Abella, *Soldiers of Reason: The RAND Corporation and the Rise of the American Empire* (Orlando, FL: Houghton Mifflin Harcourt, 2008).

9. Andrew Marshalll, *Problems of Estimating Military Power*, P-3417 (Santa Monica, CA: RAND Corporation, August 1966).

10. Michael J. Deane, "The Soviet Concept of the 'Correlation of Forces" (Arlington, VA: Stanford Research Institute, May, 1976).

11. Eliot A. Cohen, *Net Assessment: An American Approach,* memorandum no. 29 (Tel-Aviv: Jaffee Center for Strategic Studies, April 1990); and Stephen Peter Rosen, "Net Assessment as an Analytical Concept," in *On Not Confusing Ourselves,* Andrew W. Marshall, J. J. Martin, and Henry Rowen, eds. (Boulder, CO: Westview Press, 1991), 290.

12. Thomas M. Skypek, "Evaluating Military Balances through the Lens of Net Assessment: History and Application," *Journal of Military and Strategic Studies,* 12:2 (Winter 2010), 3.

13. Paul Bracken, "Net Assessment: A Practical Guide," *Parameters,* Spring, 2006, 91.

14. [14] Cohen, *Net Assessment: An American Approach,* pp. 13–19; Bracken, "Net Assessment: A Practical Guide," 92–100; and Skypek, "Evaluating Military Balances," 6–9.

15. Quoted in Skypek, "Evaluating Military Balances," 14.

16. Still the single best description of the competitive strategies methodology and its applications is David Andre's study, already cited in note 2. Much of the discussion in this section is drawn from his analysis.

17. His classic text, first published in 1980 and now in its sixtieth printing, is Michael Porter, *Competitive Strategy: Techniques for Analyzing Industries and Competitors* (Glencoe, IL: Free Press, 1980).

18. David Andre, "Competitive Strategies: An Approach against Proliferation," in *Prevailing in a Well-Armed World: Devising Competitive Strategies against Weapons Proliferation,* Henry Sokolski, ed. (Washington, DC: Nonproliferation Policy Education Center, 2000), 7–8.

19. Bracken, "Net Assessment: A Practical Guide," 94–95.

20. Andre, "Competitive Strategies: An Approach against Proliferation," 13.

21. Ronald Reagan, *An American Life* (New York: Simon and Schuster, 1990), 287.

22. Peter Schweizer, *Victory: The Reagan Administration's Secret Strategy That Hastened the Collapse of the Soviet Union* (New York: The Atlantic Monthly Press, 1994).

23. Andre, "New Competitive Strategies Tools and Methodologies," 1.

24. *Annual Report to the Congress, FY J98* (Washington, DC: Government Printing Office, 1986), 86–87, as cited in Gary L. Guertner, "Competitive Strategies and Soviet Vulnerabilities," *Parameters,* March 1988, 26.

25. Andre, "New Competitive Strategies Tools and Methodologies," 1.

26. Phillip A. Karber, "The 'Counter-Offensive' in Competitive Strategies: Lessons from the Reagan Era," Conference Presentation, U.S. Naval War College, Newport, RI, October, 2010.

27. Andrew Krepinevich and Robert Martinage, *Dissuasion Strategy* (Washington, DC: The Center for Strategic and Budgetary Assessments, 2008), 5–6.

28. Christopher Ford and David Rosenberg, "The Naval Intelligence Underpinnings of Reagan's Maritime Strategy," *Journal of Strategic Studies,* 2: 2 (April, 2005), 379–409.

29. "The Maritime Strategy," *Proceedings Supplement,* The U.S. Naval Institute, Annapolis, 1986, 1–49.

30. Bernard Finel, "Competitive Strategies as a Teaching Tool," in Sokolski, *Prevailing in a Well-Armed World,* 41–42.

31. Defense Science Board, *The Role and Status of DoD Red Teaming Activities* (Washington, DC: Department of Defense, September 2001).

32. For example, see Gregory Hildebrand, *SDI and the Soviet Defense Burden,* N-2662-AF (Santa Monica, CA: The RAND Corporation, December 1988).

33. Andrew Krepinevich, *The Military-Technical Revolution: A Preliminary Assessment* (Washington, DC: Center for Strategic and Budgetary Assessments, 2002).

34. For example, Colin S. Gray, *Strategy for Chaos: Revolutions in Military Affairs and the Evidence of History* (London: Frank Cass, 2004).

35. Donald Rumsfeld, "Transforming the Military," *Foreign Affairs,* 81: 3 (May/June 2002), 20–32.

36. Yee-Kwang Heng, "The Return of Net Assessment," *Survival,* 49 (December 2007), 23–31.

37. Sokolski, *Prevailing in a Well-Armed World,*

38. Michael T. Flynn, Matt Pottinger, and Paul D. Batchelor, *Fixing Intel: A Blueprint for Making Intelligence Relevant in Afghanistan* (Washington, DC: Center for a New American Security, January 2010).

39. See, for example, Sameer Lalwani, *Pakistani Capabilities for a Counterinsurgency Campaign: A Net Assessment* (Washington, DC: Center for a New American Security, September 2009). Also a number of the situation assessments provided by Anthony Cordesman, including *The Afghan War at the End of 2009: A Crisis and New Realism* (Washington, DC: Center for Strategic and International Studies, January 4, 2010).

40. The Joint IED Defeat Organization, *About JIEDDO*; retrieved in August 2010 from www.jieddo.dod.mil/about.aspx.

7 SOVIET MILITARY THOUGHT AND THE U.S. COMPETITIVE STRATEGIES INITIATIVE

John A. Battilega

IN THE MIDDLE OF THE 1980s, the U.S. Department of Defense structured a formal long-term program known as "Competitive Strategies" as a method of developing and evaluating U.S. defense strategy in the context of the long-term military competition between the United States and the Soviet Union.[1]

The competitive strategies process focused on identifying and targeting key and enduring U.S. (and NATO) strengths against enduring Soviet (and Warsaw Pact) weaknesses over a time horizon five to fifteen years in the future. Candidate initiatives were evaluated in move-countermove-counter-countermove analysis that was focused on seizing and retaining U.S. initiative in key aspects of warfare. The objective was to channel the long-term U.S.-Soviet military competition into areas safer and more stable for the United States and NATO and thus to enhance deterrence by altering the Soviets' perception of their ability to conduct successful offensives.[2] Although competitive thought had been a part of defense planning for many years, the Competitive Strategies Initiative was formulated in 1985 as an adjunct to existing planning processes. The process of institutionalizing the initiative within the Department of Defense began in July 1987.[3]

This chapter interprets in retrospect the Competitive Strategies Initiative from the perspective of Soviet military thought, in the context within which it was received within the Soviet Union.[4] It develops four points:

1. First, the Competitive Strategies Initiative was a well-posed program. Because the Soviet Union viewed itself to be in a steady-state competition with the United States, a formal competitive program targeted against the Soviet Union was a program to be reckoned with.

2. Second, Soviet military strategy offered many targets for Competitive Strategies. These came from the basic Soviet approach to warfare and how that was implemented in Soviet military art. The first Competitive Strategies Initiatives directly targeted what the Soviet military viewed as key aspects of its approach.

3. Third, Competitive Strategies cannot be evaluated in isolation. The Soviets viewed the core concepts of U.S. defense initiatives within which Competitive Strategies were embedded to have originated several years earlier. Some Soviet counterinitiatives designed to deal with important gaps in defense technology development and major issues in Soviet weapon system acquisition planning and overall military strategy were already in motion.

4. Finally, Competitive Strategies was probably an effective program. The Soviet Union itself ended a few years after the U.S. program was in place, and the full cycles of moves and countermoves did not play out. Nevertheless, the Cold War ended with the United States on the initiative, moving toward control of Soviet-critical areas of the military competition, and with the machinery, momentum, and intent in place to carry that forward. It seems that the program, for as long as the Soviet Union lived, was effective.

This chapter concludes with some observations that bear on the formulation of future Competitive Strategies initiatives in the 21st century.

THE COMPETITIVE STRATEGIES INITIATIVE WAS A WELL-POSED PROGRAM

The underlying basis for the Soviet approach to interstate relations at all levels was scientific Marxism—the belief that objective laws govern all processes, including warfare. A second important Marxist concept, derived from the German philosopher Hegel, was the concept of the dialectic. In this concept, history proceeds as a result of the conflict ("struggle") between opposites, with the stronger side winning. This in turn creates the conditions for a new dialectic, and so forth.

A key derivative Soviet concept was that of the correlation of forces. The correlation of forces (*sootnosheniye sil*) was the Soviet term that expressed the relationship between the strengths of two opposing sides in a conflict situation (that is, the two sides of the dialectic). In accordance with the underlying philosophy, the result of the conflict (that is, the synthesis of the dialectic) would be determined by the greater strength: In the absence of error in execution, victory will go to the side that has the favorable correlation of forces in those aspects of strength that will actually determine outcomes in the given conflict situation.

The Soviet scientific-determinist philosophy, the concept of the dialectic, and its derivative construct of the correlation of forces were the underlying bases for Soviet international relations and its warfare component. The constant dialectic struggle between opposites has been the engine of history and has occurred in all regimes of human endeavor. Interstate relations have thus been viewed as a dialectic process. The important dimensions of strength that have determined outcomes fell into several major categories: political, economic, military, scientific-technical, and social (ideological). Each of these categories formed major regimes of conflict, and each in turn was governed by the logic of the correlation of forces.

As a result of this overarching philosophy and structure, the Soviet Union viewed itself as being in a steady-state competition with the United States, especially in the military area. Hence the Competitive Strategies Initiative was a well-posed program: against an opponent that viewed itself to be in a long-term competition and for which move-countermove-countercountermove activities were noticed, meaningful, and enduring.

SOME IMPORTANT ELEMENTS
OF SOVIET MILITARY THOUGHT

From the perspective of Soviet military thought, the Competitive Strategies Initiatives were troublesome. Before discussing those aspects that were targeted by the specific initiatives, it is necessary to summarize some important aspects of Soviet military thought that were the targets.[5]

The Soviets had a structured and stable process for planning and executing military operations that a competitor could exploit. It was founded in an overarching approach to military strategy that was firmly rooted in the underlying precepts of the objective laws of war and the process of the dialectic. The objective laws of war and the dialectic joined together in the philosophy of the correlation of forces. Furthermore, careful scientific study over time could create methods and criteria, based on the objective laws of war, which provide an objective basis for success. Hence sound military concepts and execution, based on these criteria, could create objective conditions for victory. In the military sphere, the Soviets actually framed some of the basic laws of war in terms of the correlation of forces. For example, leading Soviet military scientists, writing in 1971 in *Military Thought*, the journal of the Soviet General Staff, argued that:

> The most important and general law . . . is the law of the dependence of the course and outcome of war on the correlation of forces of the belligerents involved . . . It is known that the *correlation of belligerent forces (quantitative and qualitative) is an objective foundation on the basis of which troops accomplish their assigned missions* . . . Since the outcome of war between states (coalitions) depends on the correlation of their military strength and on the ability of the military and political leadership of each of the belligerents to establish superiority in this respect and to utilize this superiority, each military action (engagement, battle, operation) is predetermined by the same concrete conditions. *In other words, the law of dependence of the course and outcome of war on the correlation of forces of the belligerents is in effect at all levels of war and at every scale of war.*[6] [emphasis added]

The Soviets embedded this overall approach into their military art. Hence, the overarching Soviet requirement for combat was the achievement, with confidence, of a "favorable correlation of forces at decisive places and times." The underlying Soviet philosophy of combat, directly tied to the Marxist philosophy already described, saw this mandate as both necessary and sufficient for success. Soviet military scientists also believed that not only was the success of combat at specific times and places determined by the correlation of forces at the start, but also the both the course and the outcome of war were determined by the correlation of forces of the sides. The military correlation of forces in this context was based not simply on the quantity and quality of the armaments of the combatants but also on many other factors such as leadership, training, morale of the troops, terrain, and so on.

Military operations were then structured in ways that facilitated the ability of combat forces to achieve and maintain the correlation of forces necessary for success. This resulted in the major hierarchical war-fighting structures of Soviet military art.

The Major Soviet War-Fighting Structures

The overarching structural element of Soviet military art was what the Soviets termed the "Theater of Military Operations" (*Teatr Voennykh Deistvii*, or TVD, in Russian). The Soviets defined a TVD as a part of the world that had similar political, economic, military, and geographic characteristics. The similarities provide a somewhat homogeneous focus for overall military operations.[7] The similarities also provide the basis for the formulation of TVD-specific military-political goals in the event of war and, in turn, for strategic military tasks to execute those goals. A given TVD also included the contiguous air and sea space, and there was overlap between the boundaries of the TVDs. Soviet military art divided the entire world into TVDs, consistent with the overall Soviet philosophy of preparing to fight a global battle between the forces of capitalism and communism.[8]

Because a TVD itself is very large, the Soviets also divided them into smaller areas that themselves were the focus of separate components of the overall military campaign. These separate areas, or "strategic directions,"[9] defined the operational spaces of lesser-scale military actions within the TVD. The strategic directions could also be subdivided into smaller "operational directions." At sea, the roles of "strategic direction" corresponded to the naval "region" and the "operational direction" to the naval "zone."

The "Operation": The Focal Point of Soviet Military Art

The most important form of combat action within Soviet military art was the "operation" (*operatsiia*). An operation was a standard form of large-scale combat, generally combining arms in execution, which was carefully designed and orchestrated to achieve a stated predictable combat result in space and time. Operations could be either strategic or operational and were designed to be executed by very large forces. Strategic operations were orchestrated over the scale of an entire TVD; strategic directions (regions) within a TVD were the scale of combat for what the Soviets called operational-strategic large formations (for example, a front). Smaller-scale operations were executed on the scale of an operational direction (zone) by operational-tactical large formations (for example, by an army subordinate to a front). There was a canonical set of operations for which doctrinal templates were developed. Over time, Soviet military scientists revised the structure of both the TVDs and the family of canonical strategic and operational-scale operations.

In the 1980s, Soviet military art at the strategic level was structured into three strategic-scale operations: One focused on warfare in a TVD that was principally on land (but included the maritime littoral areas); a second focused on warfare in a TVD that was principally at sea (but included the land littorals); and the third focused on the defense of the Soviet homeland against direct attack from aerospace weapons.[10] The land-focused strategic operation could be principally either offensive or defensive; the other two had a principally defensive focus (even though they may have included offensive components).

A canonical set of operational-scale operations formed the building blocks of these three strategic operations. For the land-focused strategic operation, there were seven: (1) the front offensive operation, (2) the front defensive operation, (3) the air operation, (4) the antiair operation, (5) the *desant* operation,[11] (6) the anti-*desant* operation, and (7) the fleet operation, which itself may consist of one or more "naval operations."[12]

For the sea-focused strategic operation, the basic components were canonical naval operations of operational scale. There were also seven: (1) disruption of enemy ocean transportation; (2) defending areas of Soviet naval basing and lines of communications; (3) routing enemy navies adjacent to Soviet shores; (4) destroying ground targets; (5) annihilating aircraft carrier groupings; (6) annihilating groupings of antisubmarine forces; and (7) annihilating missile-carrying submarines.[13] Additionally, either strategic operation could involve some form of combination of long-range missile or air-delivered strikes of either strategic or operational scale.

Operations were the basic elements of an overall war plan. Hence, the military campaign in a given strategic geographic area consisted of a standard set of strategic operations, and supporting operational scale operations, executed in the places defined by the strategic or operational direction (region) structure and at the times determined by overall strategy.[14] Each canonical operation had its own eligible mix of forces, its own preparation requirements, and its own set of calculations of the correlation of forces.

Soviet Command and Control

The Soviet structural framework was formulated and executed from the top down. Centralized planning focused on the achievement of strategic goals, which in turn resulted in a hierarchy of tightly linked strategic, operational, and tactical scale combat missions. The overall approach to wartime command and control was to insure success at the higher levels. For example, the Soviets were willing to deliberately accept tactical defeat if that facilitated operational success.

The overall goal of Soviet military operations at all levels was to ensure adequate correlation of forces at the places and times decisive for success in a way that maximized the stability of Soviet military operations and forces. Stability was maximized if Soviet military operations were well designed, hedged, and executed so that they were minimally susceptible to disruption. The Soviets also sought high confidence in their ability to respond to offset the impact of change as it occurred. In the Soviet view, loss of control during combat was destabilizing; similarly, the potential for loss of control was destabilizing to Soviet preparations. The Soviets thus strongly emphasized predictability in their warning systems, command and control processes, and weapon systems.[15]

The Soviet process for maintaining control invoked what the Soviets called their "Troop Control System," which included command and control equipment, procedures, training of commanders and staff, and the use of automated methods to help develop and execute their war plans at all echelons. The troop control system was designed to make it possible for the Soviet command and control process not only to develop and execute plans but also to generate timely responses at the operational level to changing situations on the battlefield.[16]

Soviet military art also focused heavily on the timeline of combat, the orchestration of operations along that timeline, and hedging to ensure success. One of the fundamental precepts of Soviet command and control was to ensure the predictability of lower-level outcomes to higher-level commanders. This approach led to a very conservative formulation of the requirements that were used to develop combat operations. There were also very strict requirements placed on Soviet combat operations at all levels. They were required to create the conditions in the initial period of war that allowed the attainment, with high confidence, of the strategic goals defined for that period.[17]

To achieve these objectives, the fundamental questions asked of the operations as they were being prepared were two: Can the combat missions be achieved on a preplanned timetable, and can the critical missions be achieved with confidence in the face of a set of uncertainties that cannot be resolved in advance? In accordance with Soviet theory, achieving these conditions required that the operations be able to ensure adequate correlation of forces at decisive places and times. To facilitate this condition, over time the Soviets developed an integrating calculus of the correlation of forces.

The Calculus of the Correlation of Forces

The calculus of the correlation of forces was the glue that tied the structures of Soviet military art together. The basic logic of the military dialectic argues that success will go to the stronger side. Hence, if there are indices that capture the correct dimensions of comparative strength for a given form of combat, then there is a direct relationship between the sizes of the comparative forces at the start of combat, as measured by those indices, and the probability of mission success.

The Soviets had a well-developed calculus of the correlation of forces.[18] There was a family of indices, each designed to capture the key strengths of different forms of combat. There also was a structure for the application of those indices, for monitoring success or failure during combat and for anticipating success or failure in the future aspects of operations being executed.

In preparing for combat, the Soviets calculated the appropriate indices of the correlation of forces across the scale of combat for the command echelon for which they were preparing. This process continued down the chain of command. The indices of the correlation of forces were also used to establish many kinds of specific battle conditions. For example, relative casualty requirements for the two sides in division-level combat were one such condition that could be estimated using this approach. Correlation of forces indices were also used in some cases to establish a specified rate of advance for ground forces, based on historical data.[19] The use of correlation of forces indices as an intermediate device to estimate the requirements of these kinds of battle conditions also kept the underlying logic of the correlation of forces at the center of Soviet military art.

COMPETITIVE STRATEGIES INITIATIVES FROM
THE PERSPECTIVE OF SOVIET MILITARY THOUGHT

Within the structure and methods of Soviet military thought, there were many different kinds of operational judgments that could be targeted directly by Competitive Strategies. Major categories included:

- *Assessments of future warfare.* These included the types of military operations that should be anticipated, the force levels and length of time it would take for success in those operations, the dynamics of combat, and specific vulnerabilities in those operations and subordinate missions most critical for overall success.
- *Assessments of the adequacy of forces.* These included the overall correlation of forces, the expected correlation of forces for each operation and each phase of that operation, and the adequacy of forces for specific critical elements of combat in the face of uncertainty.
- *Requirements for development and execution of plans for operations.* These included the ability to develop and execute stable plans, with high confidence of success, that would achieve specific combat results on preplanned timetables, and the ability to modify them rapidly enough to respond to unexpected changes on the battlefield.

The Competitive Strategies Initiatives were developed to exploit these Soviet characteristics. The first initiatives were developed by a special task force that focused on global conventional war with emphasis on the European theater and on the identification of critical military tasks that Soviet military thought considered essential for prosecuting a war with NATO.[20]

The task force initially approved four initiatives. These collectively focused on improving NATO's defense posture in ways that directly targeted Soviet air and ground penetration capabilities, Soviet ability to command and control their own operations, and Soviet requirements to be able to successfully execute operations on the NATO flanks as well as in other global areas that might have come into play.[21] Each directly targeted important aspects of Soviet military thought.

Initiative 1: Countering Soviet Air Operations

This initiative included the phased attack of Soviet main operating bases and air infrastructure and strengthening NATO air and ground operations.[22] From the perspective of Soviet military thought, this could seriously erode the Soviet military leadership's confidence in its ability to plan and execute the Air Operation as a part of the Theater Strategic Operation in the Western Theater of War.

Soviet war plans depended on the successful execution of the Air Operation very early in combat to gain air superiority and to neutralize NATO strike systems and radio-electronic combat systems. These conditions were necessary for the success of the rest of the war plan. The initiative would reduce Soviet estimates of the correlation of forces for the Air Operation, reducing Soviet confidence in the ability of that operation to meet its objectives in the designated time. This, in turn, would degrade confidence in the timing of the plan for the entire Theater Strategic operation within which it was embedded, thus reducing the chance of success across the theater. From the perspective of Soviet military thought, this initiative directly threatened what the Soviets saw as the most critical element of their planned combat operations for Western Europe.

Initiative 2: Countering Soviet Penetration
of NATO Forward Defenses

This initiative included the development of an asymmetric force capability of an integrated network of long-range mobile weapons platforms and target acquisition and command and control assets capable of engaging Soviet mobile forces beyond the range of Soviet artillery and multiple-launch rocket systems.[23]

This initiative had two different impacts from the Soviet perspective. The first had to do with the strategic significance of these systems. Long-range precision weaponry linked to real-time reconnaissance and command and control systems, which the Soviets characterized as "reconnaissance strike complexes," was at the forefront of what the Soviets characterized as a new military-technical revolution underway in the West. This capability gave NATO the ability to rapidly identify and strike Soviet mobile targets throughout the battlefield. The initiative directly reduced the correlation of forces for Soviet ground combat elements and affected the stability of Soviet plans for their tactical and near-operational units, resulting in a loss of control over tactical operations. This capability also would have required a major and very costly change in the Soviet force posture to provide an equivalent capability.

The second impact was on the Soviet operational concept for rapidly capturing Western Europe. Soviet plans depended on the exertion of land-warfare pressure across the NATO front, eventually resulting in tactical penetration of NATO lines. Once the tactical penetration occurred, then an operation-level combat formation, known as an Operational Maneuver Group (OMG), was to be in place to rapidly exploit the penetration, place an operational-size force behind NATO lines, and result in the rolling up and collapse of the NATO defense. A Competitive Strategy Initiative that could identify, strike, and defeat elements of the deeper OMG before it became engaged undercut the basis for the Soviet plan for success.

Initiative 3: Stressing the Soviet Troop Control System

This initiative was focused on frustrating tactical operations by blocking the ability to execute preplanned options successfully. This would force operational-level replanning, which could be targeted by direct attack, special operations, and deception, thus countering the ability of Soviet forces to devise and execute new operational-level responses.[24]

From the perspective of Soviet military thought, this initiative threatened the structural process of troop control. It made it difficult to create a war plan that had a high confidence of success because one of the underlying precepts of the process was the ability to identify and execute preplanned options at the operational level. The process also threatened the ability to replan at the operational level and shift forces to the new plan in time to be successful.

Soviet military thought viewed the troop control process, the ability to rapidly shift to preplanned options, and the ability to create new plans when necessary to be at the heart of the Soviet approach to dealing with the fog of war. Hence this initiative would directly reduce Soviet confidence in their ability to respond to battlefield change and thus undercut Soviet confidence in the overall effectiveness, stability, and timing of the plan itself.

Initiative 4: Countering Soviet Global and Multitheater Operations

This initiative exerted military pressure on the Soviet flanks via large-scale joint and combined offensive military campaigns.[25]

In Soviet military art, the strategic operations for all TVDs were linked together to facilitate success on the main strategic direction and to insure protection of the Soviet homeland. In a war with NATO over Central Europe, the main strategic direction was the Western Theater of War, with the main theater direction being the Western TVD and secondary directions in the Northwest and Southwest TVDs. The most important secondary strategic direction was the Far East/Pacific TVDs because they were the focal point for a conflict with China and also housed portions of the Soviet SSBN force. The Competitive Strategies Initiative portended increased levels of forces and combat activities especially in the Northwest TVD, the Southwest TVD, and the Pacific TVD.

From the perspective of Soviet military thought, this possibility had three major impacts. The first was in the European Theater of War. The Theater Strategic Operation depended on the concurrent success of the strategic operations on both flanks of the Central Front. The Northwest TVD housed the conventional submarine force of the Northern Fleet. Increased combat pressures would require greater protection for that force, and the submarines would be less available for timely dispersal into the Atlantic TVD to interdict U.S. forces coming by sea from the United States to reinforce central Europe. This would be important if Soviet combat activities were unsuccessful in rapidly seizing Western Europe. The Southwest TVD included the Turkish straits and the Mediterranean southern flank of combat operations. Increased combat pressure would jeopardize Soviet plans to maintain control of the straits to facilitate access from the Black Sea Fleet into the Mediterranean and to control the Mediterranean to deny its use as a platform for NATO operations. In both cases, the results would be a reduced confidence in the ability of the overall Theater Strategic Operation to meet its goals in space and time in the main Western TVD.

The second impact affected all of the TVDs contiguous to the Soviet Union other than the Western TVD. Increased combat pressure had two effects. One was the increased threat to the Soviet homeland, and to the second echelon forces closing in the Western Theater, from the forward deployment of larger numbers of U.S. sea- and air-based strike aircraft and cruise missiles. The second effect came from the impact on the correlation of forces in each TVD from strategically mobile forces. From a conservative Soviet planning perspective, these forces were especially troublesome: They could be deployed at the brink of war to any TVD. U.S. systems with global deployment capabilities, and U.S. concepts of operation for shifts in forces at the brink of war, reduced predictability for planning purposes. As a result, the strategically mobile forces potentially reduced the correlation of forces in every TVD.

The third impact was on the Soviet nuclear SSBN force. This force was based in the Northwest TVD and the Pacific TVD. Increased U.S. antisubmarine warfare activity in these areas would mandate greater protection for the Soviet SSBN force and divert Soviet submarine and other antisubmarine warfare (ASW) assets from other missions, thus jeopardizing the confidence of success in the strategic operations in those TVDs. Hence, from the perspective of Soviet military thought, there was great strategic leverage from this initiative on the confidence of success of the overall Soviet war plan.

Finally, although the Competitive Strategies Initiatives targeted key aspects of wartime operations, from a Soviet perspective they also directly affected Soviet readiness for future war and forced them into peacetime military competition by creating requirements for investments to offset their impacts.[26] For example, the second U.S. initiative mandated Soviet technological competition to create new "reconnaissance strike complexes" to remain viable on the land battlefield of the future.

THE TIMING AND EFFECTIVENESS
OF COMPETITIVE STRATEGIES

In 1989, the Soviets published an article on Competitive Strategies in the journal *Foreign Military Review*.[27] This journal typically described and analyzed foreign military developments for internal readership in the Soviet Union. Competitive Strategies was characterized as focused on "inevitable, prolonged political, military, economic and technological confrontation as the basis of foreign policy conditions for its implementation."[28] The intent of Competitive Strategies was to take advantage of U.S. scientific-technical capabilities for the purpose of obtaining U.S. military superiority and also the economic undoing of the Soviet Union. The emphasis was on offensive systems to cause the USSR to shift resources to defensive systems.

According to the Soviet article, one of the key requirements for Competitive Strategies was to increase the gap between the United States and the USSR in the development of basic technologies, including especially stealth, superconductivity and new materials, supercomputers, target acquisition, and automated data processing. By component, systems cited for development included cruise missiles armed with nuclear or conventional warheads, the B-2 stealth bomber, improved accuracy ballistic missiles, a North American Air Defense Initiative, reconnaissance-strike-complexes of long-range precision-guided weaponry linked to real-time reconnaissance and weapons control systems, the F-117 and A-12 tactical aircraft, new naval cruise missiles and air defense systems, and improved ASW against Soviet nuclear submarines. These elements were focused on key missions in the initial period of war, including destroying Warsaw Pact air forces on airfields, neutralizing aviation command and control systems, disrupting Warsaw Pact command and control at the operational-strategic level, and implementing flank operations on the European and other theaters of war.

Although the Soviets appeared correctly to understand at least the military elements of Competitive Strategies, in fact the initiative appeared at the tail end of a stream of developments that had been underway since the late 1970s. These included the Air Launched Cruise Missile, the MX missile, the Global Positioning System, the Trident missile system, the Copperhead system, the Advanced Technology Bomber, the Seawolf submarine, the Strategic Defense Initiative, and the triad of doctrinal developments: Air Land Battle (U.S. Army), Forward Maritime Strategy (U.S. Navy), and Follow-on Forces Attack (U.S. Air Force).

Although these initiatives may appear to be a collection of general U.S. force posture upgrades, in fact each also directly targeted key aspects of the Soviet approach to warfare; they were similar in spirit to Competitive Strategies.[29] Each caught Soviet attention: The Soviet military establishment was in the midst of trying to work out countermeasures to these programs when the Competitive Strategies Initiative was tabled, adding another set of elements to the overarching U.S. force modernization portfolio of like-minded activity. As a result, evaluating the overall effectiveness of the Competitive Strategies program, and Soviet countermoves, cannot be done without considering the Soviet measures underway with respect to the overall future U.S. defense posture within which it was embedded.

Soviet Technological Countermoves

The Competitive Strategies Initiatives had a strong technological component. Technologies common to the four areas included unmanned systems, area munitions, extended range projectiles, rapidly emplaceable barriers, precision-penetrator warheads, smart submunitions, advances in automatic data processing, intelligence fusion, electronic miniaturization, stealth, and integrated command, control, and communications systems.[30]

Soviet counters to these technological developments were interpreted in the context of the full set of U.S. defense programs. Some of the required technological responses were already in motion at the time of the formal Competitive Strategies Initiative. Soviet military-technical policy of the 1980s placed high priority on the development of a new generation of mobile intercontinental systems, highly accurate weapons and reconnaissance strike systems, substantial increases in conventional firepower and ammunition, increasing the range and stealthiness of strategic nonnuclear forces, significant increases in physical and electronic survivability of all armament systems, and improvements in many operational aspects of weaponry, including size-weight ratio, mobility, controllability, habitability, and repairability.[31] The Soviet armament plans of the 1980s, designed to field weaponry by 2000–2005, focused on these areas. Some directly addressed on the designated Competitive Strategy Initiatives that were set in motion in the late 1980s.

Major Acquisition Planning Reform

The ability of the U.S. weapons systems acquisition process to seize and retain the initiative in technology and weapon systems development was an explicit element of Competitive Strategies. This logic appealed to enduring U.S. characteristics: its free market economic system, strong science and technology base, a history of technological initiative, strength in production technology across a wide range of technologies, and the flexibility of the U.S. Planning, Programming, and Budgeting System. In contrast, the Soviet weapon systems acquisition process exhibited many fewer favorable characteristics.

The Soviet research, development, and acquisition process was embedded within the structures and processes of the Soviet centrally planned economy. This economy operated on fixed five-year plans. There were derivative characteristics that guided the development process for new weaponry.[32] There were a relatively small number of decision points in the life cycle of a weapon and only one major decision: the decision to go ahead with full-scale engineering development. Once that decision was made, the program was funded to completion, even if that required committing funds for multiple five-year plans.

The Soviets had clearly recognized the need for greater flexibility and innovativeness in the weapon systems acquisition process by the late 1960s.[33] In 1968, the Soviets initiated a major program designed to significantly modify their weapon systems acquisition.[34] The intent of that change was to make the command process act as though it had much greater flexibility by implementing a stagewise adaptive process of planning and decision making. The method, known as "goal-oriented life-cycle planning," focused on a rigorous definition of a weapon systems life cycle as comprised of a system of stages, which could be executed adaptively and incrementally. The progress of an armament program through its life cycle could thus be determined incrementally based on the actual materialization over time of a variety of key technological and operational uncertainties both internal and external to the acquisition process.

The objective was to guide the process adaptively so that the full-scale engineering development and procurement decision, which represented a major commitment of resources for perhaps several five-year plans, would produce a system that met the precise need and was fielded with the most confident capability to meet that need. This approach would represent a major improvement in acquisition flexibility and in the ability to incorporate in-process innovations when compared with the previous armament processes.

It was not until the late 1970s that this new process was worked out,[35] and it was not until the mid-1980s that textbooks appeared as a guide for industrial planning.[36] The planning cycle of 1986–1990 was probably the first one scheduled to use the process in practice. This planning cycle focused on systems to be developed during the period 1991–2015. Because this planning cycle is the same period during which Competitive Strategies was formulated, Soviet concerns about the consequences of that initiative were probably a factor in the formulation of Soviet acquisition plans that would produce results during the period 1991–2015. And these plans, based on the new process, would have had a much higher degree of flexibility and adaptivity than the previous approach. In turn, it may have been easier for the Soviets to respond effectively in a move-countermove-countercountermove sequence.

Soviet Military Reform

A second class of major Soviet change dealt with their entire armed forces. During the early 1980s, the Soviets recognized the need for wholesale military change. Part of this was motivated by their conclusions about the emergence of a new military-technical revolution underway in the West based on their analysis of the Arab-Israeli wars, the Falklands conflict, and the Carter and Reagan defense modernization programs.[37] Eventually this led Soviet military leadership to conclude that wholesale "military reform" was needed.

"Military reform," in Russian history, denotes a major strategic change in the nature of the armed forces, their relationship to the state and society, their organizational structure, their technical base, their operational concepts, and, as a derivative, their force posture and their supporting industrial base. This is so sweeping a concept that, according to the Soviets, such reform had happened previously only five times in all of Russian history.[38] The argument that the strategic conditions both within and external to the Soviet Union mandated consideration of military reform received growing emphasis with the Soviet military beginning in 1985 as a part of the Gorbachev's "new thinking" and military conclusions about the need to change from a "quantitative" to a "qualitative" basis for the Soviet armed forces.

Diagnoses within the General Staff concluded that the requirement for qualitative change encompassed virtually every facet of military science. This included the qualitative characteristics of Soviet weaponry; the qualitative dimension of Soviet military art; qualitative improvements in force structure, organization, and troop control; qualitative advances in unit training; qualitative changes in military leadership methods and standards; improvements in the quality of professional education; and advances in the quality of military logistics.[39]

In 1989 a special commission created the first plan for the achievement of true comprehensive military reform, developing a three-stage timetable starting in 1991 and ending in 2000.[40] The earlier acquisition reform was also imbedded within the plan. This plan would deliberately downsize the armed forces and its supporting defense industrial base while at the same time significantly improving its qualitative capabilities to conduct modern warfare and to keep pace with the rapid advances of global technology.

Because military reform on the scale envisioned could have resulted in changes in aspects of strategy and military art on which the initial Competitive Strategies Initiative were based, it is not known what their outcome on the effectiveness of the Competitive Strategies Initiatives would have been. The results, if achieved on the Soviet timetable, would have been in place within the five-to-fifteen–year time horizon of the Competitive Strategies process.

HOW EFFECTIVE WAS THE COMPETITIVE
STRATEGIES INITIATIVE?

It seems clear that Competitive Strategies indeed targeted important elements of the Soviet approach to warfare, that the logic for those targets was well founded, and that the Soviets understood and recognized the significance of the program and its four initial initiatives. From a Soviet perspective, each of the initiatives demanded a response, not only in future combat but also in the peacetime competition to create Soviet forces that could prevail against a U.S. posture significantly strengthened by the Competitive Strategies Initiatives.

It also is clear that the Soviets had started, even years earlier, a set of peacetime countermoves in some areas, cast in response to the U.S. defense modernization program that started in the Carter administration. There were also other Soviet major initiatives for change underway that, once completed, predictably would have had some impact on at least the initial set of Competitive Strategies Initiatives and possibly on aspects of the entire concept.

Nevertheless, the United States had gained the initiative in critical aspects of Soviet military art. There was also a Department of Defense organization to shepherd that initiative forward and to react as appropriate to whatever countermoves the Soviets put forth. Although the Cold War ended in approximately 1989, and the Soviet state itself ceased to exist in 1991, the competitive trends at that time in those key areas favored the United States. It is an exercise in counterfactuals to consider what new Soviet remedial moves they would have undertaken or what counterresponses would have emanated from the Pentagon. In any event, the Cold War ended with the United States firmly moving toward control of Soviet-critical areas of the military competition, and with the machinery, momentum, and intent in place to carry that forward. It seems that the program, for as long as the Soviet Union lived, was probably effective.

OBSERVATIONS FOR THE FUTURE

With a view toward the future of competitive strategies in the 21st century, the following six observations flow from the Soviet experience. First, the Competitive Strategies program appears to have hit the mark against the Soviet Union. Hence, this appears to be a useful approach to defense planning that should be considered again on a case-by-case basis. An important issue will be the identification of a security situation suited for the long-term competitive approach. It may be best formulated as the United States versus one or more nation-states. Or, perhaps, to use a business analogy, it may be most appropriate as a strategy of competitively controlling niche-area military aspects on a global scale against all comers.

Second, the utility of the Competitive Strategies initiative against the Soviet Union was facilitated by the fact that the Soviet Union viewed itself to be in direct military competition with United States, both in peacetime and in wartime. A future U.S. competitive strategies program would probably be most effective against a target with similar competitive perspectives. Engaging a target that views itself to be in even selected military competition with the United States will ensure that the Competitive Strategies Initiatives will catch the attention of the targeted country and that the country will commit resources in response and will engage in the move-countermove-counter-countermove cycle on which the process is predicated.

Third, the U.S. Competitive Strategies program carefully targeted key aspects of Soviet military art that were well understood in the United States. As a corollary, the military art of a targeted country must be understood in enough detail to identify real competitive strategies targets from the perspective of that country. It is not adequate to mirror image using U.S. military concepts and perspectives. The most effective targets will probably be those key elements of the targeted country's concepts of operations on which they are depending for success and for which the United States has a competitive advantage in the peacetime competition for combat capabilities in those elements.

Fourth, a targeted country must have a stable enough structure in its military art to allow developing specific competitive strategies targets that will endure for many years. This suggests countries with a long history of warfare and with a relatively stable military culture.

Fifth, the comparative structure of the U.S. versus Soviet weapon system acquisition processes was a direct advantage for the United States. For the competitive process to succeed, the acquisition process, and other related processes, of the targeted country must not be more agile than those of the United States. Retaining comparative acquisition agility for the United States may become increasingly challenging for effective competition against countries that are learning to depend on commercial processes and the fruits of globalization for their military capabilities.

Finally, it should be pointed out that the Competitive Strategies Initiative was cost-imposing on the Soviets across many dimensions of "cost." For example, the first initiative (countering Soviet air operations) imposed a significant operational cost in the extended time and combat assets that would be necessary to achieve air superiority in Central Europe. The second initiative (countering Soviet penetration of NATO forward defense) imposed ruble costs, costs in development time, and the opportunity costs of scientific and technical resource commitments necessary to develop and outfit the Soviet force posture with a fundamentally new class of weaponry. The third initiative (stressing the Soviet troop control system) imposed an operational cost in the extra time necessary to replan and reposition forces to achieve combat success. Finally, the fourth initiative (countering Soviet global and multitheater operations) imposed time, resource, and opportunity costs on the combat assets necessary for success in global war, with significant ruble costs required to increase the capabilities of the Soviet forces (for example, air defense) to offset selected effects of the envisioned US operations. Future competitive strategies initiatives should think very carefully about targets and think very broadly about the classes of costs that it may be possible to impose.

NOTES

1. For discussion of the underlying rationale for the Competitive Strategies initiative, see Caspar W. Weinberger, "US Defense Strategy," *Foreign Affairs* (Spring 1986), 675–697.

2. *Competitive Strategies Primer* (Washington, DC: Office of the Secretary of Defense Competitive Strategies Office, April, 1989), 4–5.

3. Ibid., 6, 12.

4. For the last fifteen years of the Cold War, the author directed research for the Department of Defense on Soviet military art and Soviet weapon system acquisition. He was directly involved in many aspects of the Competitive Strategies Initiative. This chapter is based on his recollections and interpretations. Conclusions drawn in this paper are those of the author and do not necessarily reflect the perspectives of the Department of Defense.

5. This section is an adaptation and revision of portions of the paper by J. Battilega, "Soviet Military Art: Some Major Asymmetries Important to Net Assessment," prepared for the Conference on Net Assessment: Past, Present, and Future, in Washington, DC, on March 28–29, 2008.

6. V. Morozov and S. Tyushkevich, "The Objective Laws of War and Their Reflection in Soviet Military Science," *Military Thought*, 5 (May 1971).

7. M. M. Kozlov, "Teatr Voennykh Deistvii" [Theater of Strategic Military Action]," *Soviet Military Encyclopedia*, Vol. 8 (Moscow: Voyenizdat, 1980), 8–9. The term TVD in the West was also sometimes used to conveniently denote the "High Command of Forces in the TVD" that the Soviets had established in some theaters of war to better prepare for, and control, wartime operations. See, for example, J. Hines and P. Peterson, "Changing the Soviet System of Control," *International Defense Review*

(March 1986), 281–289. As used here, the term *TVD* refers to the strategic framework structural element and not to the wartime command headquarters.

8. The Soviet global TVD structure changed over time as conditions changed. In 1975 it included eleven: a North American TVD; Atlantic, Pacific, and Indian Ocean TVDs; Northeastern, Far Eastern, Middle Eastern, and Near Eastern TVDs; and European Northwestern, Central, and Southwestern TVDs; G. Wardak, *The Voroshilov Lectures: Materials from the Voroshilov General Staff Academy,* Vol. I (Washington, DC: National Defense University Press, 1989), Subsequent changes combined some TVDs and added new ones. By 1986 the TVD structure included fifteen TVDs: a North American and a South American TVD; a Far Eastern TVD; an African TVD; the European Northwest, Western, and Southwest TVDs; an Australian TVD; an Antarctic TVD; the oceanic Arctic, Atlantic, Pacific, and Indian Ocean TVDs; and the strategic rear of the Soviet homeland; Hines and Peterson, "Changing the Soviet System of Control." As the USSR collapsed, Soviet military scientists were debating whether outer space should be declared to be a separate TVD.

9. Unattributed, "Strategicheskoe Napravlenie" [Strategic Direction], *Soviet Military Encyclopedia,* Vol. 7 (Moscow: Voyenizdat, 1979), 555. The English term *sector* or *axis* could also be used.

10. M. L. Cherednichenko, "Strategicheskaia Operatsiia" [Strategic Operation], *Soviet Military Encyclopedia,* Vol. 7 (Moscow: Voyenizdat, 1979), 552.

11. A *desant* operation is a special type of operation that inserts forces forward at specific places and times and has special conditions associated with its execution. The two basic types of *desant* operations focused on the employment of airborne forces and the employment of amphibious landing forces.

12. Unattributed, "Morskaia Operatsiia" [Naval Operation], *Military Encyclopedic Dictionary* (Moscow: Voyenizdat, 1986), 711–712.

13. Ibid.

14. See David M. Glantz, *The Military Strategy of the Soviet Union: A History* (Abingdon, UK: Frank Cass & Co., 2001), 198–266.

15. Hence the Soviet arms control view of the U.S. Air Launched Cruise Missile as more destabilizing than the ballistic missile. The U.S. view was exactly the opposite.

16. For a discussion of the Soviet troop control process, see John Helmsley, *Soviet Troop Control* (Oxford, UK: Brasseys Publishers, 1982).

17. As a result of debates that took place within the Soviet General Staff during the late 1950s, the Soviets concluded that, in future wars, successful combat in the initial period would probably determine war outcomes; hence the Soviet emphasis on the initial period.

18. V. I. Belyakov, "Sootnosheniye Sil i Sredstv," *Soviet Military Encyclopedia,* Vol. 7 (Moscow: Voyenizdat,, 1979).

19. See, for example, A. Gaponov, "Correlation of Forces and Rates of Advance," *Voyennaya Mysl'* (October 1971).

20. Frank C. Carlucci, *Report of the Secretary of Defense Frank C. Carlucci to the Congress on the Amended FY 1988/FY 1989 Biennial Budget* (Washington, DC: U.S. Government Printing Office, February 18, 1988), 116–118.

21. John G. Roos and Benjamin Schemmer, "Revolution in NATO's Conventional Defense Looms from 'Competitive Strategies' Initiative," *Armed Forces Journal International* (October, 1988): 116–121.

22. Ibid., 117.

23. Ibid.

24. Ibid.

25. Ibid.

26. The Soviets viewed military strategy to encompass both the preparation for and conduct of warfare. Hence the Competitive Strategies Initiative engaged them directly in both arenas. For a discussion of the Soviet concept of military strategy and its peacetime and wartime components, see "Principles and Content of Military Strategy," in G. Wardak, *The Voroshilov* Lectures, chapter 1.

27. N. Ruzayev, "The Competitive Strategy of American Military Policy," *Foreign Military Review,* 8 (August, 1989), 3–8.

28. Ibid., 3.

29. This was recognized in the United States, too. In January 1987, before the formal Competitive Strategies process started, then Secretary of Defense Caspar Weinberger, in the Annual Report to Congress, cited the current defense program as containing "a number of outstanding examples of Competitive Strategies," citing specifically antisubmarine warfare, the ability of U.S. air forces to penetrate Soviet air defense, AirLand Battle, Follow-on Forces Attack, and the Strategic Defense Initiative. See "Operational Concepts: Challenges for Competitive Strategies," *Aerospace Daily,* 10 (January 15, 1987).

30. Carlucci, *Report of the Secretary of Defense,* 117–118.

31. John A. Battilega, *Development, Creation, and Production of Weapons and Military Equipment in the USSR* (Greenwood Village CO: Science Applications International Corporation, 1995).

32. Arthur J. Alexander, *Decision Making in Soviet Weapons Procurement* (London: International Institute of Strategic Studies, 1978).

33. Portions of this section and the next are adaptations and revisions of material in J. Battilega, "Innovation in the Russian Defense Industrial Base and Acquisition Process: A Russian Play in Three Acts," prepared for the Workshop on Russian Military Innovation, Central Intelligence Agency, Washington DC, January 12, 1999.

34. "On Measures for Increasing the Effectiveness of Work of Scientific Organizations and Accelerating the Utilization of Scientific and Technical Achievements in the

National Economy," *Joint Decree of the Communist Party of the Soviet Union and the Council Ministers,* Moscow, September, 1968.

35. See, for example, G. S. Pospelov and V. A. Barishpolets, *Integration of Science and Production* (Moscow: Znaniye, 1978).

36. V. I. Tikhomirov (ed.), *Organization, Planning, and Management of Aviation Scientific Production Organizations* (Moscow: Mashinostroyeniye, 1985).

37. See, for example, M. M. Kir'yan (ed.), *Progress in Military Technology and the Armed Forces of the USSR* (Moscow: Voyenizdat, 1982), and the writings of Marshall Ogarkov, especially *Always Ready to Defend the Fatherland* (Moscow, Voyenizdat, 1982).

38. These were the reforms of Ivan the Terrible (16th century), Peter the Great (18th century), Miliutin (19th century), post–Russo-Japanese War (1905–1912), and post–Civil War (1924–1925). See R. Greenwalt, J. Banks, D. Beachley, K. Blount, G. Fonda, J. R. Holbrook, and R. Nall, *Military Reform of the Soviet Armed Forces: Implications for National Security* (Greenwood Village, CO: Science Applications International Corporation, July 1991).

39. R. Greenwalt and L. Bennicelli, *The Transition from Quantitative to Qualitative Parameters as Primary Determinants of Military Development: Possible Impacts on Soviet Military Research, Development, and Acquisition* (Greenwood Village, CO: Science Applications International Corporation, July 1991). See also Glantz, *The Military Strategy of the Soviet Union,* 335–348.

40. M. A. Moiseyev, *Red Star,* November 18, 1990.

Part III

THE UNITED STATES AND CHINA

Toward Strategic Competition?

8 THE STATE OF THE U.S.-CHINA COMPETITION

James R. Holmes

THE U.S.-CHINA STRATEGIC COMPETITION is a curious one in that only one party, China, has competed in earnest since the contest's inception in the mid-1990s. China has stolen an intellectual march on the United States while rapidly acquiring the means—primarily the maritime means—to execute a strategy that turns Chinese strengths to advantage while playing on American vulnerabilities. Energy and imagination, it seems, reside more with challengers to an established status quo than with its defenders. It behooves the United States to summon up some competitive energy of its own.

Chinese strategists do not emulate the U.S. competitive strategies literature. Rather, their general approach comports with China's historic outlook on strategy. The classical Chinese theorist Sun Tzu, for instance, depicts strategy as a quest for *shih,* or strategic advantage, in relentlessly interactive surroundings.[1] True to this logic, the People's Liberation Army (PLA) has studied the U.S. military and devised strategy, forces, and operational practices meant to impose high costs on the United States at minimal cost to China. Declares Luo Yuan, deputy secretary general of the PLA Academy of Military Science:

> History tells us that the strategic game played between major powers is in the end determined by the contest of actual power and wisdom. This kind of contest is long-term and complex. As such, we should keep our minds clear . . . we need to continually improve our actual power. . . . Sunzi's *The Art of War* says "First make plans and take diplomatic measures, then demonstrate resolve to fight, then send out a portion of one's forces to fight, and if that still fails, attack the enemy's strategic points and territory."[2]

National power is a dynamic and relative thing for Beijing, always on the increase or decrease. Strategists like Luo constantly tally up "comprehensive national power," aggregating not only physical indices like economic development and military power but intangible measures like cultural appeal. Cataloging such indicators helps them track China's standing relative to other leading powers—improving Chinese performance in long-term international competition.[3]

The coming years will likely see China, on the one hand, and the United States and its allies, on the other, grapple for competitive advantage between the two offshore island chains. Each will bolster its capacity to shape events in these expanses, only to see the other reply through novel measures of its own. Beijing is acquiring the wherewithal to deny U.S. forces access to—or free movement within—the Western Pacific, a theater where the 2007 U.S. Maritime Strategy vows to stage "credible combat power" for the foreseeable future.[4] For Washington, competition means a reciprocal effort to pierce Chinese anti-access measures while denying Chinese naval forces ready access to waters between the island chains or even to the "three seas" landward of the first island chain. U.S. forces would turn the tables, denying the sea denier.

For both sides, then, the U.S.-China competition is about access.[5] Navies and shore-based forces capable of influencing events on the high seas—combat aircraft, antiship cruise and ballistic missiles, and the like—will be the chief implements for both contenders. The impending "collision of two living forces," in Carl von Clausewitz's apt metaphor for competitive interactions, will evoke a match between two wrestlers:

> Countless duels go to make up war, but a picture of it as a whole can be formed by imagining a pair of wrestlers. Each tries through physical force to compel the other to do his will; his *immediate* aim is to *throw* his opponent in order to make him incapable of further resistance.[6]

If so, Asia-Pacific seas and skies will provide the setting for a cycle of continual challenge, reply, and mutual adaptation, with each side contesting the other's access to the nautical thoroughfare while attempting to preserve its own. How the competition unfolds will depend in great measure on the resources, political resolve, and ingenuity each protagonist applies to it.

This chapter addresses three basic questions in an attempt to appraise the state of the U.S.-China competition and erect a platform for further debate. First, what is the nature of the competition? Second, what enduring strengths does the

United States possess that it can match against enduring Chinese vulnerabilities? And, third, how well is the United States doing in the strategic competition?

Some caveats and qualifications are in order at the outset. Writings on competitive strategies stress *peacetime* competition, but this chapter treats the boundary separating wartime from peacetime competition as permeable. Peacetime competition is about constructing platforms and systems useful for wartime encounters and using these tools to mold perceptions among key audiences in peacetime. In other words, peacetime strategy works in cyclical fashion, broadcasting one's war-fighting capacity to generate strategic effects in peacetime. Many of this chapter's observations and findings, accordingly, exhibit a strongly operational hue. This reflects a conscious choice.

Thinking about war and peace as a continuum along which policy is prosecuted with varying degrees of force has a long pedigree. Although Clausewitz insists that battle is the arbiter of competitive international intercourse, he also observes that "policy converts the overwhelmingly destructive element of war into a mere instrument. It changes the terrible battle-sword that a man needs both his hands and his entire strength to wield, and with which he strikes home once and no more, into a light, handy rapier—sometimes just a foil for exchange of thrusts, feints, and parries."[7] Conflict can range from "a war of extermination down to simple armed observation."[8]

Eastern thinkers are even more explicit on this point. Mao Zedong engraved his way of thinking on the Chinese way of strategy, proclaiming that "politics is war without bloodshed while war is politics with bloodshed."[9] Or, turning to antiquity, theorist Sun Tzu pronounced it the "highest excellence" or the "acme of skill" to "subdue the enemy without fighting."[10]

Many international-relations theorists also conceive of a continuum between war and peace. Thomas Schelling observes that "most conflict situations are essentially *bargaining* situations" in which strategy "is not concerned with the efficient *application* of force but with the *exploitation of potential force*" (emphasis in the original). Deterrence is "the skillful *non-use* of military forces" (emphasis in the original). Deployable military power constitutes a tool of political influence, even if no shots are fired. For Schelling, "'winning' in a conflict . . . may be done by bargaining, by mutual accommodation, and by the avoidance of mutually damaging behavior."[11]

It is thus misleading to exclude readiness for an actual trial of arms from peacetime strategic competition. Competitive strategy is about constructing relatively inexpensive wartime capabilities in peacetime to goad a prospective antagonist into costly responses, sapping that antagonist's resources while setting the terms of the game.

Edward Luttwak applies this insight to the maritime realm, portraying fleets as an implement of "naval suasion." The fleet and its political masters artfully combine words, credible war-fighting capabilities, and deeds to send a message. They convince key audiences to take—or refrain from taking—certain actions. In Schelling's terms, a peacetime naval presence is all about the nonuse of potential force. But there is no suasion absent the prospect of combat—of tapping the fleet's potential force should the adversary cross certain redlines. Luttwak insists it is "misleading to make any dichotomy between 'peacetime presence' and 'wartime' combat capabilities, since a 'presence' can have no significant effect in the absence of *any* possibility that the transition to war will be made."[12] As he puts it, "The *perceived* balance of forces that determines the outcome of 'peacetime' confrontations can only be construed by men in terms of the predicted outcome of putative battle, and it is such predictions that determine political attitudes and, therefore, decisions."[13]

Luttwak calls attention to one difficulty in prosecuting peacetime strategic competition. He observes that peacetime tallies of combat potential "can be grossly misleading indicators of true capabilities" because technical characteristics and raw numbers of platforms can disguise shortcomings in design and manufacture. The outward appearance of a weapon system can mislead. The bean-counting approach also overlooks "'dynamic' variables" such as "seamanship, maintenance standards, and sensor/weapon skills under stress," simply because "there is generally so little in the way of data to go by."[14]

NATURE OF THE COMPETITION

Naval suasion and dissuasion lie at the heart of the trans-Pacific contest. To gain the upper hand, Beijing and Washington are designing political and military measures to assure free access to critical waterways, deny access to prospective opponents, and regain access should they lose it.[15] Most Western analysts assign the initiative to Beijing, framing the competition as Chinese anti-access strategy versus American efforts to preserve access to and mobility in the Western Pacific. There is little doubt that this constitutes the major focus of Chinese maritime strategy, but Beijing also frets about a reciprocal U.S. effort to deny it access. It has historical grounds for doing so. The United States routinely used naval might to hinder Soviet and Chinese movement along the Asian seaboard during the Cold War. President Harry Truman inaugurated this practice during the Korean War, ordering the U.S. Seventh Fleet into the Taiwan Strait to prevent cross-strait war between the Nationalist regime that had fled to Taiwan and the Chinese Communist regime newly ensconced on the mainland.

Mao Zedong cared little about maritime matters. He was content to cede maritime Asia to the United States beyond Chinese territorial seas. But Mao's indifference is a thing of the past now that China sees pressing interests in seaborne resource imports and in regaining influence within its historic maritime periphery. Indeed, many Chinese thinkers construe the innocuous-seeming 2007 U.S. Maritime Strategy, titled *A Cooperative Strategy for 21st Century Seapower,* as a latter-day instrument of containment—despite its plea for cooperative policing of the global commons. Lu Rude, for instance, discerns "hegemonic thinking" in the document. Although the word *China* appears nowhere in the Maritime Strategy, Lu prophesies that the U.S. author-ities will use the strategy as a pretext for "implementing strategic encirclement of different kinds of maritime flashpoints and 'potential enemy' through mili-tary deployment in 'chokepoints' of navigation and strategic nodes."[16] He finds geopolitically charged language jarringly dissonant with the strategy's stated theme of preventing war through combined guardianship of free navigation.

The 1990–1991 Gulf War began concentrating minds among PLA leaders, showing that high-tech U.S. forces could demolish a largely Soviet-equipped military in short order while suffering few losses. Chinese strategists studied their shortcomings in minute detail after the Gulf conflict, concluding that the overthrow of Saddam Hussein's army demonstrated that China must con-struct a more professional, more mechanized, more "informatized" military to hold its own against the United States in maritime Asia.[17]

It was, however, the 1995–1996 Taiwan Strait crisis that exposed the PLA's powerlessness on the high seas in dramatic fashion, marking the beginning of the trans-Pacific competition. The PLA Second Artillery Corps, the Chi-nese missile force, lobbed ballistic missiles into the waters adjoining Taiwan. The "missile tests" represented a clumsy bid to intimidate Taiwanese voters, who were preparing to elect proindependence candidate Lee Teng-hui to the presidency. The William J. Clinton administration hurriedly dispatched the USS *Independence* and USS *Nimitz* battle groups to the theater to deter fur-ther intimidation.[18] PLA forces found themselves unable to detect—let alone target—massive task forces prowling the island's vicinity.

The crisis jolted Beijing into action. The Chinese military redoubled its competitive efforts following the standoff, in effect vowing never again to per-mit such a debacle. Its goal was to wrest some control of nearby seas from the

U.S. Navy, deterring Washington from interposing itself in future crises. To shore up its weaknesses while exploiting U.S. vulnerabilities, the PLA procured weaponry capable of detecting, tracking, and targeting U.S. battle groups in offshore waters—ratcheting up the costs of entry at minimal cost to China. One authoritative estimate places the cost of the U.S. Navy's next-generation aircraft carrier, USS *Gerald R. Ford,* at $10.5 billion, not counting its air wing or escort ships.[19] How much the PLA pays for antiship cruise missiles (ASCMs) is unknown. But even if the average Chinese missile costs as much as a U.S. Navy *Harpoon* Block II ASCM—a doubtful prospect—the PLA Navy can afford 8,750 missiles for the price of one *Ford*-class vessel.[20] This is a forbidding ratio considering the potency of modern ASCMs against surface combatants. A massive, low-cost ASCM arsenal conforms ideally to the logic of competitive strategies.

It stands to reason that China brings more industry and imagination to its maritime challenge than the United States does to its defense of the status quo. But Washington's ambivalence toward U.S.-China competition also speaks volumes about its predicament following the Cold War, when there was no obvious challenger to American primacy—least of all in the military sphere. The situation resembled that of the U.S. Navy in late 1945, when, as Samuel Huntington recalls, an overpowering fleet "floated in virtually solitary splendor upon the waters of the earth," bereft of a strong rival or any galvanizing strategic purpose.[21] Victory deprived the U.S. Navy of its raison d'être. Only the rise of a peer Soviet Navy starting in the 1960s reinvigorated American competitive energies.

U.S. diplomacy and strategy were largely rudderless after the Cold War. The large but backward Chinese armed forces were little cause for concern. Paramount leader Deng Xiaoping had launched his economic reform and openness initiative only in the late 1970s. Admiral Liu Huaqing, who commanded the PLA Navy during the 1980s, proposed a phased naval buildup that would give Beijing control of an expanding offshore belt of ocean and skies. By the middle of the 21st century China would field its first global navy, taking its place alongside the U.S. Navy. While the PLA Navy started building a credible fleet during the Cold War, then, Beijing's maritime project bore little fruit until after that conflict ended. Beijing continued the Maoist practice of assenting to de facto U.S. guardianship of Chinese maritime interests while the PLA studied U.S. strategy and forces. The PLA Navy, meanwhile, undertook a leisurely process of fleet experimentation. It built ships in small batches, took them to sea to determine what did and did not work, and incorporated the lessons learned into future classes. Incremental naval development aroused few worries in Washington.

Successive U.S. administrations, furthermore, have deliberately avoided wholeheartedly competing with China. There are both competitive and co-operative strains to the U.S.-China relationship, making a stark contrast with the overwhelmingly competitive U.S.-Soviet relationship. No administration is eager for conflict with Asia's historic leading power. Soft-pedaling the competitive aspects of the trans-Pacific relationship for the sake of cooperation appears prudent. Amicable U.S.-China relations, moreover, could help Washington manage its "elegant decline" from unquestioned primacy to something resembling parity with regional sea powers like China.[22]

To be sure, knowledgeable Western commentators sometimes opine that the United States *is* competing with China. They typically cite combined exercises between U.S. and Asian forces, upgrades to military hardware and tactics, and other evidence of military initiative.[23] But such claims miss the point of competitive strategy. Exercises display resolve and combat capacity and may balance the pretensions of prospective red teams, but in themselves they cannot steer the competition into areas favoring the United States, impose outsized costs on China, or help the U.S. military husband resources. As Schelling might say, China has displayed considerable skill at the effective nonuse of military force, fielding inexpensive yet lethal weaponry to counteract expensive, virtually irreplaceable U.S. platforms. Beijing also evinces more determination to manage events in nearby seas than any distant power like the United States will. This combination of capability and political will amplifies the effectiveness of Chinese suasion and dissuasion. Washington has yet to match this effort to shape affairs.

Although China specialists in the West have been slow to accept the reality of a seafaring China, there is ample precedent for China's ascent to naval prominence.[24] As noted before, Beijing started assembling an oceangoing navy in the early 1980s and accelerated the effort after the 1995–1996 Taiwan Strait crisis. Its naval project, consequently, has been underway for some thirty years. Thirty years after Imperial Japan opened itself to the outside world and decided to Westernize, its navy had crushed that of China's Qing Dynasty and was scant years from sinking two Russian fleets.[25] Imperial Germany's High Seas Fleet fought Britain's Royal Navy to a draw at Jutland in 1915, only seventeen years after German shipwrights commenced laying down the German battle fleet.[26] Congress authorized the first U.S. armored steam-powered combatants in 1883. The U.S. Navy defeated the Spanish Navy fifteen years later. Another fifteen years after that the U.S. Navy stood on the brink of "a navy second to none," to quote President Woodrow Wilson.[27]

Clearly, a nation with enough resources and political resolve can put to sea a great fleet in fairly short order. An authoritarian regime like China's may even hold an advantage. As Alfred Thayer Mahan observes, "Despotic power, wielded with judgment and consistency, has created at times a great sea commerce and a brilliant navy with greater directness than can be reached by the slower processes of a free people."[28] (Of note, Mahan also declares that naval power can quickly atrophy in authoritarian nations should the sovereign turn his attention away from the sea.[29])

The potential for swift realignment of the maritime order is belatedly sinking in among senior U.S. leaders. Declares Admiral Robert Willard, commander of the U.S. Pacific Command, "China's rapid and comprehensive transformation of its armed forces is affecting regional military balances and holds implications beyond the Asia-Pacific region. Of particular concern is that elements of China's military modernization appear designed to challenge our freedom of action in the region."[30] Added Willard in late 2009, "I would contend that in the past decade or so, China has exceeded most of our intelligence estimates of their military capability and capacity every year. They've grown at an unprecedented rate in those capabilities."[31]

Similarly, Admiral Mike Mullen, former chairman of the Joint Chiefs of Staff, confesses that he has "moved from curious to being genuinely concerned" about Chinese military and naval progress.[32] Mullen forecasts that U.S. forces will find themselves "increasingly challenged in securing and maintaining access to the global commons."[33] For this reason, a growing consensus within the U.S. strategic community now acknowledges that Beijing appears intent not on helping the United States uphold the liberal maritime order but on redefining or abolishing it. Washington appears set to start pushing back in the competition with Beijing—setting in motion an interactive cycle of action and reaction in maritime Asia.

ENDURING AMERICAN STRENGTHS VERSUS
ENDURING CHINESE VULNERABILITIES

What enduring strengths can the United States pit against enduring Chinese vulnerabilities to impose prohibitive costs on Beijing? Carl von Clausewitz furnishes a useful algorithm for sizing up oneself, one's competitors, and third parties:[34]

> To discover how much of our resources must be mobilized for war, we must first examine our political aim and that of the enemy. We must gauge the

strength and situation of the opposite state. We must gauge the character and abilities of its own government and people and do the same in regard to our own. Finally, we must evaluate the political sympathies of other states and the effect the war may have on them.[35]

We can merge the Prussian theorist's first and third parameters for international competition, estimating the value each contender attaches to its political goals, the magnitude and duration of the effort these goals warrant, and the urgency they command among the government and populace. A trans-Pacific mismatch probably lies in store, meaning that China is prepared to dedicate more resources to the competition commensurate with its means. This constitutes an enduring political advantage.

As a general rule, the power competing in its home region holds a lasting advantage in political resolve, owing to its proximity to the theater. Developments in or near a country directly affect its national welfare while remaining secondary for more remote powers, which probably feel tangential effects at most. Now transpose this general proposition to China. Beijing places enormous importance on restoring its stature and influence in maritime Asia, its historic periphery.[36] In particular, the urge to banish China's "century of humiliation" at the hands of seaborne invaders impels Chinese foreign policy and strategy.

Past indignities offer the Chinese Communist regime sizable reserves of popular passion to tap. With little to bind the nation together ideologically, now that communism has lost its appeal, Beijing has deliberately stoked popular fascination with the sea. Robert Ross terms this phenomenon "naval nationalism," pronouncing it a prime mover for the Chinese maritime project.[37]

No faraway power like the United States is likely to match China's sense of urgency about controlling events along Asian coastlines. For all U.S. leaders' talk about policing the globalized system of seagoing commerce—Under Secretary of Defense Michèle Flournoy declares the international commons "the fabric or connective tissue of the international system"—guaranteeing free passage through the commons appears rather abstract and far removed from the everyday lives of American citizens and public officials.[38] It inspires little popular enthusiasm absent a serious, readily intelligible challenge to freedom of the seas and skies. The commons, moreover, is a *global* medium for commercial and military movement. Unless Washington explicitly cedes the commons outside the Asia-Pacific to other powers, it can ill afford to concentrate all of its competitive endeavors on the Western Pacific. Its efforts will remain dispersed.

China is counting on this disparity in political commitment as it hones its anti-access strategy. The United States could see its superpower status seriously degraded in an afternoon if it lost much of the Pacific Fleet in combat on Taiwan's behalf. Conscious of this, a U.S. president might hesitate before committing the fleet to battle—or even decline to give the order. China might conquer Taiwan without ever confronting U.S. forces. A similar calculus would apply to most Western Pacific contingencies. Advantage: China.

Neither China nor the United States boasts a commanding edge in "strength and situation," Clausewitz's second metric for competitive enterprises. Geography is at once an asset and a liability for both competitors. Like any nation competing in its home region, China enjoys a certain "home-field advantage" over even a superior opponent operating near its coasts. Multiple bases, abundant personnel, short lines of communication, shore-based support for maritime forces, and familiarity with the physical and cultural terrain add up to a "contested zone."[39] A savvy defender can impose high if not prohibitive costs on any outsider who ventures into the theater. As noted before, the PLA has invested heavily in weaponry designed to dispute U.S. naval access to the Western Pacific and particularly to the Yellow, East China, and South China seas. If Chinese weapons engineers perfect the antiship ballistic missile (ASBM) they are reportedly testing, the PLA will boast the capacity to strike at approaching U.S. warships underway hundreds of miles distant.[40]

Shore-based fire support of such range and lethality would hone the contested-zone concept to a keener edge than ever before. An effective ASBM arsenal—an arsenal against which U.S. forces have no defense—would in effect hoist a protective shield over maritime Asia underneath which PLA fleet operations could proceed with little fear of U.S. interference. Andrew Krepinevich points out that PLA H-6K and Su-30MKK2 maritime strike aircraft outrange *all of the manned strike aircraft in the U.S. Navy's program of record carrier air wing* (emphasis in the original).[41] In other words, Beijing can start pummeling U.S. aircraft carriers or amphibious groups before these forces close to striking distance of targets along the Asian periphery. No longer can U.S. Navy carrier forces project power ashore from a safe distance. Augmenting this formidable land-based air wing with operational ASBMs would only magnify the PLA's offensive potential in China's near and far seas.

On the other hand, Beijing also confronts stubborn geographic obstacles that the United States could turn to strategic advantage. Compounding China's difficult maritime geography, the PLA has displayed a curious myopia toward antisubmarine warfare (ASW) and mine countermeasures (MCM), exposing the PLA Navy to low-cost U.S. and Japanese naval operations. This is an odd oversight given the emphasis PLA officers lay on *offensive* submarine and mine warfare. Whatever the case, clearing mines is slow, laborious work, as are detecting and countering stealthy submarines. Chinese inattention to ASW and MCM will demand years of determined effort and training to rectify, even once the PLA Navy decides to make the effort.

Japanese-held islands comprise the northward arc of the first island chain, the offshore islands that enclose the mainland coast. Roughly speaking, the island chain runs from northern Japan southward through Taiwan, its midpoint, before terminating in the Philippines. The islands remain in potentially unfriendly hands from Beijing's standpoint. As long as this remains true, Chinese strategists cannot assume merchant or military shipping will enjoy unfettered north-south mobility within the China seas or, still less, ready east-west egress into the Western Pacific. The PLA Navy clearly acknowledges the importance of narrow seas like the Miyako and Ishigaki straits, which allow shipping to pass through the Ryukyu chain off southern Japan. Miyako and Ishigaki have been PLA Navy commanders' exit points of choice through the island chain in recent years. The Luzon Strait, which connects the South China Sea with the Pacific Ocean, is another critical access point for Chinese vessels bound for the high seas. Unless the PLA Navy steps up its efforts to become proficient at ASW and MCM, the U.S.-Japan alliance could mine the straits in wartime and deploy submarines to assail Chinese shipping that essays the passage through contested narrow seas. Offensive submarine and mine warfare, then, represent promising areas for U.S.-China competition.

The United States holds geographic, diplomatic, and military advantages of its own. Its very remoteness from Asia, complemented by its history of safeguarding the commons while asking little in return, makes Washington a balancer of first resort for Asian states wary of a possible Chinese bid for regional hegemony. On the diplomatic level, then, the tyranny of distance is an asset. On the strategic and operational levels, U.S. forces' capacity to deploy across vast distances is an indispensable foundation for the U.S. forward presence in Asia. Preserving the surface fleet's capacity to maneuver in the face of Chinese anti-access measures is essential to sustaining the U.S. presence in the Western Pacific, chiefly in Okinawa and the Japanese home islands. Experimenting with concepts such as the AirSea Battle Doctrine reportedly under development by the U.S. Navy and Air Force is a must if the United States is to perpetuate this enduring advantage. Anti-access presents few problems for the all-nuclear U.S. submarine force, the world's finest on a boat-for-boat basis despite its decline in numbers. Nor should reviving an offensive mine-warfare capability present many difficulties for the U.S. Navy, although this capability has remained largely dormant for many years. Such geographic and military advantages are worth exploiting vis-à-vis Beijing.

And finally, how will third parties react to the U.S.-China competition? Commentators such as David Kang prophesy that the Asian tradition of hierarchy will reassert itself as Western dominance recedes.[42] If so, the rise of China heralds the return of a Sinocentric order in which China's neighbors reflexively defer to Beijing. Chinese officials have sought to encourage this supposed trend, waging a "soft-power" diplomacy that paints China as an inherently benign sea power, a welcome contrast with predatory Western empires. This diplomatic narrative worked well before a strong Chinese navy took to the sea, posing a potential threat. Undiplomatic Chinese conduct—Chinese foreign minister Yang Jiechi, for instance, pointedly told his Singaporean counterpart, "China is a big country and other countries are small countries, and that's just a fact"—has prompted Asian governments to start pushing back against Chinese diplomacy and to reach out to the United States for mutual support.[43] Overheated Chinese responses to maritime territorial disputes with Japan and to U.S. naval exercises in the Yellow Sea have helped little.

Chinese conduct has encouraged the U.S.-Japan alliance—the compact on which the U.S. strategic position in Asia relies—to draw together. If the alliance unraveled, depriving U.S. forces of bases in the first island chain, the United States would have little recourse other than to fall back to its redoubt on Guam, in the second island chain some 1,500 miles from the Asian mainland. U.S. officials, consequently, must direct part of their naval suasion at Tokyo in an effort to reassure Japanese leaders and citizens that the United States remains a stalwart ally and protector. Concentrating additional forces in the Pacific and devising measures to defeat Chinese anti-access strategy are central to suasion toward Japan. Working with the Japan Self-Defense Forces to inhibit Chinese access to important sea-lanes represents another way to bind together the alliance for long-term strategic competition. Washington holds at least a temporary advantage in relations with third parties, and further self-defeating Chinese behavior could convert this into a lasting advantage.

HOW IS THE UNITED STATES FARING?

The United States thus enjoys certain diplomatic, geographic, and military advantages over China. The coming years will likely witness back-and-forth interactions between the United States and China, with each side bolstering its capabilities for naval suasion and dissuasion and the other replying in kind—pushing back against its rival's innovations.

Like two wrestlers, the rival sea powers will struggle continually for advantage. As the United States improves its capacity for suasion and dissuasion, its forces can ease their access to waters within China's contested zone. As China reacts, improving its own capacity to shape trans-Pacific politics, it will thrust the culminating point farther offshore—only to see the logic of the culminating point begin to work against the PLA. Its offensive will lose momentum with distance from the mainland, with prospective adversaries like Japan and Taiwan lying to the rear of its forces and with closer proximity to U.S. bases in the Pacific. In short, constant flux will characterize the U.S.-China competition for some time to come.

NOTES

1. See, for instance, Roger Ames's commentary in Sun Tzu, *The Art of Warfare,* trans. Roger Ames (New York: Ballantine, 1993), 71–78.

2. "China Has to Be Bold Enough to 'Draw its Sword,' Exclusive Interview with General Luo Yuan, Deputy Secretary General of the People's Liberation Army Academy of Military Science," *Phoenix Weekly* 378 (October 15, 2010), Open Source Center (OSC)-CPP20101018787004.

3. Michael Pillsbury, *Chinese Views of Future Warfare* (Washington, DC: National Defense University Press, 1997), 16.

4. U.S. Navy, Marine Corps, and Coast Guard, *A Cooperative Strategy for 21st Century Seapower,* October 2007, U.S. Navy Website; available at www.navy.mil/maritime/Maritimestrategy.pdf. For a primer on Beijing's antiaccess/area-denial efforts, see Roger Cliff, Mark Burles, Michael S. Chase, Derek Eaton, and Kevin L. Pollpeter, *Entering the Dragon's Lair: Chinese Antiaccess Strategies and Their Implications for the United States* (Santa Monica: RAND, 2007); available at www.rand.org/pubs/monographs/2007/RAND_MG524.pdf.

5. Toshi Yoshihara and I advance the notion that the competition is about access and antiaccess for *both* nations in "Mahan's Lingering Ghost," U.S. Naval Institute *Proceedings* 135 (December 2009); available at www.usni.org/magazines/proceedings/2009-12/mahans-lingering-ghost.

6. Carl von Clausewitz, *On War,* ed. and trans. Michael Howard and Peter Paret (Princeton, NJ: Princeton University Press, 1976), 75.

7. Ibid., 606.

8. Ibid., 81.

9. Mao Zedong, *On Protracted War* (Beijing: Foreign Languages Press, 1972), 226–228.

10. Sun Tzu, 111, 119–120; Sun Tzu, *The Illustrated Art of War,* trans. Samuel B. Griffith (Oxford, UK: Oxford University Press, 2005), 115.

11. Thomas C. Schelling, *The Strategy of Conflict* (Cambridge, MA: Harvard University Press, 1960), 4–5, 9.

12. Edward N. Luttwak, *The Political Uses of Sea Power* (Baltimore: Johns Hopkins University Press, 1974), 12.

13. Ibid., 39.

14. Ibid., 40.

15. Andrew Erickson, "China's Evolving Anti-Access Approach: 'Where's the Nearest (U.S.) Carrier?'" *China Brief* 10 (September 10, 2010); available at www.jamestown .org/single/?no_cache=1&tx_ttnews%5Btt_news%5D=36810&tx_ttnews%5BbackPid %5D=7&cHash=2b3f00b616. A more exhaustive analysis is Andrew Krepinevich, Barry Watts, and Robert Work, *Meeting the Anti-Access and Area-Denial Challenge* (Washington, DC: Center for Strategic and Budgetary Assessments, 2003).

16. Lu Rude, "The New U.S. Maritime Strategy Surfaces," trans. Andrew S. Erickson, in *Naval War College Review* 61 (Autumn 2008), 60–61.

17. David Lai, "Introduction," in Roy Kamphausen, David Lai, and Andrew Scobell, eds., *The PLA at Home and Abroad: Assessing the Operational Capabilities of China's Military* (Carlisle, PA: Strategic Studies Institute, U.S. Army War College, June 2010), 12–16.

18. For an excellent recap, see "Taiwan Strait: 21 July 1995 to 23 March 1996," GlobalSecurity.org, www.globalsecurity.org/military/ops/taiwan_strait.htm.

19. Ronald O'Rourke, "CRS Report for Congress: Navy Ford (CVN-78) Class (CVN-21) Aircraft Carrier Program: Background and Issues for Congress," November 20, 2008; available at www.dtic.mil/cgi-bin/GetTRDoc?Location=U2&doc= GetTRDoc.pdf&AD=ADA490446.

20. Harpoons cost $1.2 million per copy. "*Harpoon* Missile," United States Navy Fact File, February 20, 2009; available at www.navy.mil/navydata/fact_display.asp?cid =2200&tid=200&ct=2.

21. Samuel P. Huntington, "National Policy and the Transoceanic Navy," Naval Institute *Proceedings* 80 (May 1954), 483–484.

22. Robert D. Kaplan, "America's Elegant Decline," *Atlantic* (November 2007); available at www.theatlantic.com/magazine/archive/2007/11/america-8217-s-elegant -decline/6344/.

23. Discussions with American scholars, Newport, RI, August 2010.

24. See chapter 9 in Toshi Yoshihara and James R. Holmes, *Red Star over the Pacific: China's Rise and the Challenge to U.S. Maritime Strategy* (Annapolis, MD: Naval Institute Press, 2010) for a retrospective look at how China has repeatedly defied Western expectations vis-à-vis its naval capacity.

25. S. C. M. Paine, *The Sino-Japanese War of 1894–1895: Perceptions, Power, and Primacy* (New York: Cambridge University Press, 2003), 165–196; Denis and Peggy Warner, *Tide at Sunrise: A History of the Russo-Japanese War, 1904–1905* (New York: Charterhouse, 1974), esp. 324–338, 494–520.

26. Paul M. Kennedy, *The Rise of the Anglo-German Antagonism, 1860–1914* (London: Ashfield, 1980), esp. 410–431.

27. George W. Baer, *One Hundred Years of Sea Power: The U.S. Navy, 1890–1990* (Stanford, CA: Stanford University Press, 1994), 9–63; Harold and Margaret Sprout, *The Rise of American Naval Power* (Princeton, NJ: Princeton University Press, 1944), 334–346.

28. Alfred Thayer Mahan, *The Influence of Sea Power upon History, 1660–1783* (1890; repr., New York: Dover, 1987), 58.

29. Ibid., 72.

30. "Statement of Admiral Robert F. Willard, U.S. Navy, Commander, U.S. Pacific Command before the House Armed Services Committee on U.S. Pacific Command Posture," March 23, 2010, U.S. House of Representatives Website; available at http://armedservices.house.gov/pdfs/FC032510/Willard_Testimony032510.pdf, p. 3.

31. Adm. Robert F. Willard, quoted in Bill Gertz, "China Estimate War," *Washington Times,* November 5, 2009; available at www.washingtontimes.com/news/2009/nov/05/inside-the-ring-70787975/.

32. Michael J. Carden, "Mullen Cites Importance of Asian Partners, Stability in Pacific Region," *JCS News,* June 10, 2010; available at www.jcs.mil/newsarticle.aspx?ID=303.

33. U.S. Office of the Secretary of Defense, *Quadrennial Defense Review Report* (Washington, DC: Department of Defense, February 2010), 103.

34. Clausewitz, *On War*, 131.

35. Ibid., 585–586.

36. Andrew R. Wilson, "The Maritime Transformations of Ming China," in *China Goes to Sea: Maritime Transformation in Comparative Historical Perspective,* Andrew S. Erickson, Lyle J. Goldstein, and Carnes Lord, eds. (Annapolis, MD: Naval Institute Press, 2009), 238–285.

37. Robert S. Ross, "China's Naval Nationalism: Sources, Prospects, and the U.S. Response," *International Security* 34 (Fall 2009), 46–81.

38. Michèle Flournoy and Shawn Brimley, "The Contested Commons," U.S. Defense Department website; available at www.defense.gov/qdr/flournoy-article.html.

39. Barry Posen, "Command of the Commons: The Military Foundation of U.S. Hegemony," *International Security* 28 (Summer 2003), 5–46.

40. Yoichi Kato, "China's Anti-Ship Missile Is Nearly Operational," *Asahi Shimbun,* August 26, 2010; available at www.asahi.com/english/TKY201008250379.html.

41. Andrew F. Krepinevich, *Why AirSea Battle?* (Washington, DC: Center for Strategic and Budgetary Assessments, 2010), 20–21. See also Thomas P. Ehrhard and Robert O. Work, *Range, Persistence, Stealth, and Networking: The Case for a Carrier-Based Unmanned Combat System* (Washington, DC: Center for Strategic and Budgetary Assessments, 2008), 137–138, 195.

42. David Kang, *China Rising: Peace, Power, and Order in East Asia* (New York: Columbia University Press, 2007).

43. John Pomfret, "U.S. Takes a Tougher Tone with China," *Washington Post,* July 30, 2010; available at www.washingtonpost.com/wp-dyn/content/article/2010/07/29/AR2010072906416.html.

9 CHINA'S APPROACH TO STRATEGY AND LONG-TERM COMPETITION

Jacqueline Newmyer Deal

WHAT IS THE SIGNIFICANCE of strategy and competition from a Chinese perspective? What are the elements of China's strategy for competing over the long term? How do Chinese political-military elites assess China's progress as a strategic competitor, and how might Chinese strategy interact with American behavior or strategy? This chapter will draw on Chinese historical and military sources to address these questions in sequence. The discussion will end with policy-relevant preliminary conclusions about possible outcomes of the interaction of the American and Chinese approaches.

The application of "competitive strategy" to U.S. defense policy originated during the Cold War and reflected the influence of American management theory. As other chapters explore, the American approach to the Soviet Union was based on an understanding that the Cold War was going to unfold as a long-term competition that would develop over years or decades. This made it appropriate to employ an approach exploiting knowledge of the USSR's fears and procurement procedures to encourage Moscow to invest in defensive systems that were relatively less dangerous for the United States while increasing costs on the Soviet Union. Long-term competitions are generic interactions in world politics, but the approaches brought to them by each competitor may not be. By analyzing China's strategy for competing with the United States in the light of the American strategy for defeating the Soviet Union, this chapter will contribute to our understanding of what is universal and what is particular in matters of long-term strategic competition.

The argument advanced here is that China's way of competing shares with the American Cold War model a concern about influencing the adversary's decision making and behavior. At the same time, China and the United States approach this task differently, and ultimately their strategies have different ends. The outcome of the interaction of the two strategies is likely to reflect their differences, which can be distilled as follows:

- Whereas the United States assumes that other actors are partners until confronted with evidence to the contrary, China's default assumption is one of strategic competition.
- When the United States does decide to employ a competitive strategies approach, the goal is to stimulate the adversary to invest in relatively less threatening defensive areas, which requires knowledge of the adversary's decision-making processes and fears. China's approach focuses on concealing Chinese intentions and decision-making processes while preparing for the moment for decisive action.
- The United States seeks to outlast the adversary in peacetime; China plans to prevail in the competition by subduing the adversary, if necessary by military means.

THE SIGNIFICANCE OF STRATEGY
AND COMPETITION FOR CHINA . . .

To understand China, a preliminary step is to understand ourselves, so a brief account of the American orientation toward matters of competition and strategy is warranted. By and large, the United States has not been self-consciously strategic in its approach to foreign relations since the fall of the Soviet Union. That is, Americans have not considered the country as being in the midst of a long-term competition requiring the use of strategy against another power. Unless or until the United States is directly threatened, it seems to be intrinsic to the American outlook to see other actors as friends or potential partners rather than as long-term rivals or enemies.

Structural and cultural reasons may explain this. Structurally, America can afford to look benevolently at the rest of the world because of our overwhelming power and because, since the defeat of the Soviet Union, we have not faced a serious state challenger. In addition, the United States is often said to have stamped on the world a system of international law and institutions that serves the American end of creating a peaceful backdrop for market-based economic interactions.

Culturally, our domestic political and economic system encourages a view of all human beings as entitled to certain basic rights and respect and as potentially contributing to the common prosperity through commerce. Similarly, Americans have faith in the impartiality of the legal institutions that protect property rights and underpin market-based economic interactions. Although it is true that political candidates and firms compete against one another and use strategies to do so, there seems to be a basic level of confidence in American institutions. Candidates manage their campaigns knowing that, on Election Day, a result will be reached, and the contest will end. Similarly, firms in competition with one another can assume a shared desire to continue to do business, and they can trust the legal system to punish foul play.

China's orientation toward these subjects is very different from that of the United States. For Chinese rulers, now as in the past, "normal" domestic political interaction does not take place in a state of comity. A strategy to deal with hostile internal competitors over the long term is always necessary, regardless of the external situation. The Chinese Communist Party (CCP) leadership presides over commoners, or subjects, not citizens.[1] There is no rule of law in China, only of men. Other experiments in human history suggest that regimes characterized by the rule of men—even expert, highly talented men—ultimately degenerate in the face of a natural human tendency toward greed and the abuse of power. Increasing reports of officials expropriating land or absconding with large amounts of cash may be interpreted as evidence that the sixty-year-old People's Republic of China (PRC) is already suffering from internal rot. When aggrieved by corruption or rapacity, ordinary Chinese people may complain to police or try their luck with bringing legal action, but in the absence of an independent judiciary branch of government, the police and politically appointed judges tend to defer to elites. Protests, of which there were more than 90,000 in each of the last three years according to official Chinese reports, are the recourse of last resort, with protesters, and particularly ringleaders of demonstrations, risking detention or worse.[2]

China lacks regular elections to provide a channel for political housecleaning, so as local officials behave in increasingly venal and predatory fashion, the party maintains stability through the use of a combination of force, stratagem, and information control. Chinese authorities fear the day when restive elements of the population across the country might overcome state-imposed obstacles to connecting and unite in rebellion. Only 75 million of China's 1.3 billion people are CCP members, and even intraparty challenges are a source of concern. For this reason, China boasts an internal security apparatus that may be the largest in world history. An estimate based on a recent leak by a security official in Inner Mongolia suggests that the number of informants per capita in China today—about 3 percent of the population—exceeds the 2.5 percent of East Germans who spied for the Stasi.[3]

To date, Chinese leaders have been effective at competing against domestic rebels or dissidents, and not only through the use of brute force and secret police methods of surveillance, interrogation, and arrest. Starting with Mao, who deliberately polarized society and turned elites against one another to weaken any opposition, party leaders have strategically sought to keep potential challengers divided and distracted.[4] Instead of mounting tumultuous nationwide campaigns like the Cultural Revolution, contemporary party elites have pitted provincial areas, cities, and major business concerns against one another while working to maintain a relatively stable climate for investment and manufacturing. As Elizabeth Perry explains:

> The post-Mao leadership, following the example set by the Great Helmsman, has proven adept at the art of creating coalitions with, and cleavages among, key social elements as a means of stimulating popular political involvement so as to bolster its own political hegemony.[5]

Mao was far from the first Chinese ruler to apply divide-and-rule techniques, as neither China's native populations nor the inhabitants of its territorial additions were ever integrated into a liberal polity. There is no Chinese analogue of the American "melting pot." Rather than acknowledge the differences of ethnic minorities while embracing universal political participation, the CCP has sought to flood Tibet and western China with Han Chinese migrants and thereby demographically extinguish any basis for unrest. Ultimately, however, members of both the Han and non-Han "mass" population dramatically outnumber the elites atop the party, so the regime's strategists must devise ways of suppressing the threat of a coordinated uprising. Optimally, the party can project an image of prosperity and invincibility, so that no one even contemplates revolt. But times are not always good, and threats inevitably emerge. Beijing then turns to its internal security apparatus to strike hard, punish rabble-rousers, and nip insurgencies in the bud.

Looking beyond China's borders, the Chinese outlook focuses on Russia, the Korean peninsula, Japan, Taiwan, Vietnam, India, and most especially the United States as posing threats. This suspicion is consistent with what Christopher Ford calls "the mind of empire," a predisposition to see the world in hierarchical terms and to place China at the center of a competition for ascendancy. Ford identifies this outlook in the Mao and Qing dynasty perspectives but traces it all the way back to China's formative Warring States period.[6]

As discussed in the following pages, the Warring States period featured both diplomatic and military competition, and clashes between defenders and invading armies, often helped by local parties whom they had co-opted, resulted in huge casualties. Today's CCP elites must thus wage a strategic competition not only against a potentially restive, numerically superior multiethnic population but also against other powers that may attack China if they are not subjugated. Internal and external challenges are connected; China's domestic enemies can be a source of trouble on their own, but they may also be supported or exploited by other actors to commit treason. This leads to a natural tendency on the part of Chinese rulers to commingle internal and external challenges and to assume that the stakes in dealing with both are very high. The Chinese strategic inheritance teaches that there are no boundaries, and periods of peace are expected to degenerate into situations requiring the use of force.

. . . AND THE ROLE OF THE UNITED STATES

In light of China's imperial legacy and preoccupation with minority populations in outlying provinces, one might think of the greatest external threats as coming from India, with its influence in Tibet, or from Central Asia, which is tied religiously and ethnically to the western Chinese "autonomous region" of Xinjiang. But it is the United States that above all is the target of Chinese fears and long-term strategy. This situation seems not to be based on the particular challenge of an independent Taiwan. Rather, Chinese defense strategists derive the American threat from the structural position of the United States in the world. To be sure, the United States has been suspect since it backed Chiang Kai-shek's (Jiang Jieshi's) Nationalist forces over Mao's Communist army in the Chinese Civil War, and the young PRC regime in Beijing considered Washington to be the main foreign enemy through the Korean War period, until the Sino-Soviet rift created a temporary alignment of American and Chinese interests. But the United States returned to the fore as the primary competitor for China starting in the 1980s. Here is the end of a discussion on "setting the main strategic direction" in *The Science of Military Strategy (Zhanlue Xue)*, one of China's main defense textbooks and the first to be translated into English by the Chinese:

> The main strategic direction of China has seen three major adjustments since the establishment of PRC [sic]. The three generations of the CPC's [CCP's]

leadership have had . . . to scientifically analyze the developments and changes of the international strategic situations and the extent of their influences over China's national security. . . . In the mid-1950s, the Party Central Committee and the Central Military Commission, in the light of the strategic encirclement on China [sic] by foreign forces led by the United States and the serious situation of possible strategic offensive launched against China, specified the southeastern coastal area of China as the main strategic direction. Between the 1960s and 1970s, as the Sino-Soviet relations broke up and the Soviet Union deployed a million troops along the Sino-Soviet border and posed an increasingly serious military threat to China, the leadership changed the main strategic direction decidedly to the three northern regions. In the 1980s, they once again adjusted the main strategic direction according to the new international situations. Through timely adjustments, China has always kept its strategically active position.[7]

Several elements in this account—representative of other Chinese sources—may strike American readers as unexpected or unusual. First, the reference to "scientifically" analyzing trends in the international landscape reflects the influence of both Marxism and China's strategic tradition, discussed in the next section. Second is the preoccupation with territory and unity. Third, the penultimate sentence obliquely refers to the return of the United States as the main challenge once the Soviet Union's decline became apparent, in a period of "very complicated and difficult conditions" for China. Even when relations with Washington were most friendly, Beijing thought of the United States as a threat to be managed. Reading between the lines, the threat arose from American preeminence in Asia, making China feel surrounded, and China had to contend with this menace even as American support was required—that is, through economic ties and technology transfer—to help China become a great power. Chinese writings thus tend to walk a fine line, designating the United States as the enemy because of its imputed aggression against China rather than, say, because of any Chinese ambition to usurp the role of the United States as the dominant power in the region.

Successive Chinese Defense White Papers have toed this line, stating that while China needs peace to continue its military and economic buildup, "great power" competition has intensified. The theme also surfaces in military guidance and doctrinal statements meant for internal use. For instance, various Chinese-language expositions of the "historic missions of the People's Liberation Army (PLA) in the new period of the new century" proclaimed by Hu

Jintao in 2004 highlight, "The Western hostile forces which have not given up their ambition to ruin our nation are stepping up implementation of their political strategy to westernize and split up our country."[8]

The United States poses the central challenge for China because of its global dominance, consistent with the emphasis on hierarchy and hegemony in China's strategic tradition. From Beijing's perspective, the long-term competition with the United States has already been underway for several decades. This raises the question of what China has been doing and might do in the future to counter the U.S. threat.

ELEMENTS OF CHINA'S "COMPETITIVE STRATEGY" APPROACH

The particular worldview that led China in the 1980s to diagnose the United States as the main strategic "direction" has informed China's response to this challenge. China's outlook encourages competing by "shaping" the adversary, just as Washington sought to influence Moscow's decision making in the Cold War. But the American approach drew on management theory, inspired by firms competing in a peaceful, market-regulated environment, while China's approach flows from a classical strategy and statecraft tradition. China's strategy for long-term competition seems to revolve around concealing China's own "shape," monitoring global trends, aligning with them selectively, and collecting intelligence about American weaknesses and plans. By such means, Beijing can mislead Washington about Chinese ambitions and capabilities, or at least create ambiguity, while preparing to execute a devastating offensive if necessary. Overall, relative to American competitive strategy precedents, the principles of Chinese strategy seem more keyed to preparing for a hot war.

What are the classical sources of China's approach to strategy and competition? Aphorisms about the importance of knowing yourself and the enemy and using deception and surprise from the legendary *Sun Zi Bingfa* (or Sun Tzu's *Art of War*) are well known, but it is important to consider why these timeless precepts appeared in a tome from ancient China. The Warring States period—from which Sun Tzu's text and other venerable Chinese works on strategy and statecraft emerged—featured a protracted competition among seven different states vying to swallow one another and become the dominant power in the realm.[9] The state that eventually conquered all the rest, Qin, was an outlier and the least developed at the beginning of the age. According to Chinese historiography, Qin benefited from its peripheral position, as the supposedly culturally superior internal states came to be dominated by venal elites and weakened one another through combat and acts of sabotage.

Several aspects of the centuries-long Warring States competition are important to recognize because they left an enduring imprint on Chinese thinking about strategy. First, the states that were in contention were proximate, relatively similar, and relatively porous. Across them, a high degree of mutual understanding was possible. Second, a population of itinerant strategists, or cosmopolitan experts on war, seems to have been available to rulers and traveled across different states in search of employment. Third, landholders in border areas appear to have been bought off by rival states—for example, to allow passage to their invading forces—with some frequency. Aside from the Qin state, which eventually found ways of enforcing loyalty, ruling houses in the warring states had difficulty ensuring the allegiance of peripheral elites. Similarly, alliances were marriages of expediency. They were built on appeals to short-term interest and did not rest on a foundation of common principles or international law. Finally, the era was marked by diplomatic jockeying and sporadic outbreaks of violence, so both diplomacy and direct uses of force were relevant to the outcome of the competition.

The traditional Chinese strategic emphasis on acquiring and exploiting superior intelligence about the environment reflects the logic of its materialist outlook and the aforementioned structural elements of the Warring States context. Consider, for example, the priority attached to prewar assessments in Sun Tzu's *Art of War* and more contemporary Chinese military texts alike. This point is often contrasted with the advice offered in seminal Western strategy books such as Clausewitz's *On War,* which highlights the fog that surrounds fighting and the lack of precise intelligence or, often, adequate situational awareness on the battlefield that would be necessary for precise assessments. But, in a Warring States–style security environment that features familiar adversaries, spies can gain access to a rival's capital and cultivate enemy elites to gather significant intelligence. Comparative assessments and strategies to exploit the enemy's weaknesses can thus realistically be executed.

The emphasis in the *Sun Zi Bingfa*—and other Chinese texts on strategy and statecraft, ancient and modern—on exploiting the adversary's inferior intelligence to achieve surprise may also strike students of Clausewitz as peculiar. But the centrality of surprise in China's strategic tradition goes together both with the assumption of the availability of good intelligence, already discussed, and with an emphasis on monitoring trends to identify moments ripe for decisive action. The focus on trends—that is, general tendencies or forces in the environment, including global norms and patterns of economic relations—flows naturally from a Chinese philosophical-religious orientation that stresses harmony with, or limited human agency relative to, physical and social surroundings. When Chinese strategic texts recommend knowing not just about the enemy per se but also about global trends, so that this knowledge can be used to garner competitive advantage, we should recall that ancient Chinese rulers were judged on the basis of their claim to the Mandate of Heaven. The mandate, in turn, was measured by objective, material factors—from the quality of the weather and harvests in the realm to the efficacy of the realm's defenses against foreign invaders. Attention to broader trends is thus built into the fabric of Chinese political culture.

The classical Chinese inheritance helps explain the emphasis not just on possessing superior intelligence but on manipulating information and perceptions—an emphasis that pervades both ancient and modern Chinese strategic texts. Monopolizing information flows is essential in a world of spies and in a domestic political culture that judges the Mandate of Heaven according to material indications. A ruler who hopes to manage perceptions of developments that augur negatively with regard to the Mandate of Heaven must dominate the data. Likewise, one who hopes to conceal military forces' "shape" or weaknesses from espionage needs tight control over what is said and written.

Space constraints preclude a full inventory even of just the modern instances in which Chinese forces have enacted the strategic guidance transmitted from the era of the Qin victory down through the centuries. Suffice it to say that China's surprise intervention in the Korean War in 1950, surprise initiation of the Sino-Indian War in 1962, ambush of Soviet forces at Zhenbao/Damansky island in 1969, and surprise invasion of Vietnam in 1979 may all be considered consistent with the counsel to conceal one's own plans, deceive the adversary, monitor trends for a moment to strike, and attack with the intent to affect the enemy's calculations.[10] Space constraints similarly preclude an examination of the occasions throughout history when Chinese strategists have seen fit to liken contemporary conditions to those of the Warring States period, but it is important to note that the last such time was in the 1980s, and the analogy continues to be invoked today.[11] This suggests that American defense analysts need to understand both enduring aspects of China's strategic tradition and what it means that the Chinese consider themselves to be competing with the United States in a Warring States–like environment.

CHINA'S POLITICAL-MILITARY STRATEGY
FOR COMPETING WITH THE UNITED STATES

The source of the latest incarnation of the Warring States period analogy seems to have been Deng Xiaoping, who presided over a renaissance of the PLA. Deng not only promoted evolution away from Mao's guerrilla, personnel-intensive, low-tech "People's War" strategy (designed for luring enemies deep into China's interior) to a leaner, modernized, high-tech force for fighting wars around China's borders, but he also encouraged renewed attention to classical Chinese teachings on war and strategy. For Deng, the end of the Cold War was ushering in a period of intense competition to identify the new order or dominant power framework, at least in Asia, and potentially globally.[12] Further, he seems to have seen his own opening of China to the world for the purpose of fostering economic development as a dangerous move that rendered China as exposed to rivals as the ancient warring states were to one another. Thanks to the broader trend of globalization, the world was becoming more porous, and now foreigners would have unprecedented access to the Chinese population. As a student of classical Chinese strategy and an observer of global trends, Deng came up with a preferred course, suited to China's position relative to competitors: "Observe calmly, secure our position; cope with affairs calmly; hide our capabilities, and bide our time; be good at maintaining a low profile; and never claim leadership."[13] Strikingly, the only other record of Deng speaking in this way was in 1943 during World War II, when he advised his Communist comrades "in enemy-occupied areas . . . to gather strength secretly by every means available and to bide their time."[14]

This advice echoed the policy of the peripheral Qin state early in the Warring States period, when Qin had not yet developed into a power capable of mobilizing superior military force. Deng's strategy also involved encouraging a preexisting American tendency to promote commerce. By opening up China, Deng was aligning with an American-led globalization trend, and, by "maintaining a low profile" and not raising fears, China would allow Americans to nurture their hope that prosperity would breed liberalism and democratization. Thus Deng's guidance was intrinsically political and military. Starting in the 1980s, he focused China not just on developing the economy and acquiring modern high-tech military capabilities but also on influencing foreign perceptions of China's rise.

It is no accident that the last chapter in the PLA's *Science of Military Strategy* is called "Fight Well Military-Political War and Political-Military War." Using military capabilities to shape American perceptions and political calculations is consistent with the stress on information management in classical Chinese strategy. The textbook offers guidance worthy of a 21st-century Sun Tzu:

> The key of political struggle in a war is to expose and disintegrate the enemy to the maximum extent. . . . Aiming at the situation inside the enemy camp and the structure of his war system, making use of contradictions, we should break the enemy's aggression alliance by every possible means and destroy his conspiracy of organizing international sanctions and making coalition for invasion. We should also use every means to restrict the enemy from making war decisions and promote anti-war power inside the enemy, therefore setting obstacles against the war.[15]

The focus of this passage, the culminating wisdom of the book, is on targeting the adversary's decision-making apparatus through a variety of means—from building up antiwar advocates in the adversary's camp to wresting away the adversary's allies.

A recent spate of books and articles from Chinese military sources provides a theoretical basis for the effort to influence American decision making. The books address "the three warfares"—psychological, media, and legal—all ways of shaping foreign perceptions and calculations. Along with extensive Chinese analysis of each of the three, "military soft power" has received increasing attention from Chinese sources since about 2006.[16] Through techniques such as advancing international legal arguments and cultivating public opinion in key places, Beijing can "prepare the battleground" well in advance of the outbreak of hostilities. Accordingly, Chinese officials and other representatives seek opportunities in public appearances and in the media to advance Beijing's interpretation of its legal claims to disputed areas. Foreigners who sympathize with Beijing's perspective are rewarded. In theory, successful efforts along these lines could prevent a prospective adversary like the United States from rallying support for challenging China or responding to a Chinese provocation.

To elaborate, a central strand of Chinese military thought on this "soft" form of warfare, or warfare in the realm of ideas, seems to be targeting the American will to compete via appeals to audiences within the United States. Just as Qin bided time and Deng advocated lying low, so China for many years has sought to avoid giving the United States reason even to diagnose that it is in a long-term competition. One of the best explanations of China's efforts in this domain is James Mann's *The China Fantasy*.[17] A rare acknowledgment of Chinese internal influence efforts appeared in a 2003 publication from a

Ministry of Foreign Affairs journal, which described both the United States and China as trying to influence each other "from within through all kinds of channels and means."[18] But, in reality, only one side—China—in this dyad has an extensive apparatus for wooing "foreign friends" and encouraging them to support the party line.[19]

Beyond reaching into the United States through well-disposed proxies, China has also been heeding the advice in the already-quoted *Science of Strategy* passage about breaking up the enemy's alliances. Efforts in this area comport with the Warring States strategic inheritance, as Qin prevailed in part by picking off members of a hostile coalition arrayed against it, encircling enemies while avoiding being flanked. While the idea of alliances and counteralliances is familiar in the West, the United States tends to forge enduring relationships with similarly liberal countries. China's relationships seem more temporary and opportunistic, following the Warring States model. For instance, China's approach differs from American alliance behavior in the Cold War, which revolved around extending security guarantees and trying to restrain allies from arms buildups, particularly nuclear arms buildups. No such nonproliferation norm guides Chinese alliance behavior. Rather, China has been transferring the antiaccess weapons that it has acquired in the past few decades to other states strategically located in areas where the United States might perceive a need to fight in the future. The Iranian antiship missile that damaged an Israeli ship in the 2006 war with Hezbollah was of Chinese origin, for example, and it is possible that Chinese antiship missiles have been or will be stored in locations along the Indian Ocean littoral where China enjoys good relations and port access—from Burma to Pakistan and Iran. Finally, delivering sophisticated antiaccess capabilities to friends and clients is consistent with what the Chinese diagnose to be a global trend toward proliferation,[20] so China's activities in this area can also be seen aligning with trends, as prescribed by China's classical tradition.

Chinese writing on American attempts to establish footholds in key regions is revealing. For instance, the Chinese interpreted the American intervention in the Balkans in the 1990s not as a temporary humanitarian operation but rather as an effort to establish a permanent U.S. military presence at a key global crossroads.[21] Chinese commentators had similar reactions to the U.S. invasion of Afghanistan. "One can hardly sleep easily when a tiger is next to the bed," a Chinese analyst summarized the situation.[22] The gap between American and Chinese perspectives on these episodes is not only striking but also revealing, insofar as the Chinese view seems to reflect an extreme sensitivity to being surrounded. Again, one can draw a line from the Warring States to today with respect to the Chinese concern about encirclement and the priority attached to counterencirclement.

From Taiwan to Central Asia and beyond, China's efforts to break out of a perceived U.S. straitjacket and extend influence have involved a range of tools.[23] In the case of Taiwan, economic integration and population flows may be designed to bring about de facto integration. A similar approach has been adopted in Southeast Asia, into which Chinese nationals have been flowing for commercial reasons and where China has been building up dual-use infrastructure. As previously mentioned, defense transfers have been a primary tool for Beijing with regard to Pakistan and states in the Middle East from Saudi Arabia to Iran, as well as in parts of Africa. Beyond direct actions, the extent to which China has enabled or acquiesced in Pakistani and North Korean nuclear and missile proliferation has not been established, but the proliferation seems to have served Chinese ends in terms of strengthening friends of China hostile to the United States or to U.S. friends—for example, in the case of transfers to Pakistan and India.

Concurrent with behavior that flouts the spirit, if not the letter, of arms control agreements, China uses legal warfare to advance its territorial claims. These claims, many of which involve natural resources, serve multiple purposes. But, from the standpoint of China's strategic tradition and the lessons of the Warring States period, one clear goal is to expand the zone from which China can exclude other actors. Beijing's assertions with respect to disputed areas of the East and South China Seas are well known. Less discussed are Chinese efforts to use archaeological and other historical data to legitimate at least cultural dominion over Asia-Pacific zones from the Korean peninsula to Borneo.[24]

While attending to the range of Chinese peacetime competitive efforts— from cultivating friends in the United States to countering perceived hostile encirclement—it is important to remember that not all of the Warring States period was devoted to diplomatic jockeying. Force was critical to resolving the competition decisively, and, as mentioned in the preceding paragraphs, China's strategic inheritance has much to say about the importance of seizing the initiative early in a conflict, managing escalation, and the like.

The final aspect of China's approach to the long-term competition is the effort to acquire military capabilities suited to inflicting a devastating attack or series of attacks on U.S. forces or those of an ally.[25] This buildup stands in

tension with the attempt to prevent the United States from even recognizing that a competition is underway. But it is also similar insofar as it aims to
manipulate American decision making. The logic is to reassure and flatter the
United States to prevent a counterbuildup, while at the same time demonstrating the capacity to target U.S. vulnerabilities. Displays of antisatellite weapons,
torpedoes, precision-guided missiles, and cyber capabilities in the past several
years thus reflect a movement away from Deng's advice on "biding time." U.S.
military planners are now expected not only to discount a China threat but
also to fear China's capacity to attack American platforms and the command,
control, communications, computer, intelligence, surveillance, and reconnaissance (C4ISR) systems and networks on which they depend. The selective
demonstration of key capabilities is consistent with a strategy of manipulating
adversary perceptions and targeting decision making. American planners do
not know the full range of Chinese weapons, so they must be very careful. If
this means not operating in disputed waters, decision makers in Washington
can rationalize ceding strategic ground by reference to Beijing's assurances
that the PLA is not looking to challenge the United States but only to defend
China's "core interests." Beijing might anticipate that the United States will
be "self-deterred" from intervening in the event of a PLA attempt to seize, for
instance, territory claimed by Japan in the East China Sea. At the same time,
China may also count on being able to paralyze American decision makers
through a devastating attack on U.S. forces that would leave Washington uncertain about what else China could do if the conflict persisted.

The aim of creating crippling psychological effects emerges clearly from
recent Chinese works on nuclear deterrence.[26] The concept of *zaoshi*, or inexorable momentum, plays a central role in Chinese doctrine, with Chinese
strategists explaining the need to create a sense that inexorable momentum
could be unleashed if a Chinese red line were crossed.[27] According to a 2007
article by two PLA senior colonels, modern warfare depends less on annihila-
tion of the enemy through the application of massed firepower and more on
the use of techniques to "isolate, limit, weaken, paralyze, cow into submission,
and disintegrate one's opponent."[28] This emphasis on psychological effects is
also apparent in the *Science of Military Strategy*:

> Demonstrating momentum by showing the disposition of strength to the en-
> emy is to display clearly one's deterrent force for bringing about psychological
> pressure . . . and thus force him to submit. Such deterrence forms as large-

scale military review, joint military exercise, and military visit, etc. are usually adopted . . . Augmenting momentum by military strike . . . [shows] one's strength and determination . . . In strategic deterrence operations one must direct against the enemy's defects and play to one's superiority in concealing one's weakness and showing the potency so as to demonstrate one's strength, determination, and volition that can terrify the opponent and to attain the effect of subduing the enemy's forces.[29]

It would be misleading to highlight the deterrence passages without mentioning that the textbook also covers conventional and nuclear operations in war, with special attention to seizing the initiative and effective targeting in offensive and defensive air operations, as well as to information and electronic warfare. These discussions similarly stress the use of surprise and attacks designed to weaken the enemy's morale while showing China's resolve. Thus Beijing's strategy for the long-term competition with the United States ranges from peacetime efforts to manipulate American views of China to military preparations for waging a war from which the PLA would emerge victorious by inflicting devastating attacks that undermine the American will to fight.

CONCLUSION: CHINESE ASSESSMENTS AND POLICY IMPLICATIONS

Before turning to the U.S. policy implications of China's approach to competing, it is necessary to ask how China measures its progress in the competition. Addressing this question will allow us to speculate about the likely interaction of China's approach and American behavior in the future.

In keeping with the logic of a strategic tradition that emphasizes possessing superior intelligence, China conceals information about its decision-making processes that could be used by an adversary to predict Chinese behavior or to target vulnerabilities. This means that we know less than we would like to about how China performs assessments. But Chinese writings do indicate the use of something called "comprehensive national power" (CNP) as a metric for judging China's standing relative to other states.[30] Although the algorithm or weighting of inputs for making this calculation is not transparent and seems to vary across different assessment bodies in China, the inputs are known to combine hard and soft factors and to include domestic variables that Western estimates of relative power tend not to consider. For instance, measures of national cohesiveness are incorporated along with traditional hard data on a country's steel production and defense budget. This suggests that, over the course of the competition, China's decision makers, consistent with the traditional Chinese focus on monitoring trends, will be alert to changes in American defense spending, economic power, and national cohesion. But they will also be sensitive to factors internal to China that may shift China's relative standing.

Some negative factors for China's internal situation that are on the horizon are wholly independent of U.S. policies—or, at least, independent of policies consciously aimed at China. Notwithstanding the official number of 90,000-plus annual demonstrations in the past few years, social stability may prove to have peaked, given that China's political elites have held out economic growth as the basis for their legitimacy, and the future for growth is unlikely to be as bright as the past. To make short work of a large subject, demographic trends, public health risks arising from conditions on farms and in Chinese cities, environmental degradation, and contracted demand for Chinese goods as a result of the global downturn all seem to pose challenges.[31] Most of these issues are the flip side of China's rise to date, and they are scarcely related to deliberate American efforts. For instance, the One Child Policy adopted by China in 1979 now means that fewer laborers will be entering the work force, and the country, which on the whole lacks a pension infrastructure, will face a growing population of elderly people with only one child to support each couple. Many of the elderly will be in rural areas, where they have been left behind by children migrating to cities for work. China may have exhausted labor migration from less productive to more productive areas as a source of economic growth at just the time when the budget will be strained by social welfare demands. The budget will also have to accommodate the costs of cleaning up China's environment or of dealing with the fallout from ignoring, for instance, pollution of an already limited water supply or the spread of a contagion more potent than SARS. Whereas Western economists prescribe further marketization and promotion of domestic consumption as future sources of growth for China, it is not clear that Chinese political authorities can or will take the necessary steps in this direction.

Regardless of American views of the situation, the United States—along with its friends and allies such as Japan, South Korea, India, and members of the Association of South East Asian Nations (ASEAN)—could be linked to threats in the eyes of party leaders who are both confident from decades of double-digit growth and nervous in the face of mounting problems. In particular, just as Chinese strategy recommends manipulating forces within the

United States to shape perceptions of China, so Chinese analysts seem to be exceptionally concerned about American infiltration. This passage from a 2006 book published by the Chinese Ministry of Foreign Affairs is representative:

> The United States peddles, through a multitude of ways, her ideology and values to China aiming to change the nature of socialist China in subtle ways. The United States adopts the "Westernization" strategy to exploit our open door and reform policies and attempts to infiltrate their thoughts and ideas into China on a grand scale. Using the excuse of "merging China into the international society," the United States propagates the "superiority" of the "separation of the three powers [sic]" in order to change the existing political structure of China. . . .[32]

But Beijing is not infallible, and more recent efforts—potentially starting with the January 2007 antisatellite test—to combine reassurance with a display of military capabilities for deterrent purposes may not have been received as planned. It is possible that more aggressive Chinese behavior has spurred, or is in the process of spurring, a counterbuildup in the region. The United States may now or soon perceive a threat that effectively galvanizes the country to develop and execute a strategy for the long-term competition with China.

It thus makes sense to consider two final questions: How, over time, will China view American behavior or strategy in this long-term competition? And how are U.S. actions likely to interact with China's execution of its strategy? Space constraints prohibit a full investigation of this issue, but on the basis of the foregoing it is possible to outline some principles that U.S. policymakers may want to keep in mind:

- Chinese political elites will make predictions about future American behavior toward China on the basis of their understanding of broad trends in American power and the global security environment, not on the basis of a deep understanding of American national security decision making.
- Chinese assessments of the international balance of power and predictions about American behavior are also likely to reflect developments internal to China, even though these developments would seem unrelated from an American perspective.
- This, in turn, suggests that China could decide to strike out at a moment that American decision makers would find surprising. A Chinese attack on a regional power would be conducted with an eye toward discouraging the United States from intervening by

convincing Americans of the capacity of the PLA and/or its partners to inflict damage on U.S. forces in excess of the stakes of allowing China to prevail. A Chinese military offensive against the United States directly would target American vulnerabilities and, again, be tied to an information campaign designed to make Washington judge the costs of challenging China to be prohibitive, and thus to surrender.

- If the United States does perceive a threat from China that mobilizes an American "competitive strategies" approach to the long-term competition, opacity around Chinese defense decision making may impede efforts to influence Chinese behavior. At the same time, like the Soviet Union, barring political change, China seems to face limits on its economic growth potential and to be prone to investing in certain sensitive areas. Washington will thus have a range of different Chinese fears—from encirclement to infiltration—to consider exploiting.

NOTES

1. The conventional term for non-CCP elites or the general population is *laobaixing,* which used to be translated consistently as "the masses" and is now often translated as "commoners." See Andrew J. Nathan and Bruce Gilley, *China's New Rulers: The Secret Files,* Second Revised Edition (New York: New York Review of Books, 2003), 31.

2. Minxin Pei, *China's Trapped Transition: The Limits of Developmental Autocracy* (Cambridge, MA: Harvard University Press, 2006).

3. Malcolm Moore, "Chinese Police Admit Enormous Number of Spies," *The Telegraph,* February 9, 2010; available at www.telegraph.co.uk/news/worldnews/asia/china/7195592/Chinese-police-admit-enormous-number-of-spies.html.

4. Elizabeth Perry, "Studying Chinese Politics: Farewell to Revolution?" *The China Journal,* No. 57, (January 2007), 10–11 and *passim.*

5. Ibid.

6. Christopher Ford, *The Mind of Empire* (Lexington: University Press of Kentucky, 2010), 80–81.

7. Peng Guangqian and Yao Youzhi, eds., *The Science of Military Strategy,* English edition (Beijing: Military Science Publishing House, 2005), 233–234.

8. For instance, see excerpt of Wo Jieming, ed., "Zhongshi Luxing Xin Shiji Xin Jieduan Wojun Lishi Shiming Bai Wen Bai Da" ["Faithfully Carry out the Military's Historic Mission—100 Questions and Answers"] in Chinese, Long March Publishing House, May 1, 2006, 1–47, 83–97, 133–199, CPP20081022325003; see also Tian Bingren, "The Scientific Development of the Historical Mission of Our Army in the New

Phase of the New Century," in Chinese, *Zhongguo Junshi Kexue*, Oct. 1, 2007, 21–27, CPP2000801235001.

9. The author has written about the Warring States period as a formative era for Chinese strategy and an analogy for today's security environment, as perceived by Beijing, in Jacqueline Newmyer, "Oil, Arms, and Influence: The Indirect Strategy Behind Chinese Military Modernization," *Orbis* (Spring 2009), 205–219.

10. Mark Burles and Abram Shulsky, *Patterns in China's Use of Force: Evidence from History and Doctrinal Writings* (Santa Monica, CA: RAND, 2000); Jacqueline Newmyer, *Regimes, Surprise Attacks, and War Initiation* (Cambridge, MA: Long-Term Strategy Project, CSBA, 2005); Jacqueline Newmyer, *The Strategy of Shi: A Model for Understanding China's Approach to Competition and Conflict* (Cambridge, MA: Long-Term Strategy Project, CSBA, 2006).

11. Michael Pillsbury, *China Debates the Future Security Environment* (Washington, DC: National Defense University Press, 2000), xxxviii, *passim*; Ford, *Mind of Empire*, 253.

12. This point and the rest of the paragraph echo arguments advanced by the author in Newmyer, "Oil, Arms, and Influence."

13. Allen S. Whiting, "Chinese Nationalism and Foreign Policy after Deng," *The China Quarterly* 142, 295–316, 301, as mentioned in Jacqueline Newmyer, "The Revolution in Military Affairs with Chinese Characteristics," *The Journal of Strategic Studies*, 33, (August 2010), 493–494.

14. Newmyer, "The Revolution" 494.

15. Peng and Yao, *Science of Military Strategy*, 471–472. Pointedly, this chapter and the book conclude with a partisan account of the Korean War and how China "won [the war] morally."

16. A few representative titles are excerpt of Yang Xuhua, *Xin Zhance* ["Psychological Warfare Strategy"], in Chinese, National Defense University Press, March 1, 2004, CPP20100729658001; excerpt of Cong Wensheng, *Faluzhan Yibaili Jingdian Anli Pingxi* ["Analysis of 100 Cases of Legal Warfare"], in Chinese, PLA Press, Nov. 1, 2004, CPP20100903658001; excerpt of Liu Gaoping, *Yulun Zhan Zhishi Duben* ["Media Warfare Textbook"], in Chinese, National Defense University Press, Aug. 1, 2005, CPP20100916318003. One of the earliest open-source studies of Chinese "legal warfare" is Larry M. Wortzel, "The Chinese People's Liberation Army and Space Warfare," American Enterprise Institute, 2007; available at www.aei.org/docLib/20071017_SpaceWarfare.pdf, 3–4.

17. James Mann, *The China Fantasy: How Our Leaders Explain Away Chinese Repression* (New York: Viking, 2007).

18. Niu Jun, "Zhong Mei: Yi Cun He Jing Zheng Zhi Zhong" ["China and the United States: Between Interdependence and Competition"], *Shijie Zhishi* ["World Affairs"], in Chinese, January 1, 2003, CPP20030110000166.

19. Mann, ibid.; Anne-Marie Brady, *Marketing Dictatorship: Propaganda and Thought Work in Contemporary China* (New York: Rowman & Littlefield, 2007); Anne-Marie Brady, *Making the Foreign Serve China: Managing Foreigners in the People's Republic* (New York: Rowman & Littlefield, 2003).

20. Xu Duixing, ed., *Shijie Dashi Yu Zhongguo Heping Fazhan* ["World Trends and China's Peaceful Development"], in Chinese, Shijie Zhishi Chubanshe ["World Affairs Publishing House"], 2006, CPP20070402478001.

21. Pillsbury, *China Debates,* cites Yan Zheng, "What Are NATO Motives in Bombing the Federal Republic of Yugoslavia?," *Renmin Luntan,* 4 (April 15, 1999), 37–39, in FBIS-CHI-1999-0516, May 16, 1999; Pillsbury also cites Zhang Dezhen, "On U.S. Eurasian Strategy," *Renmin Ribao,* June 4, 1999, 6, in FBIS-CHI-1999-0605, June 4, 1999, which explicitly mentions "encircling" Eurasia.

22. Zhao Changqing, "ASEAN, the Shanghai Cooperation Organization, and China," *Dangdai Yatai,* 11 (Nov. 15, 2003), 11–15, in Chinese, CPP20031217000170. See also Chen Xiangyang, "Draw up New 'Greater Periphery' Strategy as Soon as Possible," Liaowang, 29 (July 17, 2006), 64, in Chinese, CPP20060720710009; Gao Zichuan, "An Analysis of the Basic Situation of China's Peripheral Security Environment," *Dangdai Yatai,* 1(Jan. 1, 2004), 4–10, in Chinese, CPP20040126000141.

23. Joshua Kurlanzick, *China's Charm Offensive: How China's Soft Power Is Transforming the World* (New Haven, CT: Yale University Press, 2007).

24. For Korea, see Andrew Leonard, "The 'History War' in Northeast Asia: Who Owns the Legacy of the Kingdom of Koguryo/Gaogouli? China, Korea or Wikipedia?" Salon.com, March 14, 2007; available at www.salon.com/technology/how_the_world_works/2007/03/14/history_wars and also at www.japanfocus.org/-Yonson-Ahn/2631. For Borneo, see "Astonishing, Breaking News, Chinese Areas of Borneo Return to Borneo": available at http://junshi.xilu.com/2010/0130/news_44_63136.html.

25. This point and the points in the rest of the paragraph draw on Newmyer, "The Revolution in Military Affairs with Chinese Characteristics."

26. Timothy L. Thomas, *Dragon Bytes: Chinese Information-War Theory and Practice from 1995–2003* (Fort Leavenworth, KS: Foreign Military Studies Office, 2004).

27. This concept is also sometimes expressed as "drawing the bow but not shooting" (*yin er bufa*).

28. Wang Xingsheng and Wu Zhizhong. "JFJB Discusses 'Soft Military Power' and Its Application to PRC Military," *Jiefangjun Bao,* June 7, 2007, 6, CPP20070607710013.

29. Peng and Yao, *Science of Military Strategy,* 223.

30. Pillsbury, *China Debates,* 30, passim. See also Li Tianran, "Guanyu zonghe guoli wenti" [On the Question of Comprehensive National Power], *Guoji Wenti Yanjiu,* 2 (1999): 52–58; and, more recently, Wang Ling, "Guanyu zonghe guoli de cedu" [Measuring Comprehensive National Power], *Shijie Jingji Yu Zhengzhi* (June 2006).

31. Nicholas Eberstadt, "China's One-Child Mistake," *Wall Street Journal*, Sept. 17, 2007; Elizabeth C. Economy, "The Great Leap Backward?" *Foreign Affairs*, 86 (Sept. 2007); Victor Shih, "Why China Isn't Ready to Lead," *Wall Street Journal Asia*, Oct. 22, 2009, and Victor Shih, "China's Uphill Battle for Stronger Banks," *Far Eastern Economic Review*, 168 (Nov. 2005), 37–40; Jia Hepeng, "Antibiotic Resistance in the Developing World," Science and Development Network, March 26, 2008, available at www .scidev.net/en/south-east-asia/features/antibiotic-resistance-and-the-developing-world.html.

32. Xu Duixing, ed., *Shijie Dashi Yu Zhongguo Heping Fazhan.* (The passage is from a chapter by Pei Yuanying, a former Chinese ambassador to India and Poland.)

10 THE POWER PROJECTION BALANCE IN ASIA

Dan Blumenthal

CHINA IS POSING A SERIOUS CHALLENGE to the U.S. ability to underwrite stability in the Asia Pacific region. Since World War II, U.S. regional security strategy has relied on a forward military presence in what China calls its first island chain,[1] sea and air control of the Pacific, and the ability to "command the commons,"[2] a prerequisite for projecting substantial force into the region when necessary. China is developing military capabilities to coerce countries within the first island chain and is beginning to project power deeper into the Western Pacific, which raises the costs of U.S. power projection into the region. Over the long term, China seeks to exert control over its periphery. These developments are beginning to undermine a U.S. regional strategy that depends on projecting power quickly into East Asia.

In the short term, the security competition in Asia will be characterized by U.S. attempts to continue to project power in the region to reassure and defend allies, defend its homeland and territories, and defend the global commons against Chinese attempts to coerce U.S. allies and exert more control over its periphery. In the longer term, the Sino-U.S security competition will be characterized by Chinese attempts to project power further afield to defend sea-lanes and perhaps make a bid for regional dominance.

This chapter assesses the changes in the balance of power in Asia between China and the United States and how that change affects Washington's traditional security strategy in the region. It does so in the context of the two countries' conflicting regional security goals and the military strategies each has developed to advance their respective objectives. It uses two potential conflict scenarios—Taiwan and the South China Sea—to analyze how the interplay of conflicting goals and strategies may unfold. Finally, it argues that the particular way the military balance is changing is undermining nuclear stability in the region. In particular, the United States has few if any responses to China's growing missile force that lend themselves to strategic stability.

U.S. REGIONAL INTERESTS AND
TRADITIONAL SECURITY STRATEGY

After the defeat of Imperial Japan, the United States became the guarantor of regional security in Asia. The United States committed itself to the containment of Soviet and Chinese expansionism, the rebuilding of countries ravaged by war (most importantly Japan), and the extension of an American defense perimeter to protect the homeland, out from Hawaii to the first island chain. America underwrote regional security, ensuring that Asia would not be dominated by a regional hegemon while also encouraging its friends to embrace the post–World War II liberal international system.

In part to advance these goals, the United States fought two of its bloodiest twentieth-century wars in Korea and Vietnam, defended Taiwan (including by threatening China with nuclear weapons), and assisted Southeast Asia in defeating communist and other insurgencies. These conflicts and demonstrations of force required unfettered access to Asia's rimlands and landmass, enabled by American control of the Pacific and bases both in the first island chain and on continental Asia.

America's Asia strategy was remarkably successful. It gave Asian elites the political space to pursue paths of modernization that embraced "Western ways" without engaging in enervating arms races or acquiring weapons of mass destruction. Moreover, since America's war in Vietnam and the end of the Sino-Vietnamese war in 1979, Asia has enjoyed three decades of peace and relative stability. U.S. policy has set the stage for Asia's "rise" as the center of international politics and economics.[3]

Obviously, there is no single explanation for a long period of peace. But no peace enforces itself. The long-standing American defense commitments to Asian allies (Japan, South Korea, Australia, Thailand, the Philippines, Taiwan, Singapore), Washington's leadership in encouraging those allies to join the international economic system, and, where possible, in encouraging democratic reform, undergirded by U.S. willingness to project military power to fight wars and fend off other conflicts, have all contributed to Asia's peace.

Given its distance from the Asian continent, America's ability to project power into the region has been the sine qua non of regional stability. The United States brought to bear massive military power to prosecute the Korean and Vietnam Wars. Since 1979, the United States has projected power to help stop a coup in the Philippines in 1989, stop China's intimidation of Taiwan in 1995 and 1996, and help ensure maritime trade from the Persian Gulf to Asia, particularly in the 1980s when, during the Iran-Iraq War, both sides attacked merchant ships. It conducts large-scale military exercises in the region, such as Cobra Gold in Thailand, Valiant Shield in Guam, Foal Eagle in Korea, and the Malabar exercise in the Indian Ocean. As former Director of National Intelligence Dennis Blair has written, the U.S. military is so active in the region that it has become part of the region's geopolitical fabric.[4]

THE CHINA CHALLENGE: WHAT ARE CHINA AND THE UNITED STATES COMPETING OVER?

The character of China's rise presents Washington with a serious challenge. Although China has arguably benefitted the most from American predominance in Asia and the Pacific, it has not embraced all aspects of the international system. It finds parts of the American-led order threatening and repugnant and is gaining the strength to bend the rules more to its liking. Most alarming for regional stability are China's emerging ability to check America's attempts to project power into the region and its growing ability to project its own power around its periphery.

Because of its size, power, and dynamism, China's growing attempts to change the status quo—from unification with Taiwan to claims over resources and maritime rights in the South China Sea—make China a formidable rival. Its external objectives seem to include greater control over its periphery, which necessarily means the dilution of U.S. power, the unification of Taiwan, and perhaps, over time, the dominance of Asia. Should China achieve its goals, U.S. security and well-being would suffer. For the first time since 1941, the Western Pacific and the U.S. homeland could be threatened by an East Asian power.

The fundamental conflict between the two countries has its source in two very different visions for Asia's future and how to achieve national security. Washington continues to desire an Asia comprised of strong, independent, democratic, and free-market nations that are free from domination by any actor. Alternatively, China's primary interest is in making Asia, if not the world, safe for the continued rule of the Chinese Communist Party. It has apparently concluded that this primary strategic objective is best served by finishing its project of recovering territory lost in past wars, controlling its periphery, and slowly becoming the dominant actor in Asia—a position that for reasons of strategic culture it believes is natural.[5]

An Asia under hegemonic domination could devolve into economic or military spheres of influence from which the United States could be excluded. Or it could descend into a highly intense and destabilizing security competition—even nuclear competition—among the great powers. The latter case could well have destabilizing effects on the international economy as a whole and on the U.S. economy in particular. A nuclear arms race among Asia's powers, with shifting coalitions and varying attempts to balance China's power, could make Asia look worse than pre–World War I Europe.

Washington thus has a fundamental interest in both preventing a hegemonically dominated Asia and in fostering an Asia "whole and free," characterized by democratic nations trading among themselves and integrated into the international economy. Absent the emergence of a new benign power or coalition of powers able to underwrite Asia's security, Washington will have to continue playing the role of Asia's pacifier into the foreseeable future. To do so, the United States will need to find new and innovative ways to continue to deter conflict and coercion, reassure allies, and surge forces into the region in case of conflict.

SINO-AMERICAN CONFLICTS OF INTEREST

In the short term, the United States and China will have a fundamental conflict of interest as China seeks to deny the U.S. projection of power into many of Asia's critical regions where U.S. forces will need to continue operating. From Washington's perspective, China is trying to deny U.S. forces access to critical parts of the region. The Chinese have two interlocking concepts that seem to drive their strategic approach to the seas and territories on their periphery. First, the People's Liberation Army Navy (PLAN) wants to establish "control" over the waters extending 200 nautical miles out from Chinese shores to conduct what it calls "independent operations." These operations include the ability to attack Taiwan and secure and develop maritime resources in those waters. Second, China has been gradually moving to an "offshore defense strategy" meant to engage any potential enemy farther away from its thriving cities. This strategy includes not only the PLA's missile-centric approach[6] to both denial and coercive operations but also its so-called string of pearls strategy of developing relations along the Indian Ocean to lay the groundwork for greater control around important passageways into East Asia.

In the shorter term, the Sino-American competition will manifest itself in what Beijing calls the "three seas" (the Yellow, East China, and South China Seas) and areas where China wants to assert a measure of "control" (which for Washington means denial of military access). These geographic areas include the waters around Taiwan, where China is trying to establish freedom of action from outside pressure.

The second short-term conflict of interest is over the Korean peninsula, which has the potential to spark Sino-American conflict. Above all else, Beijing values stability along its border with Korea, and China will apparently act unilaterally to ensure that North Korea does not collapse.[7] Although North Korea is proving to be a liability for China, it appears ready to live with a nuclear Korea. In contrast, Washington and its allies value foremost a nuclear-free North Korea, and, over the longer term, a unified Korea under the governance of the Republic of Korea (ROK).

The third short-term conflict of interest is China's increasing desire to clear its periphery and exclusive economic zone (EEZ) of U.S. military activity and, related to that effort, its pursuit of expansive territorial claims in the South and East China Seas. Washington will continue to insist on its rights in the EEZs as well as stand behind its Japanese and Southeast Asian allies.

Given China's current military modernization trajectory and its stated desire to "contest" the "second island chain" (an area that includes the seas around the Philippines and much of Indonesia), it is prudent to expect that China will seek capabilities that both deny U.S. access to areas within the Western Pacific and pose a credible conventional threat to the U.S. homeland to deter U.S. intervention in a potential Chinese sphere of influence closer to China's shores. With the U.S. military relying more heavily on Guam as a base of operation, China's extended operational reach can pose serious problems for U.S power projection in the Pacific. China will also probably seek a measure of "control" in the Indian Ocean and around the Strait of Malacca. As its economic and commodities needs grow, China seeks a greater ability to control the air, sea, and land routes through which its trade passes.

In the near term, the military competition will be characterized by America's need to project power into the region to deter and defend against an attack on Taiwan, to respond to a North Korean collapse or attack on Japan or South Korea, and to keep the seas safe for shipping, peaceful exploration, and lawful military activity. In turn, China will try to deny U.S. power projection associated with these tasks as it advances its own security objectives. With its growing missile and submarine force, China will have the ability to project power of its own. It will want to project force to attack or coerce Taiwan, to respond to contingencies in Korea, and to back up its territorial claims at sea. Any one of these conflicting Sino-American interests can lead to a major regional war for which the U.S. military must prepare.

In the far term, the military competition will be characterized by growing Chinese efforts to control its periphery for longer periods, to threaten U.S. allies and press for diminished U.S. influence, and to project power to defend its increasingly far-flung investments. Washington will try to hold its position in the region, assure allies of its ability to defend them, and complicate China's ability to project power in ways that threaten U.S. interests.

ASSESSING A COMPLEX BALANCE: SOME METRICS

Given the geographic diversity and broad array of potential Sino-American situations that could bring the two countries into conflict, assessing the continued ability of the United States to project power in the region is a multifaceted and complex task. For analytical purposes it is useful to break the problem down to three broad questions: First, how effectively are U.S. forces postured to maintain the ability to operate freely in the Western Pacific and project power into the South China Sea, the Taiwan Strait, the Sea of Japan, the Yellow Sea, the East China Sea, and the key maritime choke points such as the straits of Lombok and Malacca? What are the trends? Absent the ability to project power into these regions it will be nearly impossible for Washington to meet its defense commitments to its allies or partners. The U.S. military must be able to project an enormous amount of power into the region to deter and defend Taiwan, deter and respond to a North Korea crisis, and keep open the global commons. It must do so in the face of a concerted Chinese effort to defeat the "American way of power projection in the Pacific."[8]

China has been studying how to defeat the "American way" for several decades and is building an integrated air defense system, submarine and surface fleet, and missile forces, all knitted together with a command, control, computers, communications, intelligence, surveillance, and reconnaissance (C4ISR) network that that can create kill zones for American surface ships and fixed air bases around China's periphery.

Second, over the longer term, how will the U.S. military be postured to defeat possible Chinese attempts to lock the United States out of East Asia? China can only accomplish a "lockout" or exert a semblance of control over

Asia if it projects power more deeply into the Pacific Ocean, threatens the U.S. homeland, and exerts pressure on Japan and South Korea to prohibit the presence of American forces on their homeland. To accomplish this, China would have to establish air supremacy and sea control around America's main allies.

Third, over the long term, how effectively will the United States be able to use the Indian Ocean to project power into continental Asia? In the coming decades, the Indian Ocean promises to be an area of intense Sino-American (and Sino-Indian) competition. The United States now takes for granted its ability to project power from places such as Diego Garcia and into continental Asia. It has also gone largely unchallenged in ensuring the freedom of navigation for merchant shipping from the Persian Gulf to Asia (and elsewhere). If China wants to keep the U.S. from projecting its power on the Asian continent, China may seek capabilities to, at a minimum, raise the costs to Washington of operating in the Indian Ocean.

Although the military competition in the near future will be mostly between the U.S. ability to project power over long distances and China's ability to deny U.S. military power projection, over the medium to long term, China will itself look to project more power beyond its immediate periphery.

The competition over continued U.S. power projection will span the geographic subregions and contingencies described in the preceding paragraphs. However, given space constraints, this chapter will limit the discussion to two of the most pressing scenarios: a major war with China over Taiwan and the competition for the South China Sea. The scenarios are meant to describe in more detail the main characteristics of the competition—continued U.S. capabilities to project substantial amounts of force at long distances against Chinese attempts to frustrate U.S. objectives while advancing their own goals in the first island chain.

Deterring and Defending against a Chinese Attack on Taiwan: Power Projection versus Short-Distance Denial and Control

Regarding Taiwan, China would appear to have the edge in seriousness of purpose and will power. China is clear about its goals—it wants to unify Taiwan with the mainland. The United States is more ambiguous. American policy statements go no farther than committing Washington to the peaceful resolution of differences between China and Taiwan.[9] It would seem that China has more at stake, which would affect its willingness to go to war over the issue as well as the capabilities it may bring to bear in a war.

But as Sino-American competition over the future of Asia intensifies, Taipei could take on greater geopolitical meaning for the United States. For example, as China continues to modernize its military and make assertive claims in the East, Yellow, and South China seas, and Beijing pressures countries with competing claims in those seas, Taiwan could be seen by the allies and the United States as the proverbial "canary in the coal mine": If China uses force to unify 23 million of its "compatriots," many Asians will believe that Beijing would use force to settle other disputes.

Given China's growing power and assertiveness, an attack on Taiwan could be seen as an attempt to alter the balance of power in Asia for four reasons. First, despite Washington's attempts at "strategic ambiguity" with respect to Taiwan, China and regional allies already view Taiwan as an American ally and the Taiwan Relations Act as something close to a defense commitment. Should Beijing use force to successfully unify Taiwan, Chinese confidence will increase, while allies may see China's domination as irreversible. Second, key allies such as Japan may see the prospect of a China controlling Taiwan as a serious threat to Japanese well-being. China could militarize Taiwan, bringing tremendous pressure to bear on Tokyo's sea-lanes of communications and on the Ryuku island chain. Third, China could utilize Taiwan to control the South China Sea more effectively. Finally, the Chinese concept of operations regarding Taiwan may by itself force the United States into a war.

Since the mid-1990s, when the United States sent carriers to the waters near Taiwan to stop China's missile intimidation of Taiwan, Beijing has poured money into developing capabilities to coerce Taiwan into unification. Its key instrument of coercion is its missile force, the Second Artillery Corps, which is equipped with over 1,000 ballistic and cruise missiles.[10] The force has enhanced its accuracy, lethality, and precision. As its inventory of missiles grows, it could launch a massive wave of attacks against Taiwan targets that would have both political and military consequences. It could hit key critical infrastructure in an effort to harm Taiwan's economy or could conduct strikes that in effect eliminate Taiwan's ability to defend its airspace. China would thus leave Taiwan vulnerable to a range of follow-on actions intended to coerce or invade the island.

Although China could try to confine an attack to Taiwan, it could also seek to strike devastating blows against the United States and Japan to keep these countries from coming to Taipei's assistance. Indeed, China may conduct air and missile strikes on the Kadena and Iwakuni air bases in Japan, despite the geopolitical risks of striking Japanese territory.[11]

If China decides it needs to engage American forces to win in Taiwan, the PLA would execute a sea denial strategy that threatens American aircraft carriers. China can use land-based airpower equipped with air-launched cruise missiles, attack submarines, and land-based ballistic missiles with maneuverable warheads against ships at sea. The PLA is developing an intelligence, surveillance, and reconnaissance (ISR) capability to target U.S. Navy surface forces at sea. The PLA could make use of air-launched cruise missiles to attack those forces. The PLAN will probably use its submarine force, armed with antiship cruise missiles and torpedoes, to attack U.S. surface strike groups operating within tactical aircraft range of mainland China.[12]

In conjunction with an air and missile campaign, China's undersea force could blockade Taiwan. If China cannot fully quarantine Taiwan, it can execute a "leaky" blockade that threatens commercial shipping in and out of Taiwan. Its conventional submarine force and sophisticated mining capabilities could effectively shut off maritime trade to Taiwan.

China's arsenal of ballistic and cruise missiles, fourth-generation fighters, submarines, mines, and integrated air defense system represent a major shift in the balance of power between the United States, Japan, and Taiwan on one side and China on the other. Compared to 1996, when the U.S. deployment of a carrier battle group near the Taiwan Strait quieted Chinese attempts at missile diplomacy, the amount of U.S. force that would be needed to defend its own assets and defeat Chinese coercion is now far more substantial.

Given China's air and missile capabilities, the United States can no longer just play defense because there are almost no good purely "defensive" options to end an air and missile barrage against Taiwan. This development has troubling escalatory consequences. The U.S. Air Force and Navy would probably have to "shoot the archer" rather than the arrow to stop or thin out a missile barrage. This means hitting a substantial number of targets on the Chinese mainland, particularly the enablers of PRC missile launchers (storage facilities, command and control nodes, ISR, industrial facilities, and airbases). These operations would have to be carried out against a nuclear power, which would make any U.S. president hesitant to carry them out.

To execute an operation against Taiwan successfully, China may have to inflict considerable damage on the United States and Japan. After withstanding an initial strike, U.S. and allied forces would have to project power from great distances (Oceania, Guam, Northwestern Japan, carriers out of range of Chinese missiles) to suppress the Chinese integrated air defense systems (IADS) and target the PLA's missile and air force systems. In short, an effective U.S. response—even just reestablishing air supremacy to protect Taiwan from a blockade or from follow-on forces—may now be impossible without hitting many targets on the mainland.

The United States cannot assume a high Chinese nuclear threshold if it strikes the mainland. Nor should China assume that the United States would suffer great losses at sea, an attack on Japan, or an attack on Guam without contemplating a nuclear response. Although mutual fears of escalation should in theory add a measure of stability to a potential conflict, in this case the potential for miscalculation is high.

Another cause for concern is the current shortfall in the capabilities that the United States would need to defeat a Chinese attack. These include submarines, maritime patrol aircraft, long-range penetrating bombers, aerial tankers, ballistic missile defenses, survivable satellites, autonomous unmanned systems, and escort ships.[13] If China continues to gain the conventional advantage, the United States will have very unattractive and escalatory response options.

In a scenario such as the one described here, in which China quickly gains the conventional "first strike" advantage, limiting the scope of a war as well as bringing it to a satisfactory conclusion will become more difficult. Although a U.S. president may seek to return the situation to a status quo ante bellum— a de facto independence of Taiwan—it may be difficult to do so as the war drags on. If the United States and Japan are subject to heavy losses, they are both likely to expand their war aims to something beyond a restoration of the status quo. Japan and the United States may be unsatisfied leaving China's capabilities in place. They may seek a punitive approach, such as a blockade of Chinese merchant ships to harm the Chinese economy. Or they may seek a destruction or degradation of the Chinese capabilities that were used to launch the war in the first place. Both approaches make escalation control difficult.

A Chinese military strategy that strikes hard against Japanese and U.S. forces and assets may miscalculate allied responses. The United States could come to view the war as one campaign in a long struggle over the future of Asia. If so, the United States will need to engage in a protracted conflict that seeks to inflict pain on Beijing on many fronts. Not only may it fight its way back into the "first island chain," but it may use its new relationship with India, for example, or countries in Central Asia, to threaten mainland targets in China's West or Chinese assets in Central Asia or to hold captive Chinese maritime traffic in the Indian Ocean.

It is here that the United States has its greatest potential advantage in sustaining power projection: its system of allies and partners. All share with the

United States a concern that China is growing too dominant and starting to act more aggressively. Depending on how the casus belli is perceived, a Chinese attack on Taiwan and on Japanese and American forces could exacerbate these fears of China. In many imaginable circumstances, Washington could probably secure some form of assistance from all of its allies in the region who would want China to be weakened and put in its place. That development could, over time, make up for initial losses the United States sustains or initial difficulties the United States has in projecting enough force into the Taiwan Strait.

Although there are many reasons to continue a policy of ambiguity with respect to conflict over Taiwan, the policy undermines deterrence. Deterrence is better served by making clear to China that an attack on Taiwan is not an "internal" matter but a move that would be viewed in Washington as a Chinese attempt to change the balance of power in ways highly detrimental to Washington's most vital interests in Asia. For deterrence purposes, the United States must demonstrate that a short decisive blow against Taiwan would not be the end of the conflict.

In sum, the balance of power between China's "control" capabilities in the first island chain and denial capabilities in the second island chain, and America's ability to project enough power into the Taiwan Strait to defeat Chinese objectives, has shifted markedly, and in a manner that calls into question strategic stability. China can execute a short-notice devastating blow to U.S. forces in Japan and to targets on Taiwan. It can exact a high price of entry for U.S. carriers and other surface ships seeking to enter the conflict, execute a painful blockade against Taiwan, and protect its strike assets behind a sophisticated air defense system. China may calculate that these capabilities will keep the United States from coming to Taiwan's defense. But it is also possible that Washington will view a Chinese attack on Taiwan against the backdrop of increased Chinese assertiveness and a perception that China is moving to dominate the Asia Pacific. In this case, the United States has many advantages it can use to continue to project power—most importantly its web of allies and partners who share its concerns about an aggressive and dominant China. But the challenge will be twofold—projecting power under new circumstances and doing so in a manner that does not provoke a nuclear response.

Power Projection, Anti-Access, and Far Sea Defense

Taiwan is not the extent of Chinese interest in far sea and offshore defense and area denial; Chinese military leaders have begun to take seriously the requirements of defending Beijing's claim to the South China Sea.

The area within the South China Sea claimed by China extends up to 1,800 nautical miles from China's shores and is the key passageway from the Pacific Ocean to the sea-lanes, straits, and choke points that lead into the Indian Ocean. Moreover, the sea is home to abundant natural resources to which almost all Southeast Asian nations lay claim. China claims that U.S. military activities within the sea are unlawful, an assertion that is counter to customary international law. The United States and its allies have a vital interest in freedom of navigation and the conduct of lawful military activity in the seas.

Beijing makes these claims for two main reasons. First, it does not want the U.S. military operating close to its shores. This has intensified since it began to turn Hainan Island in the South China Sea into a major Chinese nuclear submarine base—one that will perhaps house part of China's undersea nuclear force. Second, control over the South China Sea would provide China with some insurance regarding its seaborne trade—it could at least retaliate against U.S. shipping if U.S. forces blockaded Chinese shipping further afield.

China's 2004 Defense White Paper first highlighted China's desire to extend its military reach.[14] The White Paper, together with China's developing capabilities and territorial claims, opens an important window into Beijing's approach to the South China Sea. Although China does not yet have the capability to control those seas in the way Americans would understand it, the PLA can exact a price on others who enter the waters through a coercive campaign prosecuted mostly by missile, air, and undersea forces and some small surface vessels. It is also likely that within the next few decades China will begin to develop regional power projection capabilities akin to those of the American military.

As discussed in the previous section, China is developing a suite of capabilities that can target U.S. ships and bases within the first island chain, which includes much of the South China Sea. But the PLA lacks a sustained power projection capability associated with asserting full control over the area, including sufficient at-sea replenishment and aerial refueling capabilities, modern destroyers with advanced air defense capabilities, and nuclear submarines, as well as regional bases to support logistical requirements.[15]

Finally, if Beijing plans to project and sustain power at greater distances, it will need some form of sea-based air power as well as the escort ships and antisubmarine warfare capabilities that go along with them. Chinese strategists certainly write about the need to acquire these capabilities, but it is unclear how far along China is in obtaining them.[16]

Consistent with China's near-term approach to the South China Sea, countries such as Vietnam and Indonesia have seen an upswing in Chinese vessels operating closer to their shores.[17] China has also recently exercised in the region: "A large group of submarines and warships from the People's Liberation Army Navy fired guided missiles and tested anti-missile air defense systems; Navy aircraft also conducted air control operations."[18]

If Washington is to carry out a more forceful diplomacy designed to frustrate China's claims, it will need to project and sustain power into the sea for a variety of missions. These include antisubmarine warfare patrols; "freedom of navigation" and "open access" exercises that would include the escort of commercial and military vessels by Aegis destroyers and a more frequent destroyer and tactical aircraft presence in the seas to chase Chinese vessels out of other countries' EEZs. In turn, the PLA will probably increase its missile forces in areas of China from which it can target forces in and around the South China Sea. Similarly, the PLAN is likely to increase its submarine patrols in the sea and to have its submarines more aggressively shadow U.S. vessels. China may also test its new DF-21D antiship ballistic missile near these waters.

To advance its own interests in open access to the South China Sea, Washington can create institutions that strengthen defense and deterrence, taking advantage of some distinct advantages in this competition. First, China's ability to do more than harass, intimidate, or coerce for short periods of time is quite limited. Second, Washington is supporting the approach of its Southeast Asian allies to resolving the sea's disputes, while China is acting alone. Third, many of Washington's security partners are beefing up their own military capabilities.

The latter may be the most consequential for Washington. It means that Washington can find ways to diversify its basing access over time and project power by helping its allies build their own capabilities. Singapore and Australia in particular have advanced capabilities well suited for "open access" missions in the South China Sea. With its fleet of advanced fighter aircraft complemented by advanced C4ISR, targeting, precision guided munitions, Airborne Early Warning capabilities, and refueling tankers, Singapore has one of the most advanced air forces in Asia. It is set to acquire the stealthy F-35s as well, which will enhance its ability to operate against advanced air defenses. Australia, already well equipped to conduct maritime surveillance and strike missions, is beefing up its forces by doubling its purchase of conventional submarines and by acquiring 100 F-35s. Both countries are models of how smaller regional partners can acquire capabilities to conduct maritime surveillance and strike missions to protect sea-lanes and shipping.

The concern of key U.S. partners about China in the South China Sea, and their willingness to modernize their militaries, make it a propitious time for the United States to institutionalize more defense cooperation, particularly in and around the South China Sea. For example, the United States can help equip its allies and partners with unmanned aerial vehicles for persistent surveillance and perhaps even create a new coalition-wide ISR architecture that knits together growing allied and partner capabilities.[19]

In the near to medium term, the military competition over the South China Sea will be characterized by Beijing's coercive conventional strike and undersea capabilities that attempt to bully Southeast Asian states to accept its claims. The United States will need to project power into the seas to conduct "freedom of navigation" missions and protect Southeast Asian allies from Chinese intimidation. The key U.S. advantage is a set of allies capable of helping Washington project power. Countries such as Japan, Australia, and Singapore will all have stealthy precision-guided maritime strike capabilities as well as fairly robust ASW forces. Washington can begin now to institutionalize greater regional cooperation to keep the seas safe from China's expansive claims. In the longer term, China will likely develop some real sea control capabilities, in which case the United States and its allies will have to move to strategies that belt China in closer to its shores and impose costs on power projection forces.

CONCLUSION

Although China's military capabilities and objectives against Taiwan and the South China Sea differ in priority, intensity, and escalatory potential, both are illustrative of the growing Sino-American military competition. In both cases, the United States will need to project a substantial amount of power in new and innovative ways to defeat Chinese attempts at coercion. Washington will do so as China both attempts to exact a very high price on U.S. forces converging on the region and tries to execute its own coercion campaigns. Both cases illustrate the fundamental conflict of political interests that drive the military competition. In the case of Taiwan, China wants unification, while the United States wants maintenance of the status quo (a de facto independent democratic Taiwan). In the case of the South China Sea, China wants to assert control over the entire body of water, while Washington wants to access the seas for commerce and military activity and keep it open to others.

China's apparent desire to exert military control over significant parts of Asia portends greater regional resistance and less regional stability. Although

China has, over the past decade, attempted to offset American military supremacy, the balance is still—for now—in America's favor. Washington's key advantage is that most of the region shares a vision of Asia free of Chinese hegemony. To sustain a preponderance of power in its favor, Washington must sustain its power projection advantages. To do so, it will have to fashion more innovative alliance strategies that take advantage of both their growing capabilities and their wariness of China.

NOTES

1. The Chinese define the chain as formed by the Aleutians, the Kuriles, Japan's archipelago, the Ryukyus, Taiwan, the Philippines, and Borneo. It roughly conforms to what the United States used to call its "forward defense perimeter."

2. See Barry Posen, "Command of the Commons: The Military Foundation of U.S. Hegemony," *International Security* 28 (Summer 2003). 5–46.

3. Since the end of the Cold War, U.S leaders make it a practice to acknowledge the region's growing importance. For example, speaking at the 2008 Shangri-La Dialogue, Secretary of Defense Robert Gates welcomed Asia's rise, saying that "Asia has become the center of gravity in a rapidly globalizing world." Secretary of Defense Robert M. Gates, "Shangri-La Dialogue" (speech, International Institute for Strategic Studies, Singapore, May 31, 2008); available at www.defense.gov/speeches/speech .aspx?speechid=1253.

4. Dennis C. Blair, "Military Power Projection in Asia," in *Strategic Asia 2008: Challenges and Choices,* Ashley J. Tellis, Mercy Kuo and Andrew Marble, eds. (Washington, DC: National Bureau of Asian Research, 2008), 365.

5. Christopher Ford, *The Mind of Empire: China's History and Modern Foreign Relations* (Lexington: University Press of Kentucky, 2010). On China's view that it is an intense competition for regional hegemony or at least a competition to fend off American hegemony, see Jacqueline Newmyer, "Oil Arms and Influence: The Indirect Strategy behind China's Military Modernization," *Orbis* 53 (Spring 2009), 205–219.

6. This approach is probably best documented in Mark Stokes and Ian Easton, "Evolving Aerospace Trends in the Asia-Pacific Region: Implications for Stability in the Taiwan Strait and Beyond," The Project 2049 Institute, May 27, 2010.

7. See Bonnie Glaser, Scott Snyder, and John S. Park, "Keeping an Eye on an Unruly Neighbor: Chinese Views of Economic Reform and Stability in North Korea," United States Institute of Peace Working Paper, January 3, 2008.

8. Borrowed from Jan Van Tol, *Air Sea Battle: A Point-of-Departure Operational Concept* (Washington, DC: Center for Strategic and Budgetary Assessments, 2010).

9. "First United States-PRC Joint Communiqué," February 28, 1972, Taiwan Documents Project; retrieved on November 12, 2010, from www.taiwandocuments.org/

doc_com.htm; "Second United States-PRC Joint Communiqué," January 1, 1979, Taiwan Documents Project; retrieved on November 12, 2010, from www.taiwandocuments .org/doc_com.htm; "Third United States-PRC Joint Communiqué," August 17, 1982; retrieved on November 12, 2010, from www.taiwandocuments.org/doc_com.htm; *Taiwan Relations Act,* HR 2479, 96th Congress, 1st session.

10. U.S. Department of Defense, *Annual Report to Congress: Military and Security Developments Involving the People's Republic of China 2010* (Washington, DC: Office of the Secretary of Defense, 2010).

11. David A. Shlapak, David T. Orletsky, and Barry A. Wilson, *A Question of Balance: Political Context and Military Aspects of the China-Taiwan Dispute* (Santa Monica, CA: RAND, 2009); available at www.rand.org/pubs/monographs/2009/ RAND_MG888.pdf.

12. Michael McDevitt, "Coping with the Dragon: Essays on PLA Transformation and the U.S. Military," (Washington, DC: The Center for Technology and National Security at the National Defense University, December 2007).

13. Andrew Krepinevich, *Why Air Sea Battle?* (Washington, DC: Center for Strategic and Budgetary Assessments, 2010).

14. Information Office of the State Council of the People's Republic of China, *China's National Defense in 2008* (Beijing: State Council, 2009).

15. Mark Cozad, *China's Regional Power Projection: Prospects for Future Missions in the South and East China Seas* (Carlisle, PA: Strategic Studies Institute of the U.S. Army War College [SSI], 2009), 313–314.

16. See Tao Shelan, "PLA Admiral States Need for Offensive as Well as Defense Capabilities," *Zhongguo XinwenShe,* in OSC CPP200701097008003, January 9, 2007; ZhouYawen, Li Gencheng, and Tang Zhongping, "South Sea Fleet Base Enhances Ship-Borne Weaponry Support Capabilities," Beijing, China, *Jiefangjun Bao,* in OSC cpp 20080325710013, March 25, 2008; and Ju Hailong, "Can the South China Sea Issue Be Resolved Peacefully?" Beijing, China, *Shijie Zhishi,* in OSC CPP20070223329001, February 1, 2007.

17. John Pomfret, "Concerned about China's Rise, Southeast Asian Nations Build Up Militaries," *Washington Post,* August 9, 2010; available at www.washingtonpost .com/wp-dyn/content/article/2010/08/08/AR2010080802631.html.

18. See "China Conducts Naval Drill in South China Sea: Media, " *Bangkok Post,* July 30, 2010; available at www.bangkokpost.com/news/asia/188674/china-conducts-naval-drill-in-south-china-sea-media.

19. I credit Tom Mahnken with this idea.

11 ASSESSING THE UNDERSEA BALANCE BETWEEN THE UNITED STATES AND CHINA

Owen R. Coté Jr.

THIS CHAPTER WILL ASSESS the undersea balance between the United States and China by comparing their relative abilities to accomplish their respective undersea warfare objectives. This chapter will assess both the current balance and how it might evolve in the future. In the latter case, it will focus on opportunities each side will have to adopt competitive strategies, or strategies designed to exploit its unique strengths or its opponent's weaknesses in ways that create favorable asymmetries in the resources that must be committed to accomplish particular missions.

DEFINING THE UNDERSEA BALANCE

Naval warfare is at bottom a contest over who will be able to use the seas, how, where, and when. The 20th century saw submarines, aircraft, and earth-orbiting satellites add a vertical dimension to naval warfare. In addition to revolutionizing naval warfare, the introduction of the vertical dimension has also wreaked havoc with analytical efforts that would seek to break apart naval warfare into discrete, self-contained mission areas or mediums of operation. Surface, undersea, air, and space-based platforms have a role to play in almost all naval missions, and each operating medium has elements of all naval missions unfolding within it.[1]

Today, China plans on using its diesel attack submarines (SS) for coastal defense, offensive mine warfare against potential regional adversaries, and likely as a local source of communication and electronic, and perhaps acoustic, intelligence. China has a small nuclear attack (SSN) and ballistic missile (SSBN) submarine force and may seek to increase the size and capability of both forces in the near future. China also appears to be preparing to use its attack submarines to deny or limit the access of Western navies to the larger sea space between what they call the first and second island chains or, roughly speaking, the Philippine Sea.

At the same time, China has very limited ASW capabilities and appears not to be making major investments to improve them. Its ASW capabilities appear focused on coastal defense and on the threat posed by the diesel submarines of potential regional adversaries, as opposed to American SSNs.

The U.S. Navy plans on using its SSNs for intelligence collection and ASW. SSNs and a force of four converted SSBNs equipped with cruise missiles (SSGN) would be used for land attack and in support of special operations. The United States also has a robust force of SSBNs for nuclear deterrence. Although U.S. SSNs possess arguably the most potent antisurface capabilities of any naval platform, historically this has not been their primary mission.

In setting up an assessment of these opposing undersea objectives and capabilities, it is possible to make some summary judgments at the outset. First, there is little reason to discuss U.S. SSBNs because there is no reason to assume that China will ever be able to develop a strategic ASW capability against them. Second, for reasons that will be discussed in the following pages, current Chinese abilities to deny access to U.S. SSNs and SSGNs are very limited. Consequently, U.S. submarines can currently operate freely in Chinese coastal waters. Third, in contrast to current declaratory policies, Chinese diesel submarines rarely deploy outside the first island chain and essentially never deploy beyond the second, nor would these submarines be well suited for extended deployments into the Pacific or Indian oceans because of range and crew habitability constraints. Fourth, current American ASW capabilities are substantially less in Chinese coastal waters than elsewhere for two relatively intractable reasons: The Chinese can deny or greatly limit the access of opposing surface and airborne ASW platforms near their coast, and very shallow water can greatly limit the effectiveness of U.S. ASW sensors. Fifth, because neither side will have a robust ASW capability in Chinese coastal waters, those waters will constitute a zone of "contested command" in which neither side can assure its use of the sea surface for either commercial or military purposes.[2]

Beyond these judgments, there is much uncertainty about the undersea balance. In the near term, there are two major questions concerning Chinese undersea warfare capabilities. First, could they use their attack submarines to attack Taiwanese shipping and/or mine the approaches to Taiwanese ports on a scale sufficient to support a successful coercion campaign?[3] Second, could Chinese submarines deploy eastward through the barrier represented by the first island chain and successfully find and attack U.S. Carrier Battle Groups (CVBGs) operating in the Philippine Sea?

In the longer term, assuming further modernization of the Chinese submarine force, there appear two important questions regarding Chinese undersea warfare objectives and capabilities. First, might they choose to develop a larger SSBN force, and if so, how will they seek to ensure its survivability? Second, might they choose to develop a more global submarine operating posture, presumably using larger, more capable diesel submarines or, more ambitiously, nuclear submarines? Two specific objectives might be associated with more advanced submarines: the desire to break a distant blockade of Chinese shipping by U.S surface combatants operating in the Indian Ocean and the desire to acquire a precision land attack capability using conventional cruise or ballistic missiles.

There is also uncertainty regarding U.S. undersea warfare objectives and capabilities. Though there is little doubt that the United States will retain its ability to use submarines as intelligence collectors and precision land attack platforms essentially anywhere it chooses, and against opposing naval surface combatants if necessary, the submarine's role as an ASW platform against very quiet targets is more uncertain. In the more distant term, there is also the question of additional missions for U.S. submarines, to include land attack against mobile targets and missile defense. Finally, there are questions about the ASW capabilities of U.S. surface combatants, particularly the Littoral Combat Ship (LCS).

ASSESSING THE UNDERSEA BALANCE

China's submarines face two distinguishable operating environments.[4] The first is the shallow water littoral along its coast, comprising the Yellow, East China, and northern South China Seas. This operating environment is characterized by bad acoustic conditions and air space that China would contest if not control during a conflict. The second can be defined as the deep water of the Philippine Sea between the first and second island chains and in the southern part of the South China Sea. This operating environment is characterized by excellent acoustic conditions and mostly lies beyond China's ability to contest air space.[5] Taiwan pulls the first island chain in closer to China, making the Taiwan Straits the narrowest portion of China's shallow water littoral seas and giving China the ability to contest Taiwanese air space. The three main exits from the first to the second operating environment lie through the Ryukus northeast of Taiwan, through the Luzon Strait southeast of Taiwan, and southward into the deep South China Sea basin between Vietnam and the Philippines.

China's first undersea warfare objective would be to defend its coastline from opposing naval combatants and, if necessary, to interdict the commercial shipping of an opponent. In the latter case, analysts have focused specifically on a coercive, submarine-based, mine warfare campaign against Taiwan. Most if not all of such a campaign could unfold within the first operating environment.

The second undersea warfare objective would be to deter or prevent U.S. naval intervention in any conflict between China and one of its immediate neighbors, Taiwan again being the most likely contingency. In operational terms, this would in principle have both an ASW and an antisurface component. The ASW component would occur in the first operating environment, where the opponent would be American SSNs and SSGNs. The antisurface component would occur in the second operating environment, and the primary opponent would be American carrier battle groups.

The First Undersea Warfare Objective

As discussed in the previous paragraphs, China has very limited ASW capabilities, and U.S. submarines are the most difficult ASW target in the world. Thus, China would have difficulty preventing U.S. submarines from operating in its shallow coastal waters. At the same time, those waters also can significantly reduce the ASW detection ranges of U.S. submarines, the only U.S. ASW asset that could safely operate in them under many circumstances. In such cases, the approaches to Chinese submarine bases and Taiwanese ports would become the focal points where American submarines could deploy to maximize their detection opportunities against Chinese submarines.

At the same time, American SSNs would face the danger of counterdetection by the best Chinese diesel submarines if they use traditional approach-and-attack tactics that use organic sensors and torpedoes. This is already driving the American submarine force to some combination of deployable, autonomous, distributed sensor (DADS) arrays using both acoustic and non-acoustic detection methods for initial detection, and unmanned underwater vehicles (UUVs) for trailing and perhaps attacking very quiet diesels once they are located. In addition, smart mines deployed near opposing bases may play a larger role than in the past. These efforts are a sign that the American submarine force is acting to maintain its traditional tactical dominance over opposing submarines in submarine versus submarine ASW operations. If these programs are successful, the exchange rate in such operations would continue to favor the United States.

The possible purpose and course of a coercive mine warfare campaign by China against Taiwan has been much studied and debated.[6] The undersea balance would obviously play a role in its outcome, but in many cases political factors would actually be decisive. The ideal scenario from a Chinese perspective would be one in which a modest amount of pain proves sufficient to cause a domestic political collapse in Taiwan, which presumably would lead to a relatively quick negotiated solution to whatever Taiwanese "provocation" or "threat to the status quo" caused the conflict in the first place. One might call this the "weak Taiwan" scenario, in which Taiwanese domestic political conflicts over its relations with China are severe enough that it would lack the cohesion and political will to stand up to even a modest amount of punishment. In the weak Taiwan scenario, it becomes difficult to imagine an undersea balance between China and the United States that would allow the latter to prevent China from coercing Taiwan.

In a "strong Taiwan" scenario, one in which Taiwan proves as resistant to coercion as most states historically have been, a larger, more protracted coercion campaign would be required because China would need to do severe economic damage to Taiwan to achieve a favorable political outcome. If the United States came to Taiwan's assistance, American SSNs could cause significant attrition as Chinese submarines exited and returned to port. Even if initial Chinese submarine deployments occurred before a conflict started, and even assuming that direct attacks against Chinese submarines in port were avoided, submarines returning to port from mining or antishipping missions would be vulnerable to attack by U.S. submarines, submarine-launched UUVs, and/or submarine-deployed mines. Given very limited Chinese ASW capabilities, American SSNs would likely suffer significantly less attrition than Chinese submarines in such operations. Given a projected force of about sixty Chinese nonballistic missile submarines, and given other important roles these submarines play in Chinese naval strategy, it is entirely possible that over the course of a several-month conflict, Taiwan's resistance to economic pain would be greater than China's willingness to lose submarines.

Countering U.S. Carrier Battle Groups

This leads to the second main Chinese undersea warfare objective, which is to prevent the successful operation of U.S. carrier battle groups in the second operating environment. Chinese undersea warfare capabilities in this mission area will primarily depend on whether their submarines can exit the first operating area covertly and whether their ocean surveillance systems can provide accurate cues to the location of American battle groups in the second operating area. To further complicate matters, the answers to these questions will vary depending on which Chinese submarines are being discussed, how long the conflict lasts, the degree to which direct attacks from and against the Chinese mainland occur, and American willingness to incur losses.

The following assessment will focus on a "reasonable" worst-case scenario. Out of a total fleet of sixty nonballistic missile submarines, the Chinese will have fifty SS/SSGs and ten SSNs equal in capability to the best of each type in the current force; the conflict will last several months, as in the strong Taiwan scenario; attacks launched directly from and against the Chinese homeland will occur; and American stakes in the conflict will be such that they will be willing to incur the loss of major combatants as long as they retain the initiative as to the rate of such losses.

The assumption that the Chinese will have ten SSNs equivalent to today's *Shang* class, of which there are two today, is conservative because the *Shangs* have not been deployed at the rate that was earlier expected. At the same time, I assume, as ONI has described, that the *Shangs* are similar to or equivalent to the Soviet *Victor III*. Though a great improvement over its predecessors, the *Victor III* was still vulnerable to long-range, passive acoustic detection, both by ocean surveillance systems like the Sound Surveillance System (SOSUS), the Surveillance Towed Array Sensor System (SURTASS), and the Fixed Distributed System (FDS), and by ships and submarines equipped with advanced towed arrays.[7] In this case, *Shangs* could not pass into the second operating area undetected, could be tracked at long range by modern passive acoustic surveillance systems, and would be at a tactical disadvantage with ASW prosecution platforms like the *Virginia* SSN and the P-8 patrol aircraft.

Given this assumption, the worst case for American ASW efforts in the second operating area is actually a force of *Kilos* or *Yuans* that have transited from the first to the second operating area without detection and that have available to them an enduring and secure source of broad-area cuing against

American battle groups operating in the second area. More reasonable would be a case where the United States can assure a fleeting detection of Chinese SS/SSGs leaving the first operating area but cannot track them once in the open ocean of the second and where it can deny them cuing against its battle groups only if it is allowed to attack the sources of such cuing.

American Acoustic Barriers   Geography and technology favor U.S. efforts to form effective acoustic sensor barriers through which Chinese SS/SSGs must pass in transiting from the first to the second operating environment. The maritime geography is at least as favorable as that which the United States successfully exploited during the Cold War. The widest exit from China's shallow inner seas, between Vietnam and the Philippines, is little or no wider than the Iceland-UK gap. The next largest exit, the Luzon Strait, is half that size, and all the other exits are significantly narrower. In all cases, the land adjoining these exits is in friendly hands and could be used as the shore terminus for cable-based undersea surveillance arrays, and the waters in question are far enough from the Chinese mainland that maritime patrol aircraft deploying more temporary, buoy-based arrays could also operate safely. Details about the performance of current U.S. passive and active acoustic barriers are classified, but the nature of several such systems is known, and deductions regarding their potential performance can be made. The most challenging case for acoustic detection is a diesel boat without any stable low-frequency tonals and a reduced broadband signature, under tactical and operational circumstances where it need not exceed patrol or transit speeds of five to ten knots. It is likely that deep-water arrays like the FDS of the late Cold War would be effective against such a target. FDS was effective against *Akula,* the first truly quiet Soviet nuclear submarine. But this would require shore stations in countries like Vietnam and the Philippines.

The U.S. Navy has sought to replicate the performance of FDS without dependence on either seabed cables or shore processing stations, using aircraft or ships to deploy more temporary sensor arrays in a crisis. The RAP vertical line array (RAP VLA) program, now in development, aims to create such an array. The Navy is also developing buoys using a combination of acoustic and radio-frequency (RF) communications to uplink RAP VLA data to distant shore processing stations. Another temporary, rapidly deployable, deep-water array development program is the Deep Water Active Detection System (DWADS), which uses both active and passive floating buoys to detect quiet submarines.

Such an active system would trade the endurance and covertness of a passive system for better localization and less dependence on acoustic conditions.[8]

Programs like RAP VLA and DWADS show great promise as a means of assuring a fleeting detection of quiet Chinese submarines as they exit the first operating environment. But a fleeting detection opportunity is not an ocean-wide surveillance capability like SOSUS provided during the Cold War. Simply establishing an acoustic trip wire around the first operating environment will not recreate this scenario. Chinese submarines that cross the trip wire during peacetime or in a crisis will not be attacked and, once past the barrier, will blend back into the background noise of the vast Western Pacific basin. The U.S. Navy must prepare to deal with a scenario in which Chinese SS/SSGs are already deployed outside of the first operating environment when a conflict begins.

One approach would be to accept that some number of Chinese submarines would initially sortie out into the Philippine Sea and be lost to any surveillance capability. This would mean that U.S. battle groups operating in that area would have to use speed, radar flooding, their ASW escorts, and a myriad of tactical deception techniques to deny targeting solutions to submarines whose positions were unknown. At its core, this situation is analogous to that the British faced around the Falklands. The British never knew where the sole Argentine submarine they faced was located, so they constantly had to exercise essentially defensive measures that they hoped would be sufficient to frustrate the opposing submarine's effort to obtain a fire control solution.

Chinese Ocean Surveillance Submarines, and particularly diesel submarines, benefit greatly from cuing that allows them to get into position for attacks without extended high-speed runs. Cuing also enables concentration, whereby several or more submarines are able to attack simultaneously. Cuing is even more advantageous, if not necessary, for submarines launching anti-ship cruise missiles (ASCMs). Such cues are generated by surveillance systems, systems that stare at or repeatedly revisit an ocean area with sensors that are able to detect ships, identify them, and locate them with the precision and timeliness needed for them to be attacked. In many cases, different systems divide the labor of detection, identification, and location, in which case each may become a necessary but not sufficient source of effective cuing. Also, some systems perform well in peacetime or in a crisis but become terminally vulnerable once a conflict has begun. Some operate day or night and/or in all weather, whereas others may be limited by cloud cover. Some assume a cooperative adversary, such as a signals intelligence (SIGINT) system that can function only if the target uses radars and/or radios. And finally, different systems have different vulnerabilities to passive and active countermeasures.

Broadly speaking, radar and SIGINT have been the primary ocean surveillance sensors. This discussion will focus on radar because SIGINT-based ocean surveillance can be defeated by emission control (EMCON) measures.[9] The choice for radar is among ground-based over-the-horizon/backscatter (OTH/B) radars, airborne radars, and satellite radars. We know that China is experimenting with OTH/B, that it has not heretofore made major investments in long-range maritime patrol aircraft like the American P-3 (or modern, long-range ASCM aircraft like the Soviet *Backfire*), and that we can expect the already robust Chinese effort in space to include attempts at radar ocean surveillance satellite development in the future.

OTH radars are not a new technology. They use the same skywave propagation phenomenon that high frequency (HF) radios use to achieve very long range and were first developed early in the Cold War, initially as a ballistic missile warning system. Modern OTH radars include the Relocatable OTH Radars (ROTHRs) developed by the United States during the late Cold War and used now in the drug war, as well as the Australian *Jindalee* system. OTH radars use Doppler to distinguish ships and aircraft from background clutter, and their coverage consists of an annular ring that starts some 1,000 miles from the transmitter and extends out to 1,500 miles.

Under normal circumstances, OTH radars have little or no capability of distinguishing one aircraft or ship from another and would therefore require another sensor for classification.[10] Formidable signal processing techniques need to be developed for an OTH/B radar to function at all, never mind to have it function against a complicated target set in the presence of active jamming. For the purposes of this discussion I will assume that Chinese OTH/B radar is or soon will be as effective as its Western counterparts; that such radars are vulnerable to a variety of jamming techniques, but that those techniques can in turn be countered with even more sophisticated electronic countercountermeasures (ECCM); and that, as large, soft, fixed targets that must be deployed within 1,500 miles of the ocean spaces to be surveilled, such radars are inherently vulnerable to conventional precision attack by cruise missiles. Thus, Chinese OTH radars will be assumed effective unless they are physically attacked.[11]

This would provide an excellent anticarrier cuing capability to Chinese submarines in the second operating area and would put great stress on American decision makers contemplating the deployment of carriers into the Philippine Sea or the southern South China Sea in a crisis. The United States would not be in full control of its exposure to Chinese submarines in any scenario where the latter had the initiative to take the first shot or shots and where terminal defenses carry the main burden of protection against those initial salvoes. This is not an operational/tactical situation that any element of the U.S. military chooses if it can be avoided. It becomes particularly difficult in the relatively unique case of a situation where the United States finds itself drawn into a conflict between China and one of its neighbors, presumably over issues that are vital to the local actors but significantly less so for the United States.

Some may argue that I am exaggerating U.S. vulnerabilities. U.S. ASW escorts are formidable enough in deep water that Chinese submarines might not be able to get into attack position undetected and would also be unlikely to survive their exposure if they were able to conduct an attack. Also, a conflict would not simply end after even a successful attack against a single or even several U.S. battle groups, and of course the barriers through which Chinese submarines have to pass to and from the second operating area in a more protracted conflict would become much less congenial once that conflict had started. Nevertheless, there would be tremendous pressure on American political leaders to strike Chinese OTH radars so as to deny cuing to Chinese submarines if the United States decided to send carrier battle groups into the second operating area.

The United States has the capability to strike these radars with submarine-launched cruise missiles. And certainly the United States would be justified in attacking those radars if China had begun using land-based ASBMs to attack U.S. carrier battle groups. The difficulty would arise in a crisis or in a conflict that had remained limited to the sea, such as the canonical mine warfare coercion campaign against Taiwan described in the preceding pages. To dampen the danger of escalation that would exist in any conflict between nuclear-armed powers, the United States would like to avoid being the first to launch strikes ashore.[12]

Conclusions Regarding the Near–Term Balance

Assumptions regarding political will end up dominating an assessment of the near-term undersea balance. Specifically, if China seeks to use submarines to coerce one of its neighbors and deter U.S. intervention on behalf of that neighbor, it will be the balance of wills in both cases that will most determine the outcome. If the target of Chinese coercion is divided politically over its relationship with China, then a fairly rapid, successful coercion campaign becomes more plausible, and there is very little that the United States could do to counter such a short campaign even if it was completely undeterred by Chinese submarines and other sea denial measures. That is because the United States can do little to stop an initial sortie by a large portion of the Chinese submarine fleet.

If the target of Chinese coercion is more robust politically, then it is more likely that a coercion campaign would induce a nationalist response and that the ensuing conflict would become more protracted. All aspects of the undersea balance improve from a U.S. perspective in that case. Chinese submarines would have to run several times in each direction through SSN barriers near their home bases and through the barriers established at the exits from the first operating area, where they would be prosecuted by patrol aircraft and surface combatants. The exchange ratios in both types of barrier would likely favor the United States, perhaps significantly.

Yet, as in the case where the state being coerced is politically weak, if U.S. stakes in the conflict are low and its aversion to risk high, U.S. decision makers might still be deterred from initially committing carrier battle groups to the second operating area. Reasonable people will disagree over the consequences of such an outcome, or the perception in the region in advance of a conflict that such an outcome was likely. Importantly, and unlike the case where the coercee is politically weak, there are steps the United States could take that would make successful deterrence of even a weakly committed United States unlikely. There are also steps the United States could take that would leverage areas of enduring advantage to increase the threat that U.S. submarines pose to mobile targets in China and decrease the threat that a future Chinese ocean surveillance radar satellite system would pose to American naval forces.

TODAY'S BALANCE AND COMPETITIVE STRATEGY
AND THE FUTURE UNDERSEA BALANCE

The main step that the United States could take to reduce further or even eliminate the threat posed by quiet Chinese diesel submarines in the second operating area is to maintain persistent, overt, active trails of them once they have passed through the barriers separating the two operating areas. Such a step would not necessarily be an example of a competitive strategy because it would be relatively asset intensive, but it would greatly increase the odds that the U.S. Navy would prevail in a "battle of the first salvo" in the Philippine Sea.

The United States also has at least two means of generating additional areas of military competition with China that would be relevant to the undersea balance where the imbalance in resources expended by both sides would favor the United States. The first new area of competition would be between U.S. submarines and Chinese mobile anti-access systems such as modern surface-to-air missile (SAM) batteries. The second would be a competition to see which party could become least militarily dependent on satellites in general, and particularly those in low earth orbit (LEO).

On the other side of the balance, the Chinese could decide to give their submarine fleet additional missions and attempt to reduce its vulnerability to existing and planned U.S. ASW capabilities. In the former case, China might expand its commitment to ballistic and cruise missile submarines, for nuclear deterrence, conventional land attack, and/or antiship operations. In the latter case, China might seek to develop further its nuclear submarine technology with the aim of achieving a truly quiet boat.

Improving Today's Balance

Holding Chinese submarines at risk once they enter the second operating area would have obvious benefits. The United States would either know where the submarines were at all times or know where to concentrate ASW assets to search for and reacquire those submarines that somehow escaped an active trail. The assets engaged in active trailing would be very close to a fire control solution on their targets and could therefore prevent them from approaching and attacking American battle groups or, in cases where they did get close, launching more than one weapon. Most importantly, the political threshold for attacking submarines trying to get into firing position against U.S. battle groups would be much lower than for attacking the land-based radars used to cue those attacks. With such a capability, the United States could effectively manage its exposure to risk if it deployed carrier battle groups into the second operating area in a crisis or early in a conflict with much less concern about escalation.

The United States already has ASW assets that could perform this mission. The problem is either that those assets are scarce, multimission platforms that are the sole means of performing other important missions or that they are dependent on the use of expendable sensors that could be exhausted in a protracted crisis or conflict. For example, an *Arleigh Burke* (DDG-51)-class destroyer with the latest version of the SQQ-89 ASW combat system can maintain an active trail of even the most modern diesel submarines at stand-off ranges of at least thirty miles and, if necessary, maintain a continuous or near-continuous fire control solution with its helicopters. The problem is that DDG-51s are also primary fleet air and missile defense assets, as well as cruise missile shooters.

Likewise, P-3s and, soon, P-8s equipped with advanced, active, multistatic acoustic systems will be very effective in deep-water operations. The problem is that these systems also arguably provide the most effective shallow-water ASW prosecution capability in the U.S. inventory. Additionally, all fixed-wing air ASW assets are dependent on expendable sonobuoys for the acoustic side of their mission, and these may be difficult to procure in numbers sufficient to sustain continuous trails, as opposed to pouncing operations where contact on the target is maintained only as long as it takes to attack it or for a more persistent surface ship to arrive and take over the trail.

For all these reasons, the United States should look carefully at both the numbers and, perhaps more important, the capabilities of the Littoral Combat Ship's (LCS) ASW module and the sea frame itself. Contrary to many expectations, American surface ships will not play much if any ASW role in the shallow waters of the first operating environment in a conflict with China, but the LCS's ASW module is optimized for a shallow water environment, and the sea frame lacks a powerful midfrequency sonar like the SQS-53.[13] On the plus side, LCS will have a tremendous air operations capability, and its often-maligned fifty-knot top speed will, if combined with a torpedo warning system, reduce its vulnerability to wake homing torpedoes.

New, More Favorable Areas of Military Competition

Of the two proposed new areas of military competition, the submarine versus air defenses competition is directly relevant to the undersea balance. The proposed competition to reduce dependence on LEO satellites is of more general relevance and will therefore also provide an opportunity to assess the Chinese ASBM threat and methods of countering it.

U.S. Submarines Versus Chinese Air Defenses   Most Chinese anti-access systems are mobile. Mobile, precise land attack weapons can evade the crushing U.S. ability to destroy fixed targets while simultaneously holding at risk the U.S. ability to use land bases. Combined with an ocean surveillance system and a terminal guidance capability, land mobile missiles can also hold U.S. naval forces at risk.

Defeating mobile targets requires a persistent network of surveillance sensors and strike assets. Unlike fixed targets that can be targeted well in advance of a conflict, mobile targets can normally be found and targeted only when they generate a specific signature associated with their mission.

Persistence is thus key to locating mobile targets. In the surveillance realm it means sensors or sensor networks that can approximate an unblinking, wide-area stare, while in the weapons realm it means weapons that combine range, speed, and basing mode in such a way that they are always available in timely fashion. Surveillance sensors need to be persistent because the mobile target signatures they exploit occur only intermittently, and the weapons need to be prompt because striking mobile targets is usually possible only when they are stationary. Thus, for example, if a targeting solution will last for only twenty minutes, the weapon to exploit it should not be more than twenty minutes away.

In the access-unconstrained environment that has characterized the War on Terror, this has led to an explosion of unmanned aerial system (UAS) use as a source of persistent surveillance. Air-breathing surveillance platforms will likely remain the primary sensor platform for dealing with mobile targets. The problem is that modern air defense systems will eliminate the sanctuary that airborne sensor platforms currently enjoy. To be specific, the increased missile range associated with modern SAM systems will force airborne radar platforms like JSTARS, U-2, and *Global Hawk* to stand off beyond the range of their radars and will prevent airborne electronic intelligence (ELINT) platforms like RC-135, EP-3, and Global Hawk from geolocating RF emissions with precision.[14]

Absent these persistent surveillance capabilities, it is impossible to deal with mobile targets, so dealing with modern SAMs is a major anti-access challenge. The problem is that current approaches to destroying modern SAMs all depend on land- and sea-based tactical fighters whose access to the theater presumes a prior solution to the access denial challenge posed by mobile, precision land attack, and antiship missiles. This in turn presumes persistent airborne surveillance, which in turn presumes a solution to the modern SAM problem.

Submarines have become uniquely capable of breaking this vicious circle because of the relatively recent development of time and frequency-difference-of-arrival (T/FDOA) ELINT signal processing techniques that can now be implemented using networks of even the smallest tactical UAS, which would be invulnerable to modern SAMs. Combined with a submarine's traditional ability to provide a stealthy and persistent source of weapons in even the most access-constrained littoral environment, an organic UAS will provide submarines a fully organic capability to detect, identify, precisely locate, and quickly strike modern SAM engagement radars.[15]

The Defense Advanced Research Projects Agency's (DARPA) Advanced Tactical Targeting Technology (AT3) program successfully demonstrated T/FDOA signal processing that exploited the vast computational power now available in even the smallest package. AT3 enables the formation of a true T/FDOA ELINT network using very small omnidirectional receivers deployable even on very small UAS.

A fast, coordinate seeking weapon is equally important for Destruction of Enemy Air Defenses (DEAD) from under the sea. AT3 can quickly locate and identify the radar as soon as it emits, but that will be of no use if a weapon arrives only after the radar has relocated. Air-breathing weapons cannot provide such promptness from any kind of standoff distance, but tactical ballistic missiles (TBMs) can.

Like AT3-equipped UAS, a GPS-guided TBM can be acquired off the shelf and deployed in existing submarine and surface combatant launchers for immediate experimentation and initial operational use in the War on Terror. A TBM based on the Standard Missile could provide a range of 300 miles and be traded one-for-one for Tomahawks, and a TBM based on the GPS-guided multiple launch rocket system (GMLRS) could provide a range of fifty miles and be traded several for one. Over the longer term, a new TBM could be developed that might build on the DARPA long range antiship missile (LRASM) program's investments in precision guidance in a GPS-denied environment.

Submarines equipped with organic, AT3-equipped UAS and TBMs may provide the only way to perform DEAD in an access-constrained environment. They constitute the only potential source of DEAD capability that is as persistent as the airborne surveillance platforms in need of continuous protection, they are the only platform assured access in even the most contested littoral environment, and they are the only platform whose DEAD capability would itself be immune to the air defenses it would be attacking.

Of course, in addition to its direct benefits, a submarine-based DEAD capability would greatly expand the threat posed by U.S. submarines to China's overall military objectives in a conflict with the United States. From a competitive strategies perspective, this would likely have one or both of two very positive effects for the United States. First, it would greatly increase deterrence, in that there is little in the near term the Chinese could do to counter such a capability. Second, should the Chinese decide in the longer term to try to counter this capability, it would force them into major investments in shallow water ASW against very quiet, fast, nuclear submarines. This is a mission area where the ratio between input and output is among the least favorable, and, even if the investments were made, success would not be guaranteed.

WHICH SIDE CAN BECOME LEAST DEPENDENT ON LEO?

As discussed in the preceding section, cuing is important for submarines seeking to engage fast surface targets in the open ocean, and denying such cuing is thereby an important ASW measure. Today, Chinese OTH radar provides the best near-term source of such cuing against American carriers and other surface combatants in the second operating environment. But all OTH radars are inherently vulnerable to physical attack, and basic bistatic OTH radars like the current system in China are vulnerable to electronic attack and spoofing.[16] Thus, many analysts reasonably predict that China will seek to develop radar ocean surveillance satellites. Formidable technical challenges stand in the path of such an effort, but for this discussion I will assume that the Chinese could eventually surmount them.[17] I will first show why the Chinese might be motivated to pursue development for reasons other than the need for submarine cuing and then discuss how the United States might respond.

In addition to the need for submarine cuing, the Chinese need to develop a means of targeting their ASBMs, which recently achieved initial operating capability.[18] One issue that is rarely fully discussed regards the target location error (TLE) associated with the various candidates identified as potential sources of Chinese ASBM targeting. Whatever TLE is, it adds to the area of uncertainty already created by shooting a ballistic missile at a moving target and the inevitable delays caused by centralized command and control. In the case of both OTH radar and space-based SIGINT, the two candidates most often mentioned, TLE can be quite large.[19]

This is why the Chinese will likely develop a real aperture, MTI radar satellite constellation in LEO if they are serious about ASBMs. MTI radar satellites would provide much better geolocation capabilities than OTH radars and, unlike ELINT satellites, would not be vulnerable to EMCON measures. MTI satellites might still need some help with classification, but imaging satellites could do this once provided the all-important initial cue by the MTI network. MTI satellites would still, like OTH radars, be vulnerable to ECM and would thus provoke an additional ECM-ECCM competition.

Essentially all of these ocean surveillance, identification, location, and targeting functions can be done better from airborne platforms, assuming one has control over the relevant air space. Airborne radars can be made more powerful than space-based radars, and they are much less costly, so they can be deployed in much greater numbers, which more than compensates for the reduction in radar horizon involved. And, of course, a reduction in radar horizon also translates into a reduction in the area from which a jammer can get a line-of-sight to the side lobes of an airborne radar's or communication relay's antenna. Indeed, this is the approach that the United States has historically taken. High Altitude Long Endurance (HALE) UAVs that combine radar, SIGINT, and optics, like the Navy's Global Hawk–derived Broad Area Maritime Surveillance (BAMS) system, represent the future of this approach.

This combination of control of the air, assured in the end by carrier aviation, and distributed, persistent airborne surveillance by manned platforms like the P-3 and the P-8 and now unmanned platforms like BAMS, constitutes a huge asymmetry in favor of the United States. That is because, in the end, the United States does not need access to LEO to control the seas that constitute the second operating area, while the Chinese will likely need access to LEO simply to contest control of those seas, never mind control them.

This directly raises the difficult question of LEO as a sanctuary in any conflict between China and the United States, both of which have just recently demonstrated direct ascent antisatellite (ASAT) capabilities. Few assumptions are more widely and firmly held than that which says the U.S. military is much more dependent on access to space than any of its potential adversaries, including China. This in turn leads to the belief that the United States would never be the first to use ASATs in a conflict because it would have much more to lose.

From DOD's perspective, and more specifically from the U.S. Navy's perspective, it is worth asking whether the conventional wisdom about which side is more dependent on space, and on LEO in particular, is correct. More to the point, it is worth asking how much any current dependencies in this regard are inescapable under modern technological and operational conditions, or merely a legacy of the past, and, in the case of the inescapable ones, how hard it would be to repair or replace them should they be lost.[20]

The consequences regarding a possible future Chinese MTI radar satellite constellation are obvious. Such a constellation would likely provide a necessary part of future Chinese efforts to deny the United States use of the seas in the second operating area. This will require great investments, and these investments, if they are made, will likely be based on the assumption that LEO is a sanctuary. If the United States is able to render that assumption obsolete after the system is developed, it will likely have accomplished a major coup of competitive strategy.

New Missions for Chinese Submarines and/or Better Submarines?

Just as the United States could seek new areas of military competition with China by giving its submarines new missions, the Chinese might seek to do the same. But the situation for the Chinese is different because they would not be building on a situation of current or inherent advantage as the United States would be. New, larger, and longer-range SSBs and SSGs would still be vulnerable to modern U.S. acoustic barriers and to overt, active trailing if they sought to exit the first operating area. Likewise, new SSBNs or SSGNs that were no more acoustically stealthy than the best current nuclear submarine, the *Shang*, would still be vulnerable to traditional, Cold War–style, passive acoustic approaches to ASW, whether by American SSNs searching SSBN operating areas or by SOSUS-like systems tracking them in deep water.

Prior to a decision to seek new missions, or the ability to operate much further away from home, the Chinese would almost certainly need to ask the prior question of whether they could make their submarines less vulnerable to American ASW. In acoustic terms, they have already reached the point of diminishing returns with regard to quieting their diesel submarines, so there is unlikely to be any way of eliminating their vulnerability to modern acoustic barriers. So, it would appear that the crucial questions are whether the Chinese could make their nuclear submarines as quiet as their diesel submarines, how much such an investment would cost, and what the consequences would be if they succeeded.

Starting with the last question first, truly quiet nuclear submarines would still be vulnerable to detection while exiting and entering their bases and while transiting between the first and second operating areas. The main difference would be that the United States would no longer be able to track them in deep water on an oceanwide scale, and they would be much less vulnerable to trailing, whether covert or overt. Once in range of a carrier battle group, the consequences would be less significant, because battle group ASW escorts have all already made the transition to bi- or multistatic active acoustics, where the target's acoustic source levels are irrelevant. Thus, if quiet nuclear submarines were simply introduced into the current Chinese submarine mission set, replacing the fleet of *Shangs* on a one-for-one basis, the consequences would not be positive from a U.S. perspective, but they would not be revolutionary either because they would essentially return the United States to the position it currently occupies, in which the basic problem is risk management early in a conflict, not the ultimate outcome of a conflict.

But if one posits the addition of new missions and/or expanded deployment areas on top of the development of truly quiet nuclear submarines, then the consequences become more dramatic. Nuclear submarines that can neither be tracked from a distance nor trailed can go wherever they want at high transit speeds. The main remaining source of vulnerability is that they must expose themselves when they use their weapons. As noted in the preceding pages, this will remain a dangerous activity for even quiet nuclear submarines facing the ASW screen of a carrier battle group, but the capabilities of that screen are not replicable across wide areas. Thus, for example, a force of quiet Chinese SSGNs could deploy throughout the Pacific, holding high-value, fixed military targets in Alaska, Hawaii, and the west coast of CONUS at risk of precision attack. Those attacks will be risk free unless appropriate wide-area, active ASW forces are deployed with sufficient density and breadth to protect the entire area. Quiet SSNs could obviously pose a similar threat to commercial shipping of all sorts. Alternately, a force of quiet SSNs could challenge a distant blockade of Chinese shipping by American surface ships operating on the Indian Ocean side of the approaches to the Malacca and Sunda Straits.[21] By comparison, quiet Chinese SSBNs would probably be the least of the U.S. concerns under the circumstances.

Looking at this scenario from a competitive strategies perspective, the Chinese would need to commit at the outset to what would be both an extremely expensive and still technologically uncertain program of nuclear submarine quieting in return for the prospect of imposing the larger costs associated with wide-area ASW against quiet targets when geography doesn't provide natural chokepoints or focal areas. As already noted, this is a different decision than the one faced by the U.S. Navy and its submarine force when they contemplate new submarine missions. The United States has already demonstrated, since the introduction of the *Thresher* class SSN fifty years ago, the ability to establish and consistently maintain significant acoustic advantages for its nuclear submarines in a competition with a peer competitor, and they have already reached absolute levels of silencing such that their passage at close range can actually cause a dip in noise levels because background noise is being blocked by the submarine's hull. The Chinese are still far from that position, but, as in other areas, it would almost certainly be a mistake to assume that they won't eventually get there if they decide to try.

CONCLUSIONS

There are many uncertainties attendant on the future undersea balance between the United States and China. For example, there has never been a naval competition between great powers both wielding fleets of quiet nuclear submarines because the Cold War ended before the Soviets could fully participate in their half of the competition. More broadly, there has never been a competition between two submarine-equipped great powers both of which were also economically dependent on the sea. In the end, uncertainties abound as to how these competitions might play out should they occur.

This chapter makes two basic arguments regarding how the United States could reduce those uncertainties in its favor by exploiting areas of enduring U.S. advantage and Chinese disadvantage. The first is to give U.S. submarines the capability of destroying modern air defenses, and the second is to eliminate or greatly reduce the Navy's and DOD's wartime dependence on LEO. DEAD from under the sea leverages the U.S. Navy's historic advantage in submarine quieting, as well as new ELINT technology, and would likely force the Chinese into major ASW investments that they have heretofore eschewed. The second would leverage the U.S. Navy's superiority in aircraft carriers to protect air-breathing ocean surveillance assets, deny them to others, and thereby eliminate any sanctuary to ocean surveillance satellites in LEO.

NOTES

1. Nuclear deterrence using ballistic missile submarines is perhaps the main exception to this rule.

2. On contested command, see Bernard Brodie, *A Layman's Guide to Naval Strategy* (Princeton, NJ: Princeton University Press, 1942), 75.

3. Taiwan is the contingency most discussed, but this analysis applies to any conflict between China and one of its neighbors in the South China Sea basin.

4. For more technical background relevant to the following discussion, see Owen R. Coté Jr., "Assessing the Undersea Balance between the U.S. and China," February 2011, SSP Working Paper WP11-1, 3-7; available at http://web.mit.edu/ssp/publications/papers.html.

5. In using the terms *first* and *second* operating environments I am intentionally avoiding the more common usage of "inside the first island chain" and "between the first and second island chains" because I believe they fail to capture the variance in

operating conditions in the South China Sea. Most of the South China Sea is deep water and outside Chinese fighter range and therefore more akin to the operating conditions in the Philippine Sea.

6. See Tom Christenson, "Posing Problems without Catching Up: China's Rise and Challenges for U.S. Security Policy," *International Security* 25:4 (Spring 2001), 5–40; Michael Glosny, "Strangulation from the Sea," *International Security* 28:4 (Spring 2004), 125–160; and Andrew S. Erickson, Lyle J. Goldstein, and William S. Murray, *Chinese Mine Warfare: A PLA Navy "Assassin's Mace" Capability,* U.S. Naval War College, China Maritime Studies, 3, June 2009.

7. From the second batch, or "Flight II," of Victor IIIs produced, all but the lowest-frequency tonals had been eliminated, and the broadband signature was much reduced. On the Flight II Victor IIIs, see testimony by then CNO Admiral James D. Watkins in U.S. Senate Armed Services Committee, *Hearings on the FY1985 Defense Budget, Part 8,* 3889; and Coté, SSP Working Paper 11-1, 11–12 and note 10. For a general discussion of Cold War ASW, and particularly the importance of barriers, see Owen R. Coté Jr., *The Third Battle: Innovation in the U.S. Navy's Silent Cold War Struggle with Soviet Submarines,* Newport Paper 16 (Newport, RI: Naval War College Press, 2003).

8. On RAP/VLA and DWADS, and the progress made with both programs in just one year, see the briefing by Joe Johnson, PEO IWS 5A, Advanced Development for Underseas Systems Office, "Reliable Acoustic Path Vertical Line Array (RAP/VLA)," October 8, 2008, retrieved on November 18, 2010, from www.ceros.org/documents/briefings/JOHNSON%20RAPVLA%20SUBPAC.pdf; and the briefing by Alan Boyd, PEO IWS 5ADEP, Advanced Development for Undersea Systems Office, 2009 National Defense Center of Excellence for Research in Ocean Sciences Industry Day, September 14, 2009, retrieved on November 18, 2010, from www.ceros.org/documents/FY09%20Industry%20Day%20Briefings/Boyd%20IWS5A%20FY10.pdf. On the key performance parameters for RAP/VLA and DWADS, the range of institutions involved in their development, and current and projected funding levels, see the RDT&E Project Justification for Project 3197 *Undersea Superiority* in the Navy's Proposed Fy 2011 Budget, February 2010, 33–35, retrieved on November 18, 2010, from www.dtic.mil/descriptivesum/Y2011/Navy/0603561N_PB_2011.pdf.

9. This is not to say that SIGINT has no role, just that it cannot be relied on as the source of initial detections against an uncooperative target. For a brief discussion of U.S. EMCON procedures during the late Cold War, see Norman Friedman, *Seapower and Space* (Annapolis, MD: U.S. Naval Institute Press, 2000), 193–198.

10. Aircraft carriers may be an exception to this rule because their signature uniquely involves both ships and aircraft in close proximity to each other during flight operations.

11. These are heroically conservative assumptions. My intent is not to argue that they are realistic but to show below that even with these assumptions it is possible

to come up with means of denying the Chinese submarines success in their second undersea warfare objective.

12. On this problem, see the chapter on the 1973 war in Joseph F. Bouchard, *Command in Crisis: Four Case Studies* (New York: Columbia University Press, 1991).

13. There are indications that the Navy is taking steps to rectify this weakness by adding a variable-depth sonar and a towed array to LCS's ASW suite.

14. The best unclassified source on modern SAMs is *Jane's Land-Based Air Defense, 2009–2010,* 22nd Edition (Alexandria, VA: Jane's Information Group, 2009), 214–215, which cites a range of over 200 miles. JSTARS' MTI radar is cited as having a range "in excess of 124 miles" in "Air Force Almanac," *Air Force Magazine* 93 (5) (May 2010), 131.

15. For a fuller discussion of submarine-based DEAD see, Owen R. Coté Jr., "Submarines in the Air Sea Battle (U)," paper presented to Submarine Technology Symposium 2010, Johns Hopkins University Applied Physics Laboratory, May 11, 2010; available at http://web.mit.edu/ssp/publications/conference.html.

16. More complex multistatic OTH radars would be the next step in the ECM-ECCM contest. They would reduce the vulnerability to jamming and spoofing but would remain physically vulnerable.

17. The United States has tried and failed twice to deploy moving target indicator (MTI) radar satellites that use essentially the same technology as would be required for ocean surveillance. For the history of these efforts, see Dwayne Day, "Radar Love: The Tortured History of American Space Radar Programs," *The Space Review,* January 22, 2007; retrieved on November 16, 2010, from www.thespacereview.com; Jeffrey Richelson, "Ups and Downs of Space Radars," *Air Force Magazine,* January 2009, 67–70; and U.S. Congressional Budget Office, *Alternatives for Military Space Radar* (Washington, DC: U.S. Government Printing Office, January 2007), 14–15. Synthetic aperture radar (SAR) satellites that image fixed targets are much easier to develop and are already widely deployed, but these are not useful for ocean surveillance.

18. See, for example, Andrew S. Erickson and David D. Yang, "Using the Land to Control the Sea: Chinese Analysts Consider the Antiship Ballistic Missile" 53–86; and Eric Hagt and Matthew Durnin, "China's Antiship Ballistic Missile: Developments and Missing Links," 87–115, *Naval War College Review* 62:4 (Autumn 2009); and Marshall Hoyler, "China's 'Anti-Access' Ballistic Missiles and U.S. Active Defense," *Naval War College Review* 63:4 (Autumn 2010), 84–105.

19. For more on TLE see Cote, SSP Working Paper WP11-1, 23.

20. For more on this point see ibid., 25–26.

21. For an analysis of such a distant blockade, see Douglas Peifer, " China, the German Analogy, and the New AirSea Operational Concept," *Orbis,* 55, 1 (Winter 2011), 114–131

12 A COMPETITIVE STRATEGY WITH CHINESE CHARACTERISTICS?

The Second Artillery's Growing Conventional Forces and Missions

Michael S. Chase and Andrew S. Erickson

THE TRANSFORMATION OF THE Second Artillery Force (SAF)—the part of the PLA responsible for most of China's conventional and nuclear ballistic and land-attack cruise missiles—is one of the centerpieces of the PRC's military modernization program. In a relatively short period, China has progressed from a limited and vulnerable nuclear ballistic missile capability to one of the world's most impressive nuclear and conventional ballistic missile programs. As the U.S. Department of Defense's report on Chinese military and security developments puts it, "China has the most active land-based ballistic and cruise missile program in the world."[1]

In doing so, China is filling the vacuum created when the United States and Russia—still the world's most capable missile producers in some respects—signed the Intermediate-Range Nuclear Forces (INF) Treaty on December 8, 1987. This prohibited both sides from producing nuclear and conventional ground-launched ballistic and cruise missiles with ranges between 500 and 5,500 kilometers (300 to 3,400 miles) and forced them to destroy their existing inventories.

According to the U.S. National Air and Space Intelligence Center (NASIC), China is "developing and testing offensive missiles, forming additional missile units, qualitatively upgrading certain missile systems, and developing methods to counter ballistic missile defenses."[2] Chinese writers rarely offer detailed descriptions of China's deployed or developmental missile systems, but they appear increasingly confident about China's missile capabilities. As one Chinese source states,

With the remarkably swift development of science and technology, the weapons of the Second Artillery are being replaced by better models, one after the other. New models and new equipment series are being distributed among the troops, and old equipment is given a longer life and heightened effectiveness through technological updates.[3]

According to the SAF's authoritative *Science of Second Artillery Campaigns*, "Nuclear weapons are the most important tools of national deterrence strategy."[4] But nuclear deterrence is subject to a number of limitations. As the book's authors point out, "Nuclear deterrence plays a huge role in terms of its shock value, but it is clearly restrained by international public opinion."[5] Consequently, the threshold for nuclear deterrence and nuclear counterattack operations is very high. Conventional missiles are much less destructive than nuclear weapons, however, and there are therefore fewer constraints on their use. Chinese military writers state that this makes conventional missiles much more flexible instruments of deterrence.[6] Indeed, according to *Science of Second Artillery Campaigns*, "In the primary direction of military struggle the means of deterrence against the primary operational opponent are conventional weapons; and the main components of conventional means of deterrence are conventional missiles."[7]

For all these reasons, conventional missiles have emerged as the centerpiece of a PLA strategy that seeks to increase China's ability to assert control over contested areas of its maritime periphery, foremost among them Taiwan. The essence of this strategy is to develop weapon systems and strategies that match Chinese strengths against the weaknesses of potential opponents in a cost-effective manner. Conventional missiles promise to further these ends by holding both land-based targets and surface ships at risk. The main goals of this approach appear to be deterring Taiwan from pursuing independence and raising the potential costs of U.S. intervention in the event of a regional crisis or conflict. The authors have found no Chinese sources that use the term *competitive strategy* to define this approach, but from a U.S. perspective the concept may offer a valid description of what Beijing seeks to accomplish. This chapter surveys the emerging doctrine, force structure, and operations of the Second Artillery's conventional forces to offer insights into the challenges that they may pose to U.S. military operations in the Western Pacific.

DOCTRINAL DIRECTION: SHIFTING TO
"DUAL DETERRENCE, DUAL OPERATIONS"

China's interest in the development of conventional ballistic missile forces grew out of its need to respond to the threat of a Soviet invasion in the 1980s. The PLA's desire to supplement China's relatively weak capability to conduct air strikes was thus one of the main motives for China's early research and development work on conventional short-range ballistic missiles (SRBMs), which began in 1984. Another motive was the possibility of profiting from exports to customers in the developing world.[8]

After the 1991 Gulf War, the Central Military Commission assigned the Second Artillery the mission of "dual deterrence and dual operations," which emphasizes the importance of deterrence and combat roles for both the conventional and nuclear missile forces.[9] China's first conventional ballistic-missile-force unit was established in 1993.

Within a few years, China's nascent conventional missile capability reached the forefront of its coercive diplomacy toward Taiwan. During the 1995–1996 Taiwan Strait crisis, the conventional missile force conducted two "large-scale conventional deterrence firing exercises."[10] Chinese sources generally evaluate the missile launches as a successful display of force that deterred Taiwan from moving further toward formal independence.

Several factors have subsequently driven the development of China's conventional missile force. These include a desire to influence politics in Taiwan and deter U.S. intervention in a regional crisis or conflict and the relative advantages offered by emphasizing missile force modernization as opposed to attempting the development of capabilities such as stealth aircraft to conduct precision strikes.

Chinese military publications underscore that the operational strength of the missile force is the foundation of missile force deterrence. According to *Intimidation Warfare,* a detailed volume published by former Second Artillery deputy commander Lt. General Zhao Xijun, "Deterrence must take reliable strength as its foundation."[11] The requirements include appropriate force size, high-quality weapons and equipment, efficient means of command and control, and advanced operational theories.

Some bluff and bluster may be involved, but deterrence is impossible without real strength to support threats and ensure that they will be credible enough to influence enemy decision makers. The basic requirement of deterrence is credibility, and for a modern missile force this translates into striking power and survivability. Consequently, Chinese strategists view continuously improving the missile force's survivability, rapid response capability, ability to penetrate missile defense systems, and destructiveness as indispensible elements of deterrence.[12]

FORCE STRUCTURE

Since its formal establishment in 1993, the conventional missile force of the Second Artillery has grown rapidly, to the point where its missiles outnumber their nuclear counterparts by a ratio of roughly seven to one. "Augmented by direct acquisition of foreign weapons and technology, [defense industry] reforms have enabled China to develop and produce advanced weapon systems that incorporate mid-1990s technology in many areas," states the U.S. Department of Defense, "and some systems—particularly ballistic missiles— that rival any in the world today."[13] At present, China's rapidly expanding conventional ballistic missile force includes DF-15 (CSS-6) and DF-11 (CSS-7) SRBMs and DF-21 (CSS-5) medium-range ballistic missiles (MRBMs). China is also developing and deploying an antiship ballistic missile (ASBM) based on a variant of the DF-21 (CSS-5) MRBM. In addition, China has deployed the DH-10 land-attack cruise missile (LACM) to enhance the PLA's regional precision strike capabilities.

Short-Range Ballistic Missiles

Since the early 1990s, when the conventional missile force component of the Second Artillery was established, China's SRBM forces have expanded dramatically. Indeed, estimates presented in the U.S. Department of Defense's annual reports on Chinese military power reveal that the number of deployed SRBMs has tripled over the past eight years (see Table 12.1). By December 2010, China's arsenal consisted of 1,000 to 1,200 solid propellant road-mobile SRBMs, all deployed in areas opposite Taiwan.[14] This includes about 350 to 400 CSS-6 SRBMs and about 700 to 750 CSS-7 SRBMs.[15] NASIC estimates that China has deployed more than 200 mobile launchers for its SRBMs.[16] Similarly, the Department of Defense provides an estimated order of battle of 200 to 250 total SRBM launchers,[17] including 90 to 110 CSS-6 and 120 to 140 CSS-7 launchers.[18]

The conventional missile force is continuing to grow, but China is "increasing its inventory at a slower rate than in past years."[19] DoD expanded on this judgment in its 2011 report, indicating that the number of SRBMs

Table 12.1. China's growing SRBM forces, 2001–2010.

Year	Number of deployed SRBMs	Year	Number of deployed SRBMs
2001	350	2006	900
2002	450	2007	990–1,070
2003	500	2008	1,050–1,150
2004	650–730	2009	1,050–1,150
2005	710–790	2010	1,050–1,150

SOURCES: Department of Defense, *Military Power of the People's Republic of China*, 2002, p. 2; Department of Defense, *Military Power of the People's Republic of China*, 2003, p. 29; Department of Defense, *Military Power of the People's Republic of China*, 2004, p. 23; Department of Defense, *Military Power of the People's Republic of China*, 2005, p. 4; Department of Defense, *Military Power of the People's Republic of China*, 2006, p. 3; Department of Defense, *Military Power of the People's Republic of China*, 2007, p. 3; Department of Defense, *Military Power of the People's Republic of China*, 2008, p. 2; Department of Defense, *Military Power of the People's Republic of China*, 2009, p. 66; and Department of Defense, *Military and Security Developments Involving the People's Republic of China*, 2010, p. 66.

appears to be holding relatively steady but that China is replacing older missiles with newer, more accurate, and more capable models. The increase in deployed SRBMs has also been accompanied by organizational expansion. In 2000, China's SRBM force consisted of only one regimental-sized unit. By 2008, this had expanded to seven brigades, including five controlled by the Second Artillery and two directly subordinate to PLA ground forces (one in the Nanjing MR and another in the Guangzhou MR).

In addition to growing numbers of SRBMs and an increase in the number of brigades, there have been improvements in quality as China has upgraded the capabilities of its SRBMs. According to the Department of Defense, China's first-generation SRBMs are not true precision-strike weapons, but later generations of Chinese SRBMs feature "greater ranges, improved accuracy, and a wider variety of conventional payloads, including unitary and submunition warheads."[20] According to an unclassified estimate released by NASIC, China currently fields at least five different types of conventional SRBMs (see Table 12.2).

China can also be expected to continue to improve the accuracy and lethality of its SRBMs and to develop an even greater variety of warheads.

Conventional Medium-Range Ballistic Missiles

China has deployed conventional MRBMs and is developing and deploying an ASBM. According to NASIC, "China is also acquiring new conventionally-armed MRBMs to conduct precision strikes at longer ranges. These systems are likely intended to hold at risk, or strike, logistics nodes and regional military bases including airfields and ports."[21] China's DF-21 (CSS-5) conventional MRBM is a two-stage solid propellant mobile missile with a maximum range of 1,750 or

Table 12.2. Types and ranges of China's deployed SRBMs.

Missile type	Maximum range (km)	Maximum range (miles)
CSS-6 Mod 1	600	370
CSS-6 Mod 2	885	550
CSS-6 Mod 3	725	450
CSS-7 Mod 1	300	185
CSS-7 Mod 2	600	370

SOURCE: National Air and Space Intelligence Center, *Ballistic and Cruise Missile Threat*, NASIC-1031-0985-09, April 2009, 11.

more kilometers (1,100 or more miles). China has deployed eighty-five to ninety-five missiles on seventy-five to eighty-five launchers.[22] Future developments may include further expansion of the conventional MRBM force and possibly conventional IRBMs. According to the Defense Department, "China's ballistic missile force is acquiring conventional medium-range and intermediate-range ballistic missiles, extending the distance from which it can threaten other countries with conventional precision or near-precision strikes."[23]

Perhaps of greatest significance, China is developing and deploying an ASBM based on a variant of the DF-21 (CSS-5). The ASBM is a two-stage solid-propellant mobile missile with "a range exceeding 1,500 km" (932-plus miles).[24] On July 11, 2011, PLA Chief of General Staff General Chen Bingde became the first Chinese government official to confirm publicly that China is developing the DF-21D ASBM.[25] Taiwan's 2011 National Defense Report states that "a small quantity of" DF-21D ASBMs "were produced and deployed in 2010."[26] Articles published by researchers affiliated with the Second Artillery Engineering College indicate that the ASBM would use midcourse and terminal guidance to strike a moving target like an aircraft carrier and employ submunitions to damage or destroy aircraft on the flight deck and other important targets. They may believe that this approach would allow the PLA to achieve a "mission kill" without actually sinking an aircraft carrier, potentially limiting escalation.[27]

Land-Attack Cruise Missiles

China is also developing and deploying air- and ground-launched LACMs to enhance the PLA's conventional long-range precision-strike capabilities. According to the Department of Defense, "The PLA is acquiring large numbers of highly accurate cruise missiles, such as the domestically produced ground-launched DH-10 land attack cruise missile." DoD estimates that by December

2009 China had deployed about 200 to 500 2,000-kilometer-range DH-10 LACMs and 45 to 55 launchers.[28]

China's land attack cruise missile capabilities also include air-launched LACMs such as the YJ-63 and a new long-range missile. The YJ-63 reportedly has a range of about 200 kilometers and is carried by the PLAAF's B-6 bombers.[29] China is currently enhancing this capability with an upgraded bomber and new long-range air-launched cruise missile. According to the 2010 DoD report, "China is upgrading its B-6 bomber fleet (originally adapted from the Russian Tu-16) with a new, longer-range variant that will be armed with a new long-range cruise missile."[30] The B-6 armed with this new LACM will extend the reach of China's regional precision strike capabilities out to 3,000 kilometers, bringing U.S. bases on Guam within range of China's conventional anti-access capabilities.[31]

CONVENTIONAL MISSILE DETERRENCE OPERATIONS AND ATTACK CAMPAIGNS

The establishment of China's first conventional ballistic missile brigade in 1993 required the Second Artillery to define and develop plans for conventional missile force deterrence operations and conventional missile attack campaigns.

Conventional Missile Force Deterrence Operations

Chinese military publications emphasize that the conventional missile force plays an important role in deterrence. Chinese writers also underscore that conventional missile force deterrence operations must be closely aligned with the diplomatic struggles they are intended to support. According to Zhao Xijun, "Like war, deterrence is an extension of politics; the employment of missile weapons to carry out military deterrence is a tool for achieving political objectives."[32]

Zhao indicates that conventional missile force deterrence operations can be divided into three categories based on the level of pressure they place on the adversary: low-, medium-, and high-intensity conventional deterrence, respectively.[33] Low-intensity conventional missile force deterrence "usually does not have a very strong confrontational nature." It involves methods such as using the media to transmit propaganda about the missile force and changing the disposition of the conventional missile force units. In contrast to low-intensity conventional deterrence, medium-intensity conventional missile force deterrence is imbued with a "definite confrontational quality."

One type of medium-intensity deterrence is "using military force to create momentum." Another method is conducting conventional missile force exercise launches. High-intensity conventional missile force deterrence has a "very strong confrontational nature." It is implemented through "close proximity or critical deterrence strikes," which involve firing missiles toward an area near an enemy state or into the waters off of an enemy-occupied island to cause the enemy to feel an even greater sense of psychological pressure.[34]

The objective of conventional missile force deterrence operations is to influence the enemy's decisions by convincing them that China's missile force has powerful strike capabilities and that Beijing has the will to use them if necessary to prevent the enemy from challenging China's interests or to compel the enemy to accept Beijing's demands. Chinese military publications underscore that the conventional missile force is a powerful instrument of deterrence in this respect. But they also note that, if deterrence fails to achieve China's political objectives, the troops must be prepared to quickly make the transition to conducting conventional missile strikes as part of a conventional missile attack campaign.

Conventional Missile Attack Campaigns

Science of Second Artillery Campaigns defined conventional missile attack campaigns as:

> . . . the offensive operational action of conventional firearm strikes on the enemy's key targets that is implemented by the conventional missile large formation of the Second Artillery based on the operational intention of the higher level as well as being under the uniform command in order to achieve specific strategic goals or campaign goals.[35]

Conventional missile campaigns are subject to a variety of political constraints and require high-level decision-making. According to *Science of Second Artillery Campaigns*,

> Because its campaign objectives and strategic objectives are closely connected, the operations of the Second Artillery conventional missile strike campaign involve the overall strategic situation. There are many campaign activities under the jurisdiction of campaign commanders at the current level that must be decided by commanders at a higher level or even by strategic commanders at an even higher level.[36]

Authoritative publications list a number of potential targets for Second Artillery conventional missile strikes, including enemy command centers, communications hubs, radar stations, other information and communications-related targets, missile positions, air force bases, naval facilities, railway stations, bridges, logistical facilities, energy and electrical power centers, and aircraft carrier strike groups.

The objectives of a conventional missile strike campaign are to "paralyze the enemy's command systems, weaken the enemy's military strength and its ability to continue operations, create psychological shock in the enemy and sway its operational resolve and halt the powerful enemy's military interventionist activities."[37]

Attacks will combine conventional cruise and ballistic missile strikes. The Second Artillery also has electronic warfare forces, and missile firepower strikes will increasingly be integrated with network and electronic warfare.[38] Information warfare will "pave the way" prior to the initiation of firepower strikes. First targets will include information systems such as command and control centers, radar stations, and communications networks. Not only are such targets are "the core of the operational system," they are also its weakest parts. By striking these targets first, the Second Artillery aims to achieve the effect of "striking one point and paralyzing a large part of the body."[39]

According to both *Science of Second Artillery Campaigns* and the 2006 edition of *Science of Campaigns,* the conventional missile strike campaign may be organized and implemented independently, but it is usually carried out as part of a joint campaign. As the former puts it, "The Second Artillery conventional missile strike operation is usually implemented in the context of the joint campaign. It engages in coordinated operation with other armed services and service arms, implementing strike against the enemy's important targets."[40] It may be part of a joint firepower strike campaign, joint blockade campaign, joint island landing campaign, joint border counterattack campaign, or joint anti-air-raid campaign.[41]

The Second Artillery plays a crucial role in joint operations by helping to achieve electromagnetic dominance, air supremacy, and sea control, as well as facilitating ground operations if required. The role of the Second Artillery's conventional missile force in enabling the other services to successfully carry out their missions is seen as particularly critical in the island landing campaign. According to *Science of Second Artillery Campaigns,* in the island landing campaign, the PLA "must first depend on the navy to seize the command of the sea, yet the securing of the command of the sea must depend on the air force and other aviation forces to seize air dominance; as for the seizing of air dominance and electromagnetic dominance, the Second Artillery conventional missile force can have critical effects."[42]

The role of the Second Artillery becomes even more important if a "powerful enemy" intervenes in a conflict along China's periphery. According to *Science of Second Artillery Campaigns:*

> The operation of resisting a powerful enemy's military intervention refers to the implementation of a fire strike operation of an expulsion quality against the enemy under the unified plan of the joint campaign command element, and which centers on the use of naval, aerial, and Second Artillery long range firepower.[43]

Chinese writers state that potential types of military intervention by a "powerful enemy" may include a show of military strength through deployment of one or more carrier battle groups, establishment of no-fly areas and restricted sea zones, direct intervention by air and naval forces, and strategic air strikes. The main actions to be conducted in response to U.S. intervention would include "firepower harassment," "frontal firepower deterrence," "flank firepower expulsion," "concentrated fire assaults," "information offensives," and "long-range warning strikes."

CONCLUSION

Chinese strategists have clearly devoted a considerable amount of time and attention to thinking about conventional missile force campaigns. Since the assignment of the mission of "dual deterrence, dual operations" to the Second Artillery and the establishment of China's rapidly growing conventional missile force, Chinese military thinkers have published several key volumes that address these issues in detail and provide some previously unavailable insights into the types of activities that Second Artillery missile force units would conduct as part of a conventional missile strike campaign, as well as how these activities would fit into a broader joint campaign.

Notwithstanding these impressive advances, Second Artillery conventional missile force campaigns would still face some limitations. For example, the number of conventional ballistic missiles in China's inventory has grown rapidly in recent years, but even with approximately 1,000 to 1,200 SRBMs in its inventory the Second Artillery still faces operational constraints. Indeed, authoritative sources emphasize that Second Artillery planners and operators would need to pay careful attention to the rate of missile consumption during conventional missile campaigns.[44]

Whatever limitations conventional Second Artillery forces still face, however, this is a challenge that the U.S. military must take seriously. Already conventional missiles offer the PLA the prospect of being able to largely destroy Taiwan's air force and other key land targets in a preemptive strike, allowing its own air force a far less contested position in the event of a cross-strait conflict. Even more significantly for U.S. planners, China appears to be on the verge of being able to threaten U.S. surface vessels with the world's first land-based conventional ballistic missiles capable of targeting a moving ship at sea. While Chinese strategists would probably use a very different term, this might be described as a "competitive strategy." This is because it exploits the fact that missiles are typically far easier and cheaper to attack with than to defend against to pose challenges that could be very difficult and expensive for the United States and its friends and allies to address effectively. The United States should avoid playing into Beijing's hands by investing disproportionately in technologies that could leave it on the wrong end of an arms race that might prove too costly to continue to wage. Instead, U.S. planners must develop their own asymmetric approaches that exploit China's vulnerabilities, and given current and expected budgetary constraints they must do so cost effectively.

NOTES

The views expressed in this chapter are those of the authors alone.

1. Office of the Secretary of Defense, *Military and Security Developments Involving the People's Republic of China 2010* (Washington, DC: Department of Defense, 2010), 1.

2. National Air and Space Intelligence Center, *Ballistic and Cruise Missile Threat* (Dayton, OH: National Air and Space Intelligence Center, April 2009), 3.

3. Wang Yongxiao, Cao Jienbing, and Tao Shelan, "Second Artillery Uses Science and Technology to Strengthen Forces—Rapid Missile Strike Capability Makes New Strides," *China News Agency,* July 23, 2007.

4. Second Artillery Force of the People's Liberation Army, *Science of Second Artillery Campaigns* (Beijing: People's Liberation Army Press, 2004), 274.

5. Ibid., 273.

6. Ibid., 273.

7. Ibid., 274.

8. John Wilson Lewis and Hua Di, "China's Ballistic Missile Programs: Technologies, Strategies, Goals," *International Security* 17:2 (Fall 1992): 6.

9. Second Artillery Force, *Science of Second Artillery Campaigns,* 54.

10. Ibid., 54.

11. Zhao Xijun, *Intimidation Warfare: A Comprehensive Discussion on Missile Deterrence* (Beijing: National Defense University Press, 2005), 83.

12. Ibid. , 77–78.

13. Office of the Secretary of Defense, *Military and Security Developments Involving the People's Republic of China 2010*, 43.

14. Office of the Secretary of Defense, *Military and Security Developments Involving the People's Republic of China 2011*, 78.

15. Office of the Secretary of Defense, *Military and Security Developments Involving the People's Republic of China 2010*, 66.

16. National Air and Space Intelligence Center, *Ballistic and Cruise Missile Threat*, 13.

17. Office of the Secretary of Defense, *Military and Security Developments Involving the People's Republic of China 2011*, 78.

18. Office of the Secretary of Defense, *Military and Security Developments Involving the People's Republic of China 2010*, 66.

19. Ibid., 31.

20. Ibid., 31.

21. National Air and Space Intelligence Center, *Ballistic and Cruise Missile Threat*, 14.

22. Office of the Secretary of Defense, *Military and Security Developments Involving the People's Republic of China 2010*, 66.

23. Ibid., 33.

24. Office of the Secretary of Defense, *Military and Security Developments Involving the People's Republic of China 2011*, 3.

25. "Press Availability with General Chen Bingde," Transcript of Remarks by Admiral Michael Mullen, Chairman of the Joint Chiefs of Staff and General Chen Bingde, Beijing, China, 11 July 2011; available at www.jcs.mil/speech.aspx?ID=1626.

26. National Defense Report Editing Committee, Ministry of National Defense, *2011 ROC National Defense Report* (Taipei: Ministry of National Defense, August 2011), 71; available at www.mnd.gov.tw/2011mndreport/en/minister.html.

27. See "DF-21D ASBM Deployed, but China Daily Probably Incorrect in Claiming '2,700km Range'; Gen. Chen Bingde Never Said That"; available at www.andrewerickson.com/2012/01/df-21d-asbm-deployed-but-china-daily-probably-incorrect-in-claiming-2700km-range-gen-chen-bingde-never-said-that/.

28. Office of the Secretary of Defense, *Military and Security Developments Involving the People's Republic of China 2010*, 66.

29. See "KongDi-63 Air-Launched Land Attack Cruise Missile," *China's Defence Today*, October 20, 2008; available at www.sinodefence.com/airforce/weapon/kd63.asp.

30. Office of the Secretary of Defense, *Military and Security Developments Involving the People's Republic of China 2011*, 4.

31. Ibid., 31.

32. Zhao, *Intimidation Warfare*, 167.

33. Ibid., 171.

34. Ibid., 171.

35. Second Artillery Force, *Science of Second Artillery Campaigns*, 46.

36. Ibid., 318.

37. Ibid., 318.

38. Ibid., 78–79.

39. Ibid., 79.

40. Ibid., 327.

41. Ibid., 317.

42. Ibid., 323–324.

43. Ibid., 400.

44. Zhang Yulang, *The Science of Campaigns* (Beijing: National Defense University Press, 2006).

13 JAPAN'S COMPETITIVE STRATEGIES AT SEA

A Preliminary Assessment

Toshi Yoshihara

CHINA'S GROWING CAPACITY to disrupt the maritime order in Asia and the associated operational dilemmas that U.S. forces are likely to encounter in the Western Pacific are well documented. An emerging consensus holds that Beijing could erect a no-go zone to preclude American maritime entry into waters along the East Asian littoral. Consequently, American defense planners have energetically debated the implications of China's emerging anti-access and access denial strategy. In contrast, there is scant evidence that Japanese strategists have engaged seriously in a discourse on coping with China's ascent at sea. Tokyo remains unprepared intellectually and materially to cope with Beijing's maritime prowess.

This inertia owes in large part to the conventional wisdom that the Maritime Self-Defense Force (MSDF) and its sister services will continue to enjoy a nearly insurmountable qualitative superiority over the People's Liberation Army (PLA) for the foreseeable future.[1] Japan, according to the prevalent narrative, has plenty of time readjust and stay ahead of China. Yet, as Chinese military modernization proceeds apace, this upbeat assumption is coming under increasing strain. Indeed, China's race to parity in several critical indices of naval power suggests that Japan may soon be in a disadvantaged position.

In short, Tokyo can no longer afford to pursue a naval strategy that hews closely to the status quo. Staying the course would likely incur unacceptable strategic risks, including shakier access to sea-lanes and insecure maritime flanks. Such an ominous prospect demands a departure (perhaps a radical one) from the sanguine assumptions that have underwritten Japanese assessments since the end of the Cold War. This chapter contends that the competitive strategies concept offers a useful point of departure for developing new approaches to meeting China's naval rise. By effectively capitalizing on Tokyo's underlying strengths while accentuating Beijing's fundamental vulnerabilities at sea, Japan could severely complicate Chinese maritime ambitions.

A COMPETITIVE STRATEGIES FRAMEWORK FOR JAPAN

To paraphrase Stephen P. Rosen's formulation in Chapter 2 of this volume, competitive strategies seek to induce an opponent to play a game that is stacked in favor of the defender. The game maximizes the defender's comparative advantages while exploiting the adversary's enduring weaknesses, frailties that it cannot quickly reverse without enormous financial, material, and intellectual outlays. Attempts by the opponent to shore up its position in such a game would result in the diversion of substantial resources away from its inherent strengths. Ideally, such a lopsided reallocation would undercut the adversary's ability to undertake offensive action or the most dangerous moves against the defender.[2] The competitive strategies approach assumes that the opponent possesses deeply embedded predispositions that can be manipulated by the defender. The objective for the defender is to set conditions or to furnish incentives that stimulate those preprogrammed preferences, thus inclining the adversary to carry out self-defeating behaviors.

Competitive strategies can be understood as a subset of a larger cost-imposing strategy outlined in Bradford A. Lee's Chapter 3. A cost-imposing strategy increases or threatens to increase the pain of initiating or continuing a course of action to such an extent that the adversary renounces its objectives or changes its behavior. In theory, the defender can raise the barriers to achieving certain goals well above the exertions that the opponent is willing or able to expend. If the adversary bows to the defender's will, then the latter wins. By comparison, the diversionary effects of competitive strategies may not be as decisive. As Lee suggests, shifts in resource allocations by themselves may be a necessary but insufficient step to achieving favorable and durable outcomes for the defender.

This analytical distinction between a competitive strategy and a cost-imposing strategy is not a minor quibble. A cost-imposing strategy employed in a hot or cold war presumes that tangible outcomes are desired, even if poorly articulated or understood. Yet it is not clear that Tokyo has any kind of meaningful end state in mind for China. In the absence of objectives that could be defined as victory over Beijing, a cost-imposing strategy may not (yet) be appropriate for Tokyo. By contrast, competitive strategies promise to buy time for Japan in a period when the future course of China is uncertain and probably unknowable. By diverting Chinese resources away from capabilities and options that most threaten Japan, Tokyo is afforded some strategic breathing space to better position itself in an increasingly competitive peacetime environment.

This chapter considers a range of potential competitive strategies that Japan could employ at sea. In particular, it identifies operational concepts designed to steer China toward disproportionately costly countermeasures or to mitigate the risks posed by the PLA's most effective naval capabilities. The analysis is limited to peacetime preparations for crisis or conflict in the maritime domain. These proposed options do not presume either the imminence of hostilities or the inevitability of conflict between Japan and China. Indeed, it is a central contention of this chapter that the anticipated diversionary effects produced by competitive strategies at the operational level are likely to dissuade and deter Beijing from naval adventurism, thus stabilizing regional strategic dynamics.

SINO-JAPANESE THREAT PERCEPTIONS AT SEA

Japan's defense community has been increasingly open about its ambivalence toward China's naval modernization. A major turning point in Japanese attitudes can be traced to 2004, when a Chinese *Han*-class nuclear attack submarine sailed through Japan's territorial waters. The tense standoff between the Chinese submarine and Japanese antisubmarine units produced a crystallizing effect on Tokyo's threat perceptions. Some of the subsequent maritime incidents are worthy of attention:

- In October 2008 a surface action group led by a *Sovremennyy*-class destroyer steamed through the Tsugaru Strait (the first time People's Liberation Army Navy, or PLAN, units had conducted such a transit), circumnavigated Japan, and circled back to port by way of the international strait between Okinawa and the Miyako Islands.
- In June 2009 a flotilla centered on a *Luzhou*-class guided-missile destroyer—a vessel armed with an advanced air defense system— voyaged to waters near Okinotorishima through the same maritime gateway.
- In April and July of 2010, Chinese squadrons transited the Miyako Strait, evidently Chinese commanders' passage of choice. In the former case, the JMSDF destroyers *Choukai* and *Suzunami*

unexpectedly encountered eight PLAN warships and two submarines in international waters southwest of Okinawa, near the Ryukyus.

Though modest compared to U.S. naval operations, these expeditions demonstrate the PLAN's capacity to operate east of the Japanese archipelago and its growing reach in the Western Pacific. Consequently, in its annual White Papers, Japan's Ministry of Defense has reported with increasing granularity on the character of PLA operations in or near Japanese waters. The 2009 issue for the first time included charts depicting the courses taken by China's flotillas. The graphics revealed the patterns of Chinese naval penetrations through the southern Ryukyu island chain.[3] For some Japanese, then, recent Sino-Japanese encounters offer a troubling foretaste of East Asia's nautical future.[4]

Not only has Japan taken notice, but it may also be actively hedging against China's rise. Japan's recent defense modernization efforts appear to be tailored specifically to emerging Chinese military capabilities.[5] A senior official claims that Japan's recent naval acquisitions are designed "to have China's submarines in check."[6] Looking ahead, Tetsuo Kotani of the Ocean Policy Research Foundation, an outspoken advocate of a more assertive Japanese maritime strategy, urges Japan to invest in submarines and antisubmarine platforms now as an answer to China's nascent aircraft carrier program.[7] In December 2010, Japan's Ministry of Defense issued its long-awaited National Defense Program Guidelines, which furnish the long-term basis for the nation's defense policy. The planning document directs the MSDF to expand the submarine force from sixteen boats to twenty-two, substantially breaching a numerical ceiling that had been fixed since the 1976 guidelines.[8] The unprecedented decision was widely interpreted as a direct response to the Chinese navy's activism.[9]

Chinese strategists, too, increasingly view Asia's complex maritime geography—and Japan's place in it—as a barrier to their nation's rightful ambitions. A glance at the map of the Western Pacific rim shows that PLAN formations cannot reach the Pacific high seas—whether to menace the east coast of Taiwan or to interdict U.S. forces—without passing through the islands that enclose the Chinese coastline. A substantial body of Chinese writings perceives an island barrier obstructing China's entry into the oceanic thoroughfare. In the eyes of some analysts, the first island chain—which runs southward from the Japanese archipelago to the Philippine islands—compromises the mainland's long coastline by restricting Beijing's nautical activities. As two senior officers of the PLA observe, "Because of the nature of geography, China can be easily blockaded and cut off from the sea, and Chinese coastal defense forces are difficult to concentrate."[10]

Japan in particular stands out to the Chinese as a potential impediment to Beijing's seaward advances. To some, the Japanese archipelago is home to the combined military power of the U.S.-Japan alliance, a strategic bloc that possesses the resolve and the capability to frustrate and even contain Chinese maritime ambitions.[11] One author frets, "The geographic conditions arising from the westward extension of the Japanese islands also confer to this 'aircraft carrier' a combat range that virtually covers eastern China, virtually all of China's oceanic exists and sea lines of communications."[12] The Japanese archipelago constitutes not only the northern segment of the first island chain but also the northern terminus of the second island chain, which meanders southward from northern Japan to Papua New Guinea. As PLA forces start operating between the inner and outer island chains, it will be increasingly commonplace for them to pass through Japanese-held narrow seas and cruise along Japan's eastern maritime frontier. As the PLAN extends its operations, Chinese analysts expect encounters with Japanese naval forces within the relatively confined spaces of the Yellow, East, and South China Seas to increase.[13]

Geopolitically minded commentators also pay special attention to the Ryukyu Islands. Some worry that this crescent-shaped archipelago essentially closes off China from the Pacific Ocean. Three naval combat-systems engineers from the Marine Design and Research Institute describe Beijing's maritime predicament in stark geopolitical terms. Of the sixteen major straits and channels critical to China's oceanic access, they claim, eleven are located along the Ryukyus, under Japanese control.[14] Shen Weilie conceives of Okinawa as the "forward position" of the U.S. "westward strategy" in Asia.[15] He argues that cities such as Shanghai, Hangzhou, and Xiamen are within striking distance of the island, while the Osumi and Miyako straits could be monitored and blockaded from there. Chinese strategists have been quite candid about this redoubt's operational importance to Japan during a cross-strait scenario. Aviation units forward-deployed along the Ryukyu chain, contends Li Zhi, would play a critical part in contesting Chinese control of the air and sea.[16] As such, analysts carefully track the military disposition of the Self-Defense Forces on the Ryukyus. Every shift in posture, including minor deployments, is assessed under a microscope.[17]

Geography, therefore, has situated two seafaring nations in close quarters, leaving both astride each other's access to the maritime commons. China cannot fulfill its maritime destiny without breaching this natural obstruction, a major portion of which is controlled by a historical nemesis and a distrusted neighbor. Clearly, elements of competition already animate Sino-Japanese maritime interactions, and the waters bounded by the Ryukyu island chain will likely be the physical locus of this rivalry.

JAPAN'S LEGACY STRATEGY

During the late Cold War, Japan helped advance one of the key competitive strategies employed by the United States. The U.S. Navy aggressively employed its superior antisubmarine warfare (ASW) capability against vulnerable Soviet strategic ballistic missile submarines (SSBNs). The goal was to compel Moscow to adopt a defensive posture, thereby steering the Soviet fleet away from more offensively oriented deterrent patrols.[18] This stratagem dovetailed with the larger offensive maritime strategy that came to dominate U.S. naval thinking in the 1980s. In the event of a superpower conflagration, the U.S. Navy planned to open a new front in Asia, where it would unleash tremendous striking power ashore and at sea against Soviet forces in the Far East. Given that a large proportion of the Soviet Union's high-value SSBNs operated in the Pacific, the United States sought to divide Moscow's attention between a secondary theater to its east and the primary contest in Europe.[19]

Japan would have figured prominently in any U.S.-led offensive sea control operation.[20] Despite the MSDF's relatively modest naval capabilities, it was able effectively to exploit Japan's geographic features and leverage the operational advantages of the assets it already possessed. In particular, the MSDF deployed modern diesel-electric submarines and honed undersea tactics that proved invaluable to the needs of the maritime strategy.[21] By blocking key chokepoints with submarines, fixed- and rotary-wing ASW units, and an elaborate undersea monitoring system, the MSDF in effect bottled up Soviet submarines in the Sea of Japan. At the same time, Japan's naval gatekeepers guaranteed that the same thoroughfares stayed open for U.S. offensive operations in the Far East.

Japan's supporting role in the U.S. regional strategy against the Soviet Union produced a world-class regional navy in Asia, a position that the maritime service retains today. Indeed, as currently postured, the MSDF would certainly exact a high price in a naval contest with the PLAN.[22] Not surprisingly, Cold War–era legacy systems and operational concepts continue to dominate Japanese naval planning. Yet doing more of the same may no longer be sufficient for Tokyo. Many of the tools that served Japan so well during the Cold War could be forced into obsolescence as the PLA fields ever more advanced weapons to contest command of the air and the seas along China's maritime periphery.

Japanese airborne ASW units, which have enjoyed pride of place in the MSDF's strategy, are likely to suffer diminishing returns in the coming years. Although ASW is a core competency of the maritime service, submarine warfare is arguably the most vibrant dimension of China's military modernization. The PLAN's submarine fleet has been growing larger, quieter, and more lethal over the past decade. Owing to the extraordinary demands that submarine hunting places on human skill and on naval assets, those conducting ASW are inherently disadvantaged. Pitting strength against strength in a symmetrical contest does not, by definition, dovetail with competitive strategies.

At the same time, the platforms and locations from which Japanese airborne ASW units would be launched are already more vulnerable today to Chinese regional strike than just a decade ago.

As the size of the PLA's theater missiles increases, the SDF will be deprived of its sanctuaries in eastern portions of the Japanese archipelago, including Yokosuka naval base and Misawa air base. If China were to prosecute preemptive missile strikes against regional bases, then airborne ASW units could be precluded from taking to the air, at least during the initial stages of a conflict. Japanese ASW flattops and destroyers that are in port and at pierside—essentially fixed targets—may also be vulnerable to bolt-from-the-blue missile attacks.

Japanese units at sea and in the air would be no safer in the future. When China's antiship ballistic missiles (ASBMs) enter service, the PLA might lock its crosshairs on Japan's ASW helicopter carriers. As Admiral Yamazaki warns, "If the ASBMs are simply programmed to track large ships, then the large 22DDH [the next-generation helicopter carrier] would be an attractive target second only to the US aircraft carrier in the Japan-US fleet conducting joint operations."[23] China's growing integrated air-defense systems along the coastline and onboard major surface combatants suggest that fixed-wing ASW aircraft may not be very survivable when operating in airspaces close to Chinese shores. In short, the big-ticket defense items that have been the centerpiece of Japan's modernization drive over the past decade could become— to borrow Andrew Krepinevich's evocative term—"wasting assets."[24]

ALTERNATIVE COMPETITIVE STRATEGIES

The potential for Japan's existing forces to undergo a severe depreciation in operational value suggests that Tokyo may need to introduce new capabilities and concepts to compete effectively over the long term. To do so would require Japan to overturn some of the defense-dominant approaches to the maritime competition. The following are a few proposals that could aid Japanese and U.S.

planners in developing new roles for the SDF. These alternative courses of action are not intended as substitutes for existing capabilities, such as the airborne ASW units, that are already available to the Japanese. Rather, they would supplement or expand on the existing force structure. It is worth emphasizing that these options loosen, for the purposes of this analysis, the political constraints that would likely stand in the way of Tokyo. The aim is to facilitate some thought experiments about optimal strategies in a peacetime competition.

One legacy system that would feed into Japan's competitive strategy at sea is submarines. Tokyo could exploit China's conspicuous weaknesses in ASW by increasing the size of its submarine fleet, threatening to hold the PLAN's surface and undersea fleets at greater risk with a larger and thus more persistent undersea presence. Tokyo might be able to enlarge its undersea forces without imposing excessive burdens on Japan's fragile fiscal position. The MSDF has traditionally decommissioned submarines unusually early, introducing more advanced boats to replace older ones. To support the expanded mission, the maritime service could easily extend the service life of its fleet by at least ten years. Keeping boats at sea longer would allow for a steady growth in fleet size without substantially increasing acquisition costs.

An offensively oriented submarine posture could nudge China in directions that tilt the naval balance in favor of Japan and the United States. Beijing might be compelled to devote far more resources in ASW than it has in the past to protect its surface combatants and submarines operating within the first island chain. Historically, China has paid little attention to ASW capabilities, preferring to invest in other naval programs such as submarines and area air defense warships. This peculiar neglect may reflect Chinese recognition that attaining mastery of ASW would incur exorbitant costs in personnel as well as organizational and material resources. It is thus possible that Beijing has rejected ASW as a viable mission, conceding this undersea contest to its more capable adversaries.[25] Investments in defensive systems, such as ASW aviation units, might deprive the PLAN of the finances that would otherwise be available to keep up the production rate of its submarines and other offensive platforms. A more defensively oriented posture could keep Chinese naval forces confined behind the island barrier, freeing up maneuver room for the U.S. and Japanese navies. If, on the other hand, the PLAN is impervious to allied attempts to prod it into a defensive posture, then Chinese inaction on the ASW front would likely confer mounting, perhaps overwhelming, undersea advantages to Japan and the United States. In other words, China's maritime position would erode whether it elects to respond to the submarine challenge or not.

The defensive use of Japan's maritime geography might also go far to secure an advantage over China. Tokyo could seek to preclude Chinese entry into the Pacific along the Ryukyu island chain with offensive mine warfare. The MSDF already boasts a world-class minesweeping fleet that could be refitted and retrained to lay mines. Large quantities of cheap sea mines could threaten Chinese surface ships and submarines attempting to break through the narrow and shallow straits of the archipelago.[26] The Air SDF could also employ long-range, heavy-lift aircraft to conduct high-volume aerial mining across the length of the Ryukyus to quickly seal off transit routes in a conflict. Air delivery would be particularly useful for plugging wide gaps, such as the Miyako Strait. A mix of bottom mines and deep-sea mines could be laid to account for the varying depths of the nautical corridors. The operational aim would be to keep Chinese naval forces hemmed in behind the first island chain, compressing the zone of Chinese anti-access/access denial to the maximum extent possible. Such an island barrier would reduce surface and subsurface threats to U.S. and Japanese naval forces operating east of the first island chain.

Japanese offensive mine warfare holds promise as an element of a competitive strategy. As in ASW, the PLAN has fared poorly in mine countermeasures (MCM). An excellent study on Chinese mine warfare states that, "Chinese naval strategists are cognizant of China's traditional weakness in MCM and of resulting vulnerabilities . . . Chinese MCM will not reach the technological level of Western MCM in the near future."[27] Minesweeping operations are by nature "a time-consuming and arduous process" that demand advanced equipment, high technical proficiency, endurance, and patience.[28] Moreover, Chinese sea control and air superiority—both doubtful prospects near defended Japanese territories—would be necessary conditions to clear mines effectively and at acceptable risk. A credible threat to close off the Ryukyus would thus exploit a critical Chinese vulnerability that cannot be quickly remedied.

Another major comparative strength of Japanese mine warfare is that China would not be able to retaliate in kind, at least not without severe risks. Most of Japan's population centers, economic hubs, and military bases are located on the eastern seaboard of the Japanese archipelago. The MSDF enjoy easy egress into the Pacific and the Sea of Japan from Sasebo and Kure naval bases. For the PLAN to sow mines near Japanese access points, its warships and aircraft would have to cross several hundred kilometers of open waters. Mine-laying units en route to their target areas would be vulnerable to Japanese defenders in the air and at sea. Indeed, PLA forces would not likely survive in contested environments without substantial numbers of escorts.

Whether Japanese mine warfare would thus encourage risk aversion among Chinese naval leaders is unclear.

It is possible that China would seek to neutralize the mine threat even at the risk of incurring high costs. Psychologically, an impenetrable island chain plays on prevalent Chinese fears that the PLAN could be shut out of the most direct route to the high seas. Questions about the Chinese navy's ability to secure the nation's critical sea lines of communications—the lifeblood of China's economic vitality—as well as public pressure to do something about China's potential energy and commercial insecurity would surely mount. The prospect that Japan could potentially dictate the terms of this competition might be politically unbearable. To a lesser extent, the sunk costs in developing the frontline submarine fleet might condition Chinese naval leaders to balk at conceding the contest over access to the Pacific high seas. These are matters of national and institutional pride that could galvanize the PLAN to act.

If Beijing were to assign much higher priority to mine-clearing missions, then the PLAN would have to invest heavily in MCM platforms and technologies. Additionally, the Chinese navy would need to develop the tactics, techniques, and procedures for performing a highly complex task. An aggressive turn to MCM could impose opportunity costs on other buildup plans, like China's submarine and carrier programs, potentially blunting developments that could enhance the PLA's offensive power. The PLAN would also need to dedicate a capable task force to protect the virtually defenseless MCM vessels against air and naval threats. In times of hostilities, PLA forces could suffer substantial losses in the contest for sea control and air dominance over areas where Chinese minesweeping operations would be taking place. In short, Japan stands to reap significant dividends should China succumb to temptations to defeat mine warfare.

To shore up its submarine and offensive mine warfare capabilities, Tokyo could militarily fortify its position along the Ryukyus, which, with the exception of Okinawa and Miyako, are largely undefended. Stouter defenses would be designed to keep Chinese aircraft and warships at bay, slamming shut an important outlet for China. From a historical perspective, Japan is certainly no stranger to island defense. Japanese tactical innovations during the Pacific War exacted a terrible toll on the American island-hopping campaign. More relevant, Japan developed powerful coastal defenses to defeat a Soviet invasion of Hokkaido Island. Shore-based fighters armed with antiship missiles and mobile antiship cruise missile (ASCM) batteries on land provided a layered defense against amphibious assault forces that would have surged across the

Sea of Japan. This Cold War–era anti-invasion strategy offers fruitful lessons that could be applied to the southwestern offshore islands.

Japan could deploy truck-mounted antiship and antiair missiles that would provide a protective umbrella over the entire island chain. For example, the Ground SDF's Type 88 SSM-1, which has been in service since the late 1980s, can strike ships at sea from launch positions located 100 kilometers inland. If redeployed to key points along the Ryukyus, a group of ASCM batteries could cover all the narrow seas in the East China Sea. Able to "shoot and scoot," these mobile platforms could quickly disperse and move by night or under cover to elude Chinese retaliatory strikes. On islands where rough terrain and limited road infrastructure are likely to constrain movement, additional force protection measures—including tunnels, hardened shelters, disguised storage sites, and decoys—would substantially undermine China's capacity to identify, target, and destroy Japanese units. Geography would also add tremendous operational burdens on the PLA: Neutralizing the Ryukyus would require it to open a new front nearly 1,000 kilometers wide.

If the defenses on the island chain were robust enough to close off or severely threaten Chinese access to the Pacific, then Japan would have at its disposal an additional competitive strategy at sea. Chinese attempts at sanitizing threats across the Ryukyu island chain with ballistic and cruise missile strikes would almost certainly accelerate the rate at which the PLA expends its finite amount of ammunition. Although China boasts a large and growing arsenal of precision strike systems, these are still nonrenewable commodities. A missile that is fired is an irretrievable asset. A wide geographic front containing numerous moving targets would thus pose both a targeting and resource challenge, particularly in a protracted conflict. A Chinese missile launched against a Japanese ASCM unit would amount to one fewer missile that might have been profitably used against other more important strategic sites. How Chinese planners would view and calculate such opportunity costs is unclear, but this interaction would clearly favor Tokyo. Japan's relatively abundant, cheap, and survivable defenses could compel China to exhaust expensive and scarce offensive weapons while still keeping the PLAN's prospects for a breakthrough in question.

In addition to defending forward along the island chain, Tokyo could adopt a defense-in-depth posture well east of the Japanese archipelago. Japan possesses thousands of offshore islands, with the farthest ones located near the Tropic of Cancer. Consequently, Japan's maritime service has long conceived of its defense perimeter in rather open-ended terms that extend far beyond the four home islands. An official history vividly describes the MSDF's area of operations: If Wakkanai, the northernmost city of Japan, is Copenhagen, then the Ishigaki, Okinotori, and Minamitori islands are the equivalents of Casablanca, Tripoli, and Alexandria, respectively. The MSDF is thus charged with patrolling and defending an expanse as large as NATO-Europe, plus the entire Mediterranean.[29] This body of water overlaps with significant portions of the U.S. Pacific Command's area of responsibility. As such, joint operations with the U.S. Navy in these common operating zones may be one way for Japan to cope with China's access denial strategies.

According to Admiral Yamazaki,

> From the standpoint of preserving an operational platform for arriving U.S. reinforcements, the strategic importance of the open fan-shaped triangular ocean area facing the main islands of Japan starting with a line drawn from Guam and extended to the Bashi Channel and then the Nansei Islands will definitely increase.[30]

A study on the future of the U.S.-Japan alliance is even more specific about potential Japanese naval missions. The authors recommend, "Japan ought to contribute to the defense of Guam, the central pillar of US strategy in the western Pacific. One option is for Japan to bear responsibility for defending sea lanes between Okinawa and Guam."[31] This bold proposal makes imminent sense because operations to secure unimpeded access to critical sea-lanes have long been a staple of the MSDF. It assumes that China might seek to contest U.S. sea control in waters out to the second island chain, disrupting transpacific lines of commercial and military communications. In response, the maritime service could clear and hold open transit corridors within the Ryukyu–Luzon Strait–Guam maritime triangle for U.S. forces in times of crisis or war.

By "defending backwards" to the second island chain, Japan would maximize its maritime strategic depth while attenuating the PLA's firepower. If the Japanese surface fleet operated farther from China's shores, the types and the volume of Chinese strike weapons capable of reaching the MSDF's combatants would concomitantly decline. At the same time, a temporary retreat to safer havens would draw out Chinese submarine and air units into the open ocean, a reaction that would play well to allied strengths in area air defense and ASW.[32] Applying Mao Zedong's guerilla tactics against the PLA, U.S. and Japanese task forces would lure their Chinese counterparts deep into the Pacific, disperse and isolate enemy units, and subject the adversary to piecemeal destruction. Japan would be able to fight on its own terms while equalizing, to a certain extent, China's home court advantage in adjacent waters.

In a major war, it can be assumed that the Chinese would target all naval bases on the Japanese archipelago, rendering them unusable for refueling, re-arming, and repairs. In this case, the allies could plan for the MSDF units to take refuge at U.S. facilities in Guam and Hawaii for resupply and other logistical support. It may even be necessary to homeport a Japanese flotilla at Guam on a rotational basis during peacetime, thus partially negating the dangers of a preemptive China missile attack against naval bases on the home islands. The maritime service would also need to substantially boost its organic at-sea replenishment fleet to support sustained operations on the high seas.

To fight effectively far from home waters, the MSDF could invest in systems that substantially enhance the range and firepower of existing platforms. For example, Japan could consider research and development in unmanned combat air systems that can be launched from the *Hyuga* helicopter carrier and the follow-on 22DDH. Designed to remain in service for at least four decades, these ships would certainly accommodate major refits and upgrades for such strike aircraft. As recent defense budgeting decisions demonstrate, Tokyo already exhibits considerable interest in the potential of unmanned aerial vehicles.[33] Allied cooperation in this area, similar to that of joint ballistic missile defense development, might pay long-term dividends.

The four purely hypothetical options reviewed in this chapter—submarine warfare, offensive mine warfare, island defense, and defense-in-depth carrier operations—can be understood as mutually supporting strategies. Japanese ASCM and SAM units based along the Ryukyus would contest China's efforts to seize sea control and air superiority over the East China Sea, thus easing the danger to the SDF's aerial and naval offensive mine operations. At the same time, these missile batteries might trigger many rounds of PLA precision strikes, potentially running down China's supply of ammunition. The minefields in the narrow seas would block or sink Chinese surface combatants and submarine forces attempting to breakout of the island chain while providing a protective screen to MSDF submarines operating near the Ryukyus. The PLA's attempts to fight through the island chain would likely reduce the number of submarines, warships, and aircraft capable of reaching the second island chain, thereby safeguarding the U.S. and Japanese task forces operating beyond China's anti-access zone.

Critics may object that these competitive strategies could well backfire. Determined to defeat Japan's access denial strategy, Beijing could redouble its efforts in ASW and MCM. The PLA could also pour more money into accumulating an even larger stock of missiles to overwhelm Japanese forces. The key risk is that China could in fact overcome its longstanding weaknesses, result-ing in an even more powerful Chinese military capable of both offensive and defensive operations within the first island chain. Although this line of reason-ing has some merit, it is also highly implausible. A countervailing response to the proposed competitive strategies combined with China's commitments to existing programs would require an unaffordable sum even for Beijing's deep pockets. China simply cannot do everything well at the same time without putting itself on what would amount to a wartime or cold war footing.

The immediate operational aim of these competitive strategies at sea is to defeat Chinese efforts at establishing and expanding its anti-access area over the waters along the first island chain in a major wartime scenario. However, a related peacetime objective is to visibly raise the potential costs to a Chinese no-go zone in the East Asian littorals. If the Chinese perceive Japanese com-petitive strategies as both effective and credible, then it is possible that China might be deterred from prosecuting the most escalatory and dangerous ele-ments of its access denial strategy. At a minimum, Japan's capacity to exact a high price in blood and treasure might condition a less confident PLA to think twice or proceed with greater caution in the event of a crisis or a conflict. As already noted, these operational preparations in peacetime are designed pri-marily to serve broader U.S. and Japanese strategic ends by enhancing crisis stability and shoring up conventional deterrence in Asia.

CONCLUDING THOUGHTS

In a long-term military competition with China, Japan is at once fortunate and disadvantaged in the maritime domain. The MSDF boasts a proud tradi-tion of excellence in antisubmarine warfare and mine countermeasures that may yield dividends in a rivalry with the PLAN. Yet, these are the same pock-ets of excellence that are likely to erode in the coming years as China's capacity to contest the air and the seas over its littoral environment leaps ahead. It is the central contention of this chapter that Tokyo must think more creatively and expansively about its future choices. One potentially fruitful approach is a competitive strategies framework.

An underlying theme of this chapter is that Japan could tremendously complicate Chinese naval planning if it chose to engage in competitive strate-gies. It is even possible to argue that Japan's past and current strategies at sea have permitted China to operate in a relatively permissive environment. Or, to put it more bluntly, Japan has not been responding competitively to China's nautical rise. Tokyo can either allow Beijing to challenge the maritime status quo free of resistance, or it could substantially raise the barriers to entry. The threat of increasing the costs to China's seaward march might be enough to signal Japanese resolve and to deter certain destabilizing Chinese behavior.

Another theme is that competitive strategies would require Tokyo to turn the tables on Beijing. Indeed, many of the options sketched out in this chapter, including submarine warfare and offensive mine warfare, essentially mimic Chinese operational preferences. The need for Japan to respond in kind stems in large part from a growing power disparity. Tokyo can no longer afford to cope with every offensive Chinese option with an exclusively defensive counter. Airborne antisubmarine warfare, mine countermeasures, missile defense, and air defense, while praiseworthy and necessary, are disproportionately expensive, difficult to perform, and cede the initiative to Beijing. Such a symmetrical approach to competition is reserved only for powers that possess absolute financial and technological advantages over their adversaries. Tokyo enjoys no such luxury.

These themes suggest an even larger strategic dilemma for Japan. It may be time for Japanese policymakers to acknowledge that Japan will become a successively weaker party vis-à-vis China. This trend is in part a result of declining U.S. military power relative to China in the Pacific theater. Short of a strategic accommodation with Beijing, Tokyo would need to respond more nimbly if it is to stay competitive in the Asian seas. The prospect of being displaced as a top-tier naval power in the region may be too difficult for many Japanese to concede at the moment. But an admission of this magnitude accompanied by a major reevaluation about Japan's place in maritime Asia may encourage more hardheaded thinking about Tokyo's long-term role in the competition with China. Now is the time to recognize this unavoidable reality.

NOTES

1. Tohru Kizu, "Japan and China—A Comparison of Their Sea Power," *Sekai no Kansen* (November 2004), 84–91.

2. See Andrew Marshall, *Long-Term Competition with the Soviets: A Framework for Strategic Analysis* (Santa Monica, CA: RAND, 1972), 21.

3. Japan Ministry of Defense, *Defense of Japan 2009*, July 2009, 56–57.

4. National Institute for Defense Studies, *East Asian Strategic Review* (Tokyo: NIDS, 2010), 127.

5. Christopher W. Hughes, *Japan's Remilitarisation* (London: IISS, 2009), 143.

6. Roundtable Discussion, "Can the SDF Protect Japan?" *Sapio*, July 22, 2009, 8.

7. Tetsuo Kotani, "The Day China Comes to Possess Aircraft Carriers," *RIPS' Eye*, 108, (March 6, 2009); available at www.rips.or.jp/from_rips/rips_eye/no108.html.

8. Government of Japan, Ministry of Defense, "National Defense Program Guidelines, FY2011–," December 17, 2010, appendix.

9. "Japan to Beef Up Submarines to Counter Chinese Power," *The Chosun Ilbo*, July 26, 2010; available at http://english.chosun.com/site/data/html_dir/2010/07/26/2010072601021.html.

10. Feng Liang and Duan Tingzhi, "Characteristics of China's Sea Geostrategic Security and Sea Security Strategy in the New Century," *Zhongguo Junshi Kexue* [China Military Science], January 1, 2007, 22–29.

11. Bai Yanlin, "The Unsinkable 'Fleet'—The First Island Chain and Navies," *Modern Navy* 10 (2007), 12.

12. Li Ziyu, "Combat Uses of Japan's Air Power," *Shipborne Weapons* (March 2007), 48.

13. Zhang Ming and Chen Xiangjun, "Collision in the Pacific: Assessing the Development of Sino-Japanese Maritime Power and Possible Confrontation in the New Century," *Shipborne Weapons* (November 2005), 19.

14. Yu Kaijin, Li Guansuo, and Zao Yongheng, "Island Chain Analysis," *Ship and Boat* 5 (October 2006), 14.

15. Shen Weilie, "Ryukyu, Island Chain, Great Power Strategy," *Lingdao Wencui* 5 (2006), 63.

16. Li Zhi, "Japanese and South Korean Aviation Units: Application to Naval Operations and Influence on China," *Shipborne Weapons* 12 (2007), 50.

17. See, for example, Gao Hui, "Japan's Military Deployment at Yonaguni Island and China's Maritime Security," *Naval and Merchant Ships* 9 (2009), 26–29.

18. See Caspar W. Weinberger, "U.S. Defense Strategy," *Foreign Affairs* 64 (4) (Spring 1986), 695; and Prepared Statement of Graham Allison, U.S. Congress, House Committee on Armed Services, *Competitive Strategies*, 101st Congress, first session, March 2–3, 1989, 18.

19. Norman Friedman, *The US Maritime Strategy* (Annapolis, MD: Naval Institute Press, 1988), 190.

20. Euan Graham, *Japan's Sea Lane Security, 1940–2004: A Matter of Life and Death?* (London: Routledge, 2006), 131.

21. Alessio Patalano, "Shielding the 'Hot Gates': Submarine Warfare and Japanese Naval Strategy in the Cold War and Beyond (1976–2006)," *Journal of Strategic Studies* 31 (6) (December 2008), 870.

22. Hideaki Matsumoto, "Ships and Aircraft of the JMSDF Today," *Sekai no Kansen* (July 2009), 152–157.

23. Makoto Yamazaki, "Thoughts about Eye-Catching 22DDH," *Sekai no Kansen*, (September 2009), 105.

24. Andrew F. Krepinevich, "The Pentagon's Wasting Assets: The Eroding Foundations of American Power," *Foreign Affairs* 88 (4) (July/August 2009), 18–33.

25. Lyle Goldstein, Miguel Martinez, and William Murray, "China's Future Airborne Anti-Submarine Capabilities: Light at the End of the Tunnel?" in *Chinese Aerospace Power: Evolving Maritime Roles,* Lyle Goldstein and Andrew Erickson, eds. (Annapolis, MD: Naval Institute Press, 2011), 186.

26. Ryohei Oga, "What the PRC Submarine Force Is Aiming For," *Sekai no Kansen* (July 2005), 99.

27. Andrew S. Erickson, Lyle J. Goldstein, and William S. Murray, *Chinese Mine Warfare: A PLA Navy's 'Assassin's Mace' Capability,* China Maritime Studies, 3 (June 2009), 46.

28. Ibid., 48.

29. MSDF Editorial Board, *Fifty-Year History of the MSDF* (Tokyo: Boeicho Kaijo Bakuryo Kanbu, 2003), 126.

30. Makoto Yamazaki, "Thoughts about Eye-Catching 22DDH," 105.

31. The Matsushita Institute of Government and Management, *A Critical Moment for the Japan-US Alliance: The Urgent Need for Progress toward a "Broad and Balanced Alliance,"* Japan-US Rising Leaders Project, MIGM Research Center, November 2008, 21.

32. Thomas P. Ehrhard and Robert O. Work, *Range, Persistence, Stealth, and Networking: The Case for a Carrier-Based Unmanned Combat Air System* (Washington, DC: CSBA, 2008), 217–218.

33. Japan Ministry of Defense, Defense Programs and Budget of Japan: Overview of FY2010 Budget, January 2010, 7.

14 STRATEGIC COMPETITION IN THE WESTERN PACIFIC

An Australian Perspective

Ross Babbage

AUSTRALIA'S DEFENSE PLANNERS face a serious challenge. The security environment in the Western Pacific is changing rapidly. Many of the military capabilities of the United States and its close allies in this theater are rapidly losing their strategic edge. In consequence, Australia's defense priorities need to be reviewed and consideration given to a series of alternative defense investment programs.

The primary driver for this rethink is the exceptionally rapid growth of China's military power. China is, for the first time, close to achieving a military capability to deny U.S. and allied forces access to much of the Western Pacific rim. Moreover, during the coming twenty years these anti-access/area denial capabilities are projected to grow stronger and reach out further.

Many of the fundamental assumptions on which Australia's and our Western allies' security planning have been based since World War II are now being seriously challenged. For instance, the assumption that the United States and its close allies will continue to enjoy an operational sanctuary in space is in serious doubt. The Peoples' Liberation Army (PLA) is actively engaged in programs to degrade or destroy the U.S. command, control, and communications (C3); the intelligence, surveillance, and reconnaissance (ISR); and the navigational systems that are all space based and critical for U.S. and Australian military operations.[1]

Second, the assumption that U.S. operational bases in Guam, Japan, and elsewhere will enjoy high levels of security in a future crisis is crumbling. This is primarily because the PLA is fielding ballistic and cruise missile systems and a number of other capabilities designed to destroy most key facilities there within a few hours and delivering persistent further attacks to prevent base resuscitation.[2] Some Australian defense facilities could also be targeted in such attacks.

Third, the assumption that U.S. and allied naval surface vessels can operate with assured security in all parts of the Western Pacific is also no longer valid. A combination of PLA long-range surveillance assets and land-, air-, and submarine-launched weaponry means that U.S. aircraft carrier strike groups and other surface vessels are now vulnerable up to 1,200 nautical miles from the Chinese coast.[3] This is further than carrier-based aircraft can fly unrefueled, so that were carrier strike groups tasked to strike targets on the Chinese coast or further inland, they would need to operate from very vulnerable locations.[4] Moreover, a new generation of Chinese submarines now poses a serious challenge to surface vessels much further out into the Pacific.[5]

Fourth, the assumption that U.S. and allied air forces would enjoy uncontested access to airspace in the Western Pacific is now also invalid. The PLA is fielding an impressive array of wide-area surveillance systems that are being integrated into a hardened air defense network and tied to a growing number of modern long-range surface-to-air missiles (SAMs) and advanced fighter aircraft.[6] The result is to make allied air operations in much of the Western Pacific vulnerable in a manner not contemplated since World War II.

Fifth, the assumption that in a crisis U.S. and allied surveillance, situational awareness, logistic, and other information networks would remain inviolate is invalid. China is working hard to develop capabilities to challenge, penetrate, or degrade a wide range of defense, national security, and logistics networks that would play key roles in any future crisis in the Western Pacific.[7]

Sixth, the assumption that, in the event of a major security crisis in the Pacific, Australia could rely on speedy and tailored military resupply from the United States is almost certainly invalid. U.S. defense planning for new security challenges in the Western Pacific makes clear that a future conflict in this theater could be extended over many months and maybe even years. Great efforts would be required to expand production of high-usage parts, precision-guided munitions, and many other supplies to sustain U.S. operations.[8] In those circumstances, the requirements of allies for resupply and support would likely be accorded modest priority.

These developments have fundamental implications for Australia's defense strategy, planning, and priorities. Some of the consequences are immediate. However, defense planners also face an even tougher task of selecting those new capabilities that will be required for 2030–2040. These decisions need to be made soon because it will take up to twenty years for any major new capabilities to be brought into service.

AUSTRALIA'S STRATEGIC CHALLENGES IN 2030

A key factor in Australia's security decision making will be judgments about what China might look like and how it might behave twenty to thirty years hence. Although there remain significant uncertainties about PLA military capabilities, strategies, and operational intentions in 2030–2040, Western defense planners have no choice but to make prudent judgments now about what should be expected in that time frame.

It is reasonable to assume that the Chinese economy twenty to thirty years into the future may be the largest in the world and that Chinese defense expenditures may exceed those of the United States. Moreover, even though Beijing will likely have broadened its strategic interests to include some concerns in distant theaters, its defense investments will probably continue to be focused heavily in the Western Pacific, where China will be seen to be the dominant military power.

Second, the PLA's strategic nuclear forces will have expanded substantially by 2030, possibly to two or three times their current size, and will include new generations of both land mobile and sea-based ballistic missiles. This larger and more sophisticated force will be broadly comparable to the greatly reduced United States and Russian strategic nuclear arsenals of the time and provide an effective deterrent against strategic nuclear attack.

Third, by 2030 most of the space, land-based, and maritime wide-area sensor systems deployed by China will have been further upgraded. Particularly strong progress is likely in surveillance of the surface and subsurface areas of the Western Pacific, although there will probably also be increased interest in surveillance and reconnaissance in some distant regions, particularly in the Indian Ocean and the Eastern Pacific. All of these upgraded sensor systems will be better integrated, and the resulting operational picture provided to senior commanders will be of significantly higher quality.

Fourth, the PLA will likely also be fielding a new generation of medium-range ballistic and cruise missiles.[9] These newer systems are likely to feature more stealthy characteristics, greater in-flight maneuverability, features to defeat missile defenses, greater accuracy, and a broader range of warhead options. These systems will have the potential to deliver a disarming first strike against allied forces in most, if not all, parts of the Western Pacific, well beyond the second island chain.

Fifth, China's submarine force will continue to grow with new classes of both nuclear and conventionally powered boats entering production during the coming two decades. The total People's Liberation Army Navy (PLAN) submarine fleet is likely to number seventy to a hundred boats in 2030.[10] The newer boats will carry a range of new and upgraded torpedoes, missiles, mines, and other weaponry. The professionalism of the PLAN crews can also be expected to have improved.

Sixth, by 2030 China will probably have been producing fifth-generation combat aircraft for five to ten years. These fighter-bomber aircraft will possess capabilities broadly similar to the United States F-22 and F-35. Hence, in this time frame, China's fighter-bomber force might comprise something like 800 fourth-generation aircraft and possibly some fifty to one hundred fifth-generation aircraft.[11] These systems, operating within China's upgraded wide-area Western Pacific sensor network, will pose a far more difficult challenge for allied forces seeking to operate in this theater.

Seventh, the PLAN's surface combatant force will also be greatly modernized, much larger, and more formidable. At this stage it is not clear whether the emphasis in Chinese naval shipbuilding during the next twenty years will be in general-purpose destroyer and frigate classes or whether China will decide to invest heavily in aircraft carrier strike groups, capable of conducting semi-self-contained combat operations in distant theaters. If it chooses the latter path, one to three aircraft carriers could be in service by 2030.

Eighth, China's air defenses in 2030 are also likely to be further modernized, better integrated, and more deeply hardened. By 2030 China will probably be manufacturing very advanced long-range SAMs with little, if any, external assistance.

Ninth, by 2030 China's antisatellite capabilities will have been further developed, and there is likely to have been at least one Chinese missile interception of a satellite in a distant geosynchronous orbit. Laser and other antisatellite systems are also likely to have reached a higher level of maturity.

Tenth, by 2030 China's cyber capabilities are likely to be world leading. This will be a reflection of the scale of the financial and human commitment to cyber programs, the quality and depth of engineering expertise committed to the effort, and the high-level strategic recognition accorded in China to the importance winning an advantage in this field.[12]

Perhaps the most difficult element of Chinese development to assess is the nature of Beijing's behavior twenty years hence. It is possible that China's international behavior may moderate as the Chinese leadership and the population at large start to feel that the country is being returned to its rightful international status. On the other hand, there is also the possibility that the achievement of clear economic and military predominance in the Western Pacific might foster the adoption of harder stances on so-called core security issues and periodically trigger aggressive actions. Prudent Western security planning should take full account of both possibilities.

Overall, then, by 2030 the PLA will probably pose a significantly stronger challenge to U.S. and allied forces in the Western Pacific. The Chinese are, however, most unlikely to try to match the Western allies in every type of military capability. They will probably continue to pursue a modified asymmetric strategy. They will likely seek to exploit perceived Western weaknesses to more effectively deny allied access to the Western Pacific, particularly within the second island chain.

In efforts to protect energy, trade, and other key interests in distant theaters, there is a prospect that selected force projection capabilities will be strengthened over time so that Chinese forces can operate more frequently and for more extended periods far removed from the homeland. In consequence, selected surface combatants, submarines, and probably some aircraft might be anticipated more frequently in the Indian Ocean, the Eastern Pacific, and possibly elsewhere.

THE CAPABILITY OF THE UNITED STATES TO RESPOND CONVINCINGLY

China's rapidly expanding military capabilities are being introduced to the Western Pacific at a time when the United States is less than ideally placed to generate an effective counter. The impact of the global financial crisis on the U.S. economy has been far deeper and potentially longer lasting than many had hitherto assumed. At the time of this writing American economic growth continues to be low, unemployment remains high (at 8.5 percent), and the U.S. budget deficit very high and still climbing. The continuing rise of government spending from 20 percent to 25 to 26 percent of GDP on a sustained basis since the 1960s[13] is converting the U.S. economy into what the prominent U.S. economist David Hale describes as "a version of a European welfare state."[14] The expected gradual economic recovery will boost tax receipts and help to slow the structural deterioration, but for the U.S. economy to be righted for the long term there is a need for serious and sustained cuts to government spending. There is little evidence at present that either the Obama administration or Congress is willing to contemplate such distasteful economic medicine.

The consequences for allied security are profound. If the outlook for the United States is of a crippled economy struggling to maintain momentum for the next decade or more, American capacities to maintain defense spending and generate an effective response to the Chinese challenge will be undermined. As David Hale argued recently:

> My message to all America's allies is don't count on US security guarantees beyond the year 2020. America's fiscal situation is so bad that Congress focuses exclusively on domestic issues, not on America's allies. I am not talking immediately but projecting out 10 years . . . I think allies such as Australia will have to accept more responsibility for their own security or form new regional alliances to buttress their security.[15]

These judgments may prove to be overstated, but they certainly give pause for thought.

A closely related problem concerns not just the scale of U.S. debt but also the fact that a large proportion of it is held by the Chinese government or Chinese commercial entities closely associated with the Chinese government. Chinese government spokespeople have stated on numerous occasions that they have no interest in exploiting this potential U.S. vulnerability.[16] Indeed, China has very strong commercial and broader economic interests in ensuring that the U.S. economy continues to thrive and absorb large numbers of Chinese products. Nevertheless, from the perspective of U.S. and allied security planners, the possibility that Beijing may be tempted to destabilize the American economy in a future crisis by manipulating this weakness should be deeply troubling.

A third constraint on decisive U.S. action in the Western Pacific is the country's distraction by major international demands in other theaters. To the extent that administration and congressional leaders have time to focus on challenges beyond America's borders, they are inclined to focus heavily on Afghanistan/Pakistan, Iraq, Iran, Israel, the Palestinians and the Middle East more generally, and then the problems just across the southern borders of the United States, particularly in Mexico. Western Pacific security planners need to appreciate that nearly all of Washington is distracted by domestic demands and by challenges in other parts of the world.

A fourth constraint is that the security analysts in the U.S. intelligence community, the Pentagon, the Department of State, and a few think tanks who appreciate the nature, scale, and momentum of the challenge posed by the PLA's rapid expansion appear to be in a distinct minority. Some progress was announced in the Obama administration's January 2012 Strategic Review, which accords a high priority to West Pacific security. Nevertheless, there remains a major challenge in maintaining the attention of administration and congressional leaders on the Chinese challenge, reviewing current policies and plans, and taking decisive action to improve the situation.

In combination, these factors are resonating in the Western Pacific. The long-held assumption of *Pax Americana* is starting to be doubted. Regional security planners are reluctantly questioning whether the United States will rise to the challenge.[17] Generally, in closed-door discussions, the credibility of the United States is being questioned, and Washington's political capital is starting to erode.

AVOIDING SELF-FULFILLING PROPHECY

This chapter is not suggesting that a major war between China and the United States is coming, nor does it wish for such a conflict. But it does argue that the Western Pacific security environment is being changed in fundamental ways by the scale and pattern of PLA development and that Australia and its allies are justified in being deeply concerned. This more challenging security environment is not one encouraged or welcomed by Australia, by the United States, or by the other Western allies, but it cannot be ignored or simply wished away. Australia, the United States, and its other close allies have no choice but to consider carefully how best to respond.

This chapter argues that in crafting a coherent Western response the United States and its close allies should not seek to confront China. Rather, the intent should be to offset and balance the PLA's more threatening force developments and operations. In part, this requires allied defense planners to "think the unthinkable" and prepare defense options for future governments that are viable, well thought out, and cost effective. While there is some possibility that such options might need to be used in a future crisis, their main purpose should be to balance the PLA, to deter adventurism, and to restore and maintain regional confidence. Our main purpose should be to ensure that the chances of war are minimized.

U.S. DEFENSE PLANNING FOR AN EFFECTIVE RESPONSE IN THE WESTERN PACIFIC

One agency of the U.S. government that clearly does recognize the challenge posed by China is the Department of Defense. The then chief of staff of the U.S. Air Force, General Norton Schwartz, and the U.S. Navy's chief of operations, Admiral Gary Roughead, reportedly signed a classified memorandum in September 2009 to develop jointly a new operational concept termed "AirSea Battle."[18] This concept appears designed to counter the growing anti-access, area denial capabilities of China and, to a lesser extent, those of Iran and North Korea. The manner, effectiveness, and speed with which the changes envisaged are taken forward will be of critical importance for Australian defense planning.

Initial reporting[19] suggests that U.S. competitive strategy and campaign planning in the Western Pacific might be composed of the following key elements.

1. Blind the Opponent

An early priority for the United States and its allies would likely be to counter the Chinese threats to allied space assets, forward bases, and forward-deployed ships and aircraft by blinding the PLA's primary intelligence, surveillance, reconnaissance, and command and control systems.

Early success in these endeavors would be critical to the prospects of all subsequent operations. Effective early operations to blind priority systems would not prevent strikes against allied bases, but they should reduce markedly the accuracy of strikes against ships at sea, planes in the air, and satellites in space. It would also make Chinese efforts to track allied forces in the theater exceptionally difficult, and it would seriously complicate battle damage assessment following an initial round of attacks. A key consequence would be to increase the miss rates of Chinese attacks and markedly increase munition wastage rates.[20]

2. Priority Defensive Measures

Many steps would need to be taken to strengthen the resilience and recuperative capabilities of U.S. and allied forces in the Western Pacific. Key measures include hardening and otherwise protecting allied space-based and other long-range ISR systems and associated command and control systems. It would be important also to have available backup surveillance and communications networks to ensure that, even in the face of heavy and sustained attacks, priority functions can still be performed. It would be appropriate, in addition, to consider upgrades to ballistic and cruise missile defenses for both priority land-based facilities and high-value ships at sea.

There would appear to be scope to disperse priority assets more widely between main and backup basing facilities. Some of these alternative facilities might be in the immediate vicinity of main bases, and others could be relatively distant. Rapid shuffling of high-value combat assets between alternative operating facilities would complicate PLA targeting substantially.

Other areas deserving consideration include the further development of decoy and other counterintelligence systems and the physical hardening of key system nodes, capabilities, and facilities.

3. Suppress PLA Medium-Range Land-Based Ballistic and Cruise Missile Forces

Success in blinding the PLA high command and then protecting most key allied forces and bases would not be sufficient to prevail in such a conflict. Also required would be the effective destruction of most PLA medium-range ballistic and cruise missile forces.

This would be a formidable undertaking. Most of these systems are road mobile and can be readily hidden in the PLA's extensive network of deep tunnels and also in the natural terrain and urban infrastructures.[21] A successful campaign to markedly reduce the threat from these forces would require exceptional and persistent surveillance of all relevant launch areas and highly responsive precision strike capabilities. Because of the PLA's capabilities to reconstitute these forces relatively rapidly, separate efforts would be required to identify and destroy missile manufacturing and storage facilities.

4. Seize the Initiative

As already indicated, sustained offensive strikes on the PLA's wide-area surveillance and command and control networks as well as medium-range cruise and ballistic missile systems would need to be planned. During the course of such operations, suppression strikes would also be required on the PLA's primary air defense networks. At sea, Chinese surface combatants would also be struck, submarine forces would be attrited, and those naval forces remaining at bases would be effectively isolated from operating areas.

Operations in this phase would be highly complex and very demanding and would probably require significant time. Moreover, many of the capabilities needed to conduct such operations are not currently held by the United States and its allies in the numbers likely to be required, or even at all.

Operations in this phase would entail the United States and its allies seizing the initiative and forcing the opponent onto the back foot. A clear allied victory could not, however, be expected to come quickly or at low cost. Combat operations would probably need to continue for months and possibly even years.

5. Sustaining Protracted Operations

Over time, substantial additional U.S. and allied forces would need to be deployed into the operational theater. These fresh forces would help to relieve and reinforce those units that take the brunt of the early exchanges. During this period many facilities would need to be repaired and many others constructed to support sustained high-tempo operations.

The defense industrial capabilities of all of the allies would be placed on emergency production footings. Although there might be scope for a small number of additional platforms (for example, ships, submarines, and aircraft) to be produced or completed during the conflict period, a higher priority is likely to be accorded to battle damage repair and to the production of additional intelligence, surveillance, and reconnaissance systems and a wide range of stand-off precision munitions.

At this stage in such a conflict interference with the opponent's nonmilitary assets is likely to become of comparable importance to dominance over the opponent's military forces. Denial of most types of international financial transactions and an effective cessation of most types of trade are likely to bring home to the opposing leadership that continuation of the conflict would result in very serious damage to the Chinese economy and, indeed, fundamental risks to the government itself.

AUSTRALIAN OPTIONS FOR CONTRIBUTING TO U.S. COMPETITIVE STRATEGY

In his seminal analysis of the AirSea Battle Concept, Jan van Tol suggests that the United States should work to encourage Australia to make the following contributions to the allied effort in the Western Pacific:

- Partner with the United States and Japan in developing the next-generation antiship/antisurface cruise missile;
- Support its fielding a fifth-generation fighter force to support combined air superiority and antisubmarine warfare (ASW) operations;
- Join the U.S. space surveillance system and build an S-Band radar to improve southern hemisphere SSA (space situational awareness); and

- Establish an offensive node for the U.S. Joint Space Operations Center to create a Combined Space Operations Center, thereby improving operational integration and enhancing C2 survivability.[22]

Although all of these suggestions appear feasible and realistic, careful consideration reveals a much broader range of options for possible Australian involvement, including the possibilities raised in the following sections.

Establishment of a Major Command, Control, Communications, Computers, Intelligence, Surveillance, and Reconaissance (C4ISR) Hub

This center would operate an extended array of sensors (including Australia's own Jindalee Over-the-Horizon Radar Network [JORN] and other sensor networks) and electronic surveillance systems and would also process, analyze, and distribute relevant products for the tactical and operational support of allied operations. The vast and relatively quiet electronic spaces across northern and offshore Australia provide an ideal environment for a diverse, dispersed, and highly resilient C4ISR network covering most of the Western Pacific.

Basing for Long-Range UAVs

High-altitude, long-endurance (HALE) uninhabited aerial vehicles (UAVs) are likely to play key roles in the evolving Air-Sea Battle concept. These systems will be required to back up satellite and other wide-area surveillance systems and also to contribute substantial resilient bandwidth for priority theater communications. The several dispersed air force bare bases across northern and central Australia would appear to offer ideal basing options for this capability.

Basing for Long-Range Strike Aircraft

One of the problems of U.S. and allied country force structures in this theater is that the stealthy, highly advanced fighter-bombers starting to enter service all possess relatively short range and endurance capabilities. Although the B-2 *Spirit* is an exception, there are only twenty of these aircraft in service. This means that the bulk of the current allied air combat force, comprising fourth-generation jet aircraft with only modest stealth capabilities, would have difficulty operating in or near Chinese air space, and the advanced aircraft that could operate with some security in that environment are small in number and mostly possess limited range capabilities.

One clear conclusion is that there is a need for a new generation of very stealthy long-endurance strike aircraft that is capable of operating for extended periods in contested air space to launch persistent attacks. These aircraft, whether manned or not, would be very valuable and would best be based in a relatively secure environment that offers both good dispersal and protection capabilities and also highly skilled local support personnel. Australia offers all of those advantages and many more, including great strategic depth, sophisticated industrial support capabilities, large expanses of relatively vacant airspace, and ready access to high-grade fully instrumented training facilities.

Basing long-range strike aircraft in Australia would also open some interesting alternative flight-path options into parts of China, not only from the east but also from the south. Generating an all-aspect air-defense challenge for the PLA has the potential to seriously complicate Chinese defense planning.

Contributing to Ballistic Missile Defense

The Australia-U.S. joint facilities in Australia already contribute to some aspects of ballistic missile defense, notably through their capabilities to provide warning of missile launches. In addition, Australia has long been a partner of the United States in the development of new ballistic missile defense technologies. Provision is being made in the Royal Australian Navy's three new *Aegis*-equipped air warfare destroyers, which are currently under construction, to be capable of carrying SM-3 air defense missiles, the U.S. Navy's primary ballistic missile interceptor.

This means that Australia may be able to contribute readily to allied ballistic missile defense operations in this theater, not least for the protection of strategically vital installations that may be located on Australian soil. There may also be scope to extend these defensive capabilities further through combined efforts.

Serving as a Major Western Pacific Arsenal

Most of the analyses so far conducted of competitive strategies in the Western Pacific have concluded that a fundamentally different pattern of strategic logistics will be required. There will be a need for extensive battle damage repair, for urgent system modifications, for fuel, for spare parts and munitions storage, and for forward stockpiles of many other key items. An optimal environment for such purposes is a large landmass just beyond range of the major combat operations but with readily available technical expertise and physical facilities to perform these essential operations with efficiency and flexibility.

Facilities in northern Japan, Alaska, or Hawaii might provide some of these services. However, Australia possesses a very comprehensive range of support capabilities, including a sophisticated range of defense manufacturing, modification, and upgrade capabilities. The Australian Defence Force already operates and supports many of the primary U.S. sensor systems, platforms, and munitions. Moreover, Australia has sufficient space and a modern transport and communications infrastructure that would permit dispersed and relatively secure logistics operations. Australia could thus reprise the role it played for much of the Pacific War as a large and secure logistic and operational base, not to mention General Douglas MacArthur's headquarters.

Basing Major Naval Units

One of the enduring features of the Western Pacific theater is the vast distance by which it is separated from the continental United States (CONUS). Sustained maritime and air operations in the Western Pacific cannot be conducted efficiently and economically across such transoceanic distances. Nowhere is the need for secure forward bases more acute than in the case of the major U.S. fleet units. For them, transiting the width of the Pacific Ocean requires passages of many days and frequently weeks. When most ships and all aircraft require access to secure base facilities to rearm, developing the appropriate pattern of forward basing must be a priority. Establishing a secure and efficient basing and support structure will have a substantial influence on sortie rates, times on station, system survival rates, and the overall effectiveness and speed of a campaign.

Several Western Pacific locations are likely to be able to play useful naval support roles. However, it is pertinent to note that western Australia already hosts the largest submarine base south of Japan and Hainan[23] and that Sydney possesses a naval dry dock capable of undertaking major hull and other repairs on U.S. aircraft carriers.[24]

APPROACHING A SEMI-INDEPENDENT AUSTRALIAN DEFENSE STRATEGY FOR 2030

This chapter does not suggest that any Australian government will wish to distance itself from the country's close alliance with the United States any time soon. Nevertheless, there is a need for Australian defense planners to conduct their own defense analyses, to consider a range of options for securing the country's vital interests, and then to reach their own conclusions on the best way forward. It is critical for Australia to develop its own strategic thinking and logic about how the PLA's challenge in the Western Pacific should best be offset and balanced.

Given the disparities in the scale and nature of Chinese and Australian societies, an optimal strategy for Australia is likely to be highly asymmetric. There would be little value in mimicking the substantial capabilities now being developed and introduced into service by the PLA. Rather, the primary intent of Australian strategy should be to focus effort and investment on those operational capabilities that are likely to provide the highest deterrence and combat leverage for given levels of investment. Those plans and capabilities should be selected not just for their potential to thwart aggressive actions by the PLA but to deter and, if necessary, do serious damage to the vital interests of the Chinese leadership.

At first sight, the prospects of Australia being able to exert significant leverage in any of these dimensions might appear to be remote, if not fanciful. However, careful analyses undertaken with a strong emphasis on creative, asymmetric, and high-leverage approaches suggest that should Australia invest in a carefully selected range of nonconventional capabilities it could, in fact, pose very serious dilemmas for any highly assertive major power.

Some of Australia's capability options might include the following:

- *Deep Engagement.* This would require a national effort to build exceptional language, culture, social, and system understanding of China and other major regional countries of relevance. Of particular importance would be the development of networks of close and friendly personal relationships with key community and national leaders. These sustained processes of deep engagement would be designed to provide high-definition understanding of political, economic, social, and military developments and also opportunities to inform and influence key decision makers on vital issues.

- *Advanced Space Warfare Capabilities.* In partnership with the United States and other close allies, this investment would be designed both to protect allied space systems that are critical for Australian operations and also to develop capabilities with the potential to interfere with Chinese space systems in ways that would complicate the opponent's risk assessments, crisis decision making, and military operations.

- *Advanced Undersea Combat Capabilities.* This option would involve heavy investment in a range of manned and unmanned undersea capabilities that would have the potential to seriously disrupt China's international trade, including its energy imports, for an extended period by interfering with shipping and other elements of infrastructure both near and distant from China's coasts. Some variants of this option would require substantial investments in very innovative unmanned systems. Other options would require a restructuring of the ADF's Future Submarine Project to purchase ten to twelve advanced nuclear attack submarines—preferably from a "hot" production line. Purchasing boats from a "hot" production line would cut unit acquisition costs markedly and also reduce very substantially contracting and delivery risks.

- *Next-Generation Large Strategic Strike Aircraft.* One of the key conclusions of the earlier discussion of competitive strategies was that the Western allies will likely need a new class of advanced, very stealthy strike aircraft that possesses very long range and an exceptional capability to loiter for extended periods in highly contested airspace. This option would entail Australia making an early decision to join with the United States in developing, building, and deploying this type of system as a matter of priority. When combined with a dispersed and hardened basing and support system, this capability should have the capacity to threaten key PLA systems and capabilities in depth.

- *Very Advanced Cyber and Information Warfare Capabilities.* This option would entail a very large and sustained investment in high-grade cyber and information warfare capabilities for use both in protecting Australian and allied systems and also for infiltrating, disrupting, and/or damaging an opponent's critical command and control and other high-value electronic systems.

- *Encouraging the Basing of Priority United States Military Capabilities in Australia.* One conclusion from the background analyses of Australia's independent strategic options that were conducted as part of this research is that the leadership of China, or of any other major power, would be deeply concerned about the risks of any conflict in the Western Pacific escalating to involve the United States. Were the leadership of any aggressor state to attack Australia or Australian forces directly, they would need to weigh the likelihood of the ANZUS treaty being invoked. One way to underline those risks to any opponent and optimise Australian (and U.S.) theater deterrence would be for selected U.S. force elements to be based in Australia. Basing U.S. combat capabilities in Australia would be a departure from long-standing Australian and U.S. policy, but given the nature of the developing regional security environment, it would appear to offer significant advantages to both Canberra and Washington.

An important first step in this direction was the joint Australia–U.S. announcement in November 2011 that a U.S. Marine force would operate for several months each year in Northern Australia. Commencing with a 250-person unit, these deployments are scheduled to rise to 2,500 U.S. personnel within a few years. More frequent aircraft and ship visits are also likely.

MERGING AUSTRALIA'S SEMI-INDEPENDENT STRATEGIC APPROACH WITH THE U.S. COMPETITIVE STRATEGY

The rapid rise of the PLA in the Western Pacific has triggered some interesting parallel thinking in the United States and Australia. The perspectives of a global superpower and a close regional ally on how to best respond to the PLA challenge will inevitably differ. However, Australia's strategic leaders will probably support the broad logic of U.S. competitive strategy. Moreover, Australia's strategic decision makers will most likely be prepared to consider many U.S. proposals for Australian involvement in the implementation of competitive strategy in the Western Pacific.

Australian strategic planners also feel a strong need to frame the country's future defense and wider security investments within a broader national logic. They will wish to convince themselves, the Australian Parliament, and the public that, so far as is possible, they can guarantee the nation's vital strategic interests, preferably with a high level of independence. As the discussion in this chapter makes clear, this broader Australian logic does not cut across the U.S. competitive strategy in any significant way.

What Australia's developing strategic approach suggests, however, is that Australia's defense and security investments will need to be selected and developed so that, if required, they can deliver priority strategic effects with a high level of independence were Australia ever forced to conduct major operations largely on its own. Secondly, in the far more likely event of Australia and the United States operating almost seamlessly within a refined competitive strategy concept, Australia will want to make its own distinct contribution. While many aspects of the Australian approach will be debated for some time, the Australian government is unlikely to be satisfied by contributing forces only on the margins of this theater. Australia will most probably wish to be a close player and a significant contributor to some of the more challenging theater operations, including in advanced cyber and information warfare operations and sophisticated underwater operations.

Why is Australia likely to adopt such a forward-leaning stance? Put simply, the country's most vital long-term security interests are riding on the outcome of this strategic competition. For Australians this is no sideshow. It looks as if it is becoming the most serious defense planning challenge that the country has faced since World War II.

NOTES

1. *Military Power of the People's Republic of China 2009* (Washington, DC: Office of the Secretary of Defense, 2009); and also Jan van Tol, *AirSea Battle: A Point of Departure Operational Concept* (Washington, DC: Center for Strategic and Budgetary Assessments, 2010).

2. *Military Power of the People's Republic of China 2009*, 25–29; and also *Military and Security Developments Involving the People's Republic of China 2010* (Washington, DC: Office of the Secretary of Defense, 2010), 29–33.

3. *Military Power of the People's Republic of China 2009*, 20–22, 25, 28–29.

4. van Tol, *AirSea Battle*, 25.

5. *Military and Security Developments Involving the People's Republic of China 2010*, 2–3; van Tol, *AirSea Battle*, 19, 40–43.

6. *Military Power of the People's Republic of China 2009*, 13, 50; and van Tol, *AirSea Battle*, 40–41.

7. *Military and Security Developments Involving the People's Republic of China 2010*, 7, 25.

8. van Tol, *AirSea Battle*, 18, 91, 93–94.

9. *Military and Security Developments Involving the People's Republic of China 2010*, 29–34.

10. *Military Power of the People's Republic of China 2009*, 21–22, 48–49. See also: *Military and Security Developments Involving the People's Republic of China 2010*, 10.

11. *Military and Security Developments Involving the People's Republic of China 2010*, 3–4; and van Tol, *AirSea Battle*, 20.

12. *Military Power of the People's Republic of China 2009*, 26–27; *Military and Security Developments Involving the People's Republic of China 2010*, 7; and Andrew Krepinevich, *Why AirSea Battle?* (Washington, DC: Center for Strategic and Budgetary Assessments, 2010), 16.

13. Paul Kelly, "US Debt a Threat to Security," *The Weekend Australian* 17–18 (July 2010), 13.

14. Ibid., 13.

15. David Hale is quoted at length in Paul Kelly, "US Debt a Threat to Security," 13.

16. Aaron Back, "China Says US Debt Not a Threat," *The Australian*, July 9, 2010: 23.

17. See, for example, the views of Kishore Mahbubani in Evelyn Goh, "What the Asian Debate about U.S. Hegemony Tells Us" (Honolulu: PacNet Report #39A, Pacific Forum CSIS, September 7, 2010).

18. Christopher P. Cavas and Vago Muradian, "New Program Could Redefine AF-Navy Joint Ops," *Air Force Times*, November 16, 2009; available at www.airforcetimes.com/news/2009/11/airforce_navy_cooperation_111509w/.

19. van Tol, *AirSea Battle*; Krepinevich, "Why AirSea Battle?"

20. van Tol, *AirSea Battle*, 61–69.

21. *China's Nuclear Missiles Hidden "Underground Maze,"* posted on December 13, 2009 at http://wuxinghongqi.blogspot.com/2009/12/chinas-nuclear-missiles-hidden.html; and L. C. Russell Hsiao, "China's 'Underground Great Wall' and Nuclear Deterrence," *China Brief* 9:25 (December 16, 2009), 1–2.

22. van Tol, *AirSea Battle*, 93.

23. For details of the facilities at HMAS Stirling see www.navy.gov.au/HMAS_Stirling.

24. For basic details concerning the Captain Cook graving dock see www.gardenisland.info/1-00-000.html.

Part IV

ALTERNATIVE STRATEGIES FOR THE COMPETITION

15 DEVELOPING A STRATEGY FOR A LONG-TERM SINO-AMERICAN COMPETITION

James P. Thomas and Evan Braden Montgomery

A SOUND COMPETITIVE STRATEGY should have three characteristics. First, it should adopt a long-term perspective, looking ahead several decades and anticipating shifts in the balance of power rather than focusing exclusively on near-term contingencies. Second, it should build on the enduring strengths of the United States, mitigate its vulnerabilities, and exploit a competitor's enduring weaknesses. In fact, an ideal competitive strategy would *align* a nation's core strengths against a rival's enduring weaknesses for maximum effect. Third, it should shape an opponent's behavior by adopting measures that channel its attention, effort, and resources toward actions and investments that are least threatening.[1] Based on these criteria, this chapter outlines a long-term, peacetime competitive strategy that would enable the United States to maintain or improve its current position relative to the People's Republic of China (PRC), preserve American influence in Asia, and forestall a more dangerous, globalized Sino-American rivalry.

For more than three decades, the Chinese economy has grown at an unprecedented rate, and since at least the mid-1990s this growth has supported an ambitious program of military reform and modernization. As Robert Kagan has aptly noted, "Few nations in history have ever moved further and faster from weakness to strength, from vulnerability to security."[2] At present, Sino-American relations are by and large amicable. Yet prudence demands that the United States hedge against the possibility that China could become more aggressive at some point in the future. Historically, the emergence of a new great power has been a disruptive event. Rising nations often see their interests expand with their capabilities and demand influence commensurate with their power, and there are few indications that China will differ from its predecessors.[3] The question for the United States, then, is what type of strategy might address the major security challenges China poses, namely its potential to overturn the military balance in Asia, the possibility that it will weaken U.S. alliances and strategic partnerships, and its apparent ambition to supplant the United States as the leading power in the Asia-Pacific region?

A "maximalist" peacetime competitive strategy—like the one the United States implemented against the Soviet Union during the 1980s—would seek to bring the competition to an end by inducing strategic overextension and economic exhaustion. A "minimalist" strategy, by contrast, would seek not to "win" in the near term but rather to limit the competition's scope, preserve the most favorable balance of power possible, and create strategic options that might be exercised in the future as opportunities present themselves. Because the former approach is both risky and unlikely to succeed against an economically dynamic power, we develop a minimalist strategy that would enhance U.S. freedom of action and constrain undesirable Chinese behavior over time.

This strategy is characterized by three core tenets. First, in the near term, the United States should bolster its military posture in the Western Pacific to enhance crisis stability, reassure its allies and security partners that the United States is committed to remaining the security partner of choice in the Indo-Pacific region, and induce China to focus the bulk of its attention on local contingencies and the bulk of its resources on anti-access/area denial (A2/AD) capabilities that have limited utility for global power projection. Second, the United States should encourage and enable partner nations surrounding China to develop countervailing military capabilities in the midterm that will deter the PRC from coercing its neighbors, complicate Chinese military planning by presenting multidirectional threats, and strengthen ties between the United States and its allies. Third, the United States should position itself to capitalize on China's internal dynamics over the longer term, encouraging changes that might prompt the regime to reallocate scare resources away from the military and toward domestic social programs to maintain internal order.

This strategy addresses several key asymmetries in the Sino-American competition. For example, China's military modernization has undermined the U.S. ability to project power into East Asia, a development that will be difficult to reverse given prevailing technological, geographic, and financial constraints. At the same time, China is surrounded by a number of regional powers that may have an incentive to check its rise, many of whom are already

U.S. allies or emerging strategic partners. Finally, to a far greater degree than the United States, China faces a host of economic, demographic, and social challenges that could disrupt its continued growth and perhaps even trigger widespread internal unrest. Equally important, all three components are mutually reinforcing. Specifically, if the United States can deter a military conflict, limit the Sino-U.S. competition to the Western Pacific, and strengthen its allies and partners, then, over time, those nations can play a greater role in maintaining regional stability, while a more global Sino-U.S. competition might be deferred until China's economic growth slows due to its many looming internal challenges.

BOLSTERING THE U.S. MILITARY POSTURE
IN THE WESTERN PACIFIC

The United States has traditionally relied on short-range combat aircraft operating from fixed bases and aircraft carriers that can maneuver close to an enemy's coastline to project air and maritime power. Yet these methods of power projection are likely to become increasingly untenable in the Western Pacific as China enhances its arsenal of anti-access/area-denial capabilities.[4] The prospects for reversing this shift in the military balance appear slim. At the very least, it is unlikely that the United States will be able to project power against China as effectively as it could over the past decade-and-a-half. In particular, many Chinese capabilities (such as ballistic missiles) are far less expensive than existing countermeasures (such as hardened aircraft shelters and ballistic missile defense systems); China can focus the majority of its attention on the United States while the United States must prepare to deter or confront a diverse array of challenges; and China can leverage the inherent advantages of a regional power confronting a global power whose forces are widely dispersed and must be transported and sustained over great distances.

The erosion of U.S. power projection will likely have three critical effects. First, it could influence the calculations of Chinese leaders, potentially emboldening them to engage in coercion or aggression in the event of a crisis over Taiwan or perhaps in other contingencies. Second, it could undermine the credibility of the United States as a reliable ally or security partner among key nations in the region, increasing the likelihood that they will adopt a more independent security strategy or align with Beijing. Third, if the U.S. military position in the region becomes increasingly untenable, China could devote more of its attention and resources toward the development of global power projection capabilities, even if Taipei maintains its de facto independence. Given these consequences, it is critical for the United States to offset the deteriorating military balance in the Western Pacific. Because of the significant challenges it faces in doing so, however, it should not attempt to restore its ability to project power and intervene in regional conflicts in the same ways as it has in the past. Instead, its objectives should be more modest and more realistic: enhancing crisis stability, reassuring allies and partners, and perpetuating China's focus on deterring Taiwanese independence.

The first two objectives—crisis stability and reassurance—are relatively uncontroversial. Stability in the Western Pacific has already been diminished over the past several years as China has increased its ability to hold at risk American bases, surface vessels, and command, control, communications, computers, intelligence, surveillance, and reconnaissance (C4ISR) assets. If these vulnerabilities grow more pronounced, Chinese leaders may become confident that they can launch successful attacks against forward-deployed U.S. forces as well as any reinforcements, delivering a "knockout blow" that would preclude the United States from retaliating effectively. The United States should therefore take steps to enable its forces to withstand a Chinese assault, strike key People's Liberation Army (PLA) targets in the aftermath of an attack, and ultimately convince Chinese leaders that the United States cannot be defeated quickly or easily.

Similarly, the United States must ensure that its allies do not begin to doubt its capabilities or its resolve, which could lead them to accommodate or even bandwagon with Beijing. If the military balance in the Western Pacific becomes increasingly unfavorable to the United States, nations in the region may question its ability and its willingness to compete over the long haul and may come to view their security relationships with a distant and declining hegemon as a liability they can no longer afford.

The third objective—perpetuating Chinese investments in A2/AD capabilities—is more contentious. In general, there appear to be two schools of thought regarding how the United States should attempt to influence China's military posture, strategy, and spending. The first maintains that China's current focus on deterring Taiwanese independence and U.S. intervention in regional contingencies benefits the United States by preventing the PRC from devoting greater resources toward power projection capabilities.[5] There are a number of very obvious reasons that the United States would not want China to invest more in power-projection capabilities. First, if China does acquire the capability to project military power globally, it would erode the important and unique U.S. advantage in this area and could therefore create or exacerbate the view of the United States as a dominant power in decline. Second, even if the PLA remains far inferior to the U.S. military, it could nonetheless gain increased leverage in select regions, particularly over nations that possess the commodities and markets that China depends on for continued economic prosperity. Third, these capabilities could prove to be a useful coercive tool in regional contingencies beyond Taiwan, for example in a conflict with China's neighbors in the South China Sea. Finally, Beijing would almost certainly gain "soft power" benefits if the PLA improved its ability to conduct disaster relief, noncombatant evacuation, or humanitarian intervention operations.

By contrast, a case can be made that the United States should actually encourage China to invest in long-range power-projection capabilities, including aircraft carriers, amphibious assault ships, and large surface combatants, as well as enabling capabilities such as aerial refueling platforms and maritime refueling and replenishment vessels.[6] The logic behind "drawing China out" rests on several assumptions. First, because the U.S. military is highly proficient in global power projection, China would be attempting to compete in an area where the United States retains a significant advantage. This approach would therefore seem to meet one of the key criteria for a successful competitive strategy. Second, developing effective power projection capabilities would require the PRC to devote enormous time, effort, and resources toward building new platforms, operating and maintaining those platforms, and training personnel for long-distance, long-duration missions and highly complex tasks such as carrier flight deck operations and underway replenishment. This would almost certainly draw resources away from A2/AD capabilities more useful in a Taiwan contingency.[7] Third, capabilities such as aircraft carriers and large surface combatants would be relatively easy targets for the U.S. military during any conflict, and supporting those vessels would also require overseas bases and an en route logistical infrastructure that would be even more vulnerable.[8] In short, at the military-operational level the United States stands to benefit if China chooses to invest in traditional power projection capabilities at a time when the value of those capabilities appears to be in sharp decline, due in large part to the proliferation of precision-guided weapons.

The United States may indeed want to draw China out at some point in the future. Nevertheless, by postponing this option for the time being, and instead bolstering the U.S. military posture in the Western Pacific to encourage China's continuing focus on local contingencies such as Taiwan, the United States could achieve three important objectives. First, it would signal

U.S. resolve to maintain the regional military balance of power, thereby reassuring its allies and partners. Second, it would strengthen the case for cooperating with allies and partners throughout the Indo-Pacific region to shore up their own military capacities, enabling them to better defend their sovereignty while limiting China's ability to project military power beyond the region. Third, if a global expansion of the Sino-American competition can be deferred, and if China's economic growth declines in the coming decades or the regime is forced to direct substantial resources toward domestic social programs to maintain growth and preserve internal stability, then the PRC may be less likely to emerge as a true peer competitor.

The principal goal for the United States should be to perpetuate the PRC's current emphasis on defensive systems and A2/AD capabilities that have little utility for extraregional power projection, including integrated air defense systems (IADS), coastal antisubmarine warfare (ASW) platforms, diesel-electric attack submarines, short-range tactical fighters, and short-range ballistic missiles (SRBMs). Although there are certainly risks associated with China's continued development of these capabilities, particularly if the United States does not adopt adequate measures to maintain crisis stability in the region, these risks are outweighed by the benefit of keeping the Sino-American military competition geographically restricted to the Western Pacific and particularly to Northeast Asia. The United States has no territorial ambitions in the region and prefers to maintain the status quo. Thus, as China continues to build and deploy A2/AD systems, the United States need only take steps that keep the regional military balance from shifting too far in China's favor and discourage the PRC's leaders from engaging in overt coercion or initiating a conflict. By encouraging China to maintain its focus on Taiwan and its near periphery, the United States would limit the resources Beijing is able to devote toward traditional air and especially maritime power projection capabilities, thus dissuading China from making a substantial investment in these areas until much later than it otherwise would have.

The United States could take several measures to enhance crisis stability, reassure its allies and partners, and maintain China's focus across the Taiwan Strait. First, it could act to counter China's growing—and increasingly accurate— inventory of ballistic and land-attack cruise missiles, which represent an acute threat given the continuing U.S. dependence on a small number of vulnerable, fixed forward bases. For instance, proliferating bases to more diverse locations and at greater ranges (that is, outside of the first island chain) would complicate China's targeting; not only would this compel China to hold more bases at risk, but it would also leave China with fewer missiles that had sufficient range to strike these targets. Similarly, hardening aircraft shelters; burying and concealing petroleum, oil, and lubricants as well as munitions stockpiles; and ensuring that bases have a significant rapid runway repair capability would increase the number of missiles required to impede flight operations. Not only would the PLA be forced to use unitary, penetrating warheads to destroy individual targets (rather than submunition warheads that can damage a host of exposed or vulnerable targets), it would also have to launch repeated salvoes to render bases inoperable over time. Together, these steps would increase the probability that China would exhaust its missile inventory and that the United States would be left with sufficient forces to mount retaliatory conventional strikes from its air bases—discouraging China from starting a conflict, reassuring U.S. allies that it can withstand a Chinese assault, and forcing China to expend greater resources to maintain an effective coercive capability.[9]

At the same time, the United States should develop and field new aerial strike platforms, including a long-range, stealthy bomber capable of penetrating defended Chinese airspace from any direction and holding both fixed and mobile targets within China at risk. Doing so would have four crucial effects: It would provide the United States with more robust strike options if forward bases are lost due to attack or political denial; it would restrain Chinese leaders by presenting a credible threat against key military targets in mainland China, including missile launchers, radars, and space launch facilities, among others; it would induce China to increase its investment in relatively nonthreatening air defense systems, to improve the quality of its systems, and to broaden their coverage beyond China's eastern approaches, where the majority of the PLA's air defenses are currently deployed; and it would force the PLA to invest in point defenses for targets that are now safely located deep within China's interior.

Second, the United States must address China's growing ability to hold U.S. surface vessels at risk, which stems in large part from investments in diesel-electric and nuclear-powered attack submarines, naval strike aircraft, a variety of wake-homing torpedoes and supersonic antiship cruise missiles, and an antiship ballistic missile (ASBM) capability.[10] Countering this threat will require a significant reorientation of the U.S. Navy away from surface ships and short-range carrier aircraft and toward undersea systems that can penetrate an A2/AD network as well as aircraft that enable carriers to operate from far greater ranges. The U.S. Navy should, therefore, proceed with its recently announced plans expand the payload capacity of its attack submarines, in addition to developing longer-endurance large-diameter unmanned underwater vehicles and new classes of submarine-launched munitions. It should also move forward as rapidly as possible with the deployment of an unmanned, stealthy, air-refuelable, carrier-based strike platform that will improve the survivability and extend the range of carrier air wings. In addition, targeting a moving ship at sea, even one as large as an aircraft carrier, depends on vulnerable surveillance and reconnaissance systems such as satellites, over-the-horizon radars, and UAVs, as well as terminal seekers. Developing both kinetic and nonkinetic means to disable these systems could severely undermine China's ASBM capability and enable carriers to maneuver more freely.

Finally, the United States must take steps to harden its own C4ISR networks, many of which depend on vulnerable space-based systems. Over the past several years China has invested in a wide range of antisatellite systems, from kinetic-energy, direct-ascent missiles, to ground-based lasers capable of dazzling or destroying spacecraft, to radio-frequency weapons that can jam or permanently disable satellites overhead. The United States should investigate a number of capabilities for reducing the vulnerability of its space systems: rapid reconstitution of satellites that have been damaged or destroyed, fractionated satellite constellations, air-breathing alternatives to space-based ISR and communications platforms, and next-generation precision navigation and timing systems as a hedge against the possibility that the global positioning system (GPS) will be unavailable or unreliable during a conflict. Perhaps most important, U.S. air and naval forces should also prepare to operate in environments where secure, reliable communications and ISR data are unavailable. One of the most significant advantages U.S. forces currently possess over potential opponents is the unparalleled quality of their education and training, which enables them to conduct decentralized operations with only general guidance from higher headquarters. Chinese forces, by comparison, are likely to be far less adept at "fighting in the dark" due to the high level of centralized control that characterizes the PLA and stifles both initiative and independent thinking. Thus the ability to blind an opponent by neutralizing its space- and computer-based C4ISR systems and operate when one's own systems are degraded can yield a net advantage. Of course, U.S. forces are at present much more dependent on vulnerable C4ISR networks than are their Chinese counterparts. Nevertheless, this gap is likely to narrow in the future as the PLA becomes increasingly reliant on complex information systems, for example those required to locate, track, and target moving surface ships at sea.

While efforts to shore up the deteriorating military balance in East Asia are crucial, the United States may need to consider other measures to dissuade Chinese aggression, not only to present Beijing with a more complex set of constraints in peacetime but also to hedge against the possibility that the steps described in the previous paragraphs prove too difficult or expensive. Thus the United States should maintain the possibility of implementing a distant blockade of Chinese seaborne commerce in the event that deterrence fails and conflicts breaks out. By conducting blockading operations in the Indian Ocean, the United States could exploit China's dependence on overseas export markets and imported natural resources, as well as its inability to control to the small number of geographic chokepoints in the Indonesian archipelago that channelize most shipping to and from East Asia. Moreover, the United States would also be in a position to use its legacy air and maritime platforms in areas where Chinese military power is weakest.

ENHANCING THE CAPABILITIES OF REGIONAL ACTORS

Perhaps the most significant advantage the United States has in its long-term competition with China stems from a confluence of geographic and diplomatic factors, including China's position as a continental power surrounded by potential counterweights, natural barriers, and maritime chokepoints that make its expansion difficult; the existing structure of American alliances and security relationships; and the U.S. status as the preferred security partner throughout much of the region. The key question for the United States is how best to exploit these advantages.

An opportunity may be emerging to transform the nature and increase the value of American alliances and security partnerships in Asia. China's rapid military modernization, coupled with a number of diplomatic missteps over the past several years, has given several nations in the region an incentive to take the initial steps toward redressing the growing military imbalance. For example, Japan is deploying ballistic missiles defenses and has announced plans to expand its submarine fleet, deploy additional forces to its southwestern islands, and acquire stealthy combat aircraft; Australia is planning to modernize and double the size of its submarine fleet; Vietnam is purchasing advanced military hardware from Russia to defend its maritime claims in the South China Sea; and India is pursuing a robust blue-water fleet. These developments provide an opening for the United States to depart from the traditional bargain in which allies provide bases, host nation support, and token forces in coalition military operations in exchange for American security guarantees. Instead, the United States should encourage and enable its allies and partners to field serious military capabilities that will allow them to assert their sovereignty over territorial waters, land borders, and airspace, limiting China's ability to project power beyond its immediate periphery. Multilateralizing the strategic competition with China could ultimately prove to be a useful component of a broader competitive strategy, one that minimizes the costs on the United States (by relying more on allies to limit the PRC's rise and counter more subtle aggression) while imposing costs on China (by multiplying the challenges it confronts).

To exploit American alliances and partnerships, China's geographic constraints, the natural tendency for neighboring countries to balance against an aspiring regional hegemon, and growing concerns within the region over the PRC's military modernization, the United States should encourage its allies and partners in the Asia-Pacific region to field select A2/AD capabilities. Coupled with the changes to U.S. force structure and posture described earlier that are intended to perpetuate China's focus on Taiwan contingencies and forestall its development of power projection capabilities, these "mini-A2/AD" complexes would further restrict China's operational freedom of action, reinforce its emphasis on regional rather than global security challenges, and help maintain this emphasis if Taiwan loses its independence.

There is no "one size fits all" prescription for what these mini-A2/AD networks might look like. Instead, a host of factors must be taken into account for each individual nation, among them the specific capabilities it needs most given its geography and its principal security challenges; supply-side constraints that will influence the cost and availability of those capabilities; the level of technology a particular nation is capable of absorbing effectively; how its neighbors (including but not limited to China) are likely to respond to its acquisition of new weapons systems; and of course what local governments are willing or unwilling to do.

Nations such as the Philippines and Vietnam, for example, should receive security assistance that is focused on improving maritime domain awareness. Working with the United States, both countries could emplace undersea surveillance assets in key areas at key chokepoints to monitor Chinese submarines and restrict their freedom of maneuver. Vietnam might benefit as well from air and ballistic missile defense systems that would enable it independently to resist coercion, at least for a short time. Hanoi should also be encouraged to acquire multirole fighters and fast-attack patrol craft armed with antiship cruise missiles. Similarly, Taiwan should improve its ability to hold hostile ships and aircraft at risk while withstanding air and missile barrages by China, in particular by investing in mobile short-range air defense systems, ballistic missile defenses, and passive radar detection systems, and by hardening air bases and other critical military infrastructure.[11]

Japan and the United States also have an opportunity to reset their alliance. Although the United States has encouraged Tokyo to play a greater role in "out of area" operations since the 1991 Gulf War, Japan's Self Defense Force should focus instead on withstanding air and ballistic missile attacks and denying the PLAN access to and freedom of operations around the smaller disputed islands of the Japanese archipelago. The United States should continue working with Japan to expand the latter's missile defenses and encourage the Japanese to expand their submarine fleet and ASW capabilities. More controversially, as Toshi Yoshihara describes in Chapter 13 of this volume, Tokyo should consider additional deployments of antiship cruise missile batteries throughout its southern islands. Such a land-based capability would complicate Chinese military planning, holding Chinese surface vessels at risk.

For its part, Australia might be encouraged to take on new roles in the nascent AirSea Battle concept.[12] As Ross Babbage describes in Chapter 14, Australia could provide bases for U.S. ISR and strike aircraft and serve as a logistical hub and arsenal, stockpiling precision munitions and other war-related materials. Along with Japan, Australia might be encouraged to pursue its own longer-range military systems, including long-range ISR/strike UAVs, extended-range sea- and air-launched cruise missiles, and nuclear-powered attack submarines for greater endurance and larger payloads.

The emerging American-Indian relationship also has significant potential. As C. Raja Mohan has observed, "Given India's deep-seated reluctance to play second fiddle to China in Asia in the Indian Ocean region and the relative comfort of working with a distant superpower" there is in fact "a structural reason for New Delhi to favor greater security cooperation with Washington."[13] The two countries, however, have taken few concrete steps to solidify, expand, or exploit this potential strategic alignment.

The United States should consider a number of measures that would bolster India's military capabilities and its influence, some of which are already underway. Relatively uncontroversial steps that could be taken include expanding bilateral and multilateral military training exercises involving American and Indian air and naval forces; welcoming Indian efforts to patrol the sea lines of communication in the northern Indian Ocean; equipping India with manned and unmanned open-ocean maritime surveillance platforms; encouraging greater military cooperation between India and Japan, to include exporting Japanese submarines to bolster India's undersea capabilities; and providing support to India in the development and deployment of missile defense systems.

OPPORTUNISTICALLY CAPITALIZE
ON CHINA'S INTERNAL DYNAMICS

The final element of this competitive strategy would cautiously account for some of the many domestic challenges confronting China's ruling Communist Party that might prompt the regime to curb its external ambitions and reallocate resources toward addressing its internal problems. More than any other element of the strategy, this leg demands a light touch. Chinese leaders have a natural fear of foreign interference in China's internal dynamics. Although this fear may be useful in a competitive strategy, excessive interference would likely trigger a counterproductive backlash, particularly if it resulted in a heightened sense of Chinese nationalism. Instead of a concerted campaign to influence internal dynamics within China, the United States and other countries should be prepared to respond opportunistically to internal developments as they present themselves.

Although conventional wisdom holds that China's economic growth will continue without interruption,[14] a number of interrelated factors could disrupt China's rise over the coming decades: an aging population; a fragile financial sector burdened by nonperforming loans and asset price bubbles; an inadequate social welfare net; growing dependencies on imported oil, metals, and food; environmental degradation; ethnic separatism; increasing income disparity between rural and urban populations; and unmet standard-of-living expectations on the part of China's growing middle class. Individually, but especially in concert with one another, these challenges could prevent China from globalizing the military competition by drawing finite resources away from the PLA and toward more pressing nonmilitary programs.[15] Moreover, if Ashley Tellis and Michael Swaine are correct that China is pursuing a "calculative strategy" that "emphasizes the primacy of internal economic growth and stability," then the accentuation of these threats to growth and stability may induce Chinese leaders to shift their focus internally.[16]

Many potential sources of instability, such as the coming demographic crisis, will manifest themselves regardless of any actions on the part of external parties and despite the best efforts of the Chinese regime to prevent or counter them. In most cases, then, the United States might simply have to exercise patience while natural forces play themselves out. In other cases, however, it may be able to take small steps—for example, simply drawing attention to various internal problems—that exacerbate these forces while incurring relatively little risk. During the Cold War, for example, the 1975 Helsinki Accords, which reified territorial boundaries throughout Europe, were viewed as innocuous at best and as a modest achievement for the Soviet Union at worst. Yet the articles on human rights unexpectedly galvanized prodemocracy groups throughout Eastern Europe. As former Secretary of Defense Robert Gates has argued, the accords "played a key role in our winning the Cold War."[17]

In this case, there may be opportunities to stimulate a "guns versus butter" debate within the Party and throughout Chinese society, one that could prompt a reallocation of state resources from military to nonmilitary programs. As Susan Shirk has noted, a "subterranean" guns versus butter debate is already underway within the Chinese Communist Party (CCP) and among policy elites.[18] It may be possible to broaden and deepen this debate over time, however, by reinforcing the proclivities of the next generation of Chinese leaders and the rising expectations of the Chinese middle class for a higher standard of living, highlighting the growing inequality in income distribution between urban populations in China's southeastern coastal areas and the population in its impoverished rural areas, and encouraging China's transition from an export-led model of economic growth to one driven by internal consumption.

The 2012 transition to the so-called Fifth Generation of China's leadership might by itself trigger a much wider and more serious debate over resource allocation. Few of the prospective Fifth Generation leaders have any significant military experience. Instead, most have risen up through the ranks as provincial governors focused on economic development issues. These leaders, according to David Lampton, "widely share the belief that Moscow's overspending on its military was a major reason for the collapse of the USSR."[19] While they are undoubtedly committed to maintaining strong military capabilities, they may be skeptical about pursuing more global military ambitions. There is also reason to believe they may be more distrustful of the PLA than previous CCP leaders. According to one Chinese scholar, whereas Deng Xiaoping "switched to more emphasis on the military, in part as a reward for June 4 [1989]" the next generation of Chinese leaders may feel less beholden to the military than its predecessors.[20]

Chinese civil-military tensions may also be a related point of leverage in the competition. A number of controversial events—including the PLA's harassment of the USNS *Impeccable* in 2009, its destruction of a meteorological satellite in 2007, the surfacing of a *Song*-class submarine near the USS *Kitty*

Hawk Carrier Strike Group in 2006, and the EP-3 collision and subsequent confinement of the American flight crew on Hainan Island in 2001—suggest that coordination between the PLA and China's civilian leadership is often inadequate. Andrew Scobell, for example, has argued that these events indicate that "the reins of civilian control over the PLA seem to be quite loose."[21] While the United States and its allies often complain about the lack of transparency on the part of the PLA externally, it is also possible that elements within the CCP have concerns about the lack of transparency internally, in addition to fears over the long-term loyalty of the military to the CCP (fears that might be particularly acute among the next generation of Communist Party leaders, who may not support the PLA's most ambitious goals). Because the United States and the CCP have a shared interest in strengthening civilian control of the military within China, the U.S. and Chinese political leadership might privately discuss sensitive information regarding PLA activities that the CCP is unaware of, disapproves of, or both.

There may also be opportunities for the United States to influence China's internal guns versus butter debate indirectly via the PRC's rising middle class. For example, the United States should make efforts to highlight the disparity in living standards between China and other great powers, not unlike the Nixon-Khrushchev Kitchen Debate of 1959. As China attempts to increase its Comprehensive National Power, it might feel compelled to narrow this gap, which would require significant domestic spending.

Changes in China's macroeconomic policy could further limit the resources available to the PLA. Over time China will be forced to shift from an export-led growth model to a greater reliance on domestic consumption, given the vulnerability of export-led economies to economic downturns and market contractions overseas. Reducing China's savings rate—a necessary step toward accomplishing this goal—will be challenging, however. The erosion of "Iron Rice Bowl" cradle-to-grave social benefits following Deng Xiaoping's shift to economic liberalization in the late 1970s has resulted in a situation today where few Chinese workers have pensions and even fewer citizens have any form of health insurance, conditions that are difficult to change absent major government investments in social programs. As a result, "precautionary" savings rates are likely to remain high. A related problem for China is the indebtedness of many state-owned companies that were created in the late 1990s to deal with the massive accumulation of nonperforming loans in state-owned banks. Although they have likely decreased over the past six years, these liabilities were estimated to equal 85 percent of Chinese GDP in 2003.[22] Ultimately, while inducing the PLA to increase investments in defensive systems or expensive military platforms such as aircraft carriers, support ships, and carrier-based aircraft would impose significant costs on the PLA, successfully encouraging China to address its internal macroeconomic challenges has the potential to dwarf any cost-imposing efforts aimed at the PLA alone.

In addition to taking steps that could trigger internal debates over how resources are allocated, the inherent tension that exists between liberalization and the regime's control over political dissent could be further exacerbated. Information technologies such as the Internet, for example, are currently fuelling China's economic growth, increasing awareness of life outside of China for a large portion of its population, and providing greater access to events and trends that the regime has long attempted to censor. As events in the Middle East over the past several years have demonstrated, the Internet and web-based social networking platforms, coupled with the ubiquity of cellular telephones, can act as catalysts for internal unrest by providing "virtual freedom of assembly" and spreading information that can quickly trigger protests against a ruling regime as well as other forms of civil disorder.

Not surprisingly, then, Chinese leaders are concerned about the threat the Internet represents.[23] In the future, there may be opportunities to exacerbate tensions between the regime's desire to control information and its need to loosen these controls to maintain economic growth. In 2006 there were approximately 126 million Internet users in China,[24] of which 30 to 50 million were bloggers.[25] The development of new information technologies and operating systems could encourage greater openness and enable unfettered access to information both internally and externally.

CONCLUSION

Many of these steps are more forceful than the policies that are currently being pursued toward China and risk generating resentment in Beijing. By pursuing them slowly and cautiously, however, the United States could avoid triggering a backlash that actually encourages China to engage in hostile behavior. It would be a mistake to assume that measures similar to those proposed here will inhibit cooperation between the United States and China. In areas of mutual interest, both sides will still have an incentive to collaborate with one another. Moreover, if Washington is able to stem the erosion of its military power and reaffirm its commitment to remaining the dominant military actor in the region, cooperation in other areas could actually improve, simply because the United States will have increased its leverage. If, however, U.S. power and influence wanes, then any agreements that are reached will increasingly reflect China's preferences, not those of the United States—a caveat that proponents of engagement often overlook.

NOTES

1. A. W. Marshall, *Long-Term Competition with the Soviets: A Framework for Strategic Analysis* (Santa Monica: RAND, April 1972); Marshall, "Competitive Strategies—History and Background," Internal Department of Defense Document, March 3, 1988; and Andrew F. Krepinevich and Robert C. Martinage, *Dissuasion Strategy* (Washington, DC: Center for Strategic and Budgetary Assessments, 2008), 5–6.

2. Robert Kagan, "Ambition and Anxiety: America's Competition with China," in *The Rise of China: Essays on the Future Competition,* Gary J. Schmitt, ed. (New York: Encounter Books, 2009), 4.

3. Richard K. Betts, "The United States in Asia," in *Strategic Asia 2008–09: Challenges and Choices,* Ashley J. Tellis, Mercy Kuo, and Andrew Marble, eds. (Seattle: National Bureau of Asian Research, 2008), 42; and Ashley J. Tellis, "China's Grand Strategy: The Quest for Comprehensive National Power," in *The Rise of China: Essays on the Future Competition,* Gary J. Schmitt, ed. (New York: Encounter Books, 2009), 44.

4. On China's military modernization and strategy, see, for example, Thomas J. Christensen, "Posing Problems without Catching Up: China's Rise and Challenges for U.S. Security Policy," *International Security* 25:4 (Spring 2001), 5–40; Roger Cliff, Mark Burles, Michael S. Chase, Derek Eaton, and Kevin L. Pollpeter, *Entering the Dragon's Lair: Chinese Anti-Access Strategies and Their Implications for the United States* (Santa Monica, CA: RAND, 2007); and Andrew F. Krepinevich, *Why AirSea Battle?* (Washington, DC: Center for Strategic and Budgetary Assessments, 2010).

5. Avery Goldstein, "Power Transitions, Institutions, and China's Rise in East Asia: Theoretical Expectations and Evidence," *Journal of Strategic Studies* 30:4 & 5 (August–October 2007), 667–688; and Larry M. Wortzel, "PLA 'Joint' Operational Contingencies in South Asia, Central Asia, and Korea," in *Beyond the Strait: PLA Missions Other Than Taiwan,* Roy Kamphausen, David Lai, and Andrew Scobell, eds. (Carlisle, PA: Strategic Studies Institute, 2009), 328.

6. David M. Lampton, *The Three Faces of Chinese Power: Might, Money, and Minds* (Berkeley: University of California Press, 2008), 55; Andrew Erickson and Lyle Goldstein, "Gunboats for China's New 'Grand Canals'? Probing the Intersection of Beijing's Naval and Oil Security Policies," *Naval War College Review* 62:2 (Spring 2009), 43; and Andrew Erickson, "The Growth of China's Navy: Implications for Indian Ocean Security," *Strategic Analysis* 32:4 (July 2008), 657.

7. Robert S. Ross, "China's Naval Nationalism: Sources, Prospects and the U.S. Response," *International Security* (Fall 2009), 75–76.

8. Erickson, "The Growth of China's Navy," 667. See also James R. Holmes and Toshi Yoshihara, "China's Naval Ambitions in the Indian Ocean," *Journal of Strategic Studies* 31:3 (June 2008), 380.

9. John Stillion, "Fighting under Missile Attack," *Air Force Magazine* (August 2009), 34–37.

10. Andrew S. Erickson and Lyle J. Goldstein, "Hoping for the Best, Preparing for the Worst: China's Response to U.S. Hegemony," *Journal of Strategic Studies* 29:6 (December 2006), 969–970; and Andrew S. Erickson and David D. Yang, "Using the Land to Control The Sea: Chinese Analysts Consider the Antiship Ballistic Missile," *Naval War College Review* 62:4 (Autumn 2009), 53–86.

11. Erickson and Goldstein, "Hoping for the Best, Preparing for the Worst," 977–978.

12. Jan Van Tol, with Mark Gunzinger, Andrew Krepinevich, and Jim Thomas, *AirSea Battle: A Point-of-Departure Operational Concept* (Washington, DC: Center for Strategic and Budgetary Assessments, 2010).

13. C. Raja Mohan, "India and the Balance of Power," *Foreign Affairs* 85:4 (July–August 2006), 30.

14. Dominic Wilson and Roopa Purushothaman, "Dreaming with BRICS: The Path to 2050," *Goldman Sachs,* Global Economics Paper No. 99 (October 2003); Jim O'Neil, Dominic Wilson, Roopa Purushothaman, and Anna Stupnytska, "How Solid Are the BRICs?" *Goldman Sachs,* Global Economic Paper No. 134 (December 2005); Dominic Wilson and Anna Stupnytska, "The N-11: More Than an Acronym," *Goldman Sachs,* Global Economics Paper No. 153 (March 2007); and Albert Keidel, "China's Economic Rise—Fact and Fiction," *Carnegie Policy Brief* (July 2008).

15. Nicholas Eberstadt, "Will China (Continue to) Rise?" in *The Rise of China*; and The National Intelligence Council, *Global Trends 2025: A Transformed World* (Washington, DC: Government Printing Office, November 2008), 29–30.

16. Michael D. Swaine and Ashley J. Tellis, *Interpreting China's Grand Strategy: Past, Present, and Future* (Santa Monica, CA: RAND, 2000), 98–98.

17. Robert M. Gates, "Remarks to the World Forum on the Future of Democracy," September 17, 2007; retrieved from www.defense.gov/speeches/speech.aspx?speechid=1175.

18. Susan L. Shirk, *China: Fragile Superpower* (New York: Oxford University Press, 2007), 74–75.

19. Lampton, *The Three Faces of Chinese Power,* 60.

20. Quoted in Lampton, *The Three Faces of Chinese Power,* 30.

21. Andrew Scobell, "Is There a Civil-Military Gap in China's Peaceful Rise?" *Parameters* 39:2 (Summer 2009), 19.

22. C. Fred Bergsten, Bates Gill, Nicholas R. Lardy, and Derek Mitchell, *China: The Balance Sheet* (New York: Public Affairs, 2006), 37.

23. US-China Economic and Security Review Commission, *2009 Report to Congress* (November 2009), 11.

24. Cheng Li, "China in the Year 2020: Three Political Scenarios," *Asia Policy* 4 (July 2007), 23.

25. Rebecca McKinnon, "The Internet in China," remarks to the Carnegie Endowment for International Peace, February 18, 2009.

16 CHINA'S MARITIME SALIENT

Competitive Strategies on the Oceanic Front
for the 21st Century

Paul S. Giarra

CHINA'S EMERGENCE WILL CONTINUE to disrupt the established world order and challenge American national interests. To protect those interests, the United States will need to design and implement a strategy to compete with China over the long term. Devising an effective strategy is more important for the United States than at any time since the demise of the Soviet Union. Dealing with China will require rebuilding military capabilities that have deteriorated markedly since the Cold War and developing new ones. Properly envisioning a future conflict with China is the first crucial step to planning for and winning it: primarily maritime, of long duration, and widespread. Such a conflict would have a minimum of three fronts: in the maritime salient defined by the strategic triangle bounded by Sakhalin, Singapore, and Guam; across the Indian Ocean; and along the SLOCS from San Diego to Singapore. U.S. forces will have to fight to pass through their own lines, fight to get forward, and fight to stay forward.

Beijing's longtime objective is establishing regional dominance in Asia, which entails preventing U.S. forces from operating in the area, an ostensibly regional goal with profound global ramifications.[1] People's Liberation Army plans and actions, focused on "active defense," have been coherent and consistent since 1993, when strategic guidelines took into account the implications of the 1991 Persian Gulf War and the collapse of the Soviet Union.[2] Over this period, the Chinese leadership has institutionalized policies and an internal political structure that cannot be redressed by American rhetoric or wishful thinking. This amounts to a Wilhelmine challenge to the United States and the current world order, and could become as tragic as its 20th-century precedent.

The challenge facing the United States is how best to deter, deflect, and defeat China's aspirations. First, an effective competitive strategy should strive for maximum competitive advantage by imposing on an opponent a set of unacceptable costs underscored by unacceptable choices. The goal of a competitive strategy should thus be to play to one's own strengths and an enemy's weaknesses. The obvious corollary is to avoid one's own weaknesses, no matter whether these are cultural inertia, doctrinal preferences, or technological hubris.

Second, it is essential that analysis of this problem be excruciatingly careful not to project American values on China. Rather, it must account for both Chinese rhetoric and actions. Building and maintaining a cadre of skilled Sinologists and China military analysts in the United States and elsewhere will be an exceptionally important component of the competition.

Third, although secrecy and surprise can serve as important elements of a competitive strategy, words and actions that telegraph strategic intent have a deterrent value all their own. They can also be used to induce an enemy to take actions that are self-defeating. The competitive strategy process is inherently dynamic because a worthy opponent no doubt has developed its own strategic communications; otherwise, there would be no need for the competition in the first place.

Formulating an effective strategy for competing with China is dependent on first overcoming domestic barriers. Rallying the American public to compete with China over decades will not be easy, no matter how compelling or necessary.

Competition with China is already well underway. With its historical precursors in mind, providing a clear and articulate explication of the task ahead will establish the basis for informed debate, public consensus, and effective resolution of strategies and resources in the American political system and national security establishment. This chapter further presupposes as an article of faith that these are feasible and worthy goals and offers in brief outline one view of a military China competitive strategy that is geographically and functionally based.

CALCULATING COMPETITIVE ADVANTAGE

The first step in the formulation of an effective competitive strategy is to recognize that the competition has begun in earnest. The China challenge facing the United States is serious and will worsen. It is global in scope, is multifaceted, and will play out primarily (but not exclusively) in a direct rivalry between two great powers, one revisionist and one status quo.

For the U.S. military specifically, this means having to fight where we achieve the greatest strategic advantage, in economy of force campaigns of fire and operational and political maneuver, with allies if possible. Properly conceived and exploited, military geography will play a determining role at the strategic and operational levels of war. As always, the costs of effective deterrence will be pennies-on-the-dollar strategic investments in peace and security.

HISTORICAL PATTERNS OF CHARACTER AND SUBSTANCE

An effective competitive strategy will recall and apply patterns of character and substance from the 20th century: a civil-military strategic posture drawing on all sources of national power, while at the same time militarily oriented beyond what is comfortable, and constantly adopting new concepts of operation, schemes of organization, and compelling technologies in innovative new combinations. Among other things, we should not be surprised by Cold War levels of effort and spending.

Sufficient opposing factors and long-term trends already suggest that the geopolitical outlines of China's rise will resemble the way in which earlier emerging powers disrupted rather than joined the existing world order. There are numerous instructive parallels in just the last several hundred years: England challenged first by Napoleonic France and then by Wilhelmine Germany; the Western allies confronted first by Germany and Japan in the 1930s and 1940s; and then the West locked in a long struggle with the Soviet Union during the Cold War.

Great Britain and later the United States exploited systemic advantages on a global scale to brilliant advantage against Napoleon, Wilhelm, Hitler, Hirohito, and the Kremlin. As one component of many, military strategies played out over time; were based in geography, economics, and culture; and exploited both time and distance in what were in every case global struggles. These were endurance contests, running their course over many decades and punctuated by intervals of violent warfare that only partially describe them.

Beijing seems to be following the same general pattern. China is an ambitious continental power with new global interests shaped by its strategic proclivities and reinforcing economic factors and driven by resource imperatives to challenge a great maritime power for leadership and control of the global system. That Beijing already is waging warfare[3] according to her own professed principles, shaping battlefields far in advance of physical combat, has immense consequences for the United States.

Early indications are that the point of contact will be in the oceanic space and its littorals, archipelagos, and maritime airspace. Meeting the military challenge of China's emergence will require deliberate and clear-eyed competitive strategies at sea—maritime but more than naval—that maximize American and allied advantages. In this planning campaign, close scrutiny of the geographic realities of China's emergence and its historic parallels can provide a solid point of departure.

A FIRST-PRINCIPLE CHALLENGE

As recently as a few years ago, during a Maritime Strategy planning conference at the U.S. Naval War College, it seemed reasonable to resist the temptation to use China as a Navy force-building case. This is precisely the course that the Sea Services chose,[4] emphasizing instead the prevention of war as a primus inter pares doctrine going forward.

What a difference a few years make. In the intervening period, the realities of China's anti-access and area denial strategy have become all too apparent. Details and implications of China's antiship ballistic missile have become increasingly public knowledge,[5] and China by declaration and demonstration has made clear its intention to challenge for dominance in its oceanic approaches.

China appears to have chosen a confrontational path, to the point where Beijing has advertised its geostrategic presumptions, including what it plans to do militarily; where it plans to do it; and the new Chinese interpretations of security and international law that challenge rather than stabilize the region and the entire global commons. China's actions speak even louder than its words: Abrasive maritime reconnaissance, extensive defense technology espionage, repetitive and persistent cyber warfare campaigns against U.S. government computer systems, building a theaterwide ballistic missile arsenal, and the launch of a navy-killing navy are not friendly gestures. Taken together, these actions have changed the strategic geometry in the Asia-Pacific, transforming an indirectly competitive China-Taiwan-United States triangle to a direct, bipolar Sino-American strategic competition. As a whole, these actions amount to undeniable strategic warning of Chinese ambitions and intentions, with the clear implication that the United States will have to resort to all sources of its national hard and soft power to preserve its traditional geostrategic advantages of global strategic mobility and economic, political, and military access.

A good competitive strategy provides for deterrence as well as for war fighting. This competitive strategy's underlying assumption is that preparing now for crisis and confrontation with China is the best way to preclude conflict later. It is far better to deter than to fight, and it is equally imperative to be ready to fight if that becomes necessary. These are long-standing and essential American strategic maxims. Failure to respond to Chinese challenges will mean falling further behind.

Recognizing that the main conflict will come in China's maritime approaches is the essential first step to understanding the nature of that conflict, to discerning those strategic choices that offer competitive advantage to the United States and its allies, to recognizing opportunities in peripheral theaters, and to outlining those necessary capabilities, force structures, and levels of effort.

This chapter lays out a competitive strategic approach to dealing with the Chinese challenge, based on a half-dozen general principles. First, given the stakes and potential consequences of not mounting a credible and convincing response to China's emergence, this is no time for American strategic lassitude, current economic conditions notwithstanding. The consequences of China misconstruing American political reserve for weakness are potentially disastrous. To the extent that Beijing already has miscalculated American staying power, it is time to assure China that the United States is serious about its commitment to freedom and security in the global commons more broadly, and in particular in the Asia-Pacific, according to long-standing American liberal democratic and free-market definitions of those interests. Integrating American military power with every other aspect of national power is an essential component of any coordinated strategic response.

Second, the geography and natural strategic advantages of proximity and depth in China's maritime approaches have dictated at least the broad outlines of both Chinese actions and American responses. Understanding and appreciating the geographic terrain in the so-called first and second island chains are essential steps in conceptualizing primary political and military responses. Third, predictable Chinese actions and natural American advantages suggest the outlines of an oceanic competition space, starting with the area defined by the first and second island chains and working outward. This initial planning space is illustrated by "China's Maritime Salient," broadly defined by the triangle bounded by Sakhalin, Singapore, and Guam (Map 16.1).

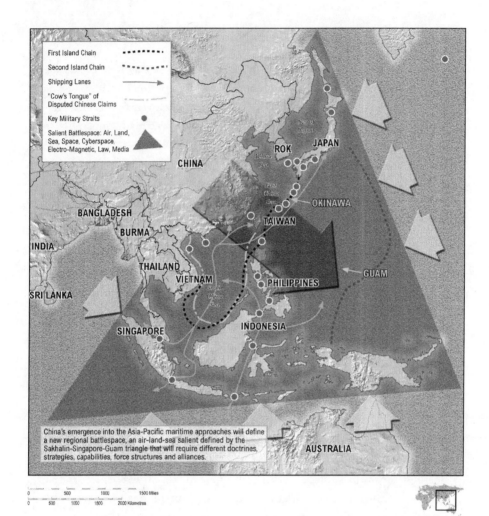

Map 16.1. China's maritime salient.
China's emergence into the Asia-Pacifice maritime approaches will define a new regional battle space, an air-land-sea salient defined by the Sakhalin-Singapore-Guam triangle, that will require different doctrines, strategies, capabilities, force structures, and alliances.

Fourth, the intellectual and emotional processes of coming to grips with new strategic challenges can take a very long time. In the case of thinking about Japan in the first half of the 20th century, this planning resolution took forty years before Japan attacked Pearl Harbor. Tellingly, in the course of this planning, the United States changed its entire operational approach to emphasize operational mobility and maneuver warfare on a broad front, while Japan hewed rigidly to doctrinal preferences for a short war and a climactic naval battle. The general effectiveness of the Cold War's containment policy notwithstanding, it took more than thirty years to establish an explicit competitive strategy process directed at the Soviet Union.[6]

Fifth, the whole point of dealing effectively with China is to preserve American strategic advantages while simultaneously leveraging them to deal with China. These include external lines of communication, global strategic mobility, continuously forward operations that exploit the power of the offensive and defense in depth, command and preservation of freedom of the global commons, compelling and enabling alliances, and a dominant strategic narrative.

Sixth, military observations are offered in the context of comprehensive whole-of-government approaches, in which robust national and allied economies are fundamental to success and effective alliances are a primary bulwark.

This may be a too muscular an approach for some. It nevertheless follows from the uncomfortable competitive position the United States finds itself in relative to China, the militarized emergence of which compels a response in the first place. After an American post–Cold War strategic latency of almost twenty years in the Pacific, exacerbated by wishful thinking and two decades of optimistic military drawdowns and compounding diversions to other theaters, China remains tone deaf to "responsible stakeholder" urgings. It is China that has turned a corner in its aggressive maritime legal and territorial claims and military operations.[7] At this clarifying moment of Chinese overreach, and with the gift of strategic warning declared and demonstrated by Beijing, the Asia-Pacific geography involved suggests competitive strategy approaches to dealing with China.

COLD WAR PARALLELS

The Fulda Gap is a powerful symbol of the Cold War, and its maritime analog is the basis for this competitive strategy. A low-lying section of the border between East and West Germany, the Fulda Gap was one of the most likely routes for Soviet tank armies to drive into the heart of Western Europe at the start of World War III. As such, the Fulda Gap almost literally was the manifestation of the Cold War. It commanded the approaches to West Germany's financial center in Frankfurt, to major NATO air bases at Rhein-Main that were key to NATO's strategy of rapid reinforcement, and to the heart of NATO military forces in Germany. This terrain was by no means the sum of Cold War military strategies—in fact, the Cold War was won when strategies emerged to challenge the Soviets everywhere but the Fulda Gap—but it had to be dealt with first and forcefully and was the pivot on which Western military credibility hinged.

Fulda was a strategic pivot because, while the West had options not open to Moscow, the Soviets were compelled by geography and their own strategy to attack through these lowlands on a few parallel axes with their tank armies in a defining thrust across Germany and to the English Channel. American and NATO war-fighting concepts, strategies of reinforcement and maneuver, combined arms doctrines, advanced tactics, and new military technologies emerged from this crucible. The Western response was to fix the Soviets in place, thereby simultaneously necessitating and enabling far broader global approaches to deterrence and war fighting. Many of these broader alternatives— Army–Air Force integration in the Air-Land Battle doctrine; a global maritime strategy that exploited external lines of communication, global strategic mobility, and persistent naval firepower; dominating space-based and stealth technologies—came hard, emerging only thirty years into the Cold War, in the context of consciously competitive strategies presaged by President Ronald Reagan's U.S. defense buildup after post–Vietnam War doldrums.

With this continental European strategic precedent in mind, numerous parallels with the Fulda Gap pertain on China's maritime approaches in the Asia-Pacific. If China is going to continue to emerge geostrategically in any meaningful way, it must do so politically and physically on the oceanic front that abuts Japan and the Korean Peninsula to the north and Southeast Asia to the south. That China must do so is incontrovertible: China has to come to sea because it is captive to its mercantilist economy. China's insatiable requirement for natural resources and access to markets has few alternatives to reliance on sea lines of communication. Although the strategic salience of China's carrying trade is typically understated in the United States because global campaigns and a wide-ranging *guerre de course* are strategically passé, in fact Chinese commerce and commodities are key strategic drivers and the physical manifestation of China's economic, political, and military emergence. Furthermore, because China has chosen to reject the notion of American sea power providing for its maritime security, the PLA is in effect a strategic gap filler.

China's emergence is no Manifest Destiny, with first priority to internal expansion. Its mercantilist economic system—like Great Britain's in the 17th and 18th centuries—is based on breakneck expansion abroad, on a global scale, in China's case without achieving underlying internal stability. Just as for mercantilist England before it, virtually every opportunity and venue for doing so—and for achieving the continuous and robust economic expansion and growth that are essential to ensuring domestic tranquility, domestic stability, and the political tenure of China's Communist Party—lie abroad. For China, sea routes to African mines and fields, and to Middle East oil, are vital. Because China does not enjoy the underlying social, political, and economic stability that was the foundation for British and American economic and geopolitical expansion, Beijing's physical expansion into the global commons is naturally tentative and necessarily vulnerable.

Beijing's strategic stance is vulnerable morally and tangibly because it is competitive and zero-sum by self-definition, challenging the international political, legal, and economic system now in place that, to the contrary, emphasizes free markets and unimpeded political and economic access. Over the last few years, this Chinese national posture has begun to manifest itself as abrasive and aggressive: securing exclusive access to raw materials and natural resources in ways that have unsettled the global economy, insisting on legal territorial rights that challenge international law, withholding key materials from the global economy in heavy-handed and maladroit displays of power, and building a navy-killing navy because all stands or falls on China's ability to control its maritime approaches, deny access to others, and secure its own strategic access to resources and markets. Hence, not only is China's emergence vulnerable, but it must be exploited.

CHINA'S OCEANIC FRONT IS A SALIENT

The practical aspects of the military component of a China competitive strategy emerge simply from looking at the map, an endeavor seldom enough practiced. China's oceanic front is roughly triangular, basically defined by the first and second island chains, with apexes at Sakhalin, Singapore, and Guam.[8] This oceanic front is a maritime salient, with all of a salient's implications for the defense (China) and the offense (the United States). Looking carefully at this salient is a useful way by which to organize strategic thinking and conceptualize competitive approaches.

The geography of China's maritime salient is not only evocative as a battlefield's topography but also strategically compelling. It is relatively contained in its Sakhalin-Singapore-Guam triangle. This gives a focus and scale to potential campaigns within it and on its periphery, sufficient to focus strategies and plans. Furthermore, geography doesn't change: The same littoral and archipelagic barriers that confounded the Soviet Union during the Cold War in the Pacific confront China today. Beijing's pronouncements concerning control of the first and second island chains are explicit recognition of this conundrum.

Second, China's maritime salient is the scene of great American military and political success during World War II and the Cold War. This heritage continues today, where American military and political presence and capabilities are enjoying a considerable resurgence for all the reasons related to China's heavy-handed emergence catalogued in the preceding pages. The U.S. Pacific Command and the Navy's Seventh Fleet are as operationally oriented as they have ever been, in direct response to Chinese naval and air operations in the Asia-Pacific.

Third, the China salient is far forward for the United States and near abroad for China. In this regard, China obviously benefits from its continental strategic depth and interior lines emanating from the relatively short Chinese coastline. Conversely, and compellingly, the United States has the profound advantage of exterior lines, an enduring military and political strategy of forward presence and strategic mobility maintained as a matter of course over global distances, and a combination of both maritime and continental strategic depth.

Great militaries leverage strategic and operational movement along external lines of communication. Great powers that do so achieve profound national competitive advantage. Control of the global external lines of communication is the essence and manifestation of forward defense and its defense in depth corollary. Ensuring this freedom of maneuver will be essential to a competitive strategy against China. Its necessity will more fully define relevant force structures, capabilities, and levels. This will place special emphasis on American sustainability and en route infrastructure, requirements exacerbated by the long decline of essential facilities and China's declared intention to target enabling fixed and mobile U.S. logistics force structure.

Fourth, the China salient composes a maritime theater, but it is far more than a naval theater. Considering that the Air Force represents a strategic flank for the U.S. Navy and vice versa, present-day analogues to the Air-Land Battle doctrine, such as the AirSea Battle concept, are absolutely essential. Even a casual glance at the China salient reveals the massive extent of littoral, island, and archipelagic land area involved. Because most political and economic activity takes place in the littorals and accounts for most American security interests, effective littoral operations present special challenges and will require new offensive and defensive capabilities.

Fifth, holding this strategic center amounts to a strategy for addressing China's maritime salient. Remarking on England's parallel strategic advantages over France at the time, Lord St. Vincent, first lord of the admiralty, famously said in 1801, "I do not say the Frenchman will not come; I say only that he will not come by sea." St. Vincent personally spent years at a time at sea to ensure this strategic result. Likewise, it will be a severe operational and technical challenge to maintain operational dominance of forward-deployed forces in a period of near-peer naval competition marked by systems and network warfare. Campaign planning assumptions will have to be recalibrated and will have to include reduction of enemy defenses over extended timelines, additional required strike and defensive capabilities, more robust force levels, new command and control doctrines defined by "silent running" and not ultimately dependent on connectivity and bandwidth, and necessary supporting S&T, R&D, and industrial capacity sufficient for a long conflict.

CHINA'S SEA LINES OF COMMUNICATION AS A STRATEGIC OPPORTUNITY

For NATO during the Cold War, the Fulda Gap was to the Soviet Union's great peripheral strategic weakness as, for the United States at present, China's maritime salient is to China's strategic maritime lines of communication. Dominating the one exposes the other to exploitation and defeat in detail.

"China's Indo-Pacific Sea Lines of Communication" (Map 16.2) illustrates one aspect of this concept of an exploitive *guerre de course* against China's maritime lifelines. China must come to sea in the first place, through its maritime salient and then breaking out onto the high seas, for one of two reasons: either precisely because it has rejected American security guarantees and decided to vouchsafe these sea lines of communication (SLOCs) itself or because the maritime salient is simply a way by which to forestall American military operations in the Asia-Pacific, and Beijing is overextended and plans neither the capability or the intention to defend its maritime SLOCs. In either case, Chinese maritime SLOCs are exceptionally vulnerable. For the United States, this presents an opportunity to dominate its Asia-Pacific competition with China through actions in so-called peripheral theaters.

Map 16.2 portrays one such theater of a China competitive strategy, the Indo-Pacific, with notional Chinese SLOCs illustrating Beijing's dependence on the raw materials market of Africa and the gas pump of the Arabian Gulf. At a glance the strategic importance of India, Australia, and the narrow seas

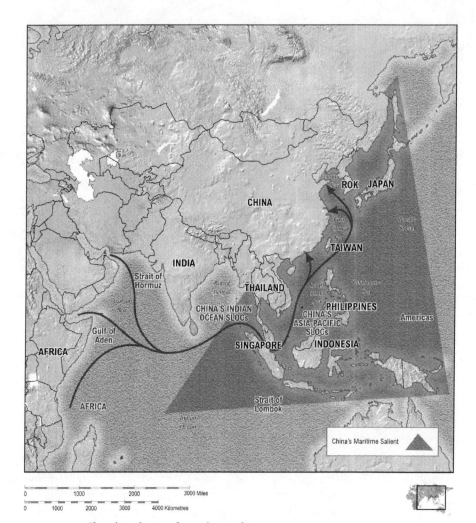

Map 16.2. China's Indo-Pacific sea lines of communication.

and straits becomes self-evident, and the geostrategic and military-operational connections between the pivotal South China Sea and the Indo-Pacific are highlighted.

The Indo-Pacific is a complementary (not secondary) theater in the Sino-American competition: part of a greater strategic whole and, after the Maritime Salient, primus inter pares on a global scale and with exceptional opportunities for dominating Chinese SLOCs en route and at their sources. As with China's maritime salient, the Indo-Pacific underscores the American military advantages of global strategic mobility, customary operations at strategic distance, and great political and military connectivity in the region.

Just as for China's maritime salient, historical analogies are important in considering the importance of the Indo-Pacific. During World War II, German U-boats were the scourge of Atlantic and Caribbean convoys. An extremely important and asymmetric aspect of their defeat in the Battle of the Atlantic occurred in the Bay of Biscay, where U-boats had to pass en route to ocean stations and back to French ports. Admiral Doenitz's submarines were defeated in large measure not just at the point of convoy attacks but by interdicting them in the Bay of Biscay, where they had to pass to and from patrol stations. By the time the Allied operational strategy was fully implemented, a long-range patrol aircraft would attack any German submarine exposed in transit for more than five minutes.

Likewise, the Chinese merchant marine, and predictably the PLA Navy, must cross the Indian Ocean to East Africa, the Strait of Hormuz, and the Gulf of Aden, and it is unlikely that they will be able to do so at feasible strength. In this way, India and Australia are the Scylla and Charybdis of the Chinese economy.

This competitive strategy is intended as a strategic straw man for subsequent consideration, blueprinting, and planning. No doubt imperfect in detail, and at this length incomplete and unsatisfactory, it is offered as an introductory provocation of subsequent commentary and embellishment.

NOTES

1. The American strategic planning literature and media commentary on this point is extensive. See, for example, Dan Blumenthal, "Sino-U.S. Competition and U.S. Security: How Do We Assess the Military Balance?" The National Bureau of Asian Research, December 2010; Annual Report to Congress, *Military Power of the People's Republic of China* (Washington, DC: Office of the Secretary of Defense, 2010).

2. U.S. Office of the Secretary of Defense, "China's Military Strategy and Doctrine" *Annual Report to Congress Military Power of the People's Republic of China,* 2007, 12.

3. The Three Warfares as expressed by China are legal warfare, media warfare, and psychological warfare. See Timothy Walton, "Treble Spyglass, Treble Spear: China's 'Three Warfares,'" *Defense Concepts* 4:4 (Washington, DC: Center for Advanced Defense Studies, 2010), 49–67.

4. U.S. Department of Defense, U.S. Navy, U.S. Marine Corps, and U.S. Coast Guard, *A Cooperative Strategy for 21st Century Seapower,* October 2007; retrieved on November 15, 2010, from www.navy.mil/maritime/Maritimestrategy.pdf.

5. See Paul S. Giarra, "China's Maritime Reconnaissance-Strike Complex: Land Mobile, MaRV'd Anti-Ship Ballistic Missiles (ASBMs): Implications for the U.S. Navy of China's Asymmetric Strategy for Control of the Sea from the Shore," presented at the China Maritime Studies Institute Annual Conference, U.S. Naval War College, December 10–11, 2008; Paul S. Giarra, "Watching the Chinese," Now Hear This Column, *Proceedings* 135:5 (May 2009); and "A Chinese Anti-Ship Ballistic Missile: Implications for the U.S. Navy," in Andrew S. Erickson, ed., *Chinese Aerospace Power: Evolving Maritime Roles* (Annapolis, MD: U.S. Naval Institute Press, 2011).

6. See Fred C. Iklé and Albert Wohlstetter, *Discriminate Deterrence: The Report of the Commission on Integrated Long-Term Strategy* (Washington, DC: U.S. Government Printing Office, January, 1988).

7. John Mearsheimer, "The Gathering Storm: China's Challenge to U.S. Power in Asia," Fourth Annual Michael Hintze Lecture in International Security, The University of Sydney, Australia, August 4, 2010, available at http://sydney.edu.au/business/ events/faculty/hintze_lecture_2010; Kenji Minemura, "China Progresses on Flattop Plan," *Asahi Shimbun,* August 8, 2010; available at www.asahi.com/english/ TKY201008110263.html; Malcolm Cook, Raoul Heinrichs, Rory Medcalf, and Andrew Shearer, *Power and Choice: Asian Security Futures* (Sydney: Lowy Institute for International Policy, June 2010), 28–29, 32–33, 51–63, 77–79; Thomas Wright, "America Must Find a New China Strategy," *Financial Times,* August 8, 2010, available at www .ft.com/intl/cms/s/0/1c9ec504-a32e-11df-8cf4-00144feabdc0.html#axzz1lnvSGzdG; Mark Helprin, "Hollow Talk in the South China Sea," *Wall Street Journal,* August 15, 2010, available at http://online.wsj.com/article/SB10001424052748704164904575542 1233581556808.html?KEYWORDS=Hollow+Talk+in+the+South+China+Sea; Eric A. McVadon, "As Beijing Digs In, How Should the U.S. React?", *Defense News,* August 20, 2010, available at www.defensenews.com/apps/pbcs.dll/article?AID=20108230311; Geoff Dyer, "Power Play in the South China Sea," *Financial Times,* August 9, 2010, available at www.ft.com/intl/cms/s/0/d0ba0580-a3e2-11df-9e3a-00144feabdc0.html# axzz1lnvSGzdG; John Lee, "China's Rise and the Road to War," *Wall Street Journal,* August 5, 2010, available at http://online.wsj.com/article/SB10001424052748703 7489045755410580240721848.html?KEYWORDS=China%27s+Rise+and+the+Road +to+War; Seth Cropsey, "Ebb Tide," *The American Interest* VI:1 (September–October 2010), 15–20, available at www.the-american-interest.com/article.cfm?piece=858; Toshi Yoshihara, "Chinese Missile Strategy and the U.S. Naval Presence in Japan: The Operational View from Beijing," *Naval War College Review* 63:3 (Summer 2010), 39–62, available at www.usnwc.edu/Publications/Naval-War-College-Review/2010 ---Summer.aspx.

8. For an early description of Chinese military thinking on the three island chains, see Alexander Huang, "The Chinese Navy's Offshore Active Defense Strategy," *U.S. Naval War College Review,* Summer 1994, 18.

17 CULTURAL BARRIERS TO IMPLEMENTING A COMPETITIVE STRATEGY

James R. FitzSimonds

CHINA'S ONGOING MILITARY BUILD-UP has generated interest within the U.S. strategic community for employing a competitive strategies approach to manage a growing military challenge in the Western Pacific. The goals of such a strategy would be to deter China from using force, impose costs to drain resources away from those Chinese military developments that the United States finds most troublesome, and ultimately provide the ability for the United States to win any conflict with China should deterrence fail.

For the past two decades, U.S. military operations have focused on projecting power from land bases and aircraft carriers on the periphery of an adversary, rapidly suppressing its air defenses, and then launching mostly manned air strikes to speedily deliver high volumes of short-range coordinate-seeking ordnance against critical enemy targets—with forces networked for exchange of sensor and command information. Having observed the United States do this twice in the Middle East since 1990, China's reaction has centered on directly neutralizing what it sees as key U.S. vulnerabilities in power projection. Official U.S. assessments provide a good summary of China's approach and critical assumptions:[1]

- China seeks to push U.S. tactical fighters and strike aircraft as well as surveillance, tanker, and electronic warfare aircraft beyond their effective ranges by holding regional air bases and aircraft carriers at unacceptable risk to precision missile and submarine attack. The People's Liberation Army (PLA) assumes that precision missiles— most notably ballistic missiles—will prove both effective in striking targets at long ranges and survivable against the best U.S. efforts to destroy the missile launchers, interrupt launch cycle communications, and intercept or neutralize the missiles in flight. The PLA assumes that its submarines will be effective in missile and torpedo attack against U.S. surface ships, while surviving the best U.S. efforts to neutralize them.

- China seeks to field a highly capable integrated air defense system that makes it extremely difficult for U.S. aircraft and missiles, even the most advanced ones, to penetrate its airspace. The PLA assumes that its active and passive air defenses will overcome any U.S. advances in aircraft stealth or drive such a significant disparity in the offense-defense cost exchange ratio that the United States cannot afford to pursue this approach.

- China seeks to assure the availability of its own communications, sensors, and navigation information during a conflict while denying the same information to the United States through signal jamming, antisatellite systems, airborne sensor pushback or destruction, and cyber network attacks. The PLA assumes that it can assure its own information for contingencies close to China's borders while denying information to U.S. forces and systems forward—and that the United States cannot respond in kind.

The ultimate validity of China's assumptions cannot be confirmed without the test of combat. But China is clearly banking on the belief that it is on the winning side of both relevant offense-defense balances and cost exchange ratios in key war-fighting areas. For the United States, the basis for a long-term, peacetime competitive strategy is to field systems and develop operational concepts that greatly reduce China's confidence that it has, and can maintain, a war-fighting advantage over U.S. forces. This requires the identification and employment of discrete capabilities that put the United States back on the winning side of the critical offense-defense balances and the posing of challenging war-fighting problems to which China is compelled to respond.

Unlike the strategic competition during the Cold War, the United States cannot count on being able to outspend China in military programs. Moreover, major changes to the U.S. force structure face huge institutional hurdles that might be too difficult to overcome in the absence of an urgent military threat. A number of proposals have been surfaced for near-term, low-cost, and potentially highly effective options that would impose disproportionate costs on China while offering significant war-fighting leverage to U.S. forces.

In these specific cases, the predominant barrier to adoption appears to derive chiefly from perceived challenges to the deeply held cultural beliefs within the U.S. military's uniformed officer corps. These examples serve to highlight how cultural impediments can inhibit even the best competitive strategies and how the ultimate success of a competitive strategy might hinge as much on its acceptance within the U.S. armed services as on its impact on the adversary.

AUTONOMOUS SEARCH-AND-ATTACK WEAPONS

Given the increasing threat to fixed facilities from precision weapons, China and other countries have made great efforts to render systems like missile launchers, sensors, and signal jammers either mobile or rapidly relocatable. This uncertainty in target location requires an attacker to conduct an active search using short-range sensors to strike enemy assets with precision weapons. Advanced surface-to-air missiles can make close-in target search by manned aircraft increasingly dangerous, and signal jammers can effectively cut sensor-to-shooter links from unmanned search-and-attack vehicles. A viable approach to holding mobile enemy systems at risk despite advanced defenses and information denial is through autonomous search-and-attack weapons.

The Low Cost Autonomous Attack System (LOCAAS), developed for the U.S. Air Force in the 1990s, is representative of a type of weapon that conducts a search and attack without the need for a "man in the loop." LOCAAS is a small, unmanned aerial vehicle that is launched from outside an enemy's air defense range. It then orbits over a predetermined area and employs an active laser-radar (LADAR) seeker to locate and identify targets matching images of hostile vehicles resident in its onboard memory. When it makes an adequate target match, the LOCAAS configures itself into an appropriate warhead and attacks. The advantages of this type of weapon include its ability to provide credible search and attack against mobile targets inside enemy air defenses at little or no risk to a human pilot, the low cost of an individual LOCAAS relative to an adversary's active air defenses, and the fact that there is no data link from the weapon back to a controlling authority that would be vulnerable to interdiction, jamming, or corruption.[2] Against an advanced opponent, the sensor-to-controller-to-weapon data link would appear to be a true Achilles' heel—and one that countries like China would seem increasingly capable of attacking. Employment of large numbers of autonomous LOCAAS-type systems would seem likely to force the defender into much more costly active and passive defense efforts to protect its critical mobile targets. Such defensive efforts might well raise the signature of the defended assets, making them even more susceptible to detection. In almost every respect, the LOCAAS concept appears to be the ideal competitive strategies approach: It exploits a U.S. technological advantage, it imposes disproportionate costs in peacetime, and it would appear to offer a clear war-fighting advantage over a high-tech opponent in key areas. The prospect of facing a LOCAAS-equipped force would also seem to offer a significant deterrent to an adversary's efforts to project power.

Despite successful operational tests, the United States has never adopted a LOCAAS-type weapon. One major reason—if not the predominant one—has been service opposition to fielding a lethal weapon that does not have a "man in the loop" to confirm the target prior to attack.[3] Since the early 1990s the United States has employed coordinate-seeking weapons like the Tomahawk Land Attack Missile (TLAM) and Joint Direct Attack Munition (JDAM), which operate without human control in flight or human verification of the target after launch. The question is why a search-and-attack weapon like LOCAAS operating in a predefined space is deemed to be different from a coordinate-seeking weapon. The apparent objection to LOCAAS is that its seeker/target algorithm could "make a mistake" in target identification—for instance, attacking a civilian vehicle. Yet there is no empirical evidence that human pilots are better at mobile target identification than a computer—and experience in actual combat suggests that pilots frequently make mistakes in identifying targets. Opposition to the autonomous weapon could be an issue of weapon control. But operators are unable to control a satellite-guided weapon after it is launched.

The primary objection to LOCAAS appears to stem from the apparent lack of accountability for a lethal action of a fully autonomous search and attack weapon—that is, the inability to peg clearly a single human, by name, with a potential human kill. A specific human pilot is responsible for his or her own attack decisions when the trigger is pulled. A specific human selects a fixed target for a cruise missile attack and theoretically accepts responsibility for what is at the target site—even though it could be a bus full of children by the time the missile arrives an hour or more after launch. By contrast, it is not clear what specific human would be responsible for a LOCAAS attack "decision"— that is, the actual "trigger puller." This aversion to autonomous attack does not appear to have been imposed from the senior ranks but nevertheless seems to pervade the bulk of the officer corps. In a survey of U.S. military officers conducted in 2005–2006, 58 percent of respondents agreed with the statement that "enemy targets should be engaged with lethal force only by systems that allow for direct human intervention or control."[4] Because the prospect of a fully autonomous weapon is relatively new, it is not clear whether this opposition is an ingrained belief or reflects a more recent post–Cold War "small conflict" mentality with its seemingly greater aversion to possible collateral damage. Although LOCAAS would significantly reduce risk to human pilots conducting strike missions inside enemy air defenses, there is also no evident push from within the pilot ranks to move from manned to unmanned attack systems even for the most dangerous missions. In the same survey, only 29 percent of aviators agreed with the statement: "I would prefer to have a UAV fly a mission that I deemed 'high risk' [defined as flying into enemy air defenses] than to fly that mission myself."[5] It is not known if aviator attitudes would be different if they actually faced contingencies featuring highly lethal air defenses like those of China (as opposed to the low air risk over Iraq and Afghanistan). Service views regarding autonomous search-and-attack weapons might change significantly if the prospect of major war were to rise and if the capabilities of LOCAAS-type technologies were better understood within the military ranks. However, the failure to adopt autonomous weapons in peacetime precludes their use as an element of a long-term competitive strategy.

PASSIVE MISSILE DEFENSES

Active defense, or "hard kill," against cruise and ballistic missiles—that is, kinetically shooting down missiles in flight—has always been a daunting challenge, with the attacker generally holding a clear advantage over the defender. A study published by the U.S. Navy's Surface Warfare Development Group in 2007 concluded that, out of more than 200 antiship missiles launched operationally by thirteen belligerents between 1967 and 2007, hard kill defeated only one, and only then after it had missed its intended target.[6] Against modern ballistic missile forces featuring exo- and endo-atmospheric maneuvers, closely timed large salvoes, and sophisticated penetration aids like decoys, active defense is ineffective. Moreover, the offense-defense cost exchange ratio likely always favors the attacking missile over the defending interceptor by a wide margin.[7]

Many proponents of active defense have continued to tout directed energy (DE) as the prospective active defense solution for missile kills—the much-hoped-for "bottomless magazine" defending at the speed of light. Directed energy for kinetic missile kills might someday prove viable, but DE countermeasures—to include air frame roll, skin hardening, and reflective coatings—coupled with persistent technological, operational employment, and environmental hurdles do not foster optimism. This persistent, and growing, asymmetric advantage of missile offense over active missile defense is no doubt a predominant reason that China has invested so heavily in a large and expanding arsenal of very sophisticated antiship and land attack cruise and ballistic missiles—an arsenal that now reportedly includes the world's first operational antiship ballistic missile.[8]

Given the limitations of active defense, the key to asset protection in a missile threat environment increasingly lies in so-called passive measures. For fixed facilities, these include asset hardening, sheltering, burial, concealment, dispersal, and the use of decoys. For mobile targets like ships at sea, passive defense options include signal emissions reduction or elimination, unpredictable movement, signature (for example, radar cross section) reduction, decoys, enemy sensor/seeker jamming, and various radio frequency obscurants (that is, "smoke screens"). The 2007 missile defense study previously cited noted that, in stark contrast to the ineffective active defense efforts, passive defenses or "soft kill" defeated more than 100 antiship missiles launched between 1967 and 2007.[9] Most passive defense measures, such as decoys and obscurants, are far less expensive than active defenses and passive defense countermeasures. For instance, a radio-frequency obscurant cloud like that produced with the U.S. Army's M56 Coyote system, which is large enough to cover multiple square kilometers, might expend some $30,000 of carbon aerosol fiber. By contrast, a single two-shot SM-3 intercept *attempt* would currently run about $18 million.

Rigorous passive defenses would challenge the sufficiency of China's missile arsenal, perhaps forcing China to field much larger numbers of missiles—including more missile launchers, more missile brigade storage sites, larger numbers of personnel, and expanded training facilities. Passive defenses would also stress China's over-the-horizon targeting, command-and-control, and existing missile seeker technology. Yet the resources and efforts that the U.S. military services devote to passive defense—and passive ship defense in particular—have been minimal compared with the resources expended on active "in-flight kill" systems.

The overriding impediment to conducting a major shift in emphasis from active to passive defense appears to be a dominant U.S. military mind-set that puts a premium on active intercept rather than hiding from the attacker's sensors. Although there is no known empirical evidence regarding officer attitudes toward passive defense, anecdotally most officers appear to equate passive defense with passivity, or even "doing nothing." This is quite logically driven by the lack of clear evidence of passive defense success—other than *not* being hit by a missile. But the fact that active and passive defense measures are not mutually exclusive—indeed they are complementary—does not seem to have increased the emphasis on employing passive measures.

Current attitudes might reflect the low quality of adversary that the U.S. Navy has faced in combat over the past two decades. The Cold War–era Fleet Deception Groups—U.S. Navy specialists in countertargeting—were disbanded in the early 1990s, ostensibly due to a lack of need.[10] But, even during the Cold War, fleet passive defense had limited funding and generally ranked well behind other considerations in fleet operations. Carrier strike group passive defense in the Cold War was normally the responsibility of a limited duty officer at the bottom of the carrier group staff hierarchy. Then, as now, upwardly mobile surface officers made their careers in surface-to-air missile operations—not passive defense or electronic warfare. Today virtually all surface officers have formal schooling in active defense but none in countertargeting. Given limited exposure to potential high-end threats like that posed by China, most U.S. officers are unaware of a need to restrict the use of distinctive and continuous radar and communications emissions. Even foreign developments touted as "game changers"—like China's antiship ballistic missile—don't generate much interest in passive defense.[11]

Beyond a possible aversion to "passive" operations in general, there are other potential cultural impacts of passive defense measures. Significant reductions in radiofrequency communications to prevent enemy targeting would drive a level of decentralization that would demand greater tactical initiative and requirements for preplanned contingencies. This would mark a decided shift away from the expectations of Network Centric Warfare and away from the increasing centralization of command and control down to the lowest levels. Moreover, increasing radio and radar silence during operations would challenge cultural norms regarding peacetime training risk—potentially closing out many useful options as simply "too dangerous" to employ outside actual combat. The overall failure to embrace passive defense as a normal operating mode during peacetime closes out a range of options that might be effectively employed as useful competitive strategies.

ANTISHIP MINES

One of the most vexing problems that the U.S. Navy has faced over the past century and a half is the antiship mine. Since 1950, mines have accounted for the damage or sinking of fourteen U.S. Navy ships, compared with five sunk or damaged by other causes.[12] The Chinese in particular have continued to invest in many different types of antiship mines, with an arsenal estimated to range from 50,000 to a 100,000 individual weapons.[13] The sophistication of sea mines continues to improve relative to mine detection and mine clearing technologies. The latest sea mines feature stealthy shapes and nonmagnetic properties to inhibit detection, delayed activation timers, ship counters, rocket propulsion, and sophisticated multisensor detonators. Advanced models will be able to bury themselves in the sea floor and even relocate after initial planting. Mines featuring encapsulated torpedoes that actively hunt for targets are also beginning to proliferate.

The threat of the sea mine is well acknowledged by the U.S. Navy. The 2010 Navy Operations Concept (NOC) deemed the mine "the greatest area-denial challenge in the maritime domain . . . capable of constraining maneuverability from deep water past the surf zone to the maximum extent of the littoral."[14] Among all the naval warfare areas, the mine versus mine countermeasures competition might represent the most radical war-fighting asymmetry and the most disproportionate offense-defense cost-exchange ratio. Yet, in stark contrast to China's efforts, the U.S. Navy's mining capability has continued to decline. At present, the only sea mines in the U.S. Navy inventory are the Mk 67 Submarine Launched Mobile Mine (SLMM) and several variants of the air-dropped Mk 60-series Quickstrike.[15] The SLMM is obsolescent, and Quickstrike can be employed only in a benign air environment.[16] Although there have been proposals for new mobile mines employing advanced navigation and control systems for deep penetration as well as new standoff air-delivered mines, there has been no concrete action to upgrade the U.S. mine inventory—or to bring mining into the mainstream of military planning and operations.[17] While the United States faces a potentially significant mining threat from China, it presents no comparable capability either to deter China or to divert China's military resources.

Despite the official recognition of the mine's effectiveness, the U.S. Navy has never embraced mine and countermine operations as primary functions. Both the 2010 Quadrennial Defense Review (QDR) and the 2010 NOC mention mines only as threats to be overcome, not as capabilities to be employed. There is no officer career path in the U.S. Navy for mine warfare as there is for submarines, aviation, and surface line—and thus no established body of expertise that is developed and maintained from the most junior to the most senior ranks. A select few junior surface officers might have a single tour in mine warfare, but the career-minded officer would not linger in that field even if more than a few billets were available. It is difficult to conclude that the principal failure of the Navy to maintain an offensive mining capability is now, and has been, anything other than cultural. To some extent, the dominant service attitude has always reflected the view of Admiral David Farragut of U.S. Civil War fame, who deemed the use of naval mines "unworthy of a chivalrous nation."[18] But, more important, mining is not perceived as a warrior function. The sea mine is set, planted, and left to its own devices—a passive rather than an active weapon. In a hostile environment, the "miner" can't shoot back. In a benign environment, the "miner" is essentially operating a delivery truck—not a fighting platform. It is possible that the low status of the mine also reflects a broader aversion to employing autonomous weapons. Sophisticated mines can do some target discrimination, but, as with LOCAAS, there is no human trigger puller—no "man in the loop" to ensure that a mine is activated only against a valid military target or to shoulder the blame should things go wrong. As in the past, the sudden exigencies of a high-intensity war will likely result in the resurgence of interest in offensive mining. Nevertheless, there is little or no peacetime deterrent value or basis for a competitive strategy in the promise of some possible future interest in weapons like mines that do not now exist.

OVERCOMING CULTURAL BARRIERS

Many, if not most, elements of competitive strategies derive from the employment of specific military systems and operational concepts that serve to provide favorable cost-exchange ratios or discrete technological advantages over an adversary. It is the very nature of a competitive strategy that these new approaches must be adopted in peacetime and implemented over a period of years to induce the competitor to make a significant and resource-intensive response. The problem with cultural impediments to the acquisition and employment of new systems or operational concepts is that, absent the common recognition of an urgent military threat, the behavior and cultural values of the U.S. military tend to resist change.[19] Such a sense of urgency generally occurs close to the point of hostilities—long after a competitive strategy might have had some deterrent or shaping effect.

But changes to military force structure and approaches—and changes to military cultures—*do* occur during peacetime. The substantial literature on the history of peacetime and wartime military innovation offers valuable insight into prerequisites and strategies for change that might fruitfully be employed for pursuing competitive strategies. Perhaps most relevant are Stephen Rosen's findings that critical factors in past peacetime innovation have been a growing understanding of critical changes in the future security environment, and "top-down" efforts within the U.S. military services to drive internal change.[20] This suggests the need for rigorous analysis and understanding of the impact of ongoing military-technical evolution, an objective evaluation of extant and emerging war-fighting balances and imbalances, and a means to expose broad segments of military officers and defense officials—both current and future U.S. military leaders—to the realities and challenges of future combat operations.

Options for consideration should include the incorporation of the theory of competitive strategies and high-end war-fighting net assessments into officer professional military education curricula. The resurgence of free-play war gaming would also appear to be important. The rigorous war gaming efforts at the U.S. Naval War College during the 1920s and 1930s are rightfully credited with revealing most of the key elements and requirements that would assure a U.S. victory over Japan in the Pacific—and likely contributed to the sense of urgency that facilitated the development of such capabilities as aircraft carrier aviation.[21] The interwar war games also served to acculturate a generation of officers to prospective major changes in the character of war fighting between the world wars, such as the critical requirements for projecting military power over thousands of miles of ocean.

Traditional free-play war gaming against a prospective high-end foe has largely atrophied in the post–Cold War era. Although past war games have not been directly associated with competitive strategies, a resurgence and widespread use of gaming today might be the best way to address ingrained cultural barriers to change by simulating, as well as possible, the visceral experience of combat. Public discussion of objective war-fighting net assessments in officer education curricula and derived from rigorous free-play war gaming could also serve as major elements of any competitive strategy by highlighting key adversary vulnerabilities that the United States has every ability and intention to exploit.

Any effort to implement a competitive strategy that will shape the behavior of an adversary must be accompanied by an internal strategy for shaping the behavior of the U.S. military. Those proposing and crafting competitive strategies must be fully cognizant of the inherent cultural impediments to the adoption of specific advanced technologies and concepts within the relevant U.S. military services or branches—and realistically assess the prospects for their acquisition and employment. Specific cultural barriers must be identified and accounted for—to include both realistic recommendations for overcoming those impediments and the very real prospect that adoption of any given system or approach might be prohibitively difficult during peacetime. Most importantly, a competitive strategy cannot be addressed simply in terms of individual and isolated technologies. A competitive strategy must be pursued as a coherent program of innovative systems and operational concepts—a comprehensive effort focused as much on generating support for adoption within the U.S. military as it is on managing the future strategic adversary.

NOTES

1. See Office of the Secretary of Defense, Annual Report to Congress, *Military and Security Developments Involving the Peoples' Republic of China,* 2010.

2. Most recent cost estimates for a large production run of LOCAAS are on the order of $70,000 per unit. It is not known what a Chinese surface-to-air missile costs them to produce, but a U.S. ESSM (Evolved Sea Sparrow Missile) terminal defense missile currently runs just over $1 million per interceptor; U.S. Department of Defense, *Program Acquisition Costs by Weapon System,* May 2009.

3. The program manager for LOCAAS at Lockheed-Martin, James Moore, stated in 2001 that fielding an autonomous weapon requires "a large paradigm shift [the Air Force is] going to have to undergo. I really think that's where the hesitation is coming in"; quoted in Frank Wolfe, "Air Force May Extend LOCAAS ATD until Next June," *Defense Daily,* April 13, 2001.

4. James R. FitzSimonds and Thomas G. Mahnken, "Military Officer Attitudes toward the Adoption of Unmanned Systems Exploring Institutional Impediments to Innovation," paper presented at the Annual Meeting of the International Studies Association, San Diego, CA, March 22–25, 2006 (unpublished).

5. FitzSimonds and Mahnken, "Military Officer Attitudes."

6. TM 3-01.1-07, *Single Ship Integrated Hard Kill and Soft Kill Tactics in Anti-Ship Missile Defense,* Surface Warfare Development Group, April 2007.

7. It is not known exactly how much a ballistic missile like the DF-21 might cost the Chinese to produce (or would cost the United States to produce). A single U.S. Navy SM-3 exo-atmospheric interceptor currently runs about $9 million; William Matthews, "Senate Subcommittee Votes to Cut LCS Buy," *Navy Times,* September 15, 2010. Even if the costs of an attacking missile and an interceptor are comparable, a high-probability intercept attempt normally requires two interceptor shots against every attacking missile, an extensive C4ISR system, and possibly an expensive launch platform like the Aegis DDG.

8. Office of the Secretary of Defense, *Annual Report to Congress, Military and Security Developments Involving the People's Republic of China* (Washington, DC: Author, 2010).

9. *TM 3-01.1-07.*

10. Sam J. Tangredi, "No Game Changer for China," *U.S. Naval Institute Proceedings,* February 2010, 27.

11. See, for instance, the minimal response by active duty officers to articles such as Andrew S. Erickson and David D. Yang, "On the Verge of a Game-Changer," *U.S. Naval Institute Proceedings,* May 2009, 26–32.

12. Bryan M. Cochran, "Mine Warfare: The Joint Commander's Achilles Heel," unpublished paper for the Joint Military Operations Department, U.S. Naval War College, February 9, 2004.

13. Andrew S. Erickson, Lyle J. Goldstein, and William S. Murray, *Chinese Mine Warfare: A PLA Navy 'Assassin's Mace' Capability,* Naval War College, China Maritime Study 3, Naval War College, Newport, RI, June 2009.

14. *Naval Operations Concept (NOC) 2010: Implementing the Maritime Strategy,* 56.

15. U.S. Navy Fact File; available at www.navy.mil/navydata.

16. The SLMM is a modification of the 1950s-era Mk 37 torpedo, a weapon that went out of the operational inventory in 1987. Published assessments indicate that SLMM has "proved to have inadequate stand-off range [a maximum of 8.5 miles] and placement accuracy"; SLMM/ISLMM (United States), Underwater Weapons: Mines, September 24, 2010,, available at www.janes.com/articles/Janes-Underwater-Warfare-Systems/SLMM-ISLMM-United-States.html. Quickstrikes date back to the early 1980s and, although effective, must be delivered by low-altitude aircraft flying directly over the planting location—clearly a low- or no-threat environment that hardly characterizes the coastline of a high-end opponent.

17. Although the U.S. Navy is reportedly carrying out analysis to explore improvement of offensive mining capabilities, the commander of Fleet Forces stated in late 2010 that offensive mine research was not at the top of the current list of Navy priorities, and he could not provide any definitive commitment to future investment in that warfare area; "Navy Examines Improved Offensive Mine Warfare Capabilities," October 18, 2010; available at insidedefense.com.

18. Quoted by J. M. Boorda, "Mine Countermeasures: An Integral Part of Our Strategy and Forces," *Surface Warfare* (March/April 1996), 5.

19. See for example, Elting E. Morison, "Gunfire at Sea: A Case Study of Innovation," chapter 2 in *Men, Machines, and Modern Times* (Cambridge, MA: The MIT Press, 1968); and Stephen Rosen, *Winning the Next War* (Ithaca, NY: Cornell University Press, 1991).

20. Rosen, *Winning the Next War.*

21. See, for instance, Michael Vlahos, *The Blue Sword* (Newport, RI: Naval War College Press, 1980); and Edward Miller, *War Plan Orange* (Annapolis, MD: Naval Institute Press, 1991).

CONCLUSION

Thomas G. Mahnken

THIS VOLUME HAS SOUGHT to stimulate interest in formulating and implementing long-term strategies for defending U.S. interests in the face of growing Chinese military power. Its chapters have described the theory of peacetime competition and its practice during the Cold War and have speculated as to its utility in the Sino-American competition.

This chapter concludes the volume by broadening the framework articulated in previous chapters and identifying avenues for further research. Specifically, it argues that greater work needs to be done to explore the contours of past peacetime competitions, understand the dynamics of Sino-American strategic interaction, and apply the competitive strategies approach to other contemporary challenges.

EXPLORING PAST PEACETIME COMPETITIONS

This volume has looked to the past to try to learn lessons for the future. Specifically, it has devoted considerable attention to understanding the dynamics of the competition between the Soviet Union and the United States during the Cold War, from both the American and Soviet perspectives. Such a focus was driven by the fact that it was during the Cold War that thinking about long-term peacetime competition crystallized in the United States. Indeed, during the late 1970s (informally) and 1980s (formally), the U.S. government developed and carried out specific strategies for competing with the Soviet Union.

More work nonetheless should be done to understand the dynamics of the Cold War. For example, both scholars and policymakers have cited the

U.S. pursuit of a manned penetrating bomber force as a cost-imposing strategy against the Soviet Union.[1] To date, however, there has been no detailed case study of this interaction, particularly one incorporating Russian sources. Similarly, scholars have viewed Washington's pursuit of ballistic missile defense as a competitive strategy, and recent scholarship indicates that President Reagan's 1983 announcement of the Strategic Defense Initiative (SDI) triggered a debate within the Soviet leadership over the wisdom of competing with the United States in space weaponry, as well as the form that competition should take. David Hoffman, for example, suggests that the announcement of SDI ultimately set up a situation by which Soviet leaders who favored a high-technology competition with the United States in space arms initially carried the day, only to be discredited by their inability to field high-technology weapons. That is, SDI put in motion a chain of events that ultimately made the Soviet leadership aware that it could not compete with the United States in high-technology weaponry.[2] Although this new scholarship is suggestive, it is not definitive; greater study is warranted.

Scholars should not, however, limit their attention to the Cold War. History contains a number of cases of long-term peacetime competition, including that between Great Britain and France from the 17th to the 19th centuries, between the United States and Great Britain from the late 19th to the early 20th centuries, between Great Britain and Germany during the same period, and between the United States and Japan during the first four decades of the 20th century. Each of these cases deserves to be examined through the lens of strategic interaction.

UNDERSTANDING SINO-AMERICAN STRATEGIC INTERACTION

More also needs to be done to understand Sino-American strategic interaction. Many discussions of Sino-American relations explicitly or implicitly reflect the assumption that interaction between the two states is tightly coupled; that is, that the Chinese government is focused on U.S. actions, perceives them accurately, and responds to them in a timely manner.

However, each element of this assumption is open to question. First, the extent to which external developments, as opposed to internal ones, drive Chinese military developments is unclear. The Chinese government clearly pays attention to the external environment; it is not strategically autistic. But it would be unusual if its decisions were not also affected by internal dynamics, to include domestic politics, bureaucratic interests, and organizational culture. What is unclear, and deserves greater study, is the extent to which these internal, as opposed to external, dynamics shape Chinese strategic decision making.

Second, to the extent that external developments drive Chinese military research, development, and acquisition, it is unclear how accurately Chinese decision makers perceive the external environment. Misperception is a common phenomenon and particularly prevalent where ideological differences further distort things.[3] This is clearly the case in Sino-American relations. Policy makers and scholars in the United States see China as opaque, whereas Chinese decision makers are suspicious of the United States, believing that it aims at overthrowing China's communist government.[4] Chinese opacity has already hindered the United States from diagnosing the state of the competition. The United States has had difficulty assessing Chinese military capabilities, frequently underestimating the pace and scope of Beijing's arms programs.[5] China, for its part, may also misperceive the military balance.[6] Of particular concern is the possibility that China may overestimate its own capability and underestimate that of the United States and its allies. It is worth recalling that parts of the People's Liberation Army last saw battle during China's 1979 war with Vietnam, and other parts have not seen combat since the Korean War. That is, the PLA is led by officers who have never faced battle using weapons that have never been tested in combat. This is, to put it mildly, a recipe for misperception and surprise.

A third issue has to do with timing. That is, the speed of Chinese reactions to external developments is unclear. Whereas parts of the Chinese economy have liberalized, centralized planning continues to reign in Chinese defense planning. This planning process, combined with bureaucratic politics, is likely to shape both the form and timing of Chinese responses to U.S. actions.

Rather than a tightly coupled action-reaction arms race, what is unfolding appears to be a looser form of interaction. Given the likelihood of continued Sino-American competition, it would be worthwhile for scholars to devote greater attention to its dynamics.

APPLICATION TO OTHER CASES

As noted in the first chapter of this volume, five features distinguish the competitive strategies approach from other methods of planning: the need for a concrete, sophisticated opponent; focus on interaction between competitors;

acknowledgment and exploitation of the fact that competitors' choices are constrained; a long planning horizon; and sufficient understanding of the competitor to formulate and implement a long-term strategy.

It would be worthwhile to explore the applicability of the competitive strategies approach to other competitors, such as North Korea and Iran.[7] Predictions of the imminent collapse of the communist regime in P'yongyang to the contrary, there is a good chance that the North Korean regime will endure in one form or another for years or decades to come. North Korea has arguably been pursuing a long-term strategy toward the United States and South Korea, one that P'yongyang has used to coerce its adversaries into providing considerable political and economic benefits to the regime.[8] By contrast, the United States and South Korea (and, for that matter, Japan) have failed to follow a coherent strategy, particularly one that focuses on pitting their considerable comparative advantages against the enduring weaknesses of North Korea. Such a strategy might, for example, emphasize taking the initiative in relations with P'yongyang by striking at the economic and political roots of the regime's power rather than, as has happened all too often in the past, ceding the initiative to P'yongyang and responding to North Korean threats and actions. It might also seek ways to exploit North Korea's status as a client of China to the detriment of the regime in P'yongyang.

A long-term competition approach might fruitfully be applied to Iran as well. It is likely that the United States and Iran face a struggle for influence in the Persian Gulf and beyond that will span decades. It is incumbent on the United States and its friends in the region to think seriously about this challenge and formulate a strategy for dealing with it. Iran has, for example, been able to use its position athwart the Persian Gulf to threaten to deny outsiders access to the region's oil. Iran's geography is, however, a two-edged sword, as Tehran itself relies on the export and reimportation of oil to serve its own needs. As Henry Sokolski has pointed out, there are a number of steps that the United States and regional powers could take to reroute oil flows and turn geography against Iran.[9]

Iran has also been able to use terrorist groups such as Hezbollah and others to inflict costs on its adversaries. The United States and others should explore options for imposing costs—economic and political as well as military—on the regime in Tehran.

A long-term competition approach may thus be applicable to a broad range of challenges that the United States faces. As the chapters in this volume have demonstrated, formulating and implementing a consistent strategy in peacetime is a difficult undertaking. However, such an approach holds the best chance of allowing the United States to marshal its limited resources in the defense of its interests in an increasingly challenging strategic environment.

NOTES

1. See the discussion in Thomas G. Mahnken, *Technology and the American Way of War since 1945* (New York: Columbia University Press, 2008), 163–164.

2. David E. Hoffman, *The Dead Hand* (New York: Doubleday, 2009).

3. Robert Jervis, "Hypotheses on Misperception," *World Politics* 20:3 (April 1968), 454–479; Kevin M. Woods and Mark E. Stout, "Saddam's Perceptions and Misperceptions: The Case of 'Desert Storm,'" *Journal of Strategic Studies* 33:1 (February 2010), 5–41; Charles A. Duelfer and Stephen Benedict Dyson, "Chronic Misperception and International Conflict: The U.S.–Iraq Experience," *International Security* 36:1 (Summer 2011), 73–100.

4. Aaron L. Friedberg, *A Contest for Supremacy: China, America, and the Struggle for Mastery in Asia* (New York: W. W. Norton, 2011), 42–45.

5. Thomas G. Mahnken, "China's Anti-Access Strategy in Historical and Theoretical Perspective," *The Journal of Strategic Studies* 34:3 (June 2011).

6. Chinese assessments of U.S. submarine programs are illustrative. See Gabriel Collins, Andrew Erickson, Lyle Goldstein, and William Murray, "Chinese Evaluations of the U.S. Navy Submarine Force," *Naval War College Review* 61:1 (Winter 2008), 68–86.

7. Henry D. Sokolski, ed., *Prevailing in a Well-Armed World: Devising Competitive Strategies against Weapons Proliferation* (Carlisle, PA: Strategic Studies Institute, 2000).

8. Narushige Michishita, *North Korea's Military-Diplomatic Campaigns, 1966–2008* (London: Routledge, 2010).

9. Henry Sokolski, "Disarming the Mullahs," *Weekly Standard* (October 23, 2006).

INDEX

A-12 tactical aircraft, 118
active missile defenses, 290, 293–95
Advanced Tactical Targeting Technology
(AT3), 198
Advanced Technology Bomber, 118
Aegis system, 247, 299n7
Afghanistan: Soviet invasion, 38, 82, 97–98;
Taliban government, 39; U.S. invasion,
38, 39, 54, 102, 158–59, 241
Air-Land Battle doctrine, 99, 118, 126n29,
282, 284
Air-Sea Battle doctrine, 142, 243–48, 267
Akhromeyev, Sergei, 84
Akula submarines, 190
Alaska, 247
Al Qaeda and Associated Movements
(AQAM), 3, 30, 38, 39, 42, 54, 56
American allies, 3, 4, 32–33, 173, 174, 260,
281; vs. Chinese allies, 158, 172; role
in U.S.-China competition, 6–7, 9–10,
142, 162, 169, 175, 177–78, 180–81, 182,
258–59, 262, 265–68. *See also* Australia;
Japan; NATO; Philippines; Singapore;
South Korea; Taiwan; Thailand
American Revolutionary War: Yorktown,
37, 41
Andre, David: *New Competitive Strategies*,
104n16
Andropov, Yuri, 77
Angola, 82
anti-ballistic missile (ABM) systems, 74
antisatellite weapons, 163, 200, 239, 264, 290

antiship ballistic missiles (ASBMs), Chinese,
140, 180, 193, 196, 199, 209, 211, 216, 225,
263, 264, 278, 294, 296
antisubmarine warfare (ASW), 126n29, 181,
205n13, 245; during Cold War, 79, 117,
118, 201, 224; in Japan's MSDF, 222, 224,
225, 226, 232, 233, 267; PLAN weakness
in, 141, 179, 185, 198–99, 226, 227, 231,
262; in U.S. Navy, 79, 117, 118, 180, 185,
186, 187–88, 189–93, 195–96, 201–3,
205n13, 224
ANZUS treaty, 250
appeasement/socialization strategy, 16, 19–20
Arab-Israeli War of 1973, 76
Argentina, 191
arms control, 74–75, 99, 159
artificial intelligence, 51–52
Assault Breaker, 99
Association of South East Asian Nations
(ASEAN), 162
asymmetry, 114, 184, 287; in attention
and persistence, 17; in Australian
strategy, 248–49; cognitive asymmetry,
15–16, 18–19; in competitive strategies
approach, 15–16, 18–19; decisive
asymmetries, 48, 49, 63n12; material
asymmetry, 16; and net assessment, 93,
94; organizational asymmetry, 15–16; in
U.S.-China competition, 200, 216, 240,
258–59, 293–94
Australia, 236–52, 285–86; intervention in
East Timor, 65n40; *Jindalee* radar system,